The Disappearing Mestizo

The Disappearing Mestizo

Configuring Difference in the Colonial
New Kingdom of Granada

JOANNE RAPPAPORT

Duke University Press | Durham and London | 2014

© 2014 Duke University Press

Text designed by Chris Crochetière, BW&A Books, Inc.
Typeset in Charis and Trade Gothic by BW&A Books, Inc.

Library of Congress Cataloging-in-Publication Data
Rappaport, Joanne.
The disappearing mestizo : configuring difference in the
colonial New Kingdom of Granada / Joanne Rappaport.
pages cm
Includes bibliographical references and index.
ISBN 978-0-8223-5629-5 (cloth : alk. paper)
ISBN 978-0-8223-5636-3 (pbk. : alk. paper)
1. Mestizos—Latin America—History.
2. Mestizaje—Latin America—History.
3. Latin America—History—To 1830.
I. Title.
F1412.R 37 2014
980'.01—dc23 2013026438

FOR MIMI

The Disappearing Mestizo

Configuring Difference in the Colonial New Kingdom of Granada

JOANNE RAPPAPORT

Duke University Press | Durham and London | 2014

© 2014 Duke University Press
All rights reserved

Text designed by Chris Crochetière, BW&A Books, Inc.
Typeset in Charis and Trade Gothic by BW&A Books, Inc.

Library of Congress Cataloging-in-Publication Data
Rappaport, Joanne.
The disappearing mestizo : configuring difference in the
colonial New Kingdom of Granada / Joanne Rappaport.
pages cm
Includes bibliographical references and index.
ISBN 978-0-8223-5629-5 (cloth : alk. paper)
ISBN 978-0-8223-5636-3 (pbk. : alk. paper)
1. Mestizos—Latin America—History.
2. Mestizaje—Latin America—History.
3. Latin America—History—To 1830.
I. Title.
F1412.R 37 2014
980'.01—dc23 2013026438

CONTENTS

ACKNOWLEDGMENTS

The archival research on which this book is based was supported by an International Collaborative Grant from the Wenner-Gren Foundation for Anthropological Research (2005–2006), a Summer Academic Grant from Georgetown University's Graduate School of Arts and Sciences (2005), and a Fulbright Fellowship in Bogotá (2007). I thank the directors and staff of the Archivo General de Indias (Seville, Spain) and the Archivo General de la Nación (Bogotá, Colombia) for their hospitality and assistance on this project; I am particularly beholden to the director of the Division of Attention to the Public of the Archivo General de la Nación, Mauricio Tovar, and his staff with whom it is a continuing joy to work.

Marta Zambrano of the Universidad Nacional de Colombia shared the Wenner-Gren grant and her ideas concerning race and mestizaje with me. She helped me to focus on mestizaje, as opposed to race, as the central argument of this book. I thank Carolina Castañeda, María Fernanda Durán, Juan Felipe Hoyos, Laura Sánchez, and Bernardo Leal for their able assistance in the Bogotá archives. Carolina, María Fernanda, Juan Felipe, and Laura transcribed the voluminous documentation of don Diego de Torres and don Alonso de Silva. I am deeply thankful to Bernardo for his patient scouring of the colonial notarial registries of Santafé and Tunja. I am also deeply appreciative of the hours of conversation I enjoyed with this team of dedicated young scholars and the space for brainstorming and speculation they so enthusiastically created.

The bulk of the archival research in this book was conducted in Bogotá. I am deeply thankful to the department of anthropology of the Universidad Nacional de Colombia for giving me a home away from home while I worked in the archives and to the Comisión Fulbright for smoothing over all those unnerving bureaucratic barriers one encounters when dealing with residence in another country. My dear friends in Bogotá, some of them colleagues (although not all of them academics), shared their dinner tables, vacation houses, and most important, their companionship and their ideas, as they have for years: Mauricio Archila, Margarita Cháves, Martha Cecilia García, Emiro González, Myriam Jimeno, Ximena Pachón, and Jaime Téllez. Marc Chernick and the late (and sorely missed) Tulia Camacho-Chernick lent me their beautiful apartment on the lively and eccentric Calle 53 during my semester in Bogotá; Francisco Ortega and Liliana Obregón allowed me to use their perch on the Carrera 7a on a later trip. I also enjoyed the continuous presence in my life of my longtime friends and compadres from Cauca: Mercedes Belalcázar, Cristóbal Gnecco, Felipe Morales, Ana Ruth Mosquera, Susana Piñacué, Abelardo Ramos, Cristina Simmonds, María Elena Tombe, and Francisco Tróchez.

The staff and fellows of Harvard University's Radcliffe Institute for Advanced Study, where I spent the 2008–2009 academic year, not only made writing easier, but forced me to think about the book in new ways. I am beholden to Dean Barbara Grosz and the fellowship program director Judith Vichniac for making Radcliffe such an inspiring place to work. Several of my co-fellows were particularly influential in my writing, including Sarah Messer, Chiori Miyagawa, Koen Vermeir, and Björn Weiler: Björn and Koen were inquiring readers with a deep knowledge of medieval and early modern history, enthusiastic about reading colonial Latin American history through a European lens; Chiori and Sarah, as creative writers, prodded me to consider ways of making my point through narrative instead of obscure academic prose, and turned me on to a vast range of narrative histories that disciplinary and area specialization had hidden from my view. The Radcliffe Institute allows its fellows to develop a close mentoring relationship with a Harvard undergraduate. Matías Iván Vera, a senior philosophy major, ably assisted me in tracing the genealogies of a series of sixteenth- and seventeenth-century Spanish families in Santafé; some of those genealogies are reproduced in this book. The writing of this book was completed during the 2011 calendar year, with the support of a Senior Faculty Fellowship from the Graduate School of Georgetown University and a fellowship from the National Endowment for the Humanities, for which I am deeply grateful.

When I first embarked on this project I was influenced by Kathryn Burns, who persuaded me to look into race in colonial Santafé. Insightful conversations with Rodney Collins, Tom Cummins, Emily

Francomano, Marta Herrera Ángel, Richard Kagan, and Jean-Paul Zúñiga, as well as careful readings of individual chapters by Luis Miguel Glave, Cristina Grasseni, José Ramón Jouve-Martín, Ruth Hill, Mercedes López, Santiago Muñoz, Luis Fernando Restrepo, and Maité Yié illuminated my understanding of the complexities of my materials, forcing me to continually question what mestizaje meant in the colonial period and to embed my microhistorical narratives in broader political and economic contexts. I am deeply beholden to the two readers for Duke University Press, one of them Nancy van Deusen and the other anonymous; their careful, illuminating readings have made this a more persuasive book.

Versions of these chapters—some of them at very preliminary stages—received perceptive commentaries and critiques at presentations I was invited to give at the annual meetings of the American Historical Association, as well as at the City University of New York Graduate Center, Dickinson College, Harvard University, Michigan State University, the Museo Nacional de Colombia, New York University, Princeton University, Queen's University, the Radcliffe Institute, the TePaske Seminar at Emory University, Universidad Autónoma de Yucatán, Universidad de los Andes, Universidad Javeriana, and the Universidad Nacional de Colombia.

As always, Valerie Millholland of Duke University Press played a key role in turning my manuscript into a book and in extending her friendship over the years; it is always a pleasure and an honor to work with her. I also welcomed the assistance of Gisela Fosado for a second time around, and I look forward to her presence at Duke and her friendship in the future. I thank Bill Nelson for preparing the map of the Santafé-Tunja area and Mark Mastromarino for writing the index.

Earlier versions of several chapters have already been published; I benefited greatly (although in the heat of the moment not always gracefully) from the commentaries of anonymous reviewers for the journals in which they appear. Chapter 1 was published in 2009 under the title, "Mischievous Lovers, Hidden Moors, and Cross-Dressers: Passing in Colonial Bogotá," *Journal of Spanish Cultural Studies* 10.1: 7–25; I thank Ruth Hill for shepherding this article to publication. Chapter 4 appeared in 2012 as "Buena sangre y hábitos españoles: Repensando a Alonso de Silva y Diego de Torres," in the *Anuario Colombiano de Historia Social y de la Cultura* 39.1: 19–48; I am beholden to the *Anuario*'s editor, Mauricio Archila, for his close attention to the manuscript. Chapter 5 was published in 2011 as "*'Asi lo paresce por su aspeto*': Physiognomy and the Construction of Difference in Colonial Bogotá," *Hispanic American Historical Review* 91.4: 601–31.

David Gow not only put up with my continuous trips to Colombia and Spain, as well as a year of commuting between Cambridge and Washington, but set aside his own interests in contemporary ethnography to read my colonial stories. As someone not firmly ensconced in the colonial period, he provided me with a critical outside reading and suggested that I include a cast of characters to help readers navigate the labyrinth of colonial people who populate the pages of this book. Miriam Rappaport-Gow, my daughter, trailed along to Bogotá and Seville with me, as well as visiting me in Cambridge; in each place she forced me out of the archive, to observe dolphins in Gibraltar, whales in Boston, to ride horses in La Calera, near Bogotá. Now that she has embarked on a college career and has taken a course in anthropology, I hope she will want to take a dip in its pages.

AUTHOR'S NOTE ON TRANSCRIPTIONS, TRANSLATIONS, ARCHIVES, AND SPANISH NAMING PRACTICES

Although I have not included the Spanish originals of most colonial documents discussed in this volume, I include some brief transcriptions in the endnotes or parenthetically. My transcriptions attempt to preserve the orthography and punctuation of the original documents while at the same time rendering them comprehensible to twenty-first-century readers. Thus, I spell out most abbreviations and generally convert the letter "f" to "s" and the initial "rr" to "r," but do not always convert "y" to "i," "u" to "v," or add the letter "h" where it is missing. I do not include accent marks in my transcriptions, as they were not used in the colonial period; for this reason, names like "Bogotá" will appear with an accent mark in the text, but without an accent in documentary citations and quotations. I do not reconcile divergent spellings of a word or a proper name, which might be written in different ways in the same document; this is particularly true for toponyms and anthroponyms in native languages, which Spanish scribes struggled to record using Castillian phonological conventions, although they were not proficient in the language in question. I also preserve the gender of certain nouns, such as "la color," in their early modern form. Colonial documentary writing frequently has run-on sentences. In the interests of making quotations in translation more readable, I have opted for dividing some run-on sentences into more coherent phrases in my translations. Likewise, I have removed "said" (*dicho/a*), which means "aforementioned," from certain translations in the interests of a more fluid reading, although I have retained it where it is central to the meaning of the sentence.

I have used the acronym AGI/S to refer to the Archivo General de

Indias, Seville, and AGN/B to refer to the Archivo General de la Nación, Bogotá; other archives and their abbreviations are listed at the beginning of the bibliography. I have also abbreviated the names of sections in the archives, such as CI for Caciques e Indios in AGN/B; a key to these abbreviations can be found at the beginning of the bibliography. I have arranged AGI documents into *legajos* (l.), *números* (n.), and *ramos* (r.); I use these abbreviations in my documentary citations. Documents from AGN frequently include a document number (doc.), which is useful for locating digitalized manuscripts on the archive's web page.

Spanish surnames combine a patronymic with a matronymic, the patronymic coming first: the first surname—the patronymic—of Próspero Morales Pradilla, a twentieth-century author I mention in passing in these pages, is "Morales," and he will appear in the bibliography under the letter "m." The matronymic (in this case, "Pradilla") is optional in everyday usage, so that Morales Pradilla can also be called "Morales." I will sometimes reduce surnames to the patronymic after initially introducing individuals by their full names, both in the body of the text and in the bibliographic references in my endnotes; complete surnames are recorded in the bibliography, alphabetized under the patronymic. However, in some cases, individuals are called by other than their first surname, a very common occurrence in the colonial period, when the conventions of naming were less strict than they are today and when some individuals did not use their patronymics, but instead went by their mothers' surnames (or even sometimes by other surnames). The colonial administrator Andrés Díaz Venero de Leiva, for example, is commonly referred to as "Venero de Leiva" or "Venero," and not "Díaz," perhaps because his second surname was less common than his first. I implore readers to try to adapt to colonial usages, instead of demanding that all persons be referred to according to the editorial conventions of twenty-first-century English-speakers.

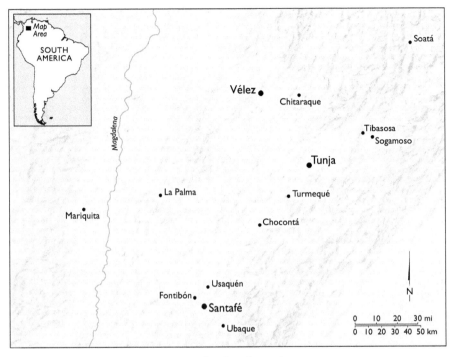

Map 1. *The Santafé-Tunja region in the early colonial period.*

INTRODUCTION

Juan Rodríguez Freile, the author of *El carnero*, a seventeenth-century satirical chronicle of Santafé de Bogotá and Tunja, provokes his readers with his recounting of the fate of Inés de Hinojosa, the beautiful and treacherous Tunja adulteress who murdered two husbands and was ultimately hanged for her crimes.[1] Inés—who Rodríguez Freile identifies as a *"doña"* (noblewoman) and as a *"criolla"* (American-born woman of Spanish descent) from Carora, in what is modern-day Venezuela—was beautiful and wealthy, but she was imprisoned in a demoralizing marriage to the gambler and heavy drinker don Pedro de Ávila, a rogue who swiftly devoured her assets while pursuing not-so-secret affairs with other women. In Rodríguez Freile's telling, Inés schemes with her dance instructor and lover, the Spaniard Jorge Voto, to kill Ávila, and after doing so, the two move to Tunja as a married couple. Once again Inés found matrimony too constraining. Don Pedro Bravo de Rivera, a well-placed Spaniard who lived across the street from Hinojosa, fell for the Venezuelan woman, and the two embarked on an affair, meeting clandestinely by way of a tunnel excavated between their houses. Bravo de Rivera's mestizo half-brother Hernán (the son of Bravo's father with a native woman) lent Inés a hand in plotting and carrying out the death of Voto so that she could once again free herself from an unwanted husband. That time, however, Inés de Hinojosa's scheme was discovered, and the two Bravo brothers and Inés were caught and condemned to death by Andrés Díaz Venero de Leiva, president of the Audiencia of Santafé (the judicial representatives of the Spanish Crown in the region that today is Colombia). Inés and Hernán were hanged. As befit his higher social status, don Pedro Bravo de Rivera was condemned to the garrote and died by strangulation.

Something of a colonial backwater, the Nuevo Reino de Granada (the New Kingdom of Granada) was an Audiencia that did not achieve autonomous status as a viceroyalty until the eighteenth century. Its indigenous populations were believed by the Spaniards to be "unorganized," a valuation given expression in the term "*behetría*," denoting confusion or disorder, which was used to classify them in relation to the native empires of Mexico and Peru. The altiplano extending between Santafé and Tunja, which was inhabited by a large and sedentary Muisca population living in close proximity to silver and emerald mines and on fertile agricultural land, was seen as a prime source of labor by the Spaniards.[2] However, in comparison to Lima or Mexico City, which generated enormous wealth with their silver mines and vibrant commercial activity, Santafé was an insignificant outpost in the far-flung empire. This is where Inés de Hinojosa's story unfolds.

Susan Herman convincingly conjectures that Rodríguez Freile's rendition of Inés's travails is a satire of the Venero de Leiva administration.[3] As the first president of the Audiencia de Santafé, Venero presided over a policy of expanding royal control over *encomenderos*, the conquistadors who had been awarded grants of indigenous tributaries in return for their services to the king.[4] *El carnero* is a chronicle of the contest between the Spanish Crown and local powerholders in the Nuevo Reino. It is a fictional narrative whose plotting does not correspond to historical events, but it nevertheless captures many of the tensions that characterized the struggle over colonial rule that pitted Spaniards against mestizos, the Nuevo Reino's two major cities—Tunja and Santafé—against each other, and local encomenderos against the Crown. In Rodríguez Freile's imagination, men were also pitted against women, and he depicts many of these conflicts by reading them through female protagonists such as Inés de Hinojosa. Whether Inés actually existed as a historical actor remains unclear, although there are abbreviated references to her punishment in the historical record.[5]

Inés de Hinojosa's story was reimagined in the 1980s by the Colombian author Próspero Morales Pradilla in *Los pecados de Inés de Hinojosa* (The Sins of Inés de Hinojosa), a steamy historical novel that later met resounding success as a television series. While Rodríguez Freile identifies Inés as a criolla, Morales envisions her as a mestiza, a woman of mixed Spanish and indigenous descent, ostensibly on the basis of his research in Venezuelan archives.[6] Morales paints a portrait of Inés as the product of the melding of two traditions and two states of being: "The color of her skin, the way she gazed at the world, the agility of her body, and the fact that she walked about freely as though she wore no clothing recalled her mother's race and was complemented by her decisive gestures, the predatory movements of her body, and her beauty, which came from her Andalusian ancestors."[7]

Morales Pradilla's embellishment of his fictional character's mestiza condition and Rodríguez Freile's portrait of Inés as a Spanish lady must each be situated in its respective historical context. If, in fact, Morales Pradilla's archival excavations constitute proof that Inés de Hinojosa was a mestiza, we cannot infer from this that Rodríguez Freile's omission of her mixed ancestry was a mistake or a purposeful elision. The colonial chronicler did not suppose that Inés's mestizo condition (assuming he was aware of it) was germane to his narrative, since as the wife of a well-placed Spaniard she automatically adopted the identity of her husband, regardless of her parentage; in fact, despite her mixed ancestry Inés may always have identified as a Spaniard. Morales Pradilla, in contrast, sensed that his readers would respond positively to a main character who was portrayed as a mestiza, given that by the late twentieth century Colombia was envisioned as a mestizo nation, even if few Colombians identify themselves individually as mestizos and racial ascriptions tend to be assigned to particular geographic regions.[8] Herein lies one of the crucial differences between sixteenth-century worldviews and those to which we moderns are more accustomed. In Rodríguez Freile's time, the qualities that distinguished a well-married elite mestiza from her plebeian sisters revolved around her ability to expunge from her person the stain of *mestizaje*; her identity was embedded in a series of profoundly malleable social categories with characteristics that adhered to individuals but not to groups.[9] In the mindset of Morales Pradilla, writing in a period in which few Colombians would use "mestizo" as an identifying marker, "mestiza" morphs into an extrasomatic symbol that transcends the individual altogether. If we hope to comprehend what "mestizo" meant in the sixteenth century, we must disentangle it from the meanings that accrued to it in the course of the subsequent four centuries. That is what I hope to accomplish in this book.

WHEN IS SOMEONE A MESTIZO?

I have opted to foreground mestizaje—as opposed to indigeneity or Africanness, which are more frequently the concerns of students of the history of race in Spanish America—as the core of my archival explorations. The mestiza Inés de Hinojosa emerges from my opening anecdote as someone who is slippery, intangible, transient, someone who repeatedly disappears from sight although she is everywhere to be seen. This is not just a literary trope; it was an essential condition of mestizos in the early colonial period of the sixteenth and seventeenth centuries, opening an unanticipated window into how difference and inequality were navigated at the time.

"Mestizo" is a label that was applied to multiple actors by colonial observers, although it was also self-ascribed. We cannot be certain that an individual who is called a mestizo in a particular documentary utterance will carry that label his entire life, nor that "mestizo" meant the same thing to him as it did to the people who surrounded him. In other words, we cannot assert that "mestizo" represented an essential and enduring quality of his very being. Sometimes, being an artisan took precedence over being a mestizo. At other times, a person who was labeled as a mestizo might foreground his Spanish noble line as opposed to his mixed parentage. Or alternately, he might have demonstrated solidarity with his neighbors by accepting their identification of him as an Indian.[10] Among members of the elite, gender played a significant role in the classification process, forcing men of mixed parentage into the mestizo slot and women into unproblematically assuming a Spanish identity. The central question before us is not "Who is a mestizo?" or "What is a mestizo?" but *"When* and *how* is someone a mestizo?" That is, we should move our gaze away from the condition of the individual, toward the context of the naming.

We tend to imagine socioracial classification in colonial Spanish America as replicating a series of eighteenth-century Mexican *casta* paintings: an orderly progression depicting different degrees of racial mixture, represented by portraits of couples with their progeny, each category with its own label and pictorial characteristics arranged systematically into a grid anchored by the primordial classes "Indian," "Spaniard," and "African" or "black." To be sure, historians are well aware that such paintings do not depict what was "out there," but that, instead, they project an idealized image meant for eighteenth-century European consumption.[11] Yet, despite the correctives offered by art historians, as well as an acceptance by historians of the fluidity of these categories, there is still a tendency in the historical literature to tacitly accept the transparency of "caste" designations as some sort of essential yet fluid marker of difference: in other words, that even if we (and colonial officials) cannot determine to which casta an individual "really belonged," there is a sense that an answer does exist, albeit just beyond our grasp. There also remains a propensity to envision caste as part of a coherent "system" that subsists across the entire colonial period and enfolds not only central Mexico, but sometimes the Andes as well.[12]

Nonetheless and to the contrary, sixteenth- and seventeenth-century classificatory practices in the Nuevo Reino de Granada were ambiguous, ragged at the edges, overlapping, and frequently displayed no center. While officials were frequently obliged to classify people in order to determine how to tax them, there is no sense in the documents that these designations were stable markers of identity, nor that they were significant for most people beyond their deployment in narrow legal and administrative situations. These classifications were not called "caste" and they were not elements of a system. Instead, they constituted a series of disparate procedures that were relational in nature, generated out of the interaction of specific people through particular speech-acts; they were highly dependent on context. Take, for instance, the example of a plebeian artisan who might silently accept being called a mestizo by a colonial official in a criminal dispute but resist a neighbor classifying him as an Indian, the latter constituting a speech-act that would directly impact his everyday relationships, making it a label worth fighting.[13] Who he was would depend on who was labeling him and for what purpose. By looking at mestizos, who frequently defy classification and whose acts of identification frequently draw on the markers used to differentiate members of the presumably more stable categories of "Spaniard," "Indian," and "black," we can begin to detect the contours of colonial practices of marking diversity and begin to ask new questions of the documents we find in the archives.

In a seminal piece entitled "Beyond 'Identity'" Rodgers Brubaker and Frederick Cooper argue that the very malleability of identity makes it difficult to define. "Identity" has too many applications, covers too much ground, envelops too many disparate practices. At the same time that it is infinitely applicable, however, the use of the word "identity" forces us to perceive a solidity and permanence where there is flux: a mestizo is always a mestizo except when he "passes" for something else, despite the fact that in the colonial period mestizos could occupy multiple slots without displaying any sense of contradiction. Brubaker and Cooper urge scholars to turn instead to more active terms like "identification," which is situational, relational, and forces us to pay closer attention to the locus of enunciation of those doing the classifying, as well as to the relationship between self-understandings and categorization by others. They argue that in some situations, processes of identification generate what they call a "groupness," a sense of commonality or connectedness that fosters the impression of a coherent group, as occurred with "Spaniards" or "Indians," but that in other cases, processes of identification are looser and more situational, more along the lines of how the concept "mestizo" operated in the early colonial period.[14] Brubaker and Cooper prod us to ask new questions that revolve not around the end result of classification—the production of the apparently stable categories "Indian," "black," "mestizo," "mulatto," and "Spaniard"—but instead to follow lines of inquiry concerning the very process of categorization: under what circumstances were individuals classified and who did the speaking? What are the diverse classificatory lexicons that colonial actors drew on to identify themselves and others, and how did these distinct sets of naming practices interact? What sorts of knowledge and what values underwrote the process of categorization?

My interest in mestizos draws on such questions. In this book I disrupt the presumed fixity of colonial sociracial classification and inquire, instead, into the process of categorization. When we look at the stories of people of mixed descent whose lives appear in the documentary record, we notice that their testimony was presented under particular legal and personal circumstances: they moved in specific social milieus, and their sociracial labels were inscribed in clearly delimited documentary genres, all of which impacted the ways in which they were classified. The identities they generated were many times transitory, frequently unvoiced (as in the case of Inés de Hinojosa). These identifications might very well have revolved around parentage, but they were also based on occupation, gender, and place of residence. And even when they turned on questions of descent, they may have skewed more toward problems of religion or noble status—the meaning of *"raza"* in the early modern era—than what we would today call "race."

I am at a bit of a loss for words in this enterprise. There is no simple gloss for the set of classificatory practices I study. These practices did not revolve exclusively around phenotype or parentage, but were also generated by numerous other cultural and social cues. For this reason, I have rejected some of the terms most commonly employed to refer to the practice of cataloguing difference in the colonial period. The available lexicon tends to fix these practices into a stable and coherent system that does not reflect what I see in the documentation from Bogotá and Tunja. "Casta," the terminology used in colonial Mexico and by Mexicanist historians to refer to a system of socioracial categories including "Indian," "mestizo," "mulatto," and so on, does not appear in the archival record of the Nuevo Reino until the eighteenth century, and then only as an umbrella term used to refer to those who were not Spaniards, Indians, or black slaves; in the sixteenth-century Andes "casta" referred to lineage in a more general sense. "Raza" (race) was another early modern term that referred to lineage, distinguishing individuals more by their status or their religion than by their color. The early modern word *"calidad"* (quality) may be most appropriate to the period, given that it transcended phenotype by revolving around questions of individual status and the behaviors appropriate to different social ranks, as well as distinguishing between categories of people generated by mixing; I will make use of this term throughout this volume.[15] I will, however, employ "socioracial" as a gloss when I intend to highlight forms of difference that today would be called "race."

We may be confining ourselves to a conceptual straitjacket when we limit our interpretation of terms like "Indian" or "mulatto" exclusively to their socioracial dimensions as part of a self-enclosed system of classification, because such usages were embedded in broader schemes of perception and categorization that both antedated the Spanish invasion of the Americas and continued to be employed on the Iberian Peninsula, taking in other markers, such as age, gender, occupation, noble or plebeian status, language, religion, and nationality, among others. The backwater of the sixteenth-century Nuevo Reino, where "casta" was not in common usage, may thus provide a constructive antidote to some of our overarching assumptions about the power and systematicity of caste in colonial Spanish America. In this sense, I appeal to historians to take a second look at the historical record, where I hope they will find something unexpected.

"MESTIZO" AS A CATEGORY

"Mestizo" is probably one of the most inscrutable categories in the colonial Spanish American documentary record. Other categories, such as "Indian" (*indio*) and "Spaniard" (*español*), functioned in the colonial period as both ascriptive classifications and as umbrella terms for groups with specific rights and obligations. These two categories functioned, along with "black" (*negro*), as major points of reference for making sense of the range of classifications of mixed people, and they appear to have displayed a good deal more coherence than did other categories, like "mestizo" or "mulatto."[16] Spaniards, for example, enjoyed the rights to certain types of citizenship, such as the status "*vecino*," a designation that permitted them to hold public office.[17] They were allowed to wear certain types of clothing and jewelry, such as capes and pearls, which Indians and members of some mixed categories were not.[18] In turn, Spaniards were required to participate in various public rituals throughout the year, ceremonial enactments that both represented and maintained Christian notions of hierarchy.[19] Similarly, "Indian" was an ascriptive category that encompassed identifiable groups with boundaries. Indians were obliged to pay tribute to the Crown but were at the same time exempt from the grasp of other intrusive colonial institutions, such as the Inquisition. They were tributaries assigned to specific native communities. Even if Indians fled their tribute obligations and sought anonymity in Santafé or Tunja, they were still at least marginally attached to a collectivity in the eyes of the colonial authorities. They also performed their Indianness in the judicial sphere, where they assumed the indio label as a vehicle for demanding those rights associated with the legal category.[20] In this sense, indios displayed a degree of "groupness," in the parlance of Brubaker and Cooper.

But it might be stretching it to infer groupness from the categories "Indian" and "Spaniard." Their existence as groups more commonly inhered in other types of classification, not in these categories themselves. That is, although they performed as Indians in the courtroom, they more likely identified themselves as members of specific *pueblos* distinguished by locality (the Muzos from the locality of Muzo, or the Sogamosos, for example). They belonged to populations (*naciones*) distinguished by language (the Muiscas of the altiplano extending between Santafé and Tunja, or the Panches to the southwest). They lived under the authority of a hereditary lord (*cacique*). Jovita Baber contends that "indio" was a constructed legal category through which the Crown was enabled to recognize "nations" (*naciones*) under its authority. Therefore, she argues, "indio" was not a racial classification, nor did it constitute a collective identity: one's identity was as a native (*natural*) of a given indigenous community and not as an indio. Promoting the corporate nature of the category "Indian" was, nevertheless, in the interests of the Crown, which was intensely preoccupied with extracting tribute and labor from native people, who were repeatedly cataloged in census documents as *indios tributarios* (tribute-paying Indians) and their dependents.[21]

Baber points out that the legal positioning of Mexican natives was similar to that of Spaniards. Spaniards—at least, Spanish men—were members of identifiable groups. Whether born in the Americas or on the Iberian Peninsula, they were labeled "vecinos" (citizens), "*residentes*" (residents), or sometimes "*estantes*" (transients) of a specific place to which they were connected by a series of privileges and duties. In addition to their affiliation with their place of residence, Spaniards born on the Peninsula also identified with particular nationalities, such as Basque or Catalán, allegiances that provoked fierce rivalries, even in the American setting.[22] Lastly, they were also distinguished by their birthplace, as naturales (natives) of Seville, Toledo, or Carmona.

Black slaves and freedpersons were sometimes identified by their origins as "Angolas," "Branes," or other African "nations." That is, they also sometimes constituted groups on the ground, notwithstanding the fact that the collectivities they belonged to had been dismembered and reorganized under slavery. Like Indians, who did not belong to the "group" of Indians but to particular "nations" or communities, Africans and African-descended people were not members of the "group" of blacks, but could be associated with specific collectivities defined by their place of origin.[23] Classification by "nation" depended, however, on who was doing the categorizing and for what purpose; it does not, moreover, always appear in the historical record. Furthermore, the rights and obligations of slaves were defined by the nature of their bondage, so that African slaves were frequently identified by reference to their owners. Mulattos could be slaves or freedpersons, but if the latter, they were subject to a special regime of taxation and were inscribed into a type of census document that imbued them, on paper at least, with a kind of groupness.[24]

None of these categories was entirely stable or homogeneous, nor were their boundaries fixed and clearly delimited, even though they sometimes constituted named entities. This is why it is more useful to think of them as exhibiting characteristics of groupness than to refer to them as groups in the sociological sense of the word. That is, they drew on some sort of commonality that led people to adopt similar behaviors, to associate with one another, to share a common and explicit definition of who they were and who did not belong with them. But even so, the porosity of their boundaries made these assemblages of individuals highly heterogeneous.

For example, nestled comfortably within the category "Spaniard" were many who did not trace their parentage exclusively to the Iberian

Peninsula, although they were assumed to be Spaniards. These individuals did not carry the label "Indian," "mulatto," or "mestizo" in the documentation, so we might think of them as "unmarked" and thus presume they belonged to the dominant Spanish category. The designation "Spaniard" was highly dependent on the space of enunciation in which it was uttered. In certain legal contexts, such as criminal records, Spaniards are labeled as such, whereas in wills and contracts they are not. Many times, individuals born in Spain are called Spaniards, while Americans of Spanish descent (infrequently called criollos or creoles in early colonial Santafé and Tunja) are not marked socioracially. Sixteenth-century Spanish women were not identified as españolas as frequently as were their brothers and husbands, which suggests to me that socioracial categories in the documentation must be construed as highly situational: they were relevant to specific legal contexts in which men, rather than women, more often participated.[25]

Notwithstanding the supposition that the class "Spaniards" referred to individuals from Spain, the unmarked category also included individuals born of mothers and fathers who were not of Iberian origin. People of mixed descent who successfully integrated themselves into Spanish social circles were frequently considered to be Spaniards when they participated in certain legal settings in which parentage was not an issue; they appear in the documentation without the "Spanish" moniker but are not identified as belonging to a different class. Similarly, we find mestizos and mulattos living in native communities who were entered into the tribute rolls, effectively becoming "Indians." So, while native people, Spaniards and their descendants, slaves, and mulattos exhibited attributes of groupness, the categories by which they were identified were in actuality heterogeneous.

Even more so than in the case of Indians or Spaniards, those assigned to the category "mestizo" fall in and out of the documentary record, leading lives in which they are only sometimes identified by their parentage. "Mestizo" was in the colonial period what I will call a disappearing category. By "disappearing," I wish to imply that under particular circumstances people classified as mestizos dropped out of the mestizo slot and into other categories, not that the population of mixed parentage disappeared from the map through a simple speech-act; indeed, by all accounts the population of those classified in the census rolls as mestizos expanded exponentially over the course of the colonial period, becoming the plurality by the late eighteenth century.

For the period I am concerned with, the mestizo population was probably minuscule in rural areas and only readily apparent in cities, although it remained small, even in Santafé and Tunja. Of course, we can only estimate mestizo populations, because they were not counted until the eighteenth century.[26] In the early colonial period, individuals might be called mestizo at one moment and Indian or Spaniard at another, sometimes by the same witness. Because there was no single group to which mestizos belonged, they could disappear from the legal record and emerge again under a different designation.

The facility with which mestizos "disappear" owes to the fact that there was no sociological group for mestizos to belong to, just a category to which they were assigned.[27] Mestizos had no specific obligations to a collectivity, as was the case with Indians and Spaniards, nor were they required as a group to pay certain kinds of taxes, as were mulattos; they were not subject to tribute, as were Indians, nor to servitude, as were African and African-descended slaves. Furthermore, the range of people who could be assigned to the mestizo slot was vast and diffuse. Many mestizos of the first generation after the Spanish invasion were not recognized by their Spanish fathers, and they often occupied lowly positions in the colonial status hierarchy as servants or laborers. These individuals are frequently identified in the documents as, for example, "Inés Mestiza" or "Juan Mestizo," as though "mestizo" were a surname. In later generations, when children were born of unions between mestizos or with members of other categories, these designations became more complicated: a child of a Spaniard and a mestiza might be identified as a mestizo, but he might also be called a *"cuarterón"* (quadroon); or, depending on his social status, he could be of unmarked calidad and taken for an American of Iberian descent. Indeed, it was very difficult for colonial observers to accurately distinguish between categories in a world where mixing was a routine occurrence.[28]

Many mestizos were also members of corporations, such as occupational groups or guilds (for example, tanners, shoemakers, or tailors) or religious fraternities (*cofradías*). They identified themselves by such varied criteria as their status as urban property-owners or the degree to which they conformed to Iberian cultural values.[29] Of course, an appeal to occupational status, membership in a religious organization, or property ownership did not preclude being labeled as mestizo, nor did it shield people of mixed parentage from discrimination, which they frequently experienced. What it did accomplish, however, was to establish in certain social contexts their affiliation with a corporate group defined by livelihood or other activities, rather than by parentage.

Many years ago, Fredrik Barth exploded the notion of ethnicity as a cultural essence or an unchanging corporate group. He pointed out that it is more relevant to examine how ethnic boundaries are maintained, negotiated, or ignored in specific circumstances than to assume ethnic allegiance as something fixed and immutable. Culture, for Barth, is something that marks differences between individuals; it is situational and relational, not stable.[30] Is this the same as my interpretation of the contextual use in the colonial period of terms like "mestizo"? On the surface, the two practices appear to be quite similar. Indeed, Barth helps us to think through why mestizos "disappear" so frequently in the documents: because classification is pertinent only at certain junctures in an individual's life and in specific documentary or legal contexts. Barth also helps us to comprehend how mestizos could surreptitiously melt into the categories "Spaniard" or "Indian" under certain legal circumstances. But the issue is more complicated. Further reflection on the differences between colonial socioracial categories and modern anthropological notions of ethnicity can help us to comprehend the specificities of classificatory practices in the Nuevo Reino.

However fluid Barth's notion of ethnic boundaries might appear, it still presupposes that there is a sociological group with which ethnics identify, even if only situationally: a collectivity across whose limits they traverse and whose (constructed) cultural essence they draw on or avoid as needed. But the category of mestizo was significantly more diffuse than an ethnic group. It functioned in the early colonial period as a loose classification of individuals, a category into which fell all those who were not indigenous, African-descendant, or European. The category "mestizo" included elites like don Diego de Torres and don Alonso de Silva, caciques with conquistador fathers, as well as plebeian laborers in Santafé, Tunja, or the rural towns that dotted the Nuevo Reino. It was a class that contained urban women of mixed parentage who wore indigenous costume but were called mestizas, as well as members of native communities fathered by mestizo or Spanish men, who spoke Muisca (also called Chibcha), the native language of their mothers, and who were entered in the tribute rolls as Indians. These individuals had little in common beyond the label "mestizo."

Stuart Schwartz and Frank Salomon eloquently elucidate the quandary faced by colonial mestizos in a passage that is worth repeating.

In colonial usage "mestizo" was not so much the name of a firm social category as a term meaning a weakly defined person, one who might occupy varied social roles depending on demand and opportunity, but who was not really entitled by his or her "nature" to any of them. In other words, "mestizo" was not a stable member of the category set *español, indio, portugués,* or *inca,* but was a term of a different order, denoting nonplacement within the legitimate set. At first Spaniards tried to regularize the situation by treating mestizos as a separate hereditary category in its own right. Toledan-era parish books sometimes carried separate registers for mixed "castes." But the idea of a mixed-caste caste was a contradiction in terms, and the term "mestizo" tended always to lapse back into usages connoting degradation.[31]

That is, "people of mixed birth formed not so much a new category as a challenge to categorization itself."[32] They were "none of the above," as the Colombian historian Víctor Álvarez comments: they were not tributaries, nor did they live in a community as did Indians; unlike African slaves, they were free; they could not claim any of the special rights due to Spaniards.[33] They had no legitimate origin—no "natural"—in comparison to Spaniards, who were naturales of named towns, or to Indians, who were sometimes referred to as naturales in a more general usage.

"MESTIZO" AS AN EXCLUSIONARY CATEGORY

"Mestizo" thus functioned as a category of exclusion. For instance, the eligibility of mestizos for the priesthood was hotly debated throughout the early colonial period; mestiza nuns could not wear the black veil.[34] Mestizos were also excluded from the corps of notaries. A royal decree granting Juan Sánchez the title of public notary came under criticism in 1563, when the city fathers of Santafé decided that Sánchez was possibly a mestizo and thus ineligible to occupy a notarial office, although the various witnesses who gave testimony could not agree as to whether he were in fact mestizo and moreover neglected to provide an account of those features that might identify him as such.[35]

The archives are full of name-calling, instances in which individuals were labeled as mestizos in order to exclude them from access to positions or rights. Sometimes these invectives turned on appearance, a pretext for pursuing power struggles that had little to do with the mestizo designation. Attributes such as clothing, language, color, and a host of other features stood in for the real terms of engagement. Name-calling was made possible by the fact that "mestizo-ness" and its difference from other categories were so difficult to determine. Don Juan, the early seventeenth-century cacique of Cunucubá, was one of these ill-fated individuals accused by his encomendera of being a mestizo and thus ineligible to continue serving as cacique.[36] Wishing to rid herself of a troublesome cacique who defended his subjects against her depredations, don Juan's encomendera declared that he was "not the same color" as his tributaries ("no es de la color de los indios") and must therefore be a mestizo. Note, however, that don Juan's color was never specified—just what color he wasn't. The encomendera also insinuated that his command of Spanish was too good for him to be an Indian, that his children dressed like Europeans and must therefore be mestizos, and that his abuse of his subjects confirmed his mestizo character.[37] In this case, "mestizo" functioned as an exclusionary vehicle precisely because it was so ambiguous.

"Mestizo" also operated as an exclusionary category based on the premise that mestizos were of illegitimate birth and could therefore be denied entry to various professions and offices or could be given short shrift when it came to inheritance. "Mestizo" fuses with the category "hijo natural" (illegitimate child) to form an assemblage in which each defines the other: if you are a mestizo, you must be illegitimate; if you are illegitimate, you might be a mestizo. Thus, don Alonso de Silva and don Diego de Torres, caciques of Tibasosa and Turmequé, respectively, were forced out of office on the basis of their illegitimate birth-status and their mixed parentage.[38] The two men defended their integrity by highlighting the superiority of their Spanish blood, inverting the more common depictions of mestizos as base individuals whose mixed parentage made them impure, but they had more trouble substantiating their status as legitimate children. Isabel Sotelo was also exposed to the slur "mestiza" because of her birth out of wedlock.[39]

Berta Ares Queija contends that illegitimacy was not as much an issue for the first generation of mestizos, because the children of conquistadors treated their illegitimate progeny as their future heirs and sometimes legitimized their status. She adds that many elite mestizos of the period, including the Inca Garcilaso de la Vega, viewed themselves as the holders of a double patrimony as children of conquistadors and heirs to the original landowners. She argues that by the mid-sixteenth century, the growth of the mestizo population posed a threat to the status quo, at which point exclusionary legislation was introduced to limit the rights of the children of mixed unions, particularly of the mestizo elite.[40] But if we focus all our attention on men like Garcilaso, Silva, and Torres, we lose sight of all the other mestizos living in the early colonial Nuevo Reino de Granada. Not all mestizos were the children of conquistadors, and even among those who were, many did not have access to powerful and well-connected families. Many mestizos were never legitimized by their fathers, nor could they aspire to the positions and perquisites available to Silva and Torres. They were simply excluded. Those born to indigenous mothers living in rural communities might, for example, be forced to abandon their families under the pretext that mestizos had a dangerous influence on native Christians. If they were the children of Spanish artisans with their native servants, they might be prevented from claiming their meager inheritance under the pretext that they were illegitimate.

THE MEANING OF MIXTURE

"Mestizo" was a label that could be contested or qualified, as it was by don Juan of Cunucubá and by Alonso de Silva and Diego de Torres, but given the fact that on the Iberian Peninsula it predated the invasion of the Americas and the process of racial mixing there, it also continued to be deployed as a floating signifier that could mean myriad things to a wide range of observers. If we want to comprehend the fluidity of the category, we need to move beyond the supposition that mestizo = Spanish + Indian, to consider the broader range of meanings that inhered in the word, and to imagine how these significations might have influenced the process of classifying individuals.

In the second half of the sixteenth century mestizos were commonly associated with rebellion. Mestizos like the caciques of Tibasosa and Turmequé were believed to constitute an imaginary fourth column capable of obliterating the colonial order. Together with other border-crossers such as *indios ladinos* (Spanish-speaking Indians) and *conversos* (converts from Islam and Judaism), mestizos were believed to be susceptible to the falsehoods propagated by idolatry; that is, their ancestry marked them as imperfectly Christianized, and they were feared as potential recruits to the ranks of an armed native revolt.[41] In short, mestizos' proximity to the indigenous population was alarming to Spaniards as a source of both spiritual and political contagion, as much to the native population as to colonial society at large. But the existence in the Spanish colonial imagination of a host of potentially aggressive mestizos does not constitute a rebellion in fact: Silva and Torres were not purveyors of armed revolution, and most mestizos led peaceful lives plying at their trades or tilling the land. Indeed, the two mestizo caciques were staunch allies of Crown officials demonized by Tunja's encomenderos.[42] More properly, then, "mestizo" functioned metaphorically, much like "Jew" did in early modern Spain, where the label was deployed as a figure of speech to defame people through a "language of political critique" that extended well beyond the boundaries of the recognizable Jewish congregation.[43] The presumed brotherhood of mestizos was a focal point for channeling similar fears and prejudices, birthing a ghostly host of rebels.

After the wave of rebellions and imagined revolts along the Andean mountain chain had cooled off in the seventeenth century, mestizos living in rural areas came to be feared by the colonial authorities, both civil and religious, because of their imagined unhealthy influence on native people: they were thought to rob native communities through trickery and to encroach on their lands, too lazy to keep their animals from destroying the crops Indians had worked so hard to plant and weed. The label "mestizo" came to serve as a metaphor for "outsider" (*forastero*) despite the fact that more often than not mestizos were born in the very native communities in which they resided.[44]

The propensity of "mestizo" to stand in for something else, its role as an empty signifier, can be observed in the definition provided by Sebastián de Covarrubias in his 1611 dictionary: "He who is engendered by diverse species of animals [El que es engendrado de diversas especies de animales]."[45] This unrestricted meaning, in which "mestizo" simply means "mixing," is preserved by the 1726 *Diccionario de autoridades*: "[That] which is applied to the animal whose father and mother are of different castes [Que se aplica a un animal de padre y madre de diferentes castas]."[46] Note that this definition makes no reference specifically to the mixing of Indians and Spaniards; instead, it conceives of a mestizo more generally as a mixture of any two animal species (as continues to be the case in modern Spanish usage, where the context of the utterance determines the more precise meaning to be attached to the word).

It is therefore no surprise that the seventeenth-century Peruvian indigenous author Felipe Guaman Poma de Ayala protests in his *Primer nueva corónica y buen gobierno* that "by marrying an *yndia mitaya*, [a cacique's] children and his descendants are mestizos."[47] A *mitayo* in the colonial context was a native man subject to the labor levy (*mita*). In this case, however, "mitaya" denotes an indigenous female commoner, an "india." Guaman Poma's act of assigning the children of chief-commoner unions to the mestizo category transcends the usual meaning of the term, because the mixing tagged by the Peruvian chronicler is reportedly between two classes of native people, not between members of distinct socioracial categories.[48] Caciques were not strictly classified as Indians, but as "Indian caciques" (*indios caciques*), their noble status qualifying their socioracial designation. Indios caciques occupied a privileged category distinct from that of their subjects, a different social status: they were exempt from paying tribute, wore European costume at a time when sumptuary laws distinguishing among categories were enforced, and enjoyed the prestige of attaching to their name the noble title of "don" or "doña." In other words, while caciques were indeed native (naturales), they were different from their subjects. Guaman Poma believed that it was unnatural for caciques to mix with commoners and tagged this behavior as a form of mestizaje.

The barb Guaman Poma flings at disorderly caciques illustrates the fact that the notion of mixing did not center exclusively on interethnic unions, but turned more generally on the question of status. How mestizaje was comprehended in the colonial period had a great deal to do with anxieties over lineage. The Iberian social hierarchy—indeed, the social hierarchies of many European countries, including France and England—was founded on the promotion and maintenance of noble lineages and on ensuring the purity of noble blood that flowed from generation to generation. The integrity of noble lineage was achieved through the policing of unions, as much with commoners or condemned heretics as with converts from Judaism and Islam, all of whom were thought to threaten the purity of noble family lines.[49]

The French notion of *mésalliance*—"misalliance" or marriage to a social inferior—crystallizes the problem of mixture alluded to by Guaman Poma. It points us away from "race" as we know it today and toward early modern notions of hierarchy in which "raza" meant "lineage."[50] In keeping with this very different appreciation of the meaning of "race," the children of French mésalliances were called "*métis*," French for "mestizo," even when the "misalliance" was between nobles and commoners.[51] This is precisely the concern voiced by Guaman Poma in his condemnation of promiscuous caciques, although in the French case the concept draws on European principles of descent. Perhaps we can better comprehend what mestizaje meant to colonial people if we ask of our documents the same questions that Jean Feerick asks of early modern English texts: "How might it affect the readings we produce if we follow this period's ascriptions and understand blood rather than skin colour to be the somatic referent anchoring this system of race?"[52]

Did the precise nature of one's parentage, rather than the simple fact of being mixed, make a difference in the colonial period? The vast majority of the children of mixed unions in the central highlands of the Nuevo Reino de Granada were the offspring of Europeans, mestizos, mulattos, or blacks with Muisca women. If they were raised in the doctrinal towns in which natives were segregated (*pueblos de indios*), these children might identify as Indian, given that descent among the Muisca was traced through the female line.[53] Alternately, they might live as mestizos in urban areas or in the countryside (even in indigenous pueblos). However, there were other mestizos in the Nuevo Reino, the offspring of unions between conquistadors and native women—sometimes members of the indigenous nobility—from Peru, Quito, or Popayán, the children of encounters that took place before the Spanish invasion of the Muisca. Marta Herrera questions whether colonial people distinguished mestizos in terms of maternal ethnicities.[54] That is, does the blanket use of the category "mestizo" dilute the specificity of parentage in the same way that "indio" ignores the various nationalities to which Indians could lay claim? Did being a mestizo with Spanish-Muisca parentage open up different possibilities than those available to individuals of Spanish-Quiteño ancestry, or was the apparently greater facility for social mobility of the mestizo children of conquistadors with native mothers from Quito a function of the high status of their fathers (and perhaps of their mothers)? It is difficult to gauge how mestizos without ties to the local native population might have been perceived at the time, although most of those I have encountered in the documentation were members of the elite or closely associated with them and were, correspondingly, able to move with ease in polite society.

But must we confine our understanding of mestizaje to the offspring of mixed unions? In the early modern period, mixture resulted not only from sexual encounters but also from other sorts of activities, both public and intimate in character. That is, mixing was not necessarily genealogical in nature. In medieval Asturias, Christians allied with the Moors, for example, were called "mestizos."[55] It was believed that European women who gazed at portraits of Ethiopians might give birth to dark-skinned infants.[56] The transmission across groups of maternal milk, which was considered to be a type of blood, was also believed to constitute a kind of mixing, as Guaman Poma points out: "The aforementioned criollos, who are fed with the milk of Indian or black women, or the aforementioned mestizos [and] mulattos, are angry and arrogant, lazy, liars, gamblers, miserly, of little charity, contemptible, deceitful, enemies of the poor Indians and of Spaniards."[57] Fray Reginaldo de Lizárraga, writing in the early seventeenth century to disparage Peruvian creoles, echoes the native Andean chronicler: "When the poor child is born, he is handed over to a dirty, lying Indian or a black woman, who nurses him. . . . How will this boy turn out? He will get his inclinations from the milk he drank. . . . He who drinks a liar's milk is a liar, he who drinks a drunkard's milk is a drunkard, he who drinks a thief's milk is a thief, etc."[58]

Mother's milk was believed to be "capable of transmitting character traits as well as lineage," and for this reason Christian children in Spain were not to be nursed by Jewish or Morisca (Muslim) wet nurses or by converts to Christianity.[59] As Sarah Pech puts it, milk provided moral nourishment as well as physical sustenance, so it was essential to choose a wet nurse who possessed the appropriate qualities.[60] Christian children who were "contaminated" by Morisca milk were said to be *"amoriscados"* or "Islamized."[61]

Of course, pragmatism frequently outweighed the moralizing discourses of theologians. The cacique Alonso de Silva decried the forced employment of indigenous wet nurses by the wife of his encomendero, who did not appear to be at all concerned that her children would imbibe impure Muisca milk.[62] Doña María Manuela de Ávila, daughter of the cacique of Guatavita, left a bequest in her will to the mulatto Frasquito, who was the son of the woman who nursed her, her *hermano de leche* (milk brother).[63] The Casa de los Niños Expósitos (Foundlings Home), established in Santafé in the mid-seventeenth century, did a brisk business in indigenous wet nurses who nourished their mostly Spanish (and sometimes noble) charges, many of whom were the illegitimate children of unmarried Spanish couples, since the illegitimate offspring of women of lower social orders were generally raised by their mothers and were not abandoned to the care of the state.[64] In other words, while wet nursing was thought to be a source of contamination, an insidious kind of mixing, in practice it was widespread among both the Spanish and indigenous elite in Santafé and

Tunja who, in the process, potentially transformed their children into mestizos.[65]

AN ETHNOGRAPHY OF COLONIAL MESTIZAJE

In the course of my research in the Bogotá archives, I discovered a civil suit filed in 1633 against Juana, the illegitimate daughter of the Santafé goldsmith Francisco Antonio de Colmenares, who was a Spaniard. Although the records indicate that Juana was a mestiza, they provide, as is often the case, no information about her mother, who is out of the picture. Juana's father married a Spanish woman and raised his daughter in a Spanish environment as a servant. According to the case record, Juana was seduced by a mestizo carpenter named Jacinto de Padilla, who took her to cohabit (*amancebarse*) with him in his house near the convent of San Francisco. Assisted by the young mestiza, Padilla proceeded to steal furniture, some tools, a blue-and-green silk skirt, a partially eaten ham, and a bouquet of roses from Colmenares and his wife (57r–v).[66] Padilla claimed that he and a companion had met Juana in the street near her father's house and that they had spent some time in a room below the stairs that was occupied by another of Colmenares's illegitimate mestiza daughters. According to his confession, after Padilla left the gathering, his companion returned and, unbeknownst to the defendant, burgled the goldsmith's house, then temporarily stored some of the stolen items at Padilla's lodgings. When he was picked up, Padilla, who was nineteen years old at the time, denied cohabiting with Juana (60v). He is depicted as the stereotypical figure of the shifty, untrustworthy mestizo.

I was struck by Juana's predicament. Despite the fact that her life transpired in the distant seventeenth century, she reminded me of a modern adolescent: she had trouble communicating with her parents and occasionally fell in with the wrong people; she liked to shoot the breeze with young men; she longed to escape the discipline of her household and believed that marriage would allow her to do so (according to her testimony, Padilla had promised betrothal) (62v). The presence of her stepmother, who likely ensured Juana's subordinated status by placing her in a servile position, provoked what I suspect was an act of revenge expressed through the theft of her household goods. In short, Juana made some bad choices. Here, I sensed, was a story, one that might enable me to explore the nuances of what it meant to be mestizo in Santafé.

Narratives like Juana's furnish ethnographic scenarios through which I explore the lives of mestizos and mulattos of the Nuevo Reino. I do so by homing in on the texture of their experiences, rather than by recurring to the condensed comparative description that characterizes so much social history, which frequently jumps from one paragraph-long case to another, each emblematic of the author's argument.[67] The stories I examine in this volume position me to inquire into how subjectivities arising out of differences of color, occupation, gender, or status generated what appears to historians centuries later as a complex and rigid system but at the time was more likely a series of highly situational and multidimensional choices. In Juana's case, I ask whether Jacinto de Padilla's mestizo moniker influenced the authorities who accused him of theft: does the simple fact that he was identified as a mestizo—defendants in criminal cases were frequently distinguished by their socioracial category—imply that authorities would be more likely to consider him a thief than they would a Spaniard, a mulatto, a black, or an Indian? Was Juana attracted to him because he was a mestizo, or, alternately, did she gravitate toward him simply because both of them lived in a plebeian milieu where they were likely to meet? Juana's narrative prods me to move beyond studying the moment of socioracial classification to consider how being mestiza impinged in a much broader and perhaps more diffuse sense on Juana's life (since in this case there is little dispute over her classification).

I opt for depth, not breadth, for something I call "ethnographic history," in an appeal to the inspiring writings of Greg Dening, who voices the following about his craft: "It begins with the most difficult thing of all to see: the experience of past actors as they experienced it, and not that experience as we in hindsight experience it for them."[68] The documents I draw from function for me as spaces of interpretation and sometimes even of speculation, as the places where I construct arguments, and not as raw data for already constructed models. As I read and reread these documents and construct narratives out of them, I repeatedly question the categories inscribed in them, engaging in a kind of "thick description" that incorporates not only the processes by which individuals were classified, but the legal contexts in which categorization took place and the spaces in which these documents might be read twenty, thirty, or a hundred years later by other colonial actors— what Dening calls history as what "actually" happened, or history as a narrative that unfolds at particular moments in historical time.[69] That is, I have tried to treat each document (or group of documents) as an ethnographic scenario, something akin to the settings that ethnographers encounter in the field, which furnish the ground on which ethnographic description and analysis is constructed.

To the extent that the documentation permits, I explore the networks of social relationships in which the protagonists move and how these relationships change over time. I inquire into the ways in which individuals shift from one form of identification to another situationally, how they speak about themselves and others in particular contexts, and how the colonial state and its legal apparatus informs this speech. In effect, given the nature of the archival record, all the ethnographic scenarios I present are legal ones in which the actions and words of the actors, as well as the recording of acts of identification or of establishing difference, are dictated by the exigencies of the procedures that are being performed and by the notaries who supervise them.[70] Both the presence and absence of markers of difference in the documentation—the purposeful silences in the ethnographic record—are relevant ethnographic facts.[71] For example, the mestizo identity of Diego García Zorro, a member of the Santafé elite, is obscured in notarial recordings of his land and slave purchases because it was irrelevant to those transactions, but it is foregrounded in his appeal to join the city council, where it played a role in the opposition he encountered; the simultaneous presence and absence of socioracial markers in the documentary record opens a window into the legal mechanisms by which García Zorro moved in and out of focus as a mestizo in late sixteenth-century and early seventeenth-century Santafé, illuminating the pathways by which mestizo men maintained their status and honor. García Zorro's experience can be juxtaposed to the story of Isabel de Sotelo, a mestiza who lived the early part of her life unproblematically as a Spaniard, until her mixed parentage was unveiled as a result of an interrupted love affair. When examined together, as in chapter 3, the two scenarios illustrate how colonial mestizaje was gendered in unexpected ways.

I also probe the documentary record to reveal the nature of historical memory. This approach is what I suggest in the vignette that opens this introduction, where I question the reasons for the absence in *El carnero* of any reference to Inés de Hinojosa's mestiza condition. In the following chapters, I return time and again to *Genealogías del Nuevo Reino de Granada*, a late seventeenth-century genealogical compendium of Santafé's most notable families, compiled by the notary Juan Flórez de Ocáriz. Flórez's entries occasionally contain references to individuals I have encountered in the sixteenth-century historical record; sometimes he identifies them as mestizos or names their parents, but in other cases he leaves their sociracial classification unmarked. By juxtaposing my documentary protagonists to these later genealogical portraits, I trace how memories of mestizaje were constructed—or erased—over time, adding a temporal dimension to my ethnography, making it into history as what "actually" happened.

In his memoir of ethnographic fieldwork among the Panare of Venezuela, Jean-Paul Dumont argues that anthropologists do not simply gather data. Instead, he asserts, there is a moment of ethnographic knowing, a juncture at which the anthropologist understands enough to know what information to collect, what to ask. This moment emerges, he reasons, from the collision of the subjectivities of the researcher and of informants who, at moments of contradiction, are forced to ask questions of one another. The act of questioning opens space for ethnographic inquiry.[72] Clearly, I cannot achieve such an intersubjective relationship with the individuals whose stories I tell in this book, but I can generate "dialogues with the dead" (to appropriate Michel de Certeau's metaphor) in an effort to imagine the kind of relationship I have enjoyed during ethnographic fieldwork.[73]

I do this by refusing to accept as self-evident the sociracial categories supplied by the documents. For example, in chapter 2 I look at the story of the criminal defendant Juan de Salazar, a cobbler identified in the documentation by some actors as a mestizo and by others as an Indian. Certainly, this information suggests the fluidity of sociracial classification. But I also inquire into some of the other qualities displayed by Salazar that might have contributed to confusion over his identity. Were the multiple markers ascribed to him due to the fact that he was a Spanish-speaker and therefore less easy to identify as indigenous? Was it because he was a Quiteño, an immigrant from the city of Quito, and thus had no attachment to a local native community? Did it depend on the status of the person doing the classifying and that individual's proximity to the shoemaker—that is, did his friends say something different from his lawyer? Could it be that Salazar's identity was less confusing to him and to his associates than it is to us? I have attempted to subject the archival materials to multiple close readings, digging deeper and deeper in order to overturn previous assumptions I might have had, using the documents as a space for ethnographic imaginings.[74]

In the end, I decided that the most productive way to explore the disappearing nature of the mestizo would be to construct ethnographic scenarios that examined the lives of a series of mestizos and mulattos in the central highlands of the Nuevo Reino de Granada. My instincts were seconded in February 2008, when I presented a first draft of what would become chapter 1 at the Radcliffe Institute for Advanced Study, where I began the writing of this book. Two of the fellows in attendance at the event, one a poet and the other a playwright, mentioned how compelling they found my stories and urged me to pursue a narrative approach. One of them pointed me to the textured history of indigenous-European relations in colonial North America by such authors as John Demos (*The Unredeemed Captive*) and Jill Lepore (*New York Burning*), although the archival documentation at my disposal did not uncover the wealth of material, much of it contained in letters and diaries, that allowed them to produce book-length narratives.[75] I discovered that by generating arguments out of the stories instead of imposing preestablished models onto the documents, even if they were not as rich and intricate as those of Demos and Lepore, I would be able to trace the paths of early colonial classificatory practice in a nuanced way.

THE STRUCTURE OF THIS BOOK

The chapters that follow narrate the stories of sixteenth- and seventeenth-century mestizos and mulattos (and one Moor) from Santafé, Tunja, Vélez, and the hinterlands of these urban centers. I briefly describe each protagonist in the Cast of Characters, which is included as an appendix to this volume.[76] Their stories serve as the ground on which I develop the following arguments.

In an effort to distinguish between the racial mindset that is a mark of our times and the distinct worldview of colonial people, I begin with epistemology. In chapter 1 I explore how notions of lineage and honor permeated classificatory practices, generating a genealogical approach to making sense of diversity and inequality that highlighted religious congregation and nobility, in addition to making sense of the mixing of American, African, and European populations. I develop a series of ethnographic scenarios in which sixteenth- and seventeenth-century Santafereños manipulate their identities in order to "pass" as others: a mulatto from Quito who disguises himself as a noble Limeño to court a Spanish noblewoman; a convert from Islam who is accused of hiding behind the façade of a wealthy encomendero; the mestiza daughter of a conquistador who in an act of rebellion against her elite family dons indigenous dress. We might easily read these cases of "disappearing mestizos" by appealing to modern notions of racial passing. However, a close look at each of these stories suggests that the terms on which these individuals passed for someone they were not had little to do with what we imagine as race in modern North America, or even in Latin America, for that matter. They more convincingly exemplify an early modern understanding of race as lineage, illustrating the distinct epistemology that underlay the process of making sense of diversity in the colonial world.

In chapter 2 I interpret how the classification of rural mestizos and mulattos emerged out of the social networks with which they interacted. In a sense, this chapter provides a familiar point of entry into my subject matter, given that the fluidity of socioracial designations is a topic that is increasingly of interest to many historians.[77] However, I intend to go beyond documenting fluidity. I probe my stories in an effort to lay bare the networks within which their protagonists moved in their daily lives. What I hope to demonstrate is that individuals labeled "mestizos" did not necessary "belong" to a sociological group identified by mixed parentage: there was no sense of groupness associated with mestizos. Instead, people bearing this classification negotiated myriad relationships, depending on the particular context in which they found themselves: some of them spent their time with other Spanish-speakers in Muisca towns; others warmed themselves at hearths tended by their indigenous wives; many walked the streets of urban centers peopled by plebeians of various socioracial designations. The nature of the different social networks in which they participated influenced, in turn, how they fashioned both their own self-images and how they were represented by others.

In order to evaluate what being a mestizo meant in the early colonial period, I examine the permeability of those categories that exhibited some degree of groupness: Indians, Spaniards, and blacks. In chapter 3 I focus on the relationship between being Spanish and being mestizo through a reading of the quandaries faced by a series of elite mestizos who strove to be accepted in Spanish social circles. These stories demonstrate that for elite women of mixed parentage, there was no identifiable boundary between "Spanish" and "mestizo." Many elite mestiza women unproblematically assumed the position of Spaniard, not in the sense of passing for Spaniards, but in that they were believed to be innately worthy of belonging to this category. This suggests that the category "Spaniard" was vastly more heterogeneous and permeable than we might at first imagine. In contrast, elite mestizo men encountered real barriers to the assumption of "Spanishness"; they were consistently demeaned by the gatekeepers of polite society and prevented from marrying Spanish women in the interests of preserving Iberian lineages and bloodlines. By deciphering the social networks drawn on by elite men and women to identify themselves as mestizos, to hide temporarily from that ascription, or to refuse to acknowledge it, as well as by looking at those who were never forced into the straitjacket of classification, I engage in an ethnographic interpretation of the contexts in which the label "mestizo" was applied, disputed, or elided. In this way I interpret "mestizo" not as a thing, but as a gendered social process.

The vignettes in the first three chapters are of necessity concise, as they are based on relatively brief documents that do not supply sufficient evidence for description-laden narratives. Furthermore, they contain accounts that are largely told in the third person by colonial officials. In chapter 4, however, I present a more comprehensive narrative, looking at two mestizo caciques of Muisca pueblos in the environs of Tunja, don Alonso de Silva and don Diego de Torres. Their first-person narratives, which comprise several thousand folios housed in Bogotá and Seville, lead me beyond the stereotypes that I had always imagined characterized mestizos in the discourse of the period: as idolaters or marginal plebeians, as hispanized elites who denied their mixed ancestry, as ignored or demeaned illegitimate children. To be sure, all of these typecasts emerge in the documentation associated with the legal suits brought by these two remarkable men, but they flow from the pens of their Spanish opponents. In contrast, Silva and Torres themselves argue for a more nuanced view of their position as mestizos in colonial society: they paint a portrait of themselves as devout Christians who despise idolatry, as the bearers of "Spanish blood" that cleansed and refined their aboriginal antecedents, as urbane and cosmopolitan gentlemen with a civilizing message for their subjects and a discourse of indigenous rights for the Spanish authorities, as the rightful heirs to the chiefdom of their communities. That is, they fashion themselves as political actors by aligning with Spanishness, as opposed to aboriginality, their objective being, paradoxically, the affirmation of their legitimacy as indigenous leaders. It was the figure of don Diego de Torres, who is almost an icon in Colombia, that persuaded me to focus my attentions on mestizos, although like so many others I first viewed him through a romantic indigenous lens. When I commenced a sustained interpretation of his legal papers, however, I discovered that what he had to say complicated my appreciation of both mestizaje and indigeneity.

Ethnography is a tool of the imagination that we can bring to bear on myriad spaces of practice, only one of which is people's daily lives and how they talk about themselves. In my archival wanderings I occasionally came across physical descriptions, oddly composed and formulaic sentences that emphasized features like beards or warts and moles, containing colors I had never heard of before such as "*loro*" or "*bazo*" (both denoting shades of brown). I discovered an enormous corpus of such descriptions in the archives in Seville, registered in documents granting permission for individuals to travel to the Indies. I noticed that these narrative portraits were frequently juxtaposed with socioracial categories classifying the applicants. In chapter 5 I examine what early modern bureaucrats thought people of different calidades looked like, inquiring into narrative portraits drawn in a variety of legal circumstances. Colonial administrators were concerned less with the characteristics of broad social categories than with the appearances of individuals, in keeping with the dictates of the early modern science of physiognomy. Detailing aspects by recourse to skin color and the presence or absence of facial hair, these descriptions frequently overflow socioracial classificatory boundaries; physiognomic conventions employed in Spain were insufficient for colonial officials to make sense of the Indians, mestizos, and mulattos they were enumerating in census records and identifying in police line-ups. I place this chapter late in the book so that readers will come to it with an appreciation of the ambivalences and complexities of early modern conventions for making sense of diversity. I hope that by this point readers will have come to understand sixteenth- and seventeenth-century physical descriptions not as transparent and self-evident, but as a fluid and ambiguous array of practices.

Laura Lewis's *Hall of Mirrors*, a study of gender and caste in early colonial Mexico, ends with a brief commentary on how the fluid classificatory practice of the sixteenth and seventeenth centuries morphed into a more elaborate (although still not rigid, not yet racial) system in the eighteenth.[78] The notion of a "caste system" has become a dominant trope in colonial historiography, notwithstanding the fact that casta may more properly reflect late colonial Mexico than Spanish America in general. Moreover, it is probably a misnomer to call the dispersed set of classifying practices a "system," particularly in the sixteenth and seventeenth centuries. In the final chapter of this volume I reflect on the problem of employing casta as an imperial model. To do so, I explore the secondary literature on eighteenth-century Nueva Granada (as the Nuevo Reino came to be called when it was elevated to viceregal status); in that century massive demographic shifts led to the emergence of a mestizo majority in the Santafé-Tunja region and to the advent of a series of classificatory practices that supplemented or supplanted earlier forms of categorization. In chapter 6 I frame this volume as being not just a case study of a region presenting substantial differences from the Mexican caste scheme, but as a rethinking of how students of colonial Spanish American history have constructed models to make sense of the regulation of diversity and inequality.

1. Mischievous Lovers, Hidden Moors, and Cross-Dressers

Defining Race in the Colonial Era

I t is difficult to determine the "groupness" of mestizos in early colonial Santafé: they defied classification by constantly "disappearing" into other categories; they did not consistently embody a clear set of attributes distinguishing them from others in colonial society; they did not enjoy special rights or obligations defining them as mestizos and facilitating their incorporation as a sociological group. Furthermore, the concept "mestizo" functioned as much as a metaphor as a social category, standing in for a broad range of types of mixing, not only between people of different socioracial categories, but also between those of different social statuses. "Mestizo" also denoted the mixing of different "blood," pure and impure, such as occurred when an African or indigenous wet nurse suckled a Spanish infant. "Mestizo" was the term used to speak about crossbred animals, such as mules. Therefore, to say that mestizos constituted a fluid socioracial category in the colonial period is insufficient. If we concentrate exclusively on how people defined themselves or were classified by others, we get only a piece of the story, a glimpse of their individual identities—themselves highly contextual and transitory—without making inroads into comprehending how the process of identification worked, and why.

The best place to begin an inquiry into the meaning of "mestizo" is to look at colonial people who pretended to be that which they were not: people who consciously "passed" for someone else. This exercise might help us to discern the nature of the boundaries that colonial people perceived between themselves and others, instead of forcing on the colonial situation a particularly modern consciousness of what those boundaries might be. Such an approach results in the observation, however startling it may be to the twenty-first-century observer, that "race" as it was understood in the sixteenth century was not what we understand it to be today. Furthermore, many of the social boundaries we would immediately tag as "racial" were founded in the colonial period on other sorts of distinctions. Race in the colonial period was inherited through the blood—not through the genes—and could not always be discerned in individual phenotypes. It characterized members of lineages, not broad social groups. And it revolved around such matters as nobility and religion.

I open my inquiry with a story that at first glance appears to be a classic narrative of racial passing: the bungled elopement of the sixteen-year-old Spanish noblewoman doña Catalina Acero de Vargas with an "*indio zambo*," a mulatto of native and African parentage.[1] In 1675 Doña Catalina escaped from her brother's house and ran off with Francisco Suárez, a young man who enticed her into marriage by telling her he was a nobleman from Lima and thus a good match for a young aristocratic woman. When the two met in person, however, she discovered that Suárez was not the Limeño noble he purported to be. The actions of doña Catalina brought dishonor upon her well-placed family.[2] Her brother, Juan de Vargas, brought accusations against Suárez to the Santafé authorities, alleging that the man "went to the houses of my dwelling and with trickery removed from them doña Catalina de Acero, my sister, a damsel of sixteen years of age, and he took her where he would, under the pretext, which he later made known, that he wanted to marry her, tricking her as though she were a child, pretending to be a great nobleman . . . although he was, as is commonly called, an *indio guauqui* or zambo [como comunmente se dize yndio guauqui o zambo]" (902r).[3] He warned the authorities to resolve the issue with haste, "both so that the aggressor did not flee and so that any of [doña Catalina's] relatives who felt offended did not pursue him and attempt to take revenge for the offense" (902r–v).

An orphan living under the tutelage of her brother, doña Catalina grumbled about the poor treatment she said she received from her sister-in-law, so it is not surprising that she was seduced by the stranger who promised to lure her out of her captivity. Suárez, a painter by trade, courted doña Catalina in a series of letters in which he attested to his noble birth, saying his parents in Peru were "well-born, of good stock [heran caualleros y jente muy principal]" (905v); who actually penned the missives is not revealed in the testimony. Slipping away from her brother's home under cover of night, doña Catalina found herself face to face with her suitor for the first time. It was then that she realized the irresoluble predicament she had gotten herself into. On closer observation, doña Catalina recognized "by the aforementioned man's color and his speech, he was not of the quality that he had told her [por el color del dicho honbre y sus palabras no ser de la calidad que se le auia dicho]" (906r). Witnesses corroborated her observations, identifying Suárez as "brown" (*moreno*) in color (903v).

This story of a dishonest suitor is an excellent example of what would today be called "racial passing," but with a telling colonial cadence. A twenty-first-century Catalina would have immediately recognized Francisco Suárez before running off with him because she would have met him in person, seen him, and heard him speak. But as befitted a high-born unmarried woman, she was sheltered (*recogida*) in her brother's house (which also likely explains why she grew weary of her sister-in-law, who was committed to preserving the family's honor by isolating her). Thus, her only experience of courtship was through letters. Given a world in which the written word was privileged over speech—indeed, was fetishized—passing could easily be camouflaged through literate communication.[4] Unfortunately for doña Catalina, her sheltered upbringing, boredom, and immaturity all interfered with the critical faculties she should have brought to an evaluation of Suárez's missives.

SITUATING FRANCISCO SUÁREZ'S BEHAVIOR

My research in the archives of Bogotá and Seville uncovered only a handful of cases of passing as we moderns would understand the practice, that is, of individuals belonging to one racial group masquerading as members of another. To be sure, I encountered examples of passing in a broader sense: conversos (new converts to Christianity or their descendants) posing as Old Christians, idolaters claiming to be pious Catholics, mestizos or native commoners serving as indigenous hereditary chiefs, mestiza women walking the streets of Santafé in native garb, slaves pretending to be free men.[5] Suárez is an anomaly in the documentary record. His deception was unusual and was easily discovered when he emerged from behind his epistles, given the tremendous gap in status that yawned between a *huauqui* (Indian from Quito) and a Lima grandee.[6]

The cases of passing I encountered did not revolve around phenotype, centering instead on religious identity or on rank, drawing on what in the colonial period was called calidad, or quality. Calidad constituted a system of social classification that bound together what we would today call "racial" markers—such as "Indian," "mestizo," and so on—with other means of distinguishing individuals: their place of residence, their costume, the language they spoke, their status as slave or free, their moral or economic status, and their rights and obligations in society, in addition to (sometimes in spite of) their color. Calidad can be understood as the intersection of multiple axes that plotted individual status according to ethnicity or race, congregation, morality, privilege, and aspect.[7] Socioracial categories were thus but one component of a broader set of classificatory practices that we might think of as being constituted more by "doing" than by "being." In other words, one's classification emerged out of the ways in which one actively engaged one's birthright or transcended it through behavior: it was a type of performance. Doña Catalina appealed to this early modern method of distinguishing among individuals in her recounting of how she discovered her error: she confessed that Suárez's color and diction betrayed his "quality." However, we should not assume that doña Catalina's interpretation of her suitor's identity was the same as our own might be.

That is to say, we would be committing a serious error if we were to assume that Francisco Suárez's crime was that of a zambo passing for white, since that racialized label does not appear in the document or in most of the sixteenth- and seventeenth-century papers I consulted. "White" was not a category comparable in the sixteenth- and seventeenth-century Nuevo Reino to "indio," "mestizo," "mulatto," or "black." Individuals of European descent were, in contrast, identified by their nationality or place of residence as Spaniards, French, English, or more commonly as vecinos (citizens) of a particular town or city or by their occupation (notary, merchant, silversmith, shoemaker). In this case, Suárez was posing as a person of noble birth (most of whom, with the exception of caciques, were Spaniards or American-born individuals of Iberian descent). The difference between "white" and "noble" is crucial, because it colors how we interpret why doña Catalina was attracted to her mysterious correspondent in the first place. If we understand calidad as reflecting nobility and general social standing, rather than reducing it exclusively to its socioracial dimension, we can enter more fully into the ethos of the period to understand more precisely the kind of subterfuge in which Suárez was engaged.

It is not only the nature of the categories across which people move that is at stake here, but that of passing itself, whose meaning in the colonial period stands at odds with modern understandings of that. Ann Twinam considers colonial-era passing to be "a dichotomy between a person's private reality and an alternative, publicly constructed status," such as, for example, a child born out of wedlock but brought up as a member of an elite household, who thus occupied an ambiguous social position with respect to his or her family.[8] Such discrepancies could be reconciled in the late colonial Spanish America studied by Twinam by means of bureaucratic arrangements like *gracias al sacar,* the institutionalized practice of petitioning to change one's birth or socioracial status, which was widely used in the eighteenth century.[9] Twinam's description of gracias al sacar is not, however, entirely appropriate to an early colonial context, because it was very rarely used in the sixteenth and seventeenth centuries. Nevertheless, she is on the mark when she rethinks passing as a process of closing the gap between public and private realities. That was more likely achieved in the sixteenth and seventeenth centuries through the public recognition by fathers of their illegitimate offspring or by officially legitimizing them by petition to the Crown, which would permit mestizo children to move with greater ease in polite society.[10] In each case, however, we are speaking of a legal fiction, not of an act of dissimulation such as that perpetrated by Francisco Suárez, in which the public-private gap was only briefly closed on the pages of a handwritten letter.

It thus behooves us to reconsider the meaning of passing in seventeenth-century Santafé. In a thoughtful critique of scholarship that treats passing as a form of deception, Sara Ahmed suggests that we would do better to refrain from viewing it as a ruse whereby a subject assumes the image of another. Instead, she entreats us to consider passing as the process by which an individual seeks to control how others perceive her, as well as, alternately, the process by which someone is recognized, and sometimes misconstrued, by others. That is to say, Ahmed urges us to keep in mind the individual intentions, as much of people who deliberately shift their identities as of those who observe the act of passing (and either tacitly accept it or call it out).[11] If we think of passing in this sense, it becomes more conceivable as a tool for comprehending the early colonial social landscape.

What did passing mean to doña Catalina Acero de Vargas, her brother, and the colonial authorities who handled her case? They could only make sense of Francisco Suárez's behavior according to culturally and historically situated cues read in light of their own positioning in the social hierarchy. For example, they would have interpreted their dilemma from their standpoint as members of the nobility. Members of the Vargas family were routinely addressed as "doña" (in the case of women) and as "don" (in the case of men), titles that were the exclusive province of the nobility (in contrast to modern-day Latin America, where "don" and "doña" are terms of respect employed in all sorts of social encounters). Whether doña Catalina's Spanish ancestors were nobles is uncertain. Perhaps they belonged to the Iberian aristocracy, or perhaps their standing issued from the heroic deeds of sixteenth-century conquistadors, as was frequently the case in Santafé, where there were relatively few nobles by birth and many who were invited into the ranks of the lesser nobility (*hidalgos* or *caballeros*) in recognition of their military service or that of their ancestors. Flórez de Ocáriz's *Genealogías del Nuevo Reino de Granada* mentions Juan de Vargas only briefly, in a note on his spouse, and does not highlight his ancestry, which suggests that he probably was not of old aristocratic stock.[12] Whatever the origins of their noble position, families like the Vargases were not subject to taxes, nor could they be imprisoned for debt; they were spared certain punishments, and their testimony was of higher value in court than was that of commoners.[13]

Descendants of conquistadors promoted their lineages by producing reports recalling their ancestors' services to the Crown (*probanzas de méritos y servicios*, or merit and service reports).[14] They endeavored to dress the part, sporting rich robes made from expensive imported textiles. They shied away from manual labor. They adorned the lintels of their houses with coats of arms to publicly proclaim their *hidalguía*, or nobility.[15] Their status was an essential aspect of their calidad, which had to be continuously maintained through lifelong performance. Ruth Hill explains how the difference between essence and exercise can be comprehended by turning to the distinction between the Spanish verbs "to be," or *ser* (a permanent or long-term attribute), and *estar* (a temporal activity or a transient attribute): the Vargases were active participants in the public performance of their nobility, that is, they had to exercise to maintain a semblance of their noble essence as though it were a permanent characteristic.[16] But, of course, blemishes on a family's honor could cause irreparable damage to its social standing. Felipe Guaman Poma de Ayala sums up the Vargases' predicament in a sentence cautioning against the dangers of a noblewoman marrying a plebeian or a Jew: "And if the man is of vile status or a Jew and the woman of a house of noblemen and Old Christians, all is lost, relatives and lineages and her sons; they are of a ruined caste, worse than a mestizo [son de rruyn casta, peor que mestizo]."[17]

Juan de Vargas undoubtedly fretted over how Francisco Suárez's ruse might impact his position in Santafereña society. The stain that the mulatto left on his honor would have consequences that ranged far beyond that fateful evening in 1675. It would adhere for decades, affecting all family members: not just Catalina herself, but especially her brother and his sons and grandsons.[18] Even if Juan de Vargas were to assuage the effect of his sister's kidnapping by forcing Francisco Suárez to keep to his word and marry her—which, in cases of couples of equal status provided a kind of compensation to the woman's family—the Vargases would have continued to suffer the affront of having a low-born "indio zambo" in their family tree, never entirely cleansing the blemish he left on their honor.[19]

In order to make sense of the Vargas family's reaction to Francisco Suárez's deception, we must also comprehend doña Catalina's position as a *mujer recogida*. *Recogimiento*, or seclusion, defined and constrained elite female identity, premised on the notion that women could not effectively control their sexuality without male supervision.[20] A woman considered to be recogida was "spiritually and morally virtuous," so that recogimiento was more than the sheltering of female members of a household in the interests of preserving family honor. Recogimiento was "a spiritual path toward God" chosen by religious mystics, as well as a means of preserving the flesh—particularly that of women—from evil. It denoted "a demure, modest demeanor," thus setting standards for female behavior that went so far as to include how a woman walked and how much she spoke.[21] As the sixteenth-century Spanish author Juan Luis Vives writes in his *Instruccion de la muger christiana* (Lessons for the Christian Woman),

> A maiden must be retiring and take care to not go out frequently on visits, and should know that it is a very bad mark on her honor to be known to many, her name shouted out over the City . . . , or to be known by her signs or marks or vices of her person, and be called white, or brown, or lame, or one-eyed, or small, or big, or fat, or one-handed, or a stutterer. All of this, good woman, it would be best if it were not known outside your walls.[22]

Doña Catalina's breaking of the terms of her recogimiento reflected poorly on the ability of her family to raise her as a proper lady, wounding their honor, endangering their elite status, and inviting the possibility of rejection by those she considered to be her social equals should she later seek a husband.[23] I was not able to trace doña Catalina's later life in the archives. Perhaps she was confined to a convent, as happened to Spanish women in Lima who found themselves in similar predicaments, or maybe she was ultimately forced to marry Suárez.[24] What is certain is that the public scandal that erupted once she discovered Francisco Suárez's true identity was further broadcast by the criminal case that Juan de Vargas brought against him, making the girl well known in a town with only three thousand Spaniards.[25]

Any interpretation of the consequences of this legal case must also take into consideration how a rising indigenous and mestizo population in Santafé and its environs might have affected the family's sense of honor as Europeans drowning in a sea of subordinates marked not only by class, but by other kinds of difference. By the end of the sixteenth century the native population in urban areas had surged, thanks to the labor levee known as the *mita urbana*, which brought thousands of indigenous tributaries, some of them becoming permanent migrants, to Santafé and Tunja to build the urban infrastructure, to work as artisans, and to serve elite families.[26] By the late seventeenth century, when doña Catalina Acero de Vargas pored over Francisco Suárez's missives, several generations of mestizos born in rural areas and in the cities constituted a marginalized urban population that was technically barred from residing in the countryside near native communities, although in fact they were also established there and to some degree had replaced a decimated indigenous population.[27] It is not by accident that this was the period when applications for recognition of noble status and declarations of pure Old Christian bloodlines surged in the Nuevo Reino.[28] The elite felt cornered and took pains to protect itself, as Juan de Vargas hoped to accomplish by means of his denunciation of Francisco Suárez.

Finally, we cannot forget that Francisco Suárez's attempt at passing unfolded in a series of letters, not in face-to-face contact, marking a dissimulation that would have been less feasible had doña Catalina met her suitor in person before running off with him. As Suárez's diction would not have been apparent in a missive, his elite Limeño identity was taken at face value by the young woman, who was in any case bound to keep his letters secret from her brother. The act of passing through writing was made possible by the constraints on women's movements, as well as by the preeminence of literate communication in the period, which undoubtedly led doña Catalina to interpret her suitor's letters as those of an attractive social equal.

In summary, this seventeenth-century case of identity fraud unfolded amid an identifiable constellation of actors and involved a particular convergence of desires, aspirations, and strategies. It was also firmly embedded in a notion of race that differed from our own. It is, precisely, this distinct set of values that makes the interrupted elopement of doña Catalina and Francisco Suárez into something other than a classic case of racial passing.[29]

THE PROBLEM OF RACE

In order to comprehend why Francisco Suárez was capable of pulling the wool over doña Catalina Acero de Vargas's eyes and how this act was such an affront to her brother (and, by her own admission, to her), we must redirect our understanding away from the genetic metaphor of discrete and phenotypically identifiable populations that has characterized the (pseudo)scientific discourse of race since the nineteenth century. Instead, we need to inquire into what "race" meant to early modern people. The epistemological basis of racial differentiation in the sixteenth and seventeenth centuries revolved around the notion that external characteristics were mutable, quite the opposite of modern notions of racial fixity (whether in North America or Latin America). For instance, drawing on Aristotle and from his own observations in Cartagena de Indias, the seventeenth-century Jesuit author Alonso de Sandoval insisted that physical characteristics were not inherited, but, instead, were products of the imagination: the color of an individual was accrued in the womb, as the mother observed and reacted to the world around her.[30]

Vanita Seth explains persuasively that it was only in the nineteenth century that the body came to be acknowledged as a transparent and measurable object, a constant that resisted the variability of time.[31] This epistemological shift made possible the emergence of what came to be viewed as a stable system of racial classification. In his study of the historical development of scientific taxonomies, Staffan Müller-Wille reveals that such an epistemological transition meant, in practice, a "shift in emphasis from diachronic ancestor-descendant relationships to synchronic relationships among members of a collective entity."[32] The early modern term "raza," which we can translate into English as "race," referred more properly to aristocratic lineage, distinguishing between those of "pure" Christian blood (Old Christians) and the descendants of converts from Judaism and Islam (New Christians). This was a moment at which important social attributes, including family honor and religion, began to be thought of as being "carried in the blood." In the sixteenth and seventeenth centuries, the public was concerned with the inheritance of spiritual purity—virtue—through blood links, not with the transmission of genetic characteristics.[33]

Raza was an accumulation of spiritual virtue that a few lucky ones inherited from their parents and grandparents, expressed through the metaphor of "blood." We can see similar referents at work in an eighteenth-century dictionary definition of calidad: "The nobility and luster of the blood [La nobléza y lustre de la sangre]."[34] The same usage comes to the fore in a discursive form employed by a member of the minor nobility (a *capitán*) of the Muisca community of Suta, in the altiplano near Santafé, to argue in favor of his legitimacy to rule over a section of the chiefdom: "It was and had been the custom to have as their authority. . . a capitán *of the very lineage and race* [un capitán de la qual linea y raza] from which issues don Juan Guayana."[35] And it is clear in how don Diego de Torres, the sixteenth-century mestizo cacique of the Muisca community of Turmequé, defended his right to govern his indigenous subjects by appealing to his genealogical connections to Christian Spaniards: "For I am of such good blood, flowing from Spaniards and Christians [Por ser de tan buena sangre proçedida de españoles y crisptianos]."[36]

Don Diego's claim to being "of good blood" is genealogical without being genetic. What he inherited from his Spanish father was his noble status and an inclination to follow Christian morals, neither of which would be considered racial attributes according to the post-Enlightenment discourse whose omnipresence in our modern lives obscures an appreciation of the meaning of lineage for this embattled cacique. The notion of blood underlay the appearance of an early modern discriminatory system operating in the Iberian and Spanish colonial world, which rooted out even the most distant manifestations of unwelcome Jewish, Muslim, or even heretic ancestors.[37] Note, for instance, how Fray Benito de Peñalosa y Mondragón's *Libro de las cinco excelencias del español* (1629) takes the Spanish preoccupation with calidad to an extreme.

Even more so, when one freely marries for passion or greed, making all the inquiries that every honorable and prudent

gentleman [cauallero] should: and to that end the most circum-
spect generally make a rigorous examination of the qualities
of the woman whom they seek to marry, informing themselves
of whose daughter she is, and of whose granddaughter, and
few come to know who were her great-grandparents, and that
is not surprising, because there are few who know them and
what their names were. So, even having done this lengthy and
difficult study, and found her to be perfect, and his neighbor, or
his enemy, hoping to destroy him, finds that a great-great-great-
great-great grandmother [sextabuela] of a great-grandmother
of his wife was (said to be) a Morisca [a Muslim], or a penitent
[confesa], and being that person honorable, and well-known,
and a gentleman married to the daughter of such persons,
his children end up as destroyed as if they themselves had
converted.[38]

Peñalosa's anxieties were not unusual at the time. He, like his contemporaries, was deeply concerned by the hazards that "impure blood"
posed to the "race" of a noble family. It is this sense of "race" that
guides my thinking in this book.

Personal appearance—skin color, but also clothing and language—
certainly fed into the determination of an individual's calidad. This
is evident in the gap that doña Catalina de Vargas's brother noted between Francisco Suárez's presumed identity as a Lima grandee and his
classification as an indio zambo. It is also noticeable in doña Catalina's
horror at his appearance and accent. But calidad was also determined
by one's status as a legitimate or illegitimate child. This was particularly problematic for mestizos and mulattos, many of whom were born
out of wedlock, and it was probably an issue for Suárez himself, who
was "outed" as a person of mixed descent. Assignment to these categories was as much a modifiable legal and social status as it was the product of the gut reaction of the observer. In a word, the identification of
Francisco Suárez was not as simple as one might think.

It has become common for scholars to employ the term "calidad" as
a gloss for socioracial category, a usage that perhaps undermines the
multivalence of the term in the colonial period. Robert C. Schwaller
suggests that the concept of calidad should be confined in the sixteenth
century to socioeconomic status, contending that it comes to denote
socioracial identities only in the second century of colonial rule.[39] This
may have been the case in the early colonial Mexico Schwaller studies,

but I have found a broad range of usages of the word "calidad" in the documentation from Santafé, where it appears to simultaneously refer to rank, behavior, and parentage. A 1575 royal communiqué to the archbishop of Santafé, commanding him to refrain from continuing to ordain mestizos as priests, notes that word has reached Madrid, that the archbishop "has given holy orders to many individuals who lack competence [*suficiencia*] for it and to mestizos and other people of this calidad, which, as you must consider, is greatly troublesome for many reasons."[40] Juan Birves, caught in 1577 in a tryst with the daughter of a prominent Spaniard in La Palma, was accused of being a mestizo and thus an unsuitable companion for the young woman; his mestizo condition was called a "calidad" by his accuser.[41] Nonetheless, Diego de Torres and Alonso de Silva appear to engage the notion of calidad as a way of setting themselves apart from indigenous caciques and mestizo commoners by emphasizing their rank and their piety. Torres, the son of a Spanish hidalgo, refers to himself as "a person of my calidad and Christianity," while Silva points out that "some [people] desire that no mestizo of the calidad and sufficiency, ability and Christianity that I possess ever be cacique."[42] Yet, in a list of questions to be posed to witnesses, Torres asks about the "calidad and condition of mestizos," implying that the term can be applied to characterize people of mixed birth. "Calidad" thus appears to encompass a broad range of referents.

Schwaller advocates the concept *géneros de gente* (genres of people), which he encounters in the early colonial Mexican documentation and which encompasses among its multiple referents socioracial classifiers like "mulatto," "mestizo," and "indio." I have also found usages in Santafé that argue for the relevance of genre in this respect. In a 1582 quarrel brought by an indio ladino couple (Spanish-speaking natives) who were assaulted at a party by municipal constables, note how "genre" encapsulates socioracial diversity, while simultaneously transcending it: "In conformity with the usages of Christians, being like them, and all of us are in our genre [*genero*] virtuous and honorable and free men, and vassals of Your Majesty."[43] This couple is more than indio: they also perceive themselves as possessing a degree of honor that rural indios could not claim; in addition, they emphasize that they enjoy autonomy from indigenous authorities, asserting instead their direct relationship as vassals of the Crown. A 1580 report on a royal inspection tour (*visita*) refers to "all genres of Indian and mestiço persons and common people [todo genero de gentes naturales y mestiços y gente comun]," suggesting that status, as well as ethnicity, was significant to the attribution of genre.[44] Magnus Mörner quotes a mid-sixteenth-century Audiencia official, who states that "there are four géneros of persons in these parts, who are encomenderos, soldiers and lost people, *calpisques* [indigenous foremen] who are the tyrants of the Indians in their labors, and doctrinal priests. All of them feed off and benefit from the blood, sweat, and labor of these miserable ones, and they and their families are clothed and triumph off their poverty and nakedness."[45] In this instance, "genre" refers simultaneously to occupation and position in the socioracial hierarchy.

In his *Tesoro de la lengua castellana o española*, Sebastián de Covarrubias includes a three-tiered definition of "género" that begins with the gender distinction between female and male, moving on to what he calls "species" (*especie*) or "type"—for example, a classification of rams by the number of horns they have—and ending with a more generalized usage: "There is a genre of men who want to be led by evil [Hay género de hombres que quieren ser llevados por mal]."[46] Although "calidad" was employed specifically to refer to status, it also appears to have overlapped with "género," as is suggested in the reference to "all genres of Indian and mestiço persons." I privilege "calidad" over "género" here: while both terms denote a simultaneous malleability and specificity, "calidad" is in broader use in the historical literature today and will thus be immediately comprehensible to many readers.

But neither "calidad" nor "género" specifically locates difference along a continuum of socioracial types, which has been one of the central concerns of modern scholars, who frequently use the term "casta" to refer to such categories. However, I did not find references to "casta" as a socioracial continuum in early colonial Santafé, and in its absence, there is no lexical term for the mode of classification that distinguished among Spaniards, Indians, mestizos, mulattos, and blacks. To some extent, "calidad" overlaps the various methods of distinguishing ethnicity, status, and even gender, because it originates, simultaneously, in visible and invisible attributes, some of them inherited and others acquired in the course of the life cycle, conveyed by clothing and rooted in geography. This makes "calidad" the most appropriate gloss, although in the absence of more specific terminology I occasionally employ the term "socioracial categories" in those instances in which I intend to highlight those categories that we moderns use to denote "race." It is, indeed, a challenge to confront a historical system that is so similar to, yet also so different from our own, in which the same words—"mestizo," "mulatto," "negro," "indio," even "race"—

carry meanings that at once connect with modern usages and yet seem so alien to us.[47] The very fact that no colonial term adequately conveys twenty-first-century concerns over sociracial classification reveals the enormous epistemological gap between the early modern world-view and our own, cautioning us to be ever conscious that our modern fixation on "race" does not sufficiently convey the ethos of the period. It is precisely a recognition of this disjuncture that makes "passing" a useful conceptual vehicle, so long as the differences, and not the similarities, between early modern epistemologies and our own are always kept in the foreground.

Two specific examples of colonial passing complicate any homology between early modern and twenty-first-century usages. First, the mid-sixteenth-century case of Diego Romero—a conquistador and an influential encomendero in Santafé who was accused of being a Morisco, a Muslim convert to Christianity passing as an Old Christian—enables further exploration of the concept of raza. The conflicting statements of witnesses in this case, some of whom testified in Santafé, while others testified in Spain, will help me to access a transatlantic genealogy of "raza." Second, *mestizas en hábito de indias*, women of mixed parentage who moved around Santafé in indigenous attire, problematize how Santafé's plebeians and aristocrats identified their fellow urbanites. These women defied colonial classifications by cross-dressing, but they were not intentionally passing in any sense of the word. Rather, they were negotiating the ambiguous and incipient category of mestizo as it emerged in the sixteenth century. Both of these cases complicate our comprehension of passing in the early colonial period and, therefore, expand our field of vision when we focus on what "mestizo" meant.

A MOOR IN BOGOTÁ

Diego Romero, a conquistador and a ubiquitous presence in sixteenth-century Santafereña elite society, was said by many to be an unpleasant man. Although he ultimately achieved a position in the colonial power structure in the mid-1570s, his first attempt, in the 1560s, at obtaining a staff of office—a position on the *cabildo*, or city council—was greeted by the following remark by an influential colonial official, Licenciate Francisco de Anuncibay: "A troubled man, a loudmouth and a slanderer [hombre inquieto, vocinglero y murmurador]."[48] He was described by witnesses as "a tall man with a large body, brown-skinned

[and] curly-headed, and with scant beard, with an eye that opens and closes frequently [vn honbre alto de cuerpo rejio moreno crespo y de pocas baruas y tiene un hojo que le abre cierra muy a menudo]."⁴⁹ Romero participated in the pacification of the native people of the Sierra Nevada de Santa Marta and in the conquest of the Nuevo Reino de Granada, as well as combating the Pizarro rebellion in Peru.⁵⁰ In return, he received a series of *encomiendas*, or royal grants allowing him to collect tribute from native communities (making him an encomendero, one of the signs of home-grown nobility in Spanish America).⁵¹ Romero was an intensely litigious individual, whose paper trail reveals a man constantly embroiled in suits over lands and tribute-earnings, as well as over the numerous debts he accumulated.⁵²

In the early 1550s, when Romero had already established himself in Santafé as a leading citizen, the state prosecutor, Licentiate García de Valverde, made a stunning accusation against the vituperative encomendero.

> He is native to the city of Oran, which is in Africa, son of a Moorish father and mother, and that Moor came to the kingdoms of Spain, to the town [*villa*] of Alcalá [de Henares], brought as a captive to Cardinal Don Francisco Tomás Ximénez. And Diego Romero was held as a captive and baptized in the town of Alcalá. After some years, Diego Romero committed a crime under the name of Diego Hurtado, so he fled said town and he changed his name and went by Diego Romero and he came to these parts without your royal license. (14r)⁵³

In short, Romero was accused of concealing his identity by changing his name from Diego Hurtado to Diego Romero so that he could escape Spain for the Americas, where he passed as a Spaniard and Old Christian, rather than presenting himself as the North African and recent convert from Islam that he presumably was. A series of seven witnesses in Alcalá de Henares, where he had lived, attested to his dark past as a slave and a murderer (20v–27v). His accusers alleged that when he was an infant he was removed from Oran in the arms of his mother, a "Mooress native to Barbary [una mora natural de Berberia]," during the 1508 conquest of the city (90r–92r), and was taken to Alcalá de Henares, where he was converted to Catholicism and freed from slavery (92r–94r); he was said to have lost the papers confirming his freed status during the conquest of Santa Marta (302v).

Why include the story of Diego Romero in a book about mestizaje in the New World, when Santafé was full of Africans, native people, Spaniards, and individuals descended from their admixtures? Sebastián de Covarrubias's early seventeenth-century dictionary, *Tesoro de la lengua castellana*, defines "raza": "The caste of purebred horses, who are marked with a brand so that they can be recognized. 2. Race in a fabric, the yarn that is differentiated from the other threads of the weft. . . . Race, in lineages, is an offense, as in having the race of a Moor or Jew."[54] As David Nirenberg convincingly asserts, this early modern definition points toward a genealogical conception of race as some sort of inherited quality; this explains Covarrubias's reference to lineage (casta), which was interchangeable with raza.[55] The dictionary entry dwells on the perception of difference, as expressed through the metaphor of the thread that stands out in a textile, like a blemish, which suggests the importance of appearance. It also conveys an anxiety over the mixing of descent lines, whether animal or human. Covarrubias's definition is intimately tied up with the Iberian project of excluding members of non-Catholic religious congregations from the Spanish world, barring their converso descendants from social privileges, and limiting their sphere of movement between Europe and the Americas (just as horses of lesser pedigree would be kept out of a line of thoroughbreds). The descendants of converts are the people called "New Christians," and this is the calidad of which Romero was accused.

New Christians—as well as heretics and their descendants—could not demonstrate "purity of blood" (*limpieza de sangre*), an invisible attribute enjoyed in particular by those of noble lineage. Purity of blood and the status of Old Christian were essential, both in Spain and in the Nuevo Reino, for those wishing to apply for public office or to join religious orders, as well as to obtain permission to travel to the Indies.[56] But even purity of blood was not entirely based on *descent* from Jews or Muslims, as David Nirenberg aptly demonstrates in his study of the widespread use of "Jew" as a metaphor for vileness in Spanish medieval literature and the politics of employing the label to disparage people and groups of people.[57] Moreover, the mixing of Christians, Jews, and Muslims (Moriscos) was so widespread in medieval Spain that the three congregations could be distinguished only by their costume.[58] In this sense, "raza" did not refer to a clearly visible population, even in the case of Jews and Moriscos. However, it did refer to an essentialized set of characteristics believed to be carried in the blood, whether those characteristics be positive (as in the case of the nobility) or negative (as in the case of conversos or heretics).[59]

Diego Romero found himself ensnarled in a trap. As a New Christian he could not hold public office, nor could he enjoy the rights to an encomienda; in fact, he should not have been in Santafé at all. But he defended himself against these allegations, pointing to his purity of blood and his services to the Crown (the latter boosting his status and calidad by foregrounding his loyalty): "Diego Romero is an Old Christian of pure lineage, born and raised in these kingdoms and more than thirty-five years ago he crossed to the Nuevo Reino de Granada and he was one of the first conquistadors of it and has served Your Highness" (6r). Moreover, even if he were proven to be a Morisco, his lawyer argued, he had arrived in the New World well before such prohibitions were established: "Before the year [fifteen] forty-two there was no law prohibiting the newly converted from being in the Indies, and my client was there well before that" (6r). Romero contended that he was a native of Toledo (41v), the illegitimate son of don Carlos de Mendoza and Inés Romero.[60]

How does one identify a man as passing for a Spaniard—which at the time meant, specifically, a Spaniard and a Catholic—when his presumed original identity cannot be distinguished by any physical markers characteristic of the group? This was precisely the problem of identifying Jews and Muslims in Spain, who were frequently singled out by their clothing, speech, and behavior, not their phenotype.[61] The difficulties of identifying Diego Romero as a convert were compounded by the fact that he had become a Catholic during his childhood and therefore demonstrated no obvious behavioral signs of his parents' religion, such as attitudes toward bathing, sartorial customs, or language use. The only feature that could possibly set him apart as a converso would be his circumcised penis. Circumcision was strictly policed in the Iberian Peninsula during the course of the sixteenth century, continuing long after Muslims were expelled and a generation or more of Catholic converts had come under the tutelage of the Church.[62] Spanish officials frequently performed physical examinations on Moriscos, since so many of them denied practicing Islam. So it was acceptable judicial practice to request, as the prosecutor did, that "the secretary of the case and two witnesses inspect said Diego Romero to see if the foreskin of his virile member is cut, because the Moors have the custom of removing it from their sons within a month or two after birth" (40v).

However, even when subjected to such scrutiny, defendants could easily argue that their foreskins had been removed for medical reasons or that they had been born that way.[63] Romero steered clear of such an examination by making this very case, arguing that his lack of a foreskin proved nothing and that attention to the issue would only cause him "notable disgrace to his honor [notable infamia y del honor]" (48r).

> A man can be missing said foreskin or part of it due to illness
> and to having had it cut due to this, [and] for this reason there
> are many in Spain and in this kingdom who do not have it, and
> for having been born this way, which happens to many, so that
> nothing can be proven by the person who is missing it. For the
> same reason there is no cause for allowing me to go through
> such a shameful procedure, since it is useless and is not among
> the purposes of this suit. (48v)

Romero's honor thence preserved, the court was forced to rely on the memories of aged witnesses in Spain, who recounted their recollections of events that had taken place twenty-five to fifty years earlier.

Charges against Diego Romero were dropped in 1578 for lack of evidence and because, in any event, he had arrived in the Nuevo Reino before the ban was enacted on travel to the Americas by New Christians (471r, 475r). However, over the course of two decades he was jailed, the tribute from his encomiendas placed in escrow, and his life disrupted by a dispute that entangled many of the other leading citizens of Santafé and neighboring Tunja, who were anxious to lay their hands on the indigenous tributaries to whom he laid claim. Romero continued to reside in Santafé after the lawsuit concluded, living well into his eighties and maintaining a roof-tile factory (which crops up as a topographic reference point in many documents of the era). The stain on his name did not inhibit his children—even his various illegitimate and mestizo ones—from achieving success in Santafereña society, since he was absolved of the charge.[64]

We will never know if Diego Romero was really a Moorish slave or if he was, indeed, a murderer, because we will never be able to state with certainty whether or not he and Diego Hurtado were the same person. What is suggestive about his predicament are the slippages it evinces in the meanings of passing in a transatlantic, early modern context, since assuming an Old Christian identity was an iconic act of passing among New Christians, one that embodied the concept of race as it was articulated in the period. Romero's case wore on for so many years in part because it involved the collection of testimony in distant Alcalá de Henares, as well as in Santafé. The core of the narrative remains the same in both locations: Romero's alleged parentage and guilt in the murder of a woman, both charges dependent on confirmation of his name change (since it was Diego Hurtado who committed these transgressions). Nonetheless, the testimonies take on a distinctly American flavor in Santafé. The discrepancies between the two sets of witnesses, separated by the vast stretches of the Atlantic Ocean, present revealing insights into how social classification operated differently across the far-flung Spanish world.

It is notable in the comparison of the testimonies from both sides of the Atlantic that several witnesses in Santafé referred to the possibility that Romero was a mulatto, the illegitimate son of the European slave-owner and his North African mother (296v, 298v, 302v); the mixture of European and North African was one of the possible permutations of the term "mulatto" in the period.[65] Of particular interest to me is not so much documenting Romero's mixed heritage as comprehending why the Santafé respondents mentioned it at all, given that it was not mentioned by the witnesses in Alcalá de Henares, who to a man (or a woman) testified to his Muslim parentage.

Covarrubias does not reference terms like "mulatto" in his definition of race, confining himself to the dangers of blood impurity among New Christians. However, his first entry refers to animal husbandry, only afterward moving to the question of noble and "offensive" family lines. What was "offensive" was the mixing of Christians and Muslims or Jews; just as animal lineages must remain pure, so, too, should human lineages. But in the New World, mixture took on additional meanings. In order to travel to the Americas from Spain, travelers were required to present certification of their purity of blood, documenting through the testimony of witnesses that they were descended in both their maternal and paternal lines from Old Christians and that there were no heretics in their family trees. Some of these certificates asserted not only that their bearers were free of the stain of conversion and heresy, but also that there were no mulattos hiding in their genealogies, thus demonstrating that even in Spain the leap was made from interreligious mixing to other kinds of mixing.[66] María Elena Martínez makes a convincing case for the resignification of purity of blood in the colonial American context. Basing her argument on Inquisition documents from Mexico, she notes that individuals seeking certificates of limpieza de sangre were scrutinized not only for their religious antecedents in Spain, but for the various mixtures of Europeans, Africans, and indigenous Americans taking place on Mexican soil.[67] In her perusal of documentation concerning Moriscos in the New World, Karoline Cook found an early seventeenth-century Mexican case in which one friar accused another of being a Moor, alternating this slur with the allegation that the man was a mestizo, which suggests a slippage between the two categories.[68]

Of note is the fact that in the Americas, as opposed to in Spain, it was presumably not sufficient to label Romero a converso passing as an Old Christian. In fact, exceedingly few conversos or Muslims were uncovered by the authorities in Santafé, where the Holy Office of the Inquisition did not maintain a tribunal (it was lodged in Cartagena de Indias, a little over a thousand kilometers to the north, where numerous cases of Judaizers were heard, but none concerning Moriscos).[69] I found no other references to Moriscos in the Santafé-Tunja vicinity, with the exception of a 1557 document decreeing the expulsion of Pedro Hernández, a highly skilled tile-worker from Hornachos (Badajoz) and a self-confessed Muslim, whose role in the construction of the church of Tocaima, however, was so vital to the city fathers that they asked he be permitted to continue his work on the temple despite his religious affiliation.[70] Muslims hardly posed a threat in the Nuevo Reino to a Church whose sights were more properly turned toward the conversion of native peoples. Consequently, Diego Romero's identity was resignified in Santafé so that it no longer adhered strictly to the early modern definition of raza (centered in lineage and congregation). Instead, some American witnesses foregrounded his mixed ancestry, situating him in the intermediate category "mulatto," a particularly perilous accusation given that Romero was a powerful encomendero, a position that mulattos (and mestizos) were barred from holding. There are clear indications that the case against him had everything to do with the desire on the part of his rivals to bring him down in order to redistribute his sources of wealth (246v–247r, 475r): a mulatto heritage could accomplish just that. Other dangers associated with racial mixing also adhered to Romero's persona, not because of his ancestors but because of his offspring. His sons Andrés and Alonso, by his native concubine Catalina Rodríguez, were among the corps of mestizo priests whose presence in native communities was predicated on their command of the Muisca language, but was fervently disputed by churchmen.[71]

Romero's mestizo offspring were, however, not mentioned in the lawsuit. At issue were not the well-documented anxieties provoked by the supposedly injurious presence of people of mixed ancestry in native communities and urban areas. To the contrary, what was at stake in this trial was the denial to a converso who could be identified as a mulatto of the right to an encomienda that could be transferred to other hands. Accusations of blood purity in Spain, likewise, had everything to do with the distribution of power, but they generally did not hinge on the questionability of mixed ancestry. Rather, it was the presence of Jewish or Muslim ancestors, not the fact of mixing itself, that produced the stain on an individual, which was precisely the fear implicit in peninsular testimony against Diego Romero.[72] The danger of passing in Alcalá de Henares resided in the converso condition, in the individual who could never achieve successful movement from one identity to another. The mulatto and the converso were both liminal categories, but of distinct character, moving in different social landscapes, which came together in unanticipated ways in the case against Diego Romero.

MESTIZAS IN INDIAN HABITS

Francisco Suárez's wooing of doña Catalina Acero de Vargas is at first glance an iconic case of passing as we understand it today (although the anxieties it evinces were very much part of the early modern ethos). In contrast, the accusations against Diego Romero typify what passing might have meant to sixteenth-century Santafereños. In both instances, racial mixing—understood in the sense of raza as lineage, rather than as genetic population—was foregrounded: Francisco Suárez was an indio zambo of indigenous and African parentage, as well as a commoner passing as a noble; Diego Romero was accused by his Santafé enemies of being some kind of a mulatto. Sixteenth- and early seventeeth-century definitions of intermediate categories like "mestizo" and "mulatto" were fluid and broad. We have only to remember Felipe Guaman Poma de Ayala's assertion that the offspring of a cacique and an indigenous commoner was a mestizo to comprehend the volatility of early colonial categories of calidad. If calidad was calculated on the basis not only of phenotype but also of behavior, then what made people mixed is compounded several times over, while at the same time the hall of mirrors created by intersecting uses of calidad also opened up new spaces into which mestizos could disappear.

Perhaps the most intriguing space in which we can investigate the broader implications of mixing is that of mestiza women dressed as Indians, whose presence on the streets of Santafé and Tunja was ubiquitous. While we might imagine the mestiza in Indian habit (mestiza en hábito de india) as a woman in pre-Columbian garb, sixteenth- and seventeenth-century indigenous costume was distinctly colonial in nature, combining local fabrics and indigenous garments with European ones. In addition to painted cotton mantles native to the region, indias wore woolen *mantas*, or shawls, made of European cloth and pinned with silver broaches (*tupus*), linen blouses, and even had textiles of Asian confection, as numerous wills display and as is stunningly depicted in the mural portrait of a *cacica* (female cacique) on the walls of the doctrinal church of Sutatausa, Cundinamarca (fig. 1.1).[73] The relatively limited wardrobe available to most people and the sumptuary laws that denied the majority the right to wear clothing made of certain textiles or to sport certain items of jewelry made native women immediately recognizable by their style of dress on any Santafé street.[74]

However, it was not easy to distinguish between an india and a mestiza in Indian habit, since their costume was identical. The documentary record frequently displays the confusion evinced by colonial officials charged with distinguishing between women bearing these two labels. Observers do not state categorically that a woman was mestiza or native, but that she "looked like" one or the other, suggesting uncertainty about her classification. There is always an "although" (*aunque*) in these documents that betrays officials' lack of clarity, as in, "She is mestiza although she goes about in Indian habit [Es mestiza aunque anda en abito de yndia]."[75] Take, for example, the case of Inés Ortiz, a mestiza born in Santafé who lived with her indigenous mother. She was picked up in 1619 by the authorities as they made their evening rounds of the San Victorino barrio in search of unmarried cohabiting couples. Discovered in the bed of the carpenter Cristóbal Enríquez—presumably a Spaniard, or perhaps a mestizo who managed to elude classification, since his calidad is not registered in the document—Inés confessed to having lived with the man for two years and having given birth to a daughter who died shortly after she was born. Enríquez described her as a "mestiza, although she wears the clothing of an Indian [es mestiza aunque anda en abito de yndia]."[76] There were also occasions when indigenous women were misidentified as mestizas in Indian habit: "[The girl] said she was named Ana and appeared to this witness to be mestiza [era al pareçer de esta testigo mestiça], and she would be about seven years old, although the girl said she was an Indian and the

Figure 1.1. *Mural with the portrait of a cacica in prayer, Church of San Juan Bautista, artist unknown, ca. 1620, Sutatausa, Cundinamarca.*

daughter of Indian parents."[77] Dress style confused colonial observers, because it easily stood in for the more ambiguous task of identifying people by their physical features.[78] "Although" (aunque) is the pivot of these utterances, the fulcrum around which the ambivalent category of mestizo rotates.

Given the strong correlation between costume and station in life in the early modern period, fugitives were frequently able to hide behind a change of clothing, a colonial form of passing that has led some scholars to argue that mestizas en hábito de indias and their male counterparts were intentionally dissimulating.[79] While this may be true for other regions of Spanish America, the mestizas in Indian habit who crop up in the Santafé documentation are not dissimulators. Instead, these women appear to have constituted an ambiguous intermediate category characteristic of the early colonial period, when population mixing fostered by urban migration was just beginning to be noticed by the authorities.[80]

"Mestiza in Indian habit" was a recognized category, but Spanish officials and elite witnesses puzzled over who, precisely, belonged to it. This was a vexing problem in the early modern period, when clothing had a "transnaturating power" that did not just reflect identity, but helped constitute it, and when costume was thought to reflect moral values, just as facial features were believed to echo the inner humors of the individual.[81] These unpretentious mestizas might have been perceived by Spanish observers as defying their station in life, as trying to pass for members of another socioracial category; on the other hand, it is more likely they confused Spanish officials because their appearance and their classification were in discord. In this sense, we might see mestizas en hábito de indias as marking the limits of the usefulness of the notion of racial passing for comprehending colonial-era mestizaje. As Karen Powers suggests, they represented a "disynchronization of race and culture" resulting from the disorder produced by urban migration and race mixture.[82] Jane Mangan notes that "habit" means not only clothing but also life-ways, implying that mestizas in Indian habit were also marked by their indigenous cultural habits, including the language they spoke and their occupations, so more than clothing was at issue here.[83] However complicated it was for Spaniards to get their minds around these women's appearance, though, it is likely that, from their own point of view, the mestizas were not passing for anyone other than themselves. Exemplifying the sometimes unconscious and overwhelming fluidity of calidad, what today might appear as "passing" was at the time more likely a way of coping with the radical cultural and social change that accompanied economic dislocation and urban migration.

Where these women fit in the colonial social fabric varies by locality and time period. Mestizas were not allowed to wear indigenous dress in Mexico City, upon pain of one hundred lashes.[84] In colonial Bolivia, mestizas en hábito de indias were market vendors living in urban areas. Exempt from paying sales taxes (alcabalas) because they sold foodstuffs grown in the countryside (productos de la tierra), they had incentive to wear indigenous costume, which identified vendors as being from rural areas (even though they were not).[85] Mestizas in Indian dress living in Cuenca, in what is today Ecuador, appear in land-sales contracts and in wills, where they are classified as "*cholas*," as opposed to "mestizas"; "chola" appears to have been a designation largely reserved for women and which, according to Jacques Poloni-Simard, was used to indicate mestiza women who had achieved an incipient degree of hispanization that was beyond the grasp of men, who were more firmly bound to their native communities by tribute obligations.[86]

The designation of "mestizas en hábito de indias" is confined in colonial documents from Santafé largely to servants in urban households. The mestizas who remained at their indigenous mothers' sides in rural settings quite likely wore the same sort of attire, but they were not identified in this way in the Santafé-Tunja region because they effectively blended into the landscape.[87] Native garb was not a useful distinguishing marker of calidad in the rural setting of the Nuevo Reino, given that so many of these women were simply reabsorbed into the indigenous population; since they were not subject to tribute, they were not singled out by the authorities. The very fact of wearing native clothing made these women into Indians, a shape-shifting practice that in neighboring Quito was probably cemented by the fact that rural parish jurisdictions were organized according to the costume of parishioners, with those in native costume assigned to friars and those in Spanish dress attending churches staffed by secular clergy.[88]

Very little is said in the documentation about these women, since they were usually marginal to the legal cases in which they appeared, cropping up for the most part as insignificant witnesses or as recipients of small bequests in the wills of their Spanish mistresses. Unlike Poloni-Simard in his study of colonial Cuenca, I did not find mestizas en hábito de indias who identified themselves as such in wills or contracts from Santafé and Tunja, and I have no way of counting how many of them lived in Santafé or Tunja, since there was no institution charged with counting mestizas in this period. Thus, it is only by testing the boundaries of the category that we can begin to understand who these women were. A 1596 suit by Catalina Tafur against Luis Bermúdez takes us some way toward solving the conundrum of these not-so-illusive racial cross-dressers.[89] Catalina, identified as a mestiza in Indian habit, was the illegitimate daughter of Captain Juan Tafur, a conquistador of noble lineage from Córdoba who later married doña Antonia Manuel de Hoyos, a noblewoman from Segovia. Juan Tafur left no legitimate offspring (although he had two illegitimate daughters, Catalina and Isabel), and he designated his widow as his sole heir.

After being widowed, doña Antonia Manuel went on to marry Luis Bermúdez, who survived her.[90] Catalina Tafur's story springs from her battle to recover one hundred pesos owed her by the estate of Antonia Manuel in return for her service to the household.

Testimony paints a portrait of a wayward girl who did not respond to the proper care proffered by her stepmother. Catalina's sister, Isabel Tafur, attests to having "known Catalina Tafur since she was born and witnessed her being raised in the house of Juan Tafur, her father and [the father] of this witness. And this witness raised her, and when captain Juan Tafur married doña Antonia, Catalina Tafur was eight years old" (996v). She began to get into trouble shortly after her father married.

> After [doña Antonia was] married for some three or four years, since Catalina Tafur roamed around, lost and in a bad way, doña Antonia threw her out of her house and she was away from there until after the death of Captain Juan Tafur. And up to three or four months before doña Antonia's death, [doña Antonia] being married to Luis Bermúdez, Catalina did not return to the house, when Luis Bermúdez brought her back against the wishes of doña Antonia. And therefore she could not perform any service worthy of consideration because for the time that Catalina Tafur was there, it would be more or less a year and a half, and she was given more in clothing and wardrobe than she would have been entitled to in exchange for her service, because she was well treated, as much in her clothing as in the food she ate, and she ruled in the house because doña Antonia was sick. And in that year and a half she would have served, she fled and disappeared with anyone that wanted to have her, because she was so lost. (996v–997r)

In this statement, which was corroborated by other witnesses, Catalina is depicted as an ungrateful dependent who refused the protection of Antonia Manuel and instead took to the streets. Witnesses denied Catalina's assertion that she was a mere servant—which was the fate of many mestiza daughters of Spanish households—arguing instead, as did the royal scribe Gonzalo Sánchez de Robledo, that "Catalina Tafur was reputed to be the daughter of Captain Juan Tafur, and as such she was protected [la recogía] and taught the Christian doctrine and educated by doña Antonia Manuel in her home, guiding her with good

customs as might be expected of a woman who was so honorable and a good Christian, as was doña Antonia Manuel" (1000r). Catalina was, stated Sánchez de Robledo, being raised as a lady.

Why would a well-cared-for daughter of a conquistador, a girl never banished to the servants' quarters, walk the streets of Santafé dressed like an india? Gaspar Enríquez, an old friend of Captain Tafur's, explained: "In the time of Captain Juan Tafur, who was said to be her father and was married to doña Antonia, she was treated well, kept in Spanish clothing [abitos de española] and doña Antonia instructed her and taught her good customs. And after the death of Captain Juan Tafur this witness saw her in Indian habit [en abitos de yndia]" (1003r). In other words, Catalina's assumption of native garb came on the heels of an abrupt change in her status in the household, provoked by the death of her father, who had left her stepmother mired in debt (996r–v). Whether the widow forced Catalina into servitude, leading her to change her costume along with her status, we do not know. But, in effect, her classification—and therefore her social situation—shifted from coddled daughter to mestiza en hábito de india who could easily be taken for native.

How, exactly, Catalina was classified before she donned the indigenous woolen *líquida* (hispanization of Quechua *lliclla*, for shawl) sheds light on how radical her shift to indigenous costume was. When Gaspar Enríquez noted that the girl was "kept in Spanish clothing," he was probably not simply identifying her as one of the multitude wearing inexpensive European garments, but referring to a more specific status, that of Spanish lady, marked by the type of cloth employed in the confection of her clothing and its relative opulence, governed by sumptuary laws that restricted the use of silk, lace, and pearls, among other materials, for the adornment of European bodies. In a 1578 suit over whether a Santafé slaveholder had recognized two mulatto girls as his daughters and freed them before his death, the witness Gonzalo García Zorro—a cleric who was, himself, mestizo—testified about one of them that "he always observed her to be well treated and in Spanish dress [abito despañola], so that she did not look like the daughter of an African."[91] African slaves did not dress in distinguishable "African" garments, but in inexpensive European clothing, so in his use of the term "Spanish habit" García Zorro was referring not only to dress style—which was common to women of all walks of life (including slaves) who wore European-style clothing—but to something more specific conveyed by the quality of the cloth and accessories, denoting a particular social status. In the case of these two mulattas, García Zorro was probably alluding to the fact that their clothing indicated the relatively high social standing of their family. Catalina Tafur, likewise, wore this style of dress, which was called "Spanish habit."

Most mestizas en hábito de indias were servants, women with no wealth or status, trying to make ends meet in a hostile urban environment. They were confusing to Spanish observers because they did not fit into established categories, which placed Indians in tribute-paying communities and relegated plebeian mestizos to the urban margins under the assumption that individuals from different walks of life looked different. Catalina Tafur's predicament was distinct from that of most mestizas in Indian habit, since she did not belong to either of these two marginal sectors. The daughter of Captain Juan Tafur was socialized to occupy elite status in the household of a conquistador. Secluded in the private quarters of the family dwelling, she was taught to be a refined woman and a good Christian, one who someday could marry a prominent Spaniard or an American-born man of Iberian descent, and ultimately abandon the epithet of "mestizo." In fact, according to Juan Flórez de Ocariz, Catalina *did* eventually marry a Spaniard.[92] In Peru, elite mestizas like Catalina were confined to convents and other public institutions in efforts to train them to be good Christians, groom them for marriage, ensure the reproduction of their fathers' lineages, and protect the capital that those without legitimate siblings would inherit (those who were recognized but not legitimized were also left a portion of the estate).[93] The Carmelite convent that was founded in Santafé some six years after the Catalina Tafur episode took in orphans, illegitimate daughters, and some mestizas, serving a somewhat similar function as the Peruvian institutions; one of its objectives was to protect vulnerable young women from undesirable unions with blacks, mulattos, and mestizos.[94] But convent life was not in Catalina's reach in her time of need, and it is unclear whether the convent would have accepted her and given her a white veil (marking her subordinate status in the convent). Catalina's life trajectory was disrupted by the death of her father and the huge debts he left his widow to repay, making Catalina placeless in terms of inheritance and leaving her nowhere to turn.

Was Catalina Tafur passing for Indian? Probably not. Everyone knew who she was despite her change in costume, and in cultural terms, she was firmly ensconced in the Spanish world where she had been raised, although with her father's death she had lost her "lineage" and was no longer socially visible. The question of passing does little to elucidate Catalina's unique situation, not to mention that of other mestizas in native dress. In order to comprehend her choice of attire, we cannot presuppose, on the one hand, that the category of mestiza to which she belonged was stable and homogeneous. Nor, on the other hand, can we assume that her actions are evidence of choices made by an individual hoping to move from one status to another, for why would Catalina opt for downward mobility? Instead of taking the social categories of Indian, mestiza, and Spaniard as givens, we can use Catalina Tafur's case to examine how they were traversed and what kinds of attitudes they triggered.

In the very fact of belonging to such an ambiguous category, Catalina Tafur defies the limitations placed by the notion of discrete socioracial types. Clothing and adornment were fundamental markers of status in the colonial period, frequently taking precedence over phenotype in the process of identifying an individual. However, the neat categorizations that accompany the equation of costume with calidad are blurred in the case of the mestiza in Indian habit, a woman who should be wearing European dress but is instead attired in indigenous costume. If mestizo is an intermediate category between Indian and European, the mestiza in Indian habit could be construed as intermediate between Indian and mestiza, or, perhaps, in Catalina's case, as someone who defies the classification entirely. Most mentions of such women in the archival documentation appear in the sixteenth and early seventeenth centuries and are associated with urban dwellers, suggesting that the existence of this group was part of an incipient moment in the constitution of colonial society, just as Andrés Sánchez Gallque's portrait *Three Mulatto Gentleman*, which depicts three dark-skinned men with indigenous jewelry, spears, and European costume, grapples with the mixture of Africans, Native Americans, and Europeans at the moment that intermediate categories were emerging.[95] From this perspective, Catalina Tafur was not passing at all. Like so many of her contemporaries, she was navigating social categories that were in formation; she was testing their boundaries.

At the moment of Catalina Tafur's costume change, socioracial cross-dressing constituted a prime scenario for working out and challenging the ethnic boundaries erected in the wake of conquest in both Spain and the Americas. The art historian Carolyn Dean interprets the use of Inca costume by indigenous nobles in seventeenth-century Corpus Christi processions in Cuzco both as an implicit recognition of the superiority of Catholicism and as a means by which the native elite drew on Incaic referents in their pursuit of power on the colonial stage.[96] The use of Moorish clothing by Spanish Christians in jousting matches and of indigenous actors to play Moors in officially sponsored public events, argues Barbara Fuchs, underline some of the fundamental "contradictions involved in translating the scripts for the emergent empires to new locales."[97] In Spain, the performance of Moorishness was shadowed by the essential difficulty of "distinguish[ing] Islamic other from Christian self."[98] In Peru, the use of Christian natives to play their pre-Christian forebears or to take the part of infidel Moors in public performances places center-stage some of the inconsistencies inherent in the conversion process.[99]

Catalina Tafur was not a cross-dresser of the sort highlighted by Dean or Fuchs, both of whom are concerned with those who adopted the costume of the other in the course of staged performances: they were meant to be observed, while to the contrary, Catalina sought to melt into the native urban populace. Nonetheless, Catalina could be considered a kind of a transvestite, a cross-dresser who, like any other mestiza, embodied in herself multiple identities that were expressed simultaneously, each continuously canceling out the other. Catalina was, essentially, playing herself: a woman of mixed descent at the dawn of mestizaje. Hers was a highly gendered performance for concrete historical reasons. I did not find other similar cases of mestizos in Indian habit in Santafé, where the category appears to have enfolded the most marginal of the marginal, the female offspring of illicit unions, themselves the future mothers of more mestizos, women whose social identity could be identified only through their absent fathers (just as Catalina's deceased father had previously determined her social standing).[100] By contrast, the positioning of their brothers was less ambiguous: they were either "Indians" or "mestizos," but never "either/or" like the mestizas in Indian habit. Men were subject to rights and obligations that rooted them more firmly in the social landscape, whether by the taxes or tribute paid by members of subordinated categories, or by the military and ceremonial obligations required of elites. Male identity was, moreover, crosscut by multiple forms of classification that incorporated men into a broader variety of occupational, ritual, and civic groups and organizations. In addition, men, especially male indigenous tributaries and conscripted laborers, are described more frequently than women in administrative records, because the Crown had a vested interest in identifying them as individuals, so they were continuously on public view.[101]

However, Catalina Tafur's predicament was differently gendered from that of other mestizas in Indian habit. As a privileged young woman, sequestered and protected by her father, she was thrust, upon his death, into a marginal social position that could only be occupied by a woman (or, perhaps, a child) without defenses. One of the few options at her disposal was to don native dress and adopt servant status—not to "pass" as an Indian, but to *become* one, since this was one of the multiple identities she could perform—moving her into a mestizo underworld, now that she had been displaced from elite Spanish society by her stepmother. Fuchs would see Catalina's predicament as a kind of early modern mimesis: "the fun-house mirror, the reflection that dazzles the impersonator, the sneaky copy, the double agent—mimesis, that is, as a deliberate performance of sameness that necessarily threatens, or at least modifies, the original."[102] However, the sameness of the mestiza Catalina Tafur lies not with her Spanish father, but with her indigenous mother (who is invisible in the documentation), whose appearance she was ultimately forced to adopt, if only for a brief time before she ultimately married a Spaniard. Her particular brand of passing—if we can call it that—threatens and modifies the original, but of the Indian, not of the elite Spanish woman she thought she could never be, or of the mestiza, for whom there was no "original."

CONCLUSION

Catalina Tafur's predicament underlines the subtleties and the ambivalences of interpreting race in the colonial American world. If we are to speak at all of passing in early Spanish America, we must understand movement across identities as part of an unfolding process of classification and of identity construction, rather than as an isolated moment of subterfuge. Francisco Suárez and Diego Romero *were* passing, but as what? In both cases, nobility and honor seem to constitute the core of their refashionings of self, more so than does "race" in the modern sense of the word. Had Suárez been a lower-status Spaniard, he would have had as little success in courting doña Catalina Acero de Vargas as he did in the role of indio zambo, although it was probably galling for the young woman's brother to discover she had been spirited away by a man of mixed native and African descent (or by a huauqui, an Indian from Quito, as Suárez is alternately identified). If Romero really was Diego Hurtado, the gulf he bridged between Muslim slave and Santafé encomendero was as great (and as improbable) as Francisco Suárez's move from indio zambo to Lima grandee—which may account for why he and his children were ultimately permitted to thrive among the Santafé elite, having weathered such terrible accusations. These two examples stand in marked contrast to modern notions of racial passing in North America, which are generally more discreet, more focused on phenotype, and do not necessarily involve the astonishing class mobility exhibited by Romero and Suárez. Narratives of racial passing in the United States, unlike the stories I have told in this chapter, are about permanent transitions between statuses that are relatively similar in socioeconomic terms but span racial gulfs, forcing their protagonists to exist in constant fear of being discovered, leading them to live constrained lives.[103] The narratives of colonial instances of passing reveal, in contrast, a constellation of classificatory practices that were so much more malleable, unfixed, and undefined.

If Romero and Suárez were dissimulators, the reverse social mobility of Catalina Tafur further disrupts the model of racial passing. She did not disguise her mestiza status, nor did she have the option to do so, given her social standing and general circumstances. It was, indeed, unusual for an elite mestiza to assume indigenous dress, but the social category Catalina came to occupy was not inhabited by passers; it was filled by women in marginal positions—as she most certainly inhabited for a time. Her experience marks the limitations of imputing to colonial actors twenty-first-century racial discourses and values.

All three cases suggest that modern notions of race do not provide a useful lens for making sense of diversity in colonial Spanish America and early modern Iberia, even if, at times, these actors effectively "passed," assuming identities other than those for which they were generally known. By locking these three individuals into a fixed racial hierarchy, we presuppose that the identities they foregrounded were uniformly perceived by observers and by the actors themselves as being stable and central to their personas, identities that they needed to hide from. It also assumes that what we would call "race" occupied the center of these individuals' identities, forcing gender, status, religion, and social condition into the background. In order to begin to comprehend who these people were, we need to interpret them, instead, on their own terms.

2. Mestizo Networks

Did "Mestizo" Constitute a Group?

J. I. Israel writes that in colonial Mexico "mestizos were many and important while apparently few and unimportant: the bulk of the mestizo population was disguised socially as something else."[1] Key to making sense of the colonial social fabric is the fact that there were many mestizos, but they were invisible—precisely the concern reflected in the title of this volume, *The Disappearing Mestizo*. However, I take issue with Israel's claim that "the bulk of the mestizo population was disguised socially as something else," because it assumes that a group of people who were mestizos existed "out there" and could be "disguised." Who was a mestizo was up for grabs: it wasn't obvious; there was no transparent "system." True, many mestizos were people of mixed indigenous-European parentage (or, in the case of mulattos, African-European or indigenous-African parentage) or of similar permutations, but some were considered part of the European population, particularly if they were members of the elite. Alternately, since the Muisca descent system was matrilineal, the child of a Muisca woman would have also been considered a member of her group, regardless of the identity of the father, so the primary identity of many mestizos was as Indians.[2] "Mestizo" was certainly a malleable social category. Moreover, a broad range of social actors participated in the process of identification of who was mestizo and who was not: people could be classified as mestizos by state or church functionaries, or they could be labeled mestizos by their masters, their enemies, their peers, or, sometimes, themselves. However, there was no *group* of mestizos in any sociological sense of the word, just an abstract class into which individuals could be sorted, or from which they could escape classification.

This distinction is crucial. Categories may reflect preexisting groups, but it is equally likely that from them new social groups might emerge, or in other cases, that the fit between category and group might not be tight.[3] The modern Andes illustrate this assertion: while "mestizo" is sometimes used to refer to people (or to refer to the nation), there is no stable group of mestizos in any of the Andean countries. This was also true in the colonial period, although the label functioned differently. By arguing that "mestizo" was a category and not a sociological group, I do not mean to imply that people did not live the consequences of being labeled (or self-identifying as) mestizos. They most certainly did suffer for occupying a marginal status, and in this sense, mestizaje was painfully real to many colonial people. Nor am I suggesting that the segment of the population comprised by mestizos was not demographically significant, which it most certainly was, increasingly, over the colonial period.

Mestizos were not "disguised socially as something else." Most of the time they *were* something else: farmers, artisans, housemaids, the wives of grandees, conquistadors, prostitutes, members of religious confraternities, priests, residents of barrios (quarters) of Santafé or Tunja, parishioners in rural or urban congregations, even caciques. They became members of a "group" of mestizos only at certain moments, in particular contexts in which they were recognized (or misrecognized) as such: when they were identified or self-identified as mestizos in a particular legal context, when they were listed in a census or another register, when their calidad was recorded in baptismal or death records, when they were accused as members of a presumed mestizo rebellion. That is, their groupness was entirely situational, as was, in practice, their identity as mestizos. Furthermore, the groups of mestizos that emerged at particular moments were not stable or homogeneous, but were, instead, purely contextual. For example, the two mestizo caciques don Alonso de Silva and don Diego de Torres moved across a series of identities based on the relationships they constructed with an array of social groups: the alliance they forged among themselves was based on their common political predicament; their standing as ethnically unmarked members of the urban elite led them to spend the majority of their time with high-placed Spaniards in Santafé and Tunja; their embeddedness in native social networks as caciques permitted them to develop a highly ritualized and rather aloof relationship with their subjects along with political alliances with other caciques. Note, however, that Silva and Torres did not dedicate themselves to cultivating relationships with other mestizos; those living in and around the pueblos of Tibasosa and Turmequé were their enemies, not their friends. So if we were to attempt to gauge their identity based on the groups of people with whom they associated on a regular basis, we would be hard-pressed to classify them as mestizos.

Perhaps it is for this reason that it is impossible to unearth figures for how many sixteenth- or seventeenth-century mestizos lived in the countryside around Santafé or Tunja, or in the urban centers themselves, although it is clear that their population was very small. I did not encounter any census of mestizos for this period in the archives, although there are population counts for the eighteenth century, when the mestizo sector began to grow exponentially.[4] However, people were certainly identified as mestizos in early colonial legal proceedings and their growing presence was decried by seventeenth-century colonial officials.[5] Seventeenth-century visitas (tribute censuses and investigations into the administration of native communities) sometimes listed the mestizos living in pueblos de indios (doctrinal towns) or on lands set aside for indigenous communities (resguardos); however, those living legally in rural areas beyond the confines of doctrinal towns and resguardos were not commonly ennumerated.[6] We have no information on how many of them there were, overall, in the provinces of Santafé and Tunja. Mestizos were, simply, an acknowledged but unspecified presence that shifted in and out of the legal record.

CONFUSED IDENTITIES

Recent scholarship has paid a great deal of attention to those moments at which individuals were misidentified by colonial officials or where their alleged identities were in question, indicating the fluidity of calidad. David Tavárez, for instance, examines two cases in which the Mexican Inquisition deliberated over whether or not their defendants were Indians—an important step in inquisitorial proceedings, as native people were not subject to the jurisdiction of the Holy Office. Tavárez looks at two men accused of bigamy in the early seventeenth century, both claiming to be Indians although they were reputed to be mestizos by their neighbors. In each case the individual in question had broken ties with his natal village, and inquisitors found it impossible to uncover genealogical documentation to substantiate his calidad. Witnesses could confirm only parts of the men's stories: some remembered them as mestizos, while others recalled knowing the couples identified as their parents but could not recollect whether they had exhibited the public behavior generally displayed by parents toward sons. In one of the cases inquisitors resorted to interviewing leaders from the defendant's alleged community of birth to establish whether or not he was born there.[7]

I encountered a similar case of mistaken identity in the archives in Bogotá, a lawsuit that indicates that when we dwell on the fluidity of the boundaries that were continually negotiated between the categories of indio and mestizo, we are only going part of the way. The case concerns the shoemaker Juan de Salazar, who was jailed in 1650 for having bitten the nose off Juan de Medina, a tanner by trade.[8] Salazar allegedly disfigured Medina in a brawl outside the house of the cacique of Fontibón, an indigenous pueblo near Santafé. The headquarters of a major Jesuit mission, early seventeenth-century Fontibón was known as a center of aboriginal ritual observance, with more than eighty *jeques*, or Muisca religious specialists, and an important temple that was sniffed out and destroyed by the Catholic Church.[9] Subsequently, Fontibón was transformed into a regional doctrinal center for the Jesuits, where the indigenous faithful were treated to the performance of elaborate Christian ceremonies, full of pomp, including processions, music, dance, choral music accompanied by an organ, and the participation of caciques from all of the neighboring towns.[10] A mission school instructed one hundred children, teaching them basic literacy and music.[11] The town was a magnet for indigenous people in the region.

But many also left Fontibón and other pueblos for urban life in the capital of the Audiencia. Numerous native men abandoned their rural homes for Santafé during the late sixteenth and the seventeenth centuries to serve Spanish households and to help build public works for periods of a month in what was called "the urban mita," bringing with them their wives and children; they built thatched-roof huts on the outskirts of the city.[12] The Jesuit Gonzalo de Lira reports that these newcomers mixed with other more permanent indigenous migrants in the capital city, many of whom "were so ladino that they loathe their language and speak always in Spanish."[13] The fluidity of movement between Fontibón and Santafé belies any assumed homogeneity in the town's population. While it was certainly an indigenous pueblo, the proximity of Fontibón to the capital and the centrifugal force exerted by Santafé on nearby towns meant that all kinds of people took up residence there. (Today Fontibón is a rough, working-class district that is part of the unrestrained expansion of Bogotá.)

Fontibón appears to have been equally rough in the seventeenth century. The scuffle between Juan de Medina and Juan de Salazar erupted in the midst of a fiesta hosted by the cacique of Fontibón, both men presumably having had their fill of *chicha*, or fermented corn beer. Men of various calidades were in attendance, including Indians, mestizos, probably mulattos; if the Jesuits had attempted to isolate the indigenous faithful from the pernicious influence of outsiders, they had not succeeded. Caciques and indigenous governors from neighboring communities also attended the fiesta, as did a range of artisans—tanners, shoemakers, barbers, and painters. Indeed, the fiesta's guests were as diverse as the population of nearby Santafé.[14]

Juan de Medina is identified in the documentation as an Indian, while Juan de Salazar's ascription shifts in the course of the criminal case brought against him. At the outset he is labeled a mestizo, but later he is called an Indian by some actors and a mestizo by others. The circumstances of this move from an intermediate designation to what could be called a "pure" category, as well as the discrepancies between how Salazar is identified by his peers as opposed to his superiors, appears at first glance to present us with an archetypal case of how the category of mestizo was navigated in the colonial period.

As in all criminal cases, the first item in the proceedings against Juan de Salazar was a description of his attack on Juan de Medina as told by an eyewitness, in this case, an indio ladino, a Spanish-speaking native. Francisco de Ortega, a painter, graphically depicts the fracas, embellishing his narration with reported speech.

> Last night, at about nine, when this witness passed by the door
> of the house of don Juan, cacique of Fontibón, he noticed that
> there were people inside dancing. He entered to take a look,
> and when he left he saw Juan de Salazar going out of the house.
> At that moment Juan de Medina, Indian, was at the door of the
> house and said to Salazar, "Ay *Yaya*"—because that's what they
> call him—and Juan de Salazar called the Indian a pig and the
> Indian answered, "You are a bigger pig than me." And with that
> Juan de Salazar seized the Indian and fell to the floor with him,
> and while he was on top of him this witness observed that he
> caught his nose in his teeth and bit off a piece of it, at which
> point a great deal of blood came flowing out of the Indian. And
> this witness saw this because it was a clear moonlit night. (125v)

Salazar was said to have off bitten Medina's nose. The verb used in the document is *desnarigar* (literally, to "un-nose") a dreadful act made only more startling by the relatively minor comment that provoked it—a familiar nickname—as well as by the copious amount of blood that streamed out of the tanner's nose.

As soon as they were informed of the offense, the authorities rushed to Salazar's workshop, where they found the shoemaker surrounded by the tools of his trade. They seized "seventy-three pairs of different types of footwear . . . and in addition, twenty-four shoe-molds, three soles already begun, some scissors and three heel-knives and other tools of little importance" (125v). Agustín de Zamora, a Spanish merchant, claimed the majority of the shoes were his because he had commissioned Salazar to cobble them, so they were placed in storage (125v–126r). The shoemaker was compelled to make a confession. He said he was twenty-five years old, a native of Quito, and married to Isabel India. He added that Medina was his friend and acknowledged that the brawl had been inflamed by Medina calling him by the nickname Yaya.[15] But, Salazar continued, he only "bit off a small piece of [Medina's nose], and then people arrived and sorted out their differences [los metieron en paz], and with that, this defendant [confesante] went home" (127v).

An investigator visited Medina, who was secluded in his sickroom, to ascertain the extent of his injuries: "Having entered in a room of [the house] we found the aforementioned lying in a bed, and I had him remove his bandages and the poultices he had on his nose and on the right side there was a piece measuring approximately two by two, something smaller than the cartilage of the nose, which it appeared to me and I was shown, is where he is missing the piece that was ripped off by teeth, as is [recorded] in these case documents" (128v). Salazar was sentenced to a fifty-patacón fine and two years of confinement in the dreaded Presidio de Carare, a military fort and forced-labor camp (131r). This was an onerous sentence that was likely to impoverish the shoemaker's family and might even prove to be life-threatening for Salazar himself.

A few months later Medina withdrew his complaint against the man whom he now called "Juan de Salaçar indio ladino" because, he confessed, "I was the one who provoked the aforementioned with offensive words" (132r). Note that here Medina identified Salazar as an Indian, not a mestizo, although Salazar's lawyer continued to use the racially mixed epithet when he referred to his client. The sentence was ultimately reduced to a twenty-five-patacón fine and a year in Carare, in spite of the lawyer's pleas to free Salazar, whose wife was bedridden and helpless (135r–137r).

Here are two men who made recourse to violence in a moment of passion. In the immediate aftermath of the incident, Salazar was dubbed a mestizo by his aggrieved acquaintance, Medina, as well as by the witnesses to his criminal act and the examining authorities. But when Medina cooled off sufficiently, he referred to his friend Salazar as an indio ladino. Medina was reflecting his changing relationship with his assailant when he shifted his description from mestizo to Indian. The threat of facial disfigurement, not to mention the fright he must have experienced as he bled onto the cacique's doorstep, drove him to slight the shoemaker by hinting at his illegitimate mixed parentage— the automatic association that anyone at the time would have made in response to the term "mestizo." However, once Medina was certain that Salazar had done him no lasting harm, he was willing to publicly demonstrate their friendship and ethnic proximity by signaling their common membership in the category of Indian. Notwithstanding the discursive shift by the complainant, Salazar remained a mestizo in the eyes of the judicial authorities. It evidently tested Spaniards' capacities of classification to distinguish between Spanish-speaking natives unattached to communities and mestizos in a semi-urban environment like Fontibón, where it was possible to attain a certain degree of anonymity through clothing, language, and profession. The lawyer's speech-act positioned Salazar at an undesirable location in the colonial social grid, in comparison to Medina's efforts at rapprochement.

Salazar did not hide from the appellation of mestizo, nor was he eliding it in any way, unlike the examples cited by David Tavárez. The Fontibón shoemaker did not contest the investigators or witnesses who called him a mestizo, nor did he contradict Medina when he referred to him as an indio ladino. What he was called does not seem to have mattered to him. The fluid movement from mestizo to Indian in Medina's speech appears to have been natural, something that occurred in the course of everyday interaction with his peers (as opposed to the more formal context of exchange with social superiors).

Both the case I present and those from David Tavárez's Mexican research demonstrate how very fluid the categories of calidad were and how much they owed to the social context in which they were uttered. Indeed, the attribution of calidad was, literally, a "speech act."[16] But we need to move beyond focusing our analysis on the decision-making that fuels the process of classification in isolated instances. We must also look into how social relations crystallize around the classificatory act. In particular, it is crucial to distinguish between the divergent classifications used to identify Salazar and the social groups that were constituted on the ground in the course of this dispute. How would we identify the group membership of partygoers at the festivities where Salazar bit Medina's nose? Certainly, the celebration had a master of ceremonies, don Juan, the cacique of Fontibón, who sponsored the fiesta. Many of his guests were Indians, although we do not know what "group" they belonged to, since we are never told if the guests were his tributaries or if they were from a neighboring pueblo. (Indeed, the visiting caciques were heads of pueblos other than that of Fontibón.) This distinction is important, since the category of Indian was not isomorphic with the group with which those who were labeled as Indians may have identified: their primary identities were as Fontibones, Sogamosos, or Ubaqueños, reflecting the pueblos in which they sustained face-to-face contact and were the subjects of specific caciques. There were also the indios ladinos, Spanish-speaking Indians living beyond the control of their caciques: they were indios, but of a different status than the Fontibones subject to the host of the fiesta. Some of the guests were called mestizos, but this was not a fiesta for mestizos, and there is no reason to assume that the revelers of mixed parentage wore this appellation on their sleeves as they imbibed their chicha and slowly drifted into drunkenness. More likely, the men congregating at don Juan's house recognized one another as artisans or as neighbors, and their most obvious common attribute at that moment was inebriation.

The judicial authorities who tried Salazar probably did infer more groupness among the shoemaker and his friends, as they shared the mistrust that most Spaniards felt toward mestizos. This may account for the lawyer's continued use of the "mestizo" epithet, even after Medina retracted it in the interests of friendship, instead calling Salazar an indio ladino. But even "indio ladino" was an ambiguous category that did not constitute a group on the ground; there were problems inherent in identifying ladinos as a collectivity. Over time, more and more indigenous people had learned Spanish, so that by 1650 it would not have been surprising to find a substantial group of them among the tributaries of the cacique of Fontibón, given its proximity to Santafé. But there were also other indios ladinos unattached to caciques, people called *forasteros* (outsiders), who made their living as hired hands, overseers, and artisans. Juan de Salazar was one of these unattached indios. In fact, like Francisco Suárez, the man who passed as a Limeño noble in his epistolary seduction of Catalina Acero de Vargas, Salazar was a particular kind of forastero: a huauqui, an Indian from Quito, a member of a group that merited its own label, which crops up period-ically in the documentary record.[17] Many huauquis, like other indios ladinos, identified more with their mestizo peers than with tributary Indians. They exerted a certain degree of authority over the indios, due to the positions they held, and they were frequently attached to powerful interests, like *hacendados*. Given these conditions, it is im-possible to state with certainty that Medina and Salazar, as indios la-dinos, would have felt themselves to be members of a collectivity of Indians, nor is it certain that the heterogeneous collection of indios la-dinos in Fontibón would have identified as a group or that they would have privileged relationships with other ladinos over friendships with mestizos.

Peer groups—sometimes relatively stable groups, such as the tribu-taries ruled by a cacique, but sometimes more fleeting, like the party-goers in Fontibón—emerged out of relationships on the ground which were, themselves, highly contextual. The people in the middle, the mestizos, mulattos, and indios ladinos, navigated this plebeian social landscape, but they were also subject to the control of other more pow-erful actors who could effectively limit how they identified themselves, like the attorney who persisted in calling Salazar a mestizo. To under-stand the dynamics of the process of naming and the social groups that coalesced around that process among members of the Nuevo Reino's lower orders, we must first understand the social contexts in which mestizaje was negotiated.

HARMONY AND CONFLICT

Sixteenth-century mestizos, most of whom were of illegitimate birth, are commonly viewed metaphorically as the children of rape, a blan-ket assertion that fosters misconceptions about the nature of social relations across social categories in rural and urban scenarios of the colonial world. It is indisputably true that field hands and retainers of Spanish hacendados, as well as their employers, forced indigenous women to grant them sexual favors, frequently spiriting them away from communities, and thus innumerable mestizos and mulattos were born of violence and rape. But others in the documentary record were the children of consensual unions and even marriages, whose every-day lives unfolded in perhaps more courteous interethnic contexts.[18] The varied experiences of mestizos in the Nuevo Reino nudge us away from stereotypical portraits of the colonial world as a series of ethnic enclaves that existed side by side, in semi-isolation from one another and bridged only by violence. The notion of heterogeneous social worlds poses a counterpoint to the persistent myth of two hermetically sealed republics, the Republic of Spaniards and the Republic of Indians, unfolding in parallel universes and conjoined only by exploitive social policy. Two distinct judicial and administrative republics certainly existed in colonial Spanish America, but members of different ethnic groups and calidades moved between indigenous pueblos and Spanish settlements, entering into continuous conversation and conflict. The very heterogeneity of colonial social life requires us to pay heed to the myriad kinds of social groups that were created and recreated in the course of social interaction.

The early seventeenth-century chronicler Pedro de Simón describes the landscape of the Nuevo Reino.

> In the two leagues surrounding [Santafé] on the side of the
> savannah, there are at least twelve pueblos de indios, implanted
> in the form of cities, with their streets, plaza, and church of
> stone with mud walls, so well built that they would look good
> in Spanish towns, [and] which do a great deal to beautify the
> countryside. In this same space there are many mills, ranches,
> or farmers' homesteads, sown with wheat, barley, root-crops,
> and vegetables of these lands and of Castile.[19]

That is to say, native people were not the sole inhabitants of the altiplano. Spaniards and others who lived in the environs of native pueblos—who, before the eighteenth century, probably occupied only 5 percent of the land, although their impact on the indigenous population was markedly greater than that—engaged the services of the doctrinal priests who were assigned to Christianize the natives.[20] Many of these small landowners were the mestizo offspring of encomenderos; they faced periodic expulsions by the authorities, while the more abusive hacendados were permitted to permanently occupy rural properties.[21] When indigenous lands were titled as resguardos in the early seventeenth century, unused plots were sold to nonindigenous settlers.[22] Some of them were eventually recognized as vecinos of the localities they inhabited; that is, they were considered citizens not of their cities of origin, but of their place of residence.[23] The continuous presence of mestizo smallholders, Spanish settlers, hacienda employees, and other outsiders fostered a constellation of interethnic relationships that were not entirely based on equality, notwithstanding the marginal status of many of these settlers themselves. The colonial state railed against their presence but also made possible their continued occupation of the land. As a result, the asymmetrical dyad "Indian-vecino" was established in the countryside, incorporating "the values of 'Spanishness' among vecinos, accentuating their difference and their 'superiority' in comparison to the 'indigenous' world, which was equally permeated by mestizaje."[24] In other words, both the "Spanish" and the "indigenous" worlds, which in any case were inextricably and uncomfortably intertwined, were spaces of both intimacy and exploitation, crosscut by the ubiquitous presence of mestizos who were obliged to deny their indigenous origins in the interests of achieving success (or at the least, survival) in colonial society.

This was not a pastoral scene of the harmonious coexistence of Spaniards, Indians, mestizos, mulattos, and black freedmen or slaves, such as was depicted in the 1930s by the Brazilian anthropologist Gilberto Freyre in *The Masters and the Slaves*. Freyre paints a portrait of colonial racial melding anchored by a plantation house presided over by a paternalistic Portuguese proprietor whose liaisons with female slaves produced *mestiços* (Portuguese for mestizos or mulattos). Similar romantic myths of racial mixing have been central to nationalist discourses across Latin America, functioning as a unifying symbol that conceals the discrimination that regularly took—and takes—place, sometimes below the surface, but also, frequently, in public view.

But colonial interethnic relationships were transculturative, however asymmetrical they may have been.[25] In-between people and their native mothers and cousins interacted on a daily basis with Spaniards, blacks, and mulattos, sometimes voluntarily and at other times against their will, constituting a cultural "middle ground" in which both indigenous and European cultural forms were continuously reinterpreted and misinterpreted.[26] Many contexts of interethnic contact took place in everyday life: relations of solidarity among the artisans of rural towns; the participation of people from different walks of life in the fiestas and celebrations sponsored by doctrinal priests; daily exchanges in the heterogeneous plebeian neighborhoods of Santafé, Tunja, or Vélez, where Spanish merchants, indigenous tailors, mestizo blacksmiths, African slaves, and mulatto servants shared not only the public space of the street or tavern, but also the more intimate domestic space of the elite urban household, the servants living in huts that dotted the property, the family itself living in the house, and merchants renting out storefronts at street level.[27]

The task at hand involves not losing sight of a number of crucial characteristics of social intercourse in an ethnically stratified society. Key is the fact that these relationships were gendered: the way a plebeian mestiza woman negotiated her own status and that of her children through strategic marriages and consensual unions differed from that of a mestizo man, whose calidad was frequently defined by his occupation instead of his sociofacial classification.[28] One's position in the social hierarchy also played a significant role in determining the classificatory terms one employed to designate others: the closer in status two individuals were to one another, the more meaningful the ethnic label given them by their counterparts (which is why Juan de Medina wavered in his identification of Juan de Salazar).[29] Finally, social indicators other than sociofacial category occupy center stage in everyday interaction. For one, the classification of individuals by language—for example, as monolingual Muisca-speaking *indios chontales* versus bilingual indios ladinos or Quechua-speaking huauquis—must be considered alongside ethnic designations and occupational identities, as yet another instance of the specificity of calidad in the colonial period.

Each of the stories that follow reflects the experiences of an individual of mixed parentage and inquires into what constituted a group for that individual, showing how sociofacial identification was counterbalanced by social interaction and pointing to the multiple, overlapping, and ever-changing circles of interaction in which people we might identify as mestizos participated. These vignettes demonstrate that the groupness of mestizos was highly variable. The movable contexts of their social interaction contributed to mestizos' propensity to disappear from the historical record: they lived as affiliates of those groups that were proximate to them, not as members of a mestizo community.

INCORPORATION INTO THE INDIGENOUS SPHERE

Many who work with colonial documentation have a gut feeling that the mestizos and mulattos born to native mothers in rural communities disappeared from the archival record because they blended into the indigenous community. In an ideal world it would be possible to document the process of reclassification by tracing the names listed across the generations in tribute censuses, identifying mestizos or mulattos who were reclassified as Indians when they reached adulthood, thus augmenting the tributary rolls. Unfortunately, tribute censuses didn't work that way. Take two hypothetical examples: Mateo Mulato, son of Catalina, *india soltera* (single indigenous woman), and Inés Mestiza, daughter of Maria, india ladina. Their mothers might be inserted into a final category of the visita register, tacked on the tails of the more extensive classes of tributaries and their families, followed by *reservados*, men exempted from tribute obligations by virtue of age or infirmity. The single mothers, grouped together with orphan children, came under the heading "*solteras y chusma*" (which I gloss as "single women and their issue," "chusma" being those who were not useful because they paid no tribute).[30] How do we trace these individuals over their life spans and those of their children? We have no surnames, except for their socioracial labels, so once they reach adulthood, they can no longer be identified through their mothers, who were not subject to tribute obligations. Furthermore, women like Inés Mestiza would probably drop out of the historical record entirely because they did not pay tribute. In the absence of such quantitative data, we must rely on anecdotal evidence.[31]

Under most circumstances, disappearance into the native world was the best option for the children of mixed unions, particularly those who had nowhere else to go and who were abandoned by their Spanish or mestizo fathers to be brought up by their Muisca mothers. Such individuals crop up often in the documentary record, particularly in the mid- to late seventeenth century, when some of them requested a change in their tributary status, often asking to be reclassified and struck from the tribute rolls.[32] In many cases, however, mestizos and mulattos were willingly incorporated as Indians by native authorities, while colonial census-takers did not know where to look for them and had no one they could ask for such information. In 1639, a visita was conducted in the town of Chocontá, located roughly halfway between the two colonial urban centers of Santafé and Tunja (Chocontá is best known to U.S. readers as the site of Orlando Fals Borda's *Peasant Society in the Colombian Andes*). A census of indigenous tributaries combined with a wide-ranging investigation of the state of secular and religious administration of an indigenous pueblo, the visita was an elaborate ceremony in which caciques and their subjects were paraded before judges called *visitadores* (visitors) who collected statistics from tributaries and examined witnesses on such topics as whether or not the doctrinal priest was fulfilling his duties, or the extent to which encomenderos committed abuses against Indians.[33] The 1639 visita in Chocontá investigated the encomienda of doña María Arias de Ugarte, widow of Captain don Francisco de Noboa Maldonado; the visitador was Licenciate don Gabriel de Carvajal. Bringing together scores of indigenous and Spanish deponents, Noboa Maldonado probed, among other issues, the presence of mestizos and mulattos in the town, which was viewed as a threat to the integrity of the native community.[34]

Because mestizo and mulatto workers were always attached to nearby haciendas in the savannah of Bogotá and the environs of Tunja, the visitador asked whether "among the Indians there lives or accompanies [them], the encomendero, his wife and children, relatives, or mestizos, mulattos, *zambaigos* [the same as zambo, an indigenous-African mixture], black slaves, indios ladinos, or Spanish settlers or temporary visitors who take or have taken their wives and daughters to abuse them, their property, or their lands, or who have committed other damages and offenses (598v)?"[35] The interlopers in Chocontá did not simply live alongside the natives on non-resguardo lands, however.

The visitador also found mulattos and mestizos living at the heart of indigenous families. For example, in the *parcialidad*, or section, of Gacha—in Muisca, the parcialidad was a kin group called an *uta*—the following families were recorded: "Luis Pasamisque, of thirty-seven years, Elvira, his wife, of fifty, the son of the aforementioned [Elvira] Francisco Mulato of nineteen years" (561v) and "Luis Guagata, of thirty-eight years, Magdalena, his wife, of thirty, Micaela, daughter of the aforementioned [Magdalena] is mestiza and this Micaela has a son, Diego, of two years" (562v).[36] These mulatto and mestizo children, raised by their indigenous mothers, would in all probability have been bilingual speakers of both Spanish and Muisca, doubtless more well versed in the Muisca culture of their immediate families than in the traditions of the dominant Hispanic society, even less in African-descendant lifeways. True, they were mulattos or mestizos, but these labels probably did not impact the texture of their daily lives, which were similar to those of their Muisca cousins. They were "disappearing mestizos" in a variety of senses. In part because they were culturally Muisca, their mixed parentage was overlooked, both by their indigenous family members, because they "fit in," and by outsiders (like the doctrinal priest, who undoubtedly spent as little time as possible in the pueblo and thus did not know his parishioners well), because they "appeared" Muisca. But they were also *legally* Muisca, inasmuch as they paid tribute as Indians, which functioned in the interests of the Crown, and because they traced their membership through their mother's line. In other words, they "disappeared" because their status as mestizos was never registered in the historical record, yet they were also not socially mestizos: they were Muiscas.

Most witnesses—caciques, *capitanes* (members of the minor nobility who ruled over the utas), and Catholic priests—could not identify any outsiders living in Chocontá, beyond a helpful blacksmith, Alvaro Cerón, who had resided there for the prior three years and who, it was noted, was a "good and quiet man, about whom there have been no complaints" (604r). The visitador made no move to dislodge this artisan from the pueblo. But then the investigators uncovered Lázaro Mulato, a free man of color who was the son of a native woman and a black father.[37] Lázaro had quietly married and lived to a ripe age in a native family. He was summarily ordered by the visitador to leave town, but he effectively asserted his case with a plea that underscores the tragedy of defending ethnic purity in a setting that was already heterogeneous in its composition.

> Lázaro, of mulatto color [de color mulato], a native [natural] of this pueblo of Chocontá, where my mother, who is now deceased, was from, responding to the charge made against me, that I have lived among the Indians of this town, contravening the decrees of Your Majesty, and in refutation I state that I must be absolved and freed because as I have stated I am a native [natural] of this pueblo, where my mother was from and my grandmother, and I was born and raised for my whole life, paying Your Majesty, until I reached the age of *reserva* [men over fifty] *requintos* [tax on blacks and mulattos] that I was obliged to pay every year. And in my youth I served in the war against the Pijaos, a soldier for sixteen years and a sergeant, as figures in the title I present [as evidence]. And I am also married in this aforementioned pueblo to an Indian with whom I have a quantity of children. Furthermore, I have lived and live in the aforementioned pueblo, quietly and peacefully, causing no damage to any Indian, even when I was a youth. What is more, I am now sixty years old and I cannot go to other parts to find a place to live. (658r)

Lázaro begged to remain in the town where he had cultivated corn and wheat in the company of his kinsfolk and where his children were registered as native tributaries. Note that he identifies himself as "of mulatto color," but also claims to be a "native" ("natural," or someone born in) of the pueblo, thereby juxtaposing two forms of identity, one by calidad and the other by place of origin. The authorities relented, allowing Lázaro to remain in Chocontá, but they charged him eight patacones in fines and legal costs and another patacón to pay for masses to be said for the souls of deceased natives (699r)—not a huge sum, but an obvious sacrifice for a poor farmer. His children continued to be considered Indians and to pay tribute, so despite the fact that their father was a mulatto, they were not classified as being of mixed descent.

MESTIZA OR INDIA?

The slightly more privileged sons and daughters of Spaniards took a different tack, which we can observe in the misclassification of Juana Galván, the mestiza daughter of the former encomendero of Chitaraque, a pueblo that lies near the city of Vélez in what is today the department of Santander. Juana was horrified to learn in 1645 that she and her children, Diego Solís and Micaela López, had been placed on the list of indigenous tributaries by the current encomendero, "who said that the aforementioned Juana Galván is an Indian and the daughter of Elvira and of don Juan."[38] This was a malicious act, charged Juana, because

> the aforementioned Juana Galván is a mestiza, daughter of
> the former encomendero. She was never placed on the list [of
> tributaries] in previous descriptions. And now her mother is not
> named in the one in which she has been included, [instead] she
> is listed as the daughter of Elvira [although] she is the daughter
> of doña Isabel, the wife of don Juan, cacique of Chitaraque, and
> the aforementioned Elvira, who is named as her mother, was
> the second wife of don Juan, and when he married doña Isabel,
> mother of Juana Galván, the aforementioned Juana Galván was
> six years old and was living in the house of her father, the en-
> comendero, because today she is forty-eight years of age, more
> or less. (747r)

In other words, Galván was misidentified as the issue of a marriage between members of the indigenous nobility, instead of as the illegitimate daughter of a native noblewoman with a Spaniard. This genealogical mistake—perhaps made on purpose by the encomendero who succeeded her father, in order to increase his tribute rolls by adding her son as a tributary—reclassified her as an Indian instead of a mestiza. In an appeal to the weight of truth of archival inscriptions in the period, Galván insisted that the judicial authorities consult earlier tribute registers compiled by Lesmes de Espinosa Sarabia and Rodrigo Zapata, where, she informed them, they would find that her name was not included; only her half siblings, who were the sons of doña Isabel with the cacique—and hence, Indians on both their mother's and father's sides—were incorporated into those lists (747r). She demanded that her name "be erased and removed from the description in which I am now placed" and that her children not be considered tributaries "given they are quarteroons [cuarterones] and the children of a Spaniard" (747v).

As in documents issuing from other disputes of the period, the initial declaration made by Juana Galván is followed by lists of questions to be addressed to witnesses (the *interrogatorio*), after which their depositions are recorded. This is a brief document, so there is only a single interrogatorio and a handful of deponents from whom we learn about the extramarital trysts that punctuated Juana Galván's life and rooted her identity in an intricate web of interethnic unions. Galván identifies herself in the questionnaire as a mestiza: "Juana Galban mestisa, daughter of Juan Lopez Galuan who was encomendero of the pueblo of Chitaraque" (474r). As the daughter of an encomendero and of a mother who would later become the wife of a cacique, Juana refused to abandon her surname, becoming "Juana Galván mestiza" instead of simply "Juana Mestiza," a way of subtly emphasizing her slightly higher status relative to mestizos who enjoyed no attachments to their Spanish fathers. Her two children, she reports, were the result of a union with Diego López, a priest who provided for them during their childhood (756r, 757r).[39] Since they were only a quarter Indian, she calls them "quarteroons," a category that occasionally appears in seventeenth-century documentation but is not as common as "mestizo," and which I have found as a term of self-description, but not of classification by colonial authorities.[40] "Cuarterón" functions here as a kind of distancing mechanism, moving Juana's children further away from indigenous or mestizo status and closer to the Spanish status of her paternal relatives: it is a kind of disappearing mechanism, whereby the bearer of the epithet ceases to be considered a mestizo (at least on paper). However, Juana subsequently married an Indian, Juan Malasmaños, who does not appear to have been affiliated with the pueblo de indios where her mother lived (756v). Her daughter, Micaela

López, married Felipe—whose surname is indecipherable in the documentation, and whose calidad is not identified—while her son, Diego Solís, remained single and served as a soldier in the conquest of the eastern plains under the command of Matías de Jeréz (756v). One of the witnesses, Gabriel Camacho, another encomendero and Galván's first cousin, states that Juana was brought up by their Spanish grandmother, Elvira López. This clears up the confusion that caused her name to be added to the tribute rolls, since it had been assumed that Elvira was her indigenous mother, not her Spanish grandmother (757r–v).[41] Juana's diverse linkages to mestizos, Indians, and Spaniards demonstrate that she navigated a diverse network of acquaintances, lovers, and relations.

Galván's genealogy underscores the difficulties in identifying a person as embodying a single, discrete calidad. She was the daughter of a Spaniard and a native noblewoman, raised by her Spanish grandmother, first cousin to an encomendero who was close enough to her to agree to serve as a witness in her favor, consort of a Spanish priest, wife of an Indian, mother of two quarteroons. Juana Galván's daily life shifted in and out of identities, back and forth between city and countryside, vacillating between an elevated social circle and a more lowly social network. This constant movement resulted, at least momentarily, in a confused legal identity, one that she was eager to define appropriately, for a designation of Indian would have had a profound and undesirable effect on her children's futures. Hence, she refused to be disappeared in the legal record, doing her best to remain a mestiza.

In this sense, we can think of archival inscription as a space in which the process of identification unfolded and was negotiated, rather than as a simple repository of historical evidence of stable identities and unchallenged genealogies. This fourteen-folio document was a site of contestation: by the visitador, the encomendero, the witnesses, and Juana Galván herself, all of whom used either oral testimony or references to previous written records (and sometimes both) to fashion an identity for Galván that was acceptable to their own interests. Juana Galván's classification as a mestiza was not so much an end result as a series of intersecting and counterposed interests that were in conflict, producing a moment observable to us almost 370 years later—a snapshot, not a film, of who she was and of who those who had vested interests wanted her to be.

While Juana Galván resisted melting into the native population of Chitaraque, Lázaro Mulato's children were absorbed by the social circle of Chocontá. But what of people like Lázaro Mulato himself? He was never recognized as a tributary although he self-identified as a mulatto-colored "natural" who shared the daily life of a pueblo de indios with his native wife and children. What "natural" meant to him was conceivably different from the visitador's interpretation of the term in this context. Lázaro was, indeed, born in Chocontá and thus a natural of the pueblo (at the time, "natural" could function as an adjective, as in "natural" of Chocontá or "originally from" Chocontá). He was a member of the community insofar as his family consisted of tributaries and their dependents. We might even say he was an informal vecino, who probably participated in public works and attended Mass and other community functions; it was not until later in the colonial period, when the mestizo population of the countryside grew exponentially, that nonindigenous residents would be formally recognized as vecinos.[42] Nonetheless, the visitador did not see Lázaro as belonging in Chocontá, a doctrinal town whose inhabitants were indigenous and were registered in the tribute records (here we have "natural" in its noun form, meaning "Indian belonging to the doctrinal town of Chocontá"). What complicated Lázaro's situation was that he was born in Chocontá of a woman who was a natural, was married to a natural, and had natural children. Thus he was definitely not an interloper (forastero); in the sense that he had deep roots there, he was an insider. But he was not a natural in the sense of being an Indian, so for the colonial administration he was an outsider. He referred to "natural" in its adjectival form, while the visitador used it as a noun. Until he was sixty, Lázaro Mulato was able to disappear into the ambiguous space that bridged the two meanings of the term, as were countless other mestizos, mulattos, and some indios ladinos.

The 1639 visita says nothing more about Lázaro, so I turn to a different case to explore further what it meant to be a mulatto in the Muisca heartland. For this, I turn to Soatá, a pueblo de indios some 115 kilometers northeast of Tunja, and to Manuel Rodríguez, a late-sixteenth-century mulatto whose life intersected for a time with the village's indigenous tributaries when he was charged with inciting a rebellion.[43] Manuel Rodríguez, unlike Lázaro Mulato, was in no sense of the word a natural. He neither self-identified nor was labeled by others as "natural," whether in its usage as a noun or a verb. The authorities did not recognize him as attached in any way to Soatá, beyond his social contacts there. He was a true forastero: if he lived in a city he might have been labeled a *transeunte*, or transient. However, Rodríguez's insertion into the social fabric of Soatá sheds valuable light on the ethnic organization of rural towns in the early colonial period. An inspection of his social networks raises intriguing questions about the groupness of people classified as being of mixed parentage, particularly when his experiences are compared to those of Lázaro Mulato and Juana Galván.

We know few facts about Manuel Rodríguez, although the document bearing his story is much longer than Juana Galván's. He was only twenty-four years old at the time of his arrest (687r). He was blind in one eye (663v). Born of mulatto parents residing in Soatá (of whom we know nothing), he had not lived in the village since his adolescence, but returned periodically to sleep at his parents' house (668r–70r), but the documentary record does not tell us if he was born there. He spent his working life in the slaughterhouse in Tunja or on the road, transporting consignments of meat for Francisco Hernández—a citizen of Tunja, perhaps a butcher or a merchant—to far-flung regions as remote as Riohacha on the Caribbean coast (676r), or driving his mules loaded with viandes to less-distant Mariquita, to the west of Tunja and Santafé along the Magdalena River (655r).

Rodríguez did not yet have offspring and thus did not produce "disappearing mulattos" as Lázaro Mulato did, nor was his own identity in question, as was Juana Galván's. No one disputes that he carried the label "mulatto." What the documentary record affords in Manuel Rodríguez's case is a glimpse at his everyday social intercourse with neighbors, providing clues about who he may have thought belonged to his peer group. This is not an altogether pleasant story. Rodríguez worked his way into the confidences of the native community of Soatá by establishing a partnership with local indios ladinos, probably to fleece native farmers and make use of their labor. He was also an aggressive and sometimes violent womanizer. But at the same time, he seems to have communicated effectively with the local aboriginal power structure, the caciques and the capitanes, most of whom did not speak Spanish. He could not be considered an organic member of the community, as was Lázaro Mulato; he was more of a hanger-on. Rodríguez's exploits provide a window into the interethnic fabric of rural society, a peek into a native space that was by no means exclusively indigenous and from which individuals of varied backgrounds could move in and out.

Manuel Rodríguez makes his appearance in the documentary record in a letter written in 1596 by the Franciscan doctrinal priest of Soatá, Fr. Francisco Sánchez. The friar accused Rodríguez of stirring up rebellion in the village. He writes that when he arrived in Soatá, on Easter Monday, he arranged for mass on the following day, but no one appeared except the captains. The others had gone to Tunja to weed the fields of Manuel Mulato, to work crops belonging to a ladino shoemaker identified as the son of Diaguillo, and to the farm of an ethnically unmarked man named Bartolomé. The priest took rash steps: "Seeing this, and that no boy would come to hear the doctrine, I locked the captains in the church" (620r). Then he advised the authorities in Tunja of his flock's misconduct, noting that in his absence "Diaguillo and the other captains met and tried to remove the cacique [from office] and put in his place don Juan Moyquitiva, saying that the cacique was dull [bobo] and a friend of Your Grace and that don Juan was a ladino and an enemy of Your Grace, and that he would return for the Indians and a thousand other evil things, which if God does not remedy I do not know what I will do with these lost souls" (620r–v). But Diaguillo "and the others I had [locked] in the church for the doctrinal lesson broke down the doors of the church at midnight and fled, bolting the door of my room from the outside" (620v). They locked the priest in, as he had locked them in. Fr. Francisco accused the group of rebellion: "These Indians only accept the rule of the mulatto and Diaguillo the little tailor and Diaguillo the shoemaker and Bartolomillo, the one with the ranch, and these are the ones who have allied themselves with my parishioners. Your Grace must arrest them as rabble-rousers [motinadores] and [when they are] imprisoned, the Indians of Soatá will be obedient and will come to hear the doctrine" (620v).[44]

Soatá was a doctrinal town, its inhabitants alerted by a bell that rang several times a day, summoning them to catechistic instruction and mass. The Jesuits, who established missions in Fontibón and Cajicá in the early seventeenth century, had indigenous initiates sit in two semicircles, oriented back to back, one of them composed of women and the other of men; how Fr. Sánchez instructed his flock is unclear.[45] Most of his congregation was composed of Muisca farmers, but there were also some mulatto residents (including Rodríguez's parents) and perhaps some mestizos and Spaniards. These outsiders, called forasteros, were the artisans who repaired shoes in the village and manufactured garments, made iron tools, and carried produce and meat throughout the province on mule-back. As in other towns, some of these forasteros probably exerted considerable influence in Soatá, leading religious confraternities and conspiring with the indigenous leadership on a variety of matters.[46] How these people came to live in the village is unclear. Some, like Manuel Rodríguez, were the children of mulattos who had arrived there a generation before; others were the children of mixed unions in the community, similar to Juana Galván or the children of Lázaro Mulato; still others may have sought out the town as an attractive spot to ply their trades or were brought as laborers by Spanish hacienda-owners.[47]

These men appear to have established friendships with local indios ladinos, the bilinguals who operated as intermediaries between the Muisca-speaking masses and the colonial administration, because unlike Chocontá, Soatá at the end of the sixteenth century still had its share of monolingual Muisca-speakers (who required the services of an interpreter to offer testimony in this criminal case). In some pueblos people identified as ladinos were subjects of the cacique (that is, they were "naturales" in all senses of the word), but in other pueblos ladinos were migrants from other jurisdictions, sometimes as far-flung as Peru or Nicaragua. The documentation of the Rodríguez case does not specify the origins of the ladino actors identified as co-conspirators by Fr. Sánchez, but their close relationship with the captains of the pueblo suggests that they might have been locals. Although the archbishop Luis Zapata de Cárdenas compelled doctrinal priests to learn the indigenous vernacular, there is no indication that Fr. Francisco Sánchez was proficient in the variety of Muisca spoken in the village, so it is likely that someone—an indio ladino or, perhaps, a bilingual mestizo or mulatto—assisted him in translating his doctrinal lessons.[48] Certainly, the judicial authorities and tribute-collectors could not complete their tasks without the intervention of an interpreter, a *lengua* (literally, "language" or "tongue"). Diego, the father of the shoemaker fingered by Fr. Francisco, was a lengua, but there were many other indios ladinos in Soatá, if the list of witnesses deposed in the case against Manuel Rodríguez is any indication (634r). Some of them were part of the close-knit group accused of rebellion. In fact, Fr. Francisco carefully points out in his missive that the cacique seated by the rabble-rousers was a ladino and, by association, an enemy of the government. He reports that the presumed rebels labeled the deposed hereditary lord a "bobo" (620r–v), which in other contexts might mean dull, but in this case probably signified someone who could not defend himself effectively in Spanish.

The dividing line between mestizos and indios ladinos was a permeable one. "Mestizo" was a designation premised on parentage, while "ladino" revolved around linguistic usage and place of origin, as many ladinos were brought by conquistadors from distant lands. Though the two referents were premised on distinct attributes, "mestizo" could nevertheless stand in for "ladino," and vice versa. The chameleon-like nature of ladinos was rendered in Pedro de Quiroga's 1562 *Coloquios de la verdad* (Colloquies of Truth), in a revealing dialogue in which a Spaniard says to the indio ladino Tito, "I admit, Tito, that I am in certain admiration of your ability and tongue and how you speak my language as if it were your own, although according to what you have told of your life, it is not so surprising. But what deception, you walk among us in the dress of an indio. Who would think such of you if they were to see you among other indios!"[49] Accused simultaneously of practicing aboriginal rituals and of betraying them, as well as of ruthless exploiting of native people, indios ladinos easily blended in with mestizos because they, too, carried the same fatal flaws. In fact, indios ladinos were barred as early as 1558 from living in pueblos de indios in the Nuevo Reino, just as the mestizos and mulattos were, because of their nefarious influence on the natives, although the royal decrees went unheeded.[50]

Witnesses testifying against Manuel Rodríguez corroborated Fr. Francisco's allegation that the mulatto and his comrades, as well as a broader circle of men in the village, were intent on organizing against encomendero abuses. One native deponent from Soatá swore that Diego, the lengua and father of Diaguillo, confronted the priest when he demanded the community send a native woman to serve Juan Chacón, the encomendero's legal guardian (the encomendero, Francisco Rodríguez Gil, being underage). Diego allegedly responded, "Off with you, Juan Chacón! [He] comes from outside, and we are here in our lands, and we don't want to give you any Indian women!" (634v).

According to witnesses for the prosecution, Rodríguez was in the habit of forcing himself on women, a behavior indiscriminately attributed in the colonial imagination to mestizos and mulattos, but which it appears Rodríguez was in fact guilty of. He reportedly stole indigenous women from their husbands, forcing them to become his concubines (646v). Thus insisted Isabel Mestiza, a sixteen-year-old mestiza who lived in Sogamoso with her Muisca husband, Laureano.

It is true that the deponent was in the house of the cacique don Luis, and upon leaving the house of the cacique one night, more or less a year ago, [when] this deponent was going to the pueblo of Tota and Guaquira, near a ranch owned by Licentiate Ruiz, going alone on the road this deponent encountered a mulatto named Manuel, a mulatto [who was] blind in one eye, who they say is from the pueblo of Soatá. And when the aforementioned mulatto approached this deponent, more or less at [the hour of] evening prayers, and the mulatto was mounted on a chestnut mare, he came on horseback toward this witness and he dismounted from the mare and he removed two necklaces of pearls and gold beads she had around her throat and he told her, "Come with me or I will cut you with this knife. I'll marry you and you won't be in the house of this dog of a cacique." And as this witness saw the knife unsheathed in the hand of the mulatto, who was angry, this deponent felt great fear and dread of the aforementioned mulatto. . . . And he snatched her up with great force and seated her on the mare that Manuel Mulato had with him and he forcibly took her to the pueblo of Soatá, to the youngest son of Juan Rodríguez Gil, and he had her there in the town of Soatá for twelve or thirteen days, forcibly availing himself of her body, telling her that she must marry him or he would stab her. And this deponent said, "I don't have to marry you. If you want to kill me, kill me." And that's when the cacique of Sogamoso arrived in the pueblo of Soatá, and he told her, "Go back to your pueblo of Sogamoso and don't stay here. There you can marry as you wish." (663v–664v)

Note that Isabel, like Lázaro Mulato, chose to inhabit an indigenous private sphere, living in a pueblo de indios with a native spouse. This was an attractive option for a mestiza from the countryside. It rooted her to a stable livelihood, with her mother nearby, and presented an option that was more appealing than abandoning her family and her childhood friends to eke out a lonely living as a maid in Santafé or Tunja. Unfortunately, the documentary record does not provide the information necessary to find out more about Isabel's daily life. It only leaves us with questions: what was Isabel's parentage, and where did she come from? Where was she raised? Was she bilingual, or was her husband a ladino? What language would she speak to her children? Would they be registered in the tributary list of Sogamoso, where she had married? What clothing did she wear? Were her garments European in style or was she a "mestiza in Indian habit," like Catalina Tafur? These questions, which are ultimately unanswerable due to lack of documentation regarding Isabel's circumstances, can serve as a guide to how we might imagine interethnic unions like hers.

Manuel Rodríguez was, unmistakably, a violent man, who kidnapped and raped Isabel, as he had done before to other women. This was not the first time that he and his friends brushed up against the law. Ten years earlier, in 1587, he was accused of assaulting Pedro Guatavita, an Indian, at a social gathering. He committed the offense with the collaboration of Cristóbal Indio, a blacksmith; Guatavita ultimately dropped charges against Cristóbal, since they were friends, and Cristóbal denied any association with Rodríguez (648r, 651v–652v). In 1591 Pedro de Cepeda, an indio ladino, brought a criminal case against Martín de Camacho Atansqui, Diego the tailor, Juan the shoemaker, Bartolomé, Juan Cogun, and all the others who were later fingered by the doctrinal priest, including a man he called "Manuel Mulato" (a.k.a. Manuel Rodríguez). The cohort was charged with locking Cepeda and his wife in their rooms and with leaving him half-dead (625v); not only did Rodríguez have criminal antecedents, but his circle of acquaintances did as well. Overall, Rodríguez operated on the wrong side of the law, moving generally in the company of other undesirables, both ladinos and, it appears from the reference to Camacho Atansqui, possibly huauquis.

The company Rodríguez kept was decidedly multiethnic, as reflected in the words of Juan Bravo, a tailor from Tunja.

It was three months ago, more or less, that this witness saw him freed from the prison where he had been held, and more or less a month ago, at the occasion of the fiesta which would be held for San Crispin and San Crispiniano, this witness . . . went in the company of the aforementioned Manuel Mulato with another three or four Indians and mestizos, and they arrived at the pueblo of Topia, which is the encomienda of doña Isabel de Quesada, who was in the lodgings she keeps there. And the aforementioned Manuel Mulato and another mestizo named Sebastián, a blacksmith who worked with Pineda the blacksmith, went to the lodgings to speak to doña Isabel de Quesada so that she would give them bulls for the fiesta, and this witness remained in the pueblo of Topia awaiting the response. And

Manuel Mulatto and Sebastian returned to where this witness was, and the aforementioned mulatto told this witness that doña Isabel had no bulls to give them. And when that happened, this witness and the rest continued on to Firavitoba in search of bulls. And this witness stayed there, and the mulatto Manuel said he was going to see an Indian [named] Pedro, servant of Bartolomé de Cepeda, who was in Sogamoso on a ranch. He said he was there with him, and the next day in the morning he came, and from there he went to Paipa. (683v–84r)[51]

Manuel Rodríguez's social network revolved around a circle of servants and artisans—blacksmiths, tailors, shoemakers—some of whom were mestizo and others ladino. We know that he broke bread with them on occasion (683v–84r). Many of these men worked in the service of Spaniards, and they moved with facility across the ethnic landscape, familiar with the inhabitants of the numerous indigenous towns that still dot the mountains around Tunja, audacious enough to make demands of local encomenderos.

To those readers familiar with the documentation of the era, none of this will be surprising: there were many free-wheeling predators in the hinterlands who operated, for the most part, with the blessings of encomenderos and hacendados. But it is notable that the vast majority of the indigenous witnesses from Soatá who testified on Rodríguez's behalf, swearing he was not in the village the day of the confrontation with the priest, were *chontales*, men who did not speak Spanish (669v–675v). Not only the artisans, but also some of the Muisca-speaking captains allied themselves with the mulatto, although we can only guess at the nature of his dealings with them. In light of the description of his meeting with Isabel de Quesada and other Spanish cattle-raisers, perhaps we can assume that he was useful in the logistical preparations for local fiestas. If he was complicit in elevating don Juan Moyquitiva to office to replace the previous cacique, he was undoubtedly a political ally of these ladino gatecrashers and their chontal followers. Was Rodríguez related to them? Mulattos were not only of mixed Spanish-black parentage, but were sometimes descended from African-indigenous unions (zambos or zambaigos), so one of Rodríguez's parents might very well have come from one of the village kin units (although the document does not indicate this). And how did he communicate with an indigenous nobility that was monolingual? Did his Soatá upbringing afford him a speaking knowledge of Muisca, or did his ladino friends serve as his interpreters? (Certainly, there were bilingual mulattos in indigenous pueblos, as the presence of mulatto lenguas in other legal cases attests.)[52] Why would the chontales trust him enough to testify on his behalf if he could not communicate directly with them?

Unfortunately, my ethnography of this case is fragmentary, the documentation unearthing more questions than answers. Only by piecing this case together with the other narratives can I begin to imagine how mestizos, mulattos, and natives interacted on a daily basis in the rural communities of Santafé and Tunja.

THE FORMATION OF GROUPS: MESTIZOS AND MULATTOS IN THE TUNJA PROVINCE

The experiences of Juana Galván and Lázaro Mulato illustrate the fluidity of classification at the bottom of the social and ethnic hierarchy in the Nuevo Reino. Neither of them had the resources—or presumably, the interest—to move higher in the social spectrum than the meager standing that was available to them as mestizos and mulattos.[53] Their concerns revolved around ensuring that their children would occupy favorable categories: somewhere in the "mestizo" range for Juana Galván's offspring, fully recognized "Indians" for Lázaro Mulato's. What their stories tell us is that the boundaries between "Indian" and "mestizo" or "mulatto" were highly permeable and subject to dispute, not transparent or fixed. These two narratives also demonstrate the pull toward "Indianness" that was exerted by the colonial system, which tended to designate people as Indians in order to expand the numbers of tribute-payers in rural areas.

Manuel Rodríguez, in contrast, does not appear to have moved between identities, nor did he establish intimate relationships with his indigenous neighbors except as a sexual predator. His dealings with Soatá's natives seem to have been entirely strategic, a variety of political collusions aimed at promoting the ascendancy of a ladino leadership in the community. His friendships cluster within the circle of ladino tradesmen living in the village and neighboring mestizos, men who provided crucial services to the indigenous population but were also responsible for numerous criminal acts—assaults, rape, kidnapping—against both Indians and Spaniards. This was an uncomfortable familiarity, in which violence was softened by political sponsorship and by fluency in the local language and lifeways.

What circumstances led certain individuals to choose to stand out as mestizos (or mulattos) while others disappeared into the indigenous population? That is, what caused Juana Galván, despite her marriage to an Indian, to opt for a mestiza identity? Why didn't Manuel Rodríguez, raised in Soatá, elect the route chosen by Lázaro Mulato, to marry locally and father children who would eventually be listed on the tribute rolls as Indians, altering his children's calidad but not his own? Of course, personal interests might explain why each of these individuals elected to identify in particular ways, but I am more concerned with the structural conditions under which certain types of groups emerged: Juana Galván's decidedly interethnic plebeian network, Lázaro Mulato's indigenous family circle, Manuel Rodríguez's band of mestizo and ladino hangers-on.

Let's proceed chronologically, beginning with Manuel Rodríguez, whose arrest took place in the late sixteenth century. Modern Tunja is a dusty and poverty-stricken backwater, bereft of water much of the year, and Boyacá—the province of which Tunja is the capital—forfeits thousands of inhabitants each month to the behemoth of Bogotá, just a few hours away by bus. Under such circumstances it is easy to lose sight of the fact that in the sixteenth century Tunja was a lively commercial center and an economic powerhouse with a dense indigenous population that was a source of both labor and tribute. Tunja was a much wealthier city than Santafé, and its colonial prominence is still evident in grand houses and convents dating to the sixteenth and seventeenth centuries. As Germán Colmenares notes, conquistadors preferred to receive encomiendas in the province of Tunja, rather than in Santafé, although over the forty-odd years following the Spanish invasion, many of these grants were acquired by wealthy merchants, not by the sons of soldiers.[54] Tunja's social landscape was marked by socioracial separation, its city dominated by elite Spaniards and its hinterland largely indigenous, ruled by an encomendero class that enjoyed vast powers, thanks to the weakness of the Crown bureaucracy and the relatively late introduction of colonial institutions that would wrest autonomy from the encomenderos and create a colonial system that was not based entirely on self-interest.[55] The dynamism of the Nuevo Reino's "second city" as a magnet for prospective servants, artisans, and laborers spurred migration from the indigenous countryside to the urban center and fostered a process of mestizaje, but a layer of mestizos also emerged in rural areas, functioning as a buffer between

Spanish urbanites and indigenous villages. These mestizos became encomienda administrators and hacienda foremen.[56]

Under such circumstances Manuel Rodríguez found ready employment in the meat trade, by means of which he circulated throughout the province and made valuable contacts with Spanish merchants and encomenderos, as well as with the overseers of haciendas and administrators of encomiendas. His interests coincided with mestizos and indios ladinos inhabiting the small towns that dotted the countryside, men who felt threatened by the chontales and promoted the rise of ladino caciques who could work more smoothly with forasteros. It is no surprise that Rodríguez chose membership in this localized group of intermediaries. At the same time, he appears to have been careful to cultivate relationships with the chontales, as the testimonies they gave in his favor suggest. But was his allegiance to a "mixed-race group," or was his mulatto designation strictly a category assigned to him? The answer is likely somewhere in between: the positioning of people of mixed parentage in the economic and political systems of the Tunja Province sometimes fostered alliances among them, a kind of temporary groupness. Their marginal—also their intermediary—status forced them into certain types of roles and relationships in rural society that came to typify their socioracial category, so that "abuser" and "intermediary" became synonymous with "mestizo."

At the same time, this groupness wasn't necessarily predicated on being mestizo or mulatto. It could just as well have been a form of plebeian solidarity, as Juana Galván's experiences in Vélez and its environs demonstrate. Remember that Manuel Rodríguez's social circle also included indios ladinos, as well as members of mixed categories. "Mestizo," "mulatto," "ladino" all convey a sense of marginality in relation to the majorities that controlled public administration and that defined space as "indigenous" or "Spanish": Muisca-speaking caciques and their subjects in the countryside, Spanish-speaking elites and their constituents in the city. Thus, again, a modern racial mindset should not be imposed on this colonial setting, as the characteristics that defined that setting were diverse.

What we do know is that Manuel Rodríguez's ties to Soatá are murky. His parents lived there, and his grandmothers may have been native to the pueblo, but it is also possible that his parents arrived in the region as employees of a large landowner or as marginal smallholders eking out a living on rented lands. There is no evidence of ties that might have drawn him toward the indigenous community for reasons other than purely pragmatic ones. Lázaro Mulato, in contrast, identified with the pueblo of Chocontá, to which he was related through his maternal line, as well as through his wife and children. It is clear that he maintained kin relationships with natives of Chocontá, because he pleads with the authorities to allow him to remain in the community on the basis of his roots and his marriage there. But unlike many mestizas, who were not subject to tribute obligations and could thus informally assume their mothers' identities beyond the reach of state scrutiny, Lázaro Mulato, being a man, could not be entered into the community census as an Indian even though he thought of himself as a "natural" of sorts. He opted instead for military service, which distanced him from the mestizos and mulattos who inhabited the fringes of all Muisca communities and who stayed at home or in nearby urban centers. Although for very gendered reasons he was never accepted as an indigenous tributary and his calidad remained that of "mulatto," imprinted in his surname-like moniker and the mulatto head-tax he paid each year, Lázaro Mulato's "group" appears to have been the native community of Chocontá: it was where he felt he "belonged." Manuel Rodríguez and Lázaro Mulato exemplify the range of possibilities for individuals of mixed parentage who lived in or spent considerable time visiting pueblos de indios: they could just as well be integrated into the native community as they could be positioned on its periphery, belonging to cofradías and renting or owning lands but fraternizing more frequently with other poor and relatively powerless outsiders.

IDENTIFYING AS A MESTIZA

Juana Galván chose to legally validate her classification as a mestiza unattached to the indigenous community of her mother. She justified her petition for recognition of her mixed parentage and for removal from the list of tributaries of Chitaraque on several grounds, all related to her status as the illegitimate daughter of the former encomendero Juan López Galván: the census-takers had maliciously identified her as the daughter of the cacique and his second wife (her mother, his first wife, married him only after Juana was born); she had never before appeared on the tributary rolls; she had been raised by her Spanish grandmother in Vélez. Her major concern was for her lineage, that her children not be identified in future censuses as tributaries, for they were the children of a mestiza and a priest.

Juana's father was connected enough to be entered into Juan Flórez de Ocáriz's series of genealogies of Santafé grandees, but was not sufficiently important to be granted his own genealogy in the tome (he is mentioned only briefly, as a distant relative of one of the major conquistadors). Flórez reports that Juan López Galván Osorio came from a line of soldiers who served in Flanders and in the Nuevo Reino, vecinos of Vélez, where Juana was raised by her Spanish relatives.[57] What status Juana occupied in her grandmother's house, however, remains unclear. Many illegitimate mestizo children were incorporated into Spanish households as servants; this might have been the case with Juana, as she provided no evidence that her father had officially recognized her as his daughter, and as the archives contain no indication that she was recogida, or groomed for elite life (as Catalina Tafur was). Moreover, Juana did not make a strategic marriage to a man of good social standing, as did mestizas, like Catalina Tafur, who were the recognized daughters of encomenderos. Instead, Galván married an Indian, suggesting that she had never been groomed for elite circles and that she may have occupied a subordinate position in the Galván household, one that eventually enabled the authorities to get away with identifying her as an india. Nonetheless, just as Lázaro Mulato's childhood was spent in an indigenous cultural milieu that pulled him toward the native sphere, Juana Galván's unfolded among elite Spaniards, which in her adulthood allowed her and her children to move in an urban milieu. She therefore had good reasons to opt for mestiza status and a position, albeit a lowly one, in the Vélez social structure.

Was Juana Galván's classification isomorphic with a "group" with which she self-identified? That is, was she both a mestiza in name and in social network? She appears to have moved in an urban plebeian social milieu that was decidedly multiethnic: her closest relatives were an Indian husband, a daughter married to an ethnically unmarked man, a soldier son. "Mestiza" certainly was her classification, but not necessarily a tangible group of people with whom she associated and with whom she identified; whether Galván emphasized her calidad as a "mestiza" in her relations with her peers—as opposed to asserting this identity in her appeals to the colonial administration—we will never know. Nonetheless, the group of which she was a member was more likely broadly plebeian than mestizo.

In *The Limits of Racial Domination* R. Douglas Cope describes mid-colonial plebeian Mexico City as a milieu in which casta affiliation was only loosely reckoned by members of the lower strata of society, since most plebeians did not possess a deep knowledge of their genealogies. He indicates, moreover, a certain fluidity between the categories "indio" and "mestizo," such that it was possible for an Indian to change his costume, hairstyle, and speech habits and "become" a mestizo. Shared economic status—living in the same neighborhood or working in the same household—fostered a kind of plebeian solidarity in which "race" (Cope's word) was not an attribute that was uniformly emphasized. While "race" was significant among Mexican plebeians, "class" frequently took precedence.[58] The caste ideology documented by Cope does not appear to have been as systematic in the mid-colonial Nuevo Reino, but Juana Galván's experience illustrates the existence of a cohesive plebeian social stratum in Vélez, in which Indians, mestizos, and others not only coexisted but shared their lives with one another.

CONCLUSION

There was no single type of mestizo in the Nuevo Reino de Granada. Some of them melded into the indigenous or Spanish worlds in which they had been socialized. In the sixteenth and seventeenth centuries, when the countryside was still largely indigenous and Muisca practices of matrilineal descent integrated mestizo children into their maternal kin group, it is likely that a considerable number of rural mestizos melted into native social circles. Only some of them were eventually exposed by visitadores; visitas were not routine occurrences, and Crown officials depended on chiefly testimony to uncover the presence of undesirables in native communities, effectively hiding many of these people from view—which is what happened to Lázaro Mulato's children. Other mestizos, particularly those who had been raised by Spaniards, were absorbed into plebeian sectors. Those who, like Manuel Rodríguez, remained in rural areas, rented lands from indigenous communities or worked on neighboring haciendas or for nearby urban merchants. Their relationships with their indigenous neighbors were not always courteous, but they very pragmatically established the alliances necessary to survive in the countryside; still, rural mestizos and mulattos appear to have lived lives more separate from their indigenous neighbors than occurred in the urban milieu. Eventually, rural "outsiders" formed parishes that coexisted alongside pueblos de indios, by the eighteenth century swallowing up the indigenous doctrinal towns. In contrast, mestizos whose Spanish parents relegated them to marginal status in their urban households melded with the plebeian majority, as occurred with Juana Galván, who certainly had mestizo friends and neighbors, even as she married an Indian and for a time was the concubine of a Spanish priest.

What did being mestizo or mulatto mean to these individuals? There were certainly moments at which colonial socioracial classifications invaded their everyday lives: when they were threatened with expulsion from their homes, when they were subject to a tributary status that they felt did not correspond to their status. But the social milieus in which they moved were varied, suggesting that while calidad did affect their lives, other forms of identification also exerted a pull on their social networks. For some of them, economic status seems to have impinged more decisively on their social lives than did their mestizo identities, determining their likely peers to a greater degree than did parentage, fashioning for them a new legacy. Others, living as slightly more privileged minorities among the majority Indians, did tend to socialize largely with their mestizo, mulatto, and ladino neighbors. There is no single mestizo narrative in the early colonial period, nor did mestizos automatically merge into single social group because they were of mixed descent. Early colonial society was both more complex and more fluid than that.

3. Hiding in Plain Sight

Gendering Mestizos

Juan de Salazar, the Fontibón cobbler accused of biting off his friend's nose, does not appear to have been fazed by the multiple labels by which he was called. Though categorized as a mestizo on some occasions during his court case, at others as an Indian, he did not dispute these contradictory appellations. When social superiors classified him, he undoubtedly lacked the power to contest them, and he may have found it in his interests to conform to peer pressure and accept his classification when friends called him an Indian. The fact that he was an indio ladino from Quito undoubtedly contributed to his ambiguous identity: he was an Indian with no local attachments and thus was out of place even among the indigenous population, being himself closer to "mestizo" or to "indio ladino" than to "indio tributario." The uncertainties inherent to labeling an indio ladino like Salazar suggest that it was not only mestizo or mulatto identities that were ambiguous, but rather that all socioracial appellations were slippery. "Indian" was not a simple birthright: it was defined in relation to "mulatto" and "mestizo." While this was particularly the case for liminal statuses like "indio ladino" or "huauqui," Lázaro Mulato's children became "full-fledged indios" when they were inscribed in the tributary record, a choice made by their parents and by census-takers. Lázaro Mulato and Juan de Salazar's stories demonstrate that there was no clear boundary dividing "Indian" from "mestizo" or "mulatto" in the early colonial period but, instead, a dynamic space in which individuals negotiated how they were to be identified. Their choices were mediated by the social and legal contexts in which they found themselves: by the identities of their adversaries and their relative positions in the social hierarchy; by their age and gender, as well as by the choices they had made in how they lived their lives; by the extent to which legal documentation afforded them an effective space of contestation—in other words, by relationships of power.[1]

The same fuzziness characterized the imaginary line separating "mestizos" from "Spaniards." Some mestizos in colonial Santafé consistently avoided identification as people of mixed parentage because their social position afforded them the influence and the social space to do so, and because it was in their interests.[2] The sixteenth-century sons and daughters of elite Spaniards and native women were frequently welcome in Santafé's more exclusive social circles and, in the case of mestizo men, sometimes precariously occupied relatively comfortable positions in the colonial hierarchy, as priests, aldermen, conquistadors, or encomenderos. Sixteenth-century elite mestizos cannot always be identified as mestizos in the documentary record, because they were able to elude such classification by foregrounding the social standing of their Spanish fathers or husbands over the ethnicity of their native mothers; that is, they were in a position to privilege certain elements of calidad over others. And sometimes calidad didn't matter: these mestizos' names frequently turn up in documentary genres like notarial registries or wills, in which calidad was rarely recorded, thus blinding readers (from any century) to the mestizos' parentage.[3] It is as though these highly placed mestizos were hiding in plain sight, although, of course, only a twenty-first-century scholar versed in racial discourse would even think to express it in this way. Only after piecing together numerous documents can one discern the mixed parentage of these individuals and begin to trace the strategies they employed to project themselves as Spaniards (or, at the least, to protect their status as ethnically unmarked) in the public arena. The capital of the Audiencia was very much a small town, and the same actors—both elite and plebeian—pop up repeatedly in a broad range of contexts in the documentary record. Under such circumstances, almost everyone in Santafé would have been aware that these individuals had native mothers and Iberian fathers. Nonetheless, the stain on their personas was effectively ignored in numerous social contexts, in the interests of polite conversation, the pursuit of economic interests, or efficient public administration.

The permeability of the category "mestizo" assumed distinct forms in the privileged circles of colonial Santafé, in comparison to the social spheres inhabited by the commoners I discussed in chapter 2, precisely because the singular nature of elite mestizo social mobility afforded access to lifestyles and to social milieus in which other people of mixed ancestry would have been unwelcome. Don Alonso de Silva—the son of the Portuguese conquistador Francisco González de Silva (also known as Francisco González de Trujillo) and doña Juana Sirita, the eldest sister of the cacique of Tibasosa—was employed as secretary to a Santafé notary and was described as "straightforward and noble . . . with much virtue [muy llano e noble . . . allegado a mucha virtud]," adjectives used to refer to a man of "calidad," in the sense of being of high social and economic status, usually a Spaniard.[4] A mestizo pretender to a Muisca *cacicazgo* (chiefdom), Silva lived as befitted a Santafé grandee: he even had a clavichord in his house.[5] Juana de Penagos, the illegitimate daughter of the conquistador Juan de Penagos and an indigenous noblewoman from Cali, married the Spaniard Alonso Valero de Tapia and owned haciendas in Tocancipá and Gachancipá, near Santafé.[6] Neither Juana de Penagos nor Alonso de Silva are identified as mestizo in much of the documentation produced by or about them during the course of their lives. What hiding in plain sight involved was perpetuating a fiction that was sustained by everyone around them: their parents and spouses, the notaries who recorded their wills and contracts, wealthy merchants who lent them money, their servants. At least, when it was convenient. Alonso de Silva's mixed ancestry became a point of contention when he sought to assume the title of cacique of Tibasosa, for it was no longer in the interests of his opponents to quietly disregard the fact that he was mestizo, now that his position could only be disputed by broadcasting the stain that Silva carried in his blood. A similar situation arose for Diego García Zorro, a mestizo, when he was appointed to the Bogotá city council (cabildo).

What, then, made someone a "Spaniard" (and, correspondingly, the unlucky others "mestizos")? Individuals born in Spain sometimes carried the label "español," particularly when they appeared in the criminal record, where socioracial origins acquired a heightened significance. In other legal genres, Spaniards were identified by their "natural," the Iberian town to which they were native. Those born in the Americas were not technically Spaniards, however, although there is little evidence in the Nuevo Reino documentation of the use of the epithet "criollo," which in other jurisdictions would have identified them as being individuals of Iberian descent born in the Americas. The American-born might have been distinguished as "vecinos" (citizens) of Santafé or Tunja, in an era in which few people of mixed parentage could hope to acquire that status (although this changed in the eighteenth century). American-born individuals might have described themselves as the "sons of the first conquerors and discoverers of this Nuevo Reino [hijos de los primeros conquistadores y descubridores de este Nuevo Reino]" and therefore used the noble title "don" to signal their membership in a new colonial elite, or they might have placed coats of arms on their lintels. And given the numerous restrictions on costume that limited certain fabrics and adornments to the Spanish population, they might have displayed their Spanishness through excessive sartorial display.[7]

The attribution of Spanishness as a label employed in legal contexts was gendered throughout the Spanish world. Unlike Alonso de Silva, Juana de Penagos remains racially unmarked in the documentary record because her gender permitted her to assume a Spanish identity throughout her lifetime. Lima's early colonial parish records specified a woman's ethnicity to a lesser extent than they did for men.[8] Lockhart intimates that behavioral cues took up the slack, noting the use of "doña" for a broad range of women in comparison to the more limited convention of calling men by the title "don," which was restricted to the high nobility.[9] Similarly, it appears to have been easier for elite mestiza women than for men to assume an unmarked socioracial status. A mestiza enjoyed much more flexibility with regard to her self-presentation than did her brothers, onto whom the stain of mixed blood adhered more permanently and persisted more doggedly over the generations. Her father could refer to her as "hija natural" (illegitimate daughter), as opposed to "mestiza." Marriage to a Spanish man further facilitated the passage of a mestiza's children into full-fledged legitimate Spanish status and sometimes ensured that she herself would be remembered as a Spaniard by future generations, although in order to accomplish this she would have had to reject entirely her mother's culture.[10] A mestiza's brothers were certainly welcome at the myriad social events frequented by the privileged—festive gatherings such as baptisms, the formality of the dinner table, proximity to the altar at holy Mass—and could freely conduct business with their Spanish relatives and their fathers' acquaintances. Nonetheless, the more intimate social universes of mestizo men, including their choice of mates and the expectations they held for their children, did not always intersect with their public performance of Spanishness.[11]

The vast majority of scholars concerned with the intersection of race and gender in the Americas privilege the study of women.[12] After all, weren't mestizos born of rape or relations of concubinage between Spanish conquerors and their native mistresses, producing an ill-fated coincidence of race, gender, and social status? Even so, the early colonial process of racial mixing can be viewed through a different, but equally gendered lens, one that contemplates the challenges of mestizo masculinity in comparison to the relative privileges of elite mestiza femininity. I do so by digging into a small number of lives of Santafé's well-placed mestizas and mestizos, tracing how they built relationships that positioned them inside Spanish social circles, as well as by traveling the paths of memory that marked them for posterity as Spaniards. The networks of public and private social interaction of elite mestizas, in particular, can be understood by studying their marital strategies and social universes.[13] The late seventeenth-century genealogical text by Juan Flórez de Ocáriz, *Genealogías del Nuevo Reino de Granada*, which traces the family lines of Santafé grandees descended from conquistadors, helps reveal the escape hatches available to mestizas but closed to mestizos. Flórez's compendium provides a vehicle for reading the film of history backward—to appropriate Marc Bloch's metaphor—opening a window into how the sixteenth-century women and men whose lives I document were remembered a century later.[14]

Among people of mixed ancestry perched in the upper strata of society, it was the men who found it almost impossible to scale socioracial barriers, while their sisters were more likely to be successfully hispanized, that is, accepted as holders of an unmarked identity. The access to elite social circles that sixteenth-century mestizos enjoyed—and largely forfeited in later centuries, when their numbers increased—was not always sufficient to propel them or their offspring into full-fledged Spanish status. It would be a century or more before they could easily avail themselves of the "gracias al sacar," a legal fiction that permitted eighteenth-century people to petition the Crown to alter their calidad through recognition of their services in commerce or war (an officially sanctioned legal alteration for which they paid a hefty sum).[15]

It was common practice in sixteenth- and seventeenth-century Lima or Cuzco for elite fathers to place their mestiza daughters in convents to "remedy" their condition through the teaching of "good customs"—prayer, needlework, sometimes reading and writing—which would prepare them for marriage with Europeans.[16] Santafé's elite mestizas had no convent dedicated to their "betterment," but they were shepherded through the intricacies of Iberian culture by their fathers' European wives in preparation for their marriage to Spaniards, as happened to Catalina Tafur. Their brothers also learned to negotiate polite society, but not as successfully. The social universes of these men were bisected. Their public lives unfolded in scenarios frequented by elite Spaniards and other people without socioracial labels, where mestizo men also enjoyed unmarked status (except, of course, in those instances in which it was inconvenient for their peers). However, their family lives took place in interethnic, plebeian milieus, where they were in intimate contact with mestizos, mulattos, and Indians. Consequently, the chameleon-like character of sixteenth-century and early seventeenth-century elite mestizaje depended in part on the gender of the individual in question.

HISPANIZED MESTIZAS

Andeanist anthropologists inquired in the 1990s into the intersection of ethnicity and gender in rural communities of highland Ecuador and Peru, questioning whether in small, Quechua-speaking villages "women were more Indian" than the men.[17] The modernization of the Andean countryside in the latter half of the twentieth century and the increased labor migration of men to urban areas shaped a social terrain in which indigenous women increasingly controlled agricultural production and adhered to more "traditional" indigenous lifeways, such as language, costume, and diet, while their husbands, who moved more freely between city and country, adopted clothing, tastes, and occupations more attuned to the dominant mestizo culture.[18] Among the mestizo elite of early colonial Santafé, social mobility trended in the opposite direction; many of the mestizas who had been recognized by their conquistador fathers, as well as the daughters of caciques, managed to hispanize themselves through strategically planned marriages to Spaniards, while their brothers were left behind.[19]

An iconic example is doña Ana de Mendoza, whose mother, doña María de Bohórques, was the niece of don Diego, the powerful cacique of Ubaque (hence, the noble titles "don" and "doña," which were commonly employed by the indigenous nobility). Doña María had been placed in the service and care of two Spanish noblewomen, doñas Leonor de Bohórques and María de Bohórques, from whom she acquired her Spanish surname and in whose residence she met the Basque nobleman Juan de Arteaga de Mendoza, who was the chief constable (alguacil mayor) of the Royal Chancellery in Santafé. Doña Ana de Mendoza was the illegitimate daughter of this affair between an Iberian aristocrat and a Muisca noblewoman. She went on to marry Pedro Diaz

Ochoa, a Spaniard, and to produce a long line of offspring who wedded Spanish nobles and forged marital ties to notaries, city aldermen, and other public officials; the children of these unions obtained *licenciaturas*, or university degrees, some becoming clerics and judges.[20]

Strategic marriages of this sort were also pursued by Iberian nobles for their mestiza daughters. Seven of the eight captains who accompanied the conquistador Gonzalo Jiménez de Quesada in his 1537 expedition to what was to become the Nuevo Reino de Granada were hidalgos, members of the Spanish minor aristocracy.[21] These men were thought to possess certain qualities inherent to nobility: good name, honor, virtue, trustworthiness, courage, a clear conscience, an orderly and moderate lifestyle, and generosity. In practice, what marked them and their descendants as aristocratic was "being generous to the church and Republic, . . . keeping up the family estate, making proper marriage linkages and performing civil and military services for the crown."[22]

Captain Juan de Penagos, who came to the Nuevo Reino in 1543 with Governor Gerónimo Lebrón, was awarded an entire genealogical tree (no. 41) in Flórez's *Genealogías*, making him one of Santafé's most influential forefathers (although he was placed near the end of the volume's forty-three total genealogies of prominent men, a list that began with the conquistador Gonzalo Jiménez de Quesada, leader of the 1537 expedition). A *caballero hijodalgo* (noble gentleman) from Santander, Penagos inherited his father's castle and lands, which he passed on to his sister and nephew, who remained on the Peninsula, and a great-grandfather's domain, which he left to his mother.[23] He also served as governor of the emerald mines of Muzo, and he appears in numerous legal briefs as the guarantor for natives who had been thrown into prison.[24] One might surmise that Penagos would have attempted to live in practice those qualities of the nobility inventoried by Flórez, but, in fact, he did not live an "orderly and moderate lifestyle." Though he never married, Penagos sired six illegitimate children, five of them with female members of the native nobility to the south of Santafé (see fig. 3.1): Pedro, Juan, Isabel, and Catalina de Penagos were the grandchildren of a cacique from Popayán; Juana de Penagos was the daughter of Isabel, the niece of the cacique of Pete, Cali; and there was his illegitimate daughter Andrea de Penagos, whose mother is not identified in the documentation.[25] The conquistador married all of his daughters to Spaniards.[26] Most is known about Juana de Penagos, who married Alonso Valero, originally from Toledo. In the will the couple

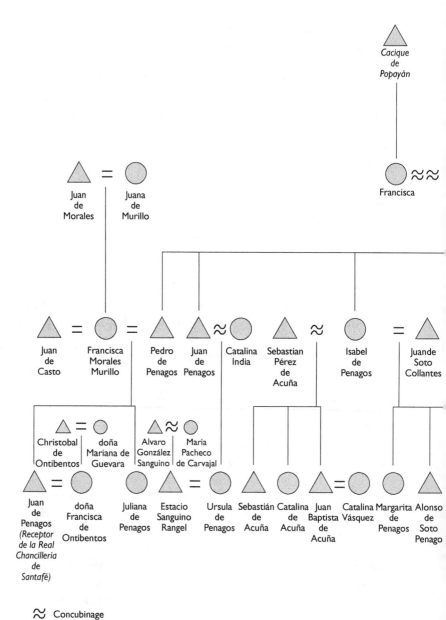

Figure 3.1. *Genealogy of Juan de Penagos.*

≈ Concubinage

═ Legitimate marriage

Figure 3.1. *Genealogy of Juan de Penagos.*

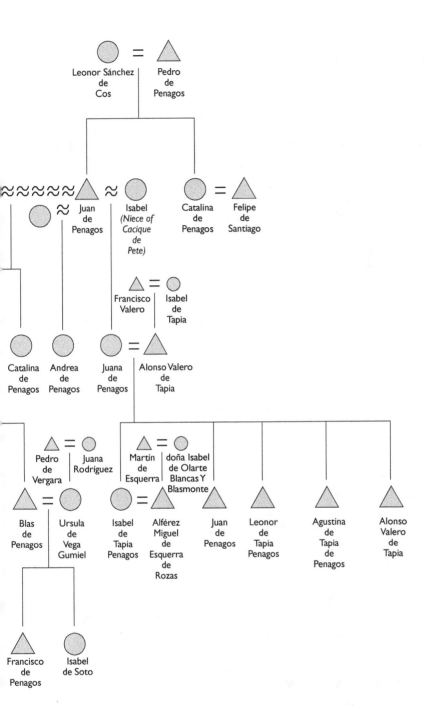

drew up together after more than four decades of married life, they list numerous ranches and haciendas inherited from Captain Penagos, some originally in Juana's dowry, others purchased from neighboring landowners. Juana identifies herself in this document as the illegitimate daughter (hija natural) of Penagos without mentioning her native mother, thus erasing her mestizo condition in an approved legal fashion that was not contradicted by the wealth she and her husband displayed.[27] I would venture to guess that the fact that her indigenous mother was not Muisca, but the daughter of a cacique from Cali, softened the edge of her mixed parentage. Juana's will recounts how she married her five children to Spaniards, distributing generous dowries to all of her sons-in-law.[28]

Elite fathers anxious to hispanize their mestiza daughters through marriage followed strategies that were also employed by conquistadors of modest birth who remodeled their humble lineages into noble ones through marriage planning.[29] As Jean-Paul Zúñiga so convincingly demonstrates, early modern notions of race (raza) were intimately bound up with a concept of lineage, out of which emerged a particular interpretation of what it meant to be of mixed parentage.[30] While twenty-first-century readers might call Juana de Penagos or doña Ana de Mendoza "mixed race," their fathers would not have considered them "half Spaniard." Instead, such women were explicitly recognized as illegitimate daughters, and their mestiza designation was conveniently set aside in the interests of constructing an aristocratic lineage, just as a humble soldier could lay the foundations for a noble family line by accumulating capital and marrying his daughters well. This was eminently possible in a colonial situation, where the local nobility was a project in process and non-aristocratic conquistadors found the road to higher status wide open. Social climbing was best accomplished by harnessing the reproductive power of women, hispanizing and Christianizing them so that they could establish unions with other well-placed families. Ultimately, the status of these women would be subsumed under that of their husbands, their mixed origins as well as their illegitimate ones swiftly forgotten, and their social standing bolstered by the acquisition of landed property, the display of heraldry, and the purchase of positions of power.[31] Kathryn Burns terms this an "evangelization of a gender-specific, strategic kind," which "redirect[ed] the energies of childrearing to increase the numbers of female Christians in Cuzco" and allowed the Spanish elite to "gain firm control over the Andes" through the reproduction of lineage, authority, and culture.[32] Such reproductive strategies had been around for a long time on the Iberian Peninsula, where the Umayyad dynasty of Córdoba kept concubines of Christian stock, who bore blond sons for the royal lineage.[33]

The hispanization of the mestiza offspring of conquistadors wrought an erasure of the memory of mixed parentage. In the case of Juana de Penagos or of doña Ana de Mendoza, the indigenous grandmother lingered as only a faint reminder of a distant sexual encounter, best swept under the rug in the interests of enhancing existing relationships, but not entirely forgotten by the coming generations, as Juan Flórez de Ocáriz's compendium reveals in his treatment of the Penagos dynasty as a noble line whose base included women explicitly identified as mestizas. Most likely, these ghostly memories were preserved because the indigenous ancestors were recalled as members of the native nobility, who could thus potentially boost the social standing of their mixed-race descendants, not to the extent that it occurred in Mexico or Peru, but via a muted and somewhat obscured facsimile of the viceregal fascination with Aztec and Inca royalty.

However, when Spaniards of high status had children with indigenous commoners, judicious marriage choices could in the best of circumstances erase the mothers from memory entirely. Take, for instance, Catalina Tafur, the young mestiza who rebelled against her father's Spanish widow by taking to the streets in Indian habit. Catalina soon came to her senses and, like her sister, married a man whose socioracial label is not stated; he was not a member of the first families of Santafé, but his ancestors had at least trod Iberian soil (whether *all* of his ancestors came from Spain, however, cannot be determined). Catalina's marriage integrated her permanently into Spanish circles, not only during her life, but for the next few generations, her memory being rearranged so that it fit neatly into an Iberian family line. About eighty years after Catalina's escapade as a mestiza in Indian habit, Flórez identifies her as Captain Tafur's "hija natural," not as his mixed-race daughter.[34] Rodríguez Freile confuses Catalina with her sister, Isabel, stating that she married Luis de Ávila, a conquistador of Santa Marta, but, like Flórez, he omits the fact that she was a mestiza and identifies her instead as Tafur's illegitimate daughter.[35] Was her mestizo identity unremarked by these authors because the memory of her indigenous mother had been erased, or was it simply neglected by the chroniclers? Had Flórez known of Catalina's Muisca mother, he likely would have noted it in his entry, given that he did so for many other mestiza daughters of conquistadors, like Juana de Penagos. Though ultimately hispanized both in her behavior and in her genealogy, Catalina is one of a very few mestizos I have come across who was able to "disappear" twice: first by embracing her mother's native identity, then by assuming her husband's Spanishness.

THE PROMISE OF BETROTHAL

The strategies employed by the cacique of Ubaque and Juan de Penagos to successfully hispanize their daughters and granddaughters can be pieced together from scattered genealogical referents, although the available details are limited. Indeed, the abbreviated entries in Flórez's *Genealogías* leave the impression that doña Leonor de Mendoza was a mere pawn in her grandfather's machinations. Juana de Penagos comes to life briefly as a political actor in the will she drew up with her husband, where she laid out the shrewd series of land acquisitions that had cemented the couple's economic influence and, consequently, their calidad (given that calidad was determined as much by nobility and economic status as by sociracial classification). Marriage served much the same function for Catalina Tafur, enveloping her in a Spanish family. We can flesh out these skeletal accounts by looking at them sideways, by probing those instances in which carefully laid strategies went terribly wrong, as they did, for a time, for Catalina Tafur. Such, too, was the case for Isabel de Sotelo, who lived in La Palma, a city nestled in the warm mountain slopes to the northwest of Santafé. Isabel's father married his daughter well, but once she was widowed, his aspirations were quashed by a dishonest suitor.[36] Accounts of this catastrophe provide hints about how important strategic marriages were, as well as about the secrets that elite families sought to conceal by marrying their daughters well. Moreover, the story of Isabel de Sotelo not only blurs the boundaries of who could be a mestizo, but opens up to debate the notion of Spanishness itself.

Picture a bedroom in a wealthy Spanish household in the wee hours, between two and three in the morning. A couple lies in a bed, their naked bodies partially obscured by bed linens: they are thirty-year-old Isabel de Sotelo and twenty-six-year-old Juan Birves. The lovers are not alone, but surrounded by a throng of spectators: the *alcalde ordinario* (a judicial magistrate elected by the cabildo) with his *alguaciles* (constables); fray Juan Baquero, a Franciscan priest; family members, most of them Isabel de Sotelo's stepchildren; permanent guests or retainers of the household; curious neighbors called in as witnesses. A few indigenous servants scurry in and out of the bedchamber. Isabel is the illegitimate daughter of Pedro del Acebo Sotelo, a conquistador from Zamora and one of the first lawyers to serve the Real Audiencia of the Nuevo Reino de Granada. Although his official obligations are in Santafé, Sotelo maintains a residence in La Palma, near his encomienda of Topaipí. Several of his fourteen children live in La Palma, including Isabel, whose first husband, the Spanish merchant Lorenzo Núñez, died and left her with three daughters, each now being of marriageable age. Isabel's brother, Alonso de Sotelo, an hijo natural, also lives there and administers his father's encomienda (although it would eventually pass to his brother Lorenzo, the legitimate son of Pedro de Sotelo). By 1577, when his daughter's trysts with Juan Birves are discovered, Pedro de Sotelo has emerged victorious and prospered after a two-year legal battle in the mid-1550s, when he was accused of libel by an investigating judge sent from Spain, subjected to torture, and led in a humiliating procession through the streets of Santafé. Sotelo had then escaped into exile, before winning absolution with the assistance of several Audiencia allies.[37]

Perhaps in the early hours of 28 October Sotelo remembered the shame to which he had been exposed on that earlier occasion and now feared he might once again suffer the same, with his daughter discovered bedded down with a man to whom she was not married. Isabel recounts in her confession that "some five months ago this complainant came home and lay down, safe and secure, in her bed" (502v).

After she extinguished the light, someone who had been hidden inside drew close to her, against the will of the complainant. . . . Whispering, she telling him to leave and that she was not a woman to be mocked and he telling her that he was not the kind of person to mock her and that he would marry the complainant and giving her his word. . . . At last, Juan Birves swore to God that no other but she would be his wife and that neither her father nor she would have cause to complain about him. After these words and urgings, she consented to his lying in the complainant's bed. And from then on, [buoyed by] the hopes and desires that he would marry her, they knew one another carnally, which she would never have consented to nor allowed if he had not given his word of betrothal. (502v–503r)

Among the crowd of spectators was Juan López, a soldier attracted by the commotion. López witnessed the alcalde tell the young man "that he should take pleasure in marrying Ysabel Sotelo because he would become the relative of such fine people and that he did not hear Juan Byrves respond, and that is when the priest came and Juan Byrvez [said he] did not want to get married" (505v). Birves confessed that he had initially agreed to the betrothal because the family members who crowded around him were armed with swords (504v), but that he had already promised himself to another woman (516v). He was shackled and thrown in prison, but escaped during the night by breaking the lock on the stocks in which he was immobilized and carrying the shackles with him (507r–509v).

The irate Audiencia lawyer and his son immediately brought criminal charges against the young intruder. They accused Birves of being a mestizo who had purchased an encomienda, contravening Crown policy that barred individuals of mixed parentage from holding tribute grants (498r). They alleged he had damaged their honor by engaging in an extramarital affair with Isabel.

> Juan Birves committed grave and awful offenses incurring
> great and grave civil and criminal penalties established by law
> and in the legislation of Your kingdoms, and he seriously libeled
> me, as I am an honorable person, a [noble] hijodalgo and one
> of the first discoverers and conquerors of this kingdom, and
> for more than forty years I have served Your Highness. And
> [Birves] libeled Ysabel de Sotelo, my daughter, given that she is
> an honorable woman, a widow who lived honestly and had been
> married to a very honorable man, of great credit, and since
> Juan Birves is of the quality [calidad] to which I have already
> referred. (498v)

Pedro de Sotelo was defamed by Birves, not only because he violated Isabel's seclusion and repeatedly engaged in sexual relations with her, and not only because he refused to honor his statement of betrothal, but also because he was "of the quality to which [Sotelo had] already referred"—that is, because Birves was a mestizo.

The first step in making sense of this sixteenth-century imbroglio is to appreciate the significance of the two concepts on which it hinges: honor and betrothal, which are intimately intertwined here. Birves stated to Isabel de Sotelo his intentions of marrying her, a promise on which he subsequently reneged, thus wounding the Sotelo family honor. In the late colonial period a complainant in a libel case brought before the authorities in Bucaramanga, to the northeast of Santafé, asked the following: "What is life without honor? Honor is the patrimony of the soul [Para qué es vida sin honra, la honra es el patrimonio del alma]."[38] For Pedro de Sotelo, honor sustained his lineage in the face of imprisonment, public humiliation, and exile. Now his honor was being attacked from within his very household, and his only option was to bring Birves up on criminal charges, making public what was private.

Margarita Garrido points out that "the public persona of individuals was built on relations of exchange with others," principally through symbolic means, including heraldry, forms of address, clothing, and diction. "These elements," she adds, "constituted the symbolic capital of people, groups, and estates, and were defended as the most valued component of one's identity." Such symbolic capital "had to be validated—recognized—by other individuals and by the community. Recognition took place in daily life, particularly in spaces that were not private."[39] But when a respected widow was discovered in bed with a man alleged to be a mestizo, the private or intimate came into public view, casting a pall over the coats of arms above doorways, the ostentatious clothing, the noble titles, and all the other everyday markers of family honor. Sotelo's only option was to attempt to control how that public narrative was fashioned by taking legal action against Juan Birves.

Legal defense of a betrothal furnished a means by which to maintain a family's honor, whether that family was commoner or noble. Until the mid-sixteenth century, when edicts by the Council of Trent obligated couples to state their marital vows before a priest, marriage involved the mutual exchange of promises, with or without the presence of a religious official. Nonetheless, even two centuries after wedding ceremonies became compulsory, the word of betrothal continued to be taken seriously.[40] The historian Pablo Rodríguez introduces readers to numerous legal cases that erupted out of the tensions that swelled between time-worn custom and ecclesiastical edict in late colonial Medellín, brought by the families of women whose suitors had reneged on their obligations. Such legal challenges were generally desperate acts of last resort, attempted only after all other solutions had been found wanting, because "in a legal suit, private shame became a public act," and in the process, the reputation of the wronged fiancée was routinely maligned: she was accused of having low morals, of drinking, of having lost her virginity. Such affronts to her honor could be resolved only through the ritual of marriage. But that marriage had to be with someone of similar social status.[41]

Early modern Spanish families also availed themselves of this legal solution in their efforts to erase the stains left on their honor by unruly daughters. In effect, they displaced blame to the male defendant. These cases hinged on a crucial distinction between honor and reputation, Abigal Dyer argues. A woman's honor (or that of her family) was subject to the actions of others, such as a man who raped her or took advantage of her innocence.[42] In contrast, her reputation inhered to her character: both adulterers and the children of adulterers were considered to be of ill repute, for example. Dyer argues that it is precisely the bifurcation between honor and reputation that facilitated the use of legal suits as vehicles for resolving women's dilemmas.

> The notion of seduction as a crime committed against—but never by—women hinged on the difference between honor and reputation, in which honor could be lost by injury while reputation could only be lost by the circumstances of one's birth or through disgraceful personal conduct. The seduced woman's successful complaint turned on this distinction, for while claiming to have been dishonored (that is, to have lost her virginity) she simultaneously had to prove herself reputable to win her case. By bifurcating the concepts of female sexual honor and a woman's reputation, secular courts provided young unmarried women with a safety net against social ruin, in the form of victim status. Spanish law shifted responsibility for premarital sexual misconduct onto the male partner, leaving any woman in possession of a good reputation before the seduction had occurred, or any woman who could fabricate a good reputation with the help of her lawyer and her witnesses, able to claim continued respectability by virtue of her victimhood.[43]

How, then, might this distinction be useful in making sense of Isabel de Sotelo's affair with Juan Birves?

Juan Birves wounded Pedro de Sotelo's honor because he slept with his daughter, reneged on his promise to marry her, and, all the while, did not let on that he was a mestizo. The throng that swarmed Isabel de Sotelo's bedroom—some of them perhaps gawking onlookers hoping to catch a glimpse of the exposed couple, others sent there as trusted witnesses—most likely expected that marriage would help cleanse the blemish of prenuptial sexual relations and mitigate the slight Birves had committed by refusing to carry through with his vows. Nevertheless, despite the goodwill of neighbors and relatives who hoped to set matters right through the good offices of Father Baquero, the marriage of his daughter to Birves was not an option available to Pedro de Sotelo. As a scion of a prominent Spanish family, of a lineage of conquistadors and hijodalgos, he could not allow for Isabel to marry her suitor, whom her father had identified as a mestizo and, therefore, as a man without a reputation.

Or could he have done so? There is much more in the documentary record that helps us to fill in the picture of the major actors in this drama. Juan Birves, we learn from the case record, was

> the hijo natural of Bartolome Hernandez Virues, deceased, who was a vecino [citizen] of the city of Tamalameque and one of the first discoverers or settlers of Veragua, Cartagena, Santa Marta, Rio Grande de la Magdalena, a principal man [hombre muy prinçipal], and Juan Virues [Birves] is a man who has served Your Highness in whatever he could offer to your Royal Person, especially in the support he gave to the provinces of Guali and Guasquia, where he served Your Highness with his person, his arms and horse, and his arquebuse, and took a slave along with him who served as a very good soldier, at his own cost, without receiving any salary, so that he spent a great quantity of gold pesos and put at risk himself and that of said slave, as is public and notorious. (532v)

If Birves was in fact mestizo, he was one of the privileged few with close ties to the conquistador elite, but even if he was the son of a leading citizen of a coastal Caribbean town, he was still a man with no means of upward mobility. He would have been well aware of that fact, which might explain why he felt no compunction to marry Isabel, although the alcalde urged him to marry into a family of "fine people." Honoring his vows would not in fact have provided Birves with a graceful means of exit, because Pedro de Sotelo would never have endorsed the marriage. Once Birves's calidad was made public by Sotelo, the same individuals who had urged him to marry Isabel backtracked, testifying that they knew he was a mestizo because "it shows in his appearance [lo muestra por su aspeto]" (577v).[44]

Isabel de Sotelo was also the hija natural of an hijodalgo. As a member of the minor nobility, her father was supposed to burnish his image by "keeping horses and retainers and very honorable households, jousting [jugando cañas] and indulging in other forms of merriment as noble gentlemen [caualleros hijos dalgo] are in the habit of doing."[45] Clearly, Isabel's tryst with Birves did not contribute to the image of an honorable household, which is precisely why her father lodged this criminal case. But not only was Isabel an illegitimate daughter: she was also alleged to be a mestiza, a fact that complicated the scenario and led otherwise staunch supporters to question the legitimacy of Pedro de Sotelo's lawsuit. Although Isabel's father never volunteered information on his daughter's calidad, probably routinely referring to her simply as his "hija natural," Birves's lawyer asked witnesses to corroborate the claim that she was a mestiza, which they did by offering statements against her much like those made against Birves (610r, 617v, 621r, 622v). For example, Adrian de Cifuentes says "that he knows she is a mestiza because she looks so in her appearance [que sabe ques mestiza porque en su aspecto lo paresçe]" (619v).

Isabel de Sotelo's late first husband, Lorenzo Núñez, had been a Spanish ship-builder from San Lúcar de Barrameda and a vecino of La Palma (561v); "vecino" indicated the highest form of citizenship in a city or town, generally reserved in this period of Nuevo Reino history for individuals of Iberian descent. According to Pedro de Sotelo, the couple had lived in a house he built for them, where Isabel had remained with her two daughters after her husband's death (and where she received the clandestine visits of Juan Birves [599r–v]). Núñez was described as "a very honorable person and of much credit [era persona muy onrrada y de mucho credito]," a statement that Pedro de Sotelo paired with the assertion that his two other legitimate daughters—he emphasized their legitimate birth, given that Isabel was born out of wedlock—were married to "two very honorable and illustrious vecinos of said city [dos vezinos muy onrrados y prinçipales en la dicha çiudad]" (562r). This is a classic case of a prominent Spaniard marrying his illegitimate daughter to the most suitable man he can find: an Iberian, a vecino, perhaps not as prominent as his other two sons-in-law, but of high enough standing that the marriage afforded him the opportunity to elide Isabel's condition as a mestiza, which, in any case, would never have been placed at center stage if, as was probably the case, he had always referred to her as an "hija natural" without emphasizing her socioracial classification.

Isabel's dalliance with Juan Birves ruined all that, spurring the household to rush to cement their marriage vows and prompting Sotelo to defend his family's honor by bringing a criminal accusation against the young man. For, as Sotelo was well aware, that honor would not be redeemed through marriage to a man with Birves's reputation; had he been simply a seducer, it might have been, but Sotelo also called him a mestizo, which indicated that he was an unwelcome marriage partner. Furthermore, Isabel's own status as a woman of good reputation was called into question by evidence of her calidad, suggesting that there was no honor to blemish in this case and no reputation to uphold. Consequently, her father used the suit as a vehicle for damaging her lover, not for preserving her reputation.

In spite of this legal skirmish, Juan Birves appears several more times in the documentary record as a prominent citizen of La Palma. In 1584 he and his wife, Inés de Olalla, were named guardians of several young Spanish orphans.[46] He is identified as the encomendero of Terama in a 1617 visita conducted in a series of native communities in the vicinity of La Palma. Birves received that grant in 1588, a decade after his dispute with Sotelo, which indicates a second encomienda, not the one Sotelo accused him of having purchased illegally.[47] The fact that Birves was awarded a second encomienda suggests that the authorities were never completely persuaded that he was a mestizo or, perhaps, that he was able to effectively mask the identity of his mother through a legal sleight of hand, providing himself with an opening for economic advancement that would not have been available to a mestizo.[48]

It may be that Sotelo's accusation was dishonest, meant to damage Birves's reputation at the moment when he was most weak. But in any case, the young suitor was not the only person embroiled in this legal drama to shy away from the mestizo label: Isabel's brother, Alonso de Sotelo, was of mixed parentage (which is why he served as administrator of his father's encomienda, but did not inherit it), as was Catalina de Truxillo, one of the family retainers—or, perhaps, a permanent guest—who gave testimony against Birves.[49] Multiple actors dropped in and out of the mestizo slot in this legal scuffle.

The Sotelo lawsuit brings to light several very important points. First, as Katherine Bonil Gómez observes in her insightful study of calidad in eighteenth-century Mariquita, to evaluate attributions of calidad in the documentation as "true" or "false" could be a significant miscalculation. What the documentary record shows, to the contrary, is that such accusations would more appropriately be assessed in terms of how effective they were. These allegations hinged not on what individuals "really" were or even what they looked like (aspect being a justification by witnesses after the fact of the original denunciation), but instead on how these people were to be considered in the future as public social beings, as public persons rather than as individuals.[50] Sotelo's accusation against Juan Birves did not succeed in the long run, given that the man from Tamalameque retained his elite status and was, by all accounts, able to live an unmarked life, even in the tiny settlement of La Palma. The libel against Isabel de Sotelo appears to have been more effective, irrevocably transforming her social status by associating her permanently with the epithet "mestiza." One of her daughters, Úrsula Núñez, was identified in a 1592 legal case as a mestiza, after her husband, the mestizo Juan de Truxillo, attempted to kill her.[51] Since Úrsula was the legitimate daughter of a Spaniard, her "mestiza" moniker would have derived from her mother, suggesting that the accusation that stained Isabel de Sotelo in 1577 had not been erased some fifteen years later.

Furthermore, in our rush to interpret Isabel and Juan as examples of the fluidity of "mestizo" as a moniker, we should not lose sight of the fact that the couple's insertion into elite circles of La Palma also demonstrates how permeable the designation "Spanish" was. Pedro de Sotelo and the late Lorenzo Núñez can be comfortably labeled "Spaniards," given that they were born on the Iberian Peninsula. But what of the other actors in this drama, including not only Isabel and Juan, but other family members and their associates whose socioracial designations go unremarked or understated? Catalina de Truxillo, for instance, emerges in the folios of this criminal case as a Spaniard or, at least, as an unmarked criolla, and it is only in another dispute some twenty years later that she is identified as a mestiza. Alonso de Sotelo cannot inherit his father's encomienda because, we learn, he is mestizo, but he serves as its administrator, thereby effectively obscuring his calidad through the public performance of his association with the Spaniard—his father and, later, his brother—who holds the royal grant to the tribute of the Indians of Topaipí.

None of these people appear to have been "pretending" or "passing": they were simply identifying with the social milieu in which they found themselves, in which they performed and were perceived as Spanish. The "Spanish fold" was as heterogeneous as the "Indian world," neither being a "pure pole" anchoring a "system." What makes Juan Birves "mestizo" in this dispute is not so much the conditions of his birth as it is the way he is distinguished in this particular legal setting as a social actor different from other "Spaniards." After all, he reenters the historical record four decades later, still an encomendero, now with two encomiendas. As this ethnographic vignette demonstrates, "Spanish," "mestizo," "Spaniard," and "Indian" were all relational categories.

ELITE MESTIZO MEN: NO EXIT

Juan Birves was able to position himself in the murky space created by the uncertainty around whether or not he was a mestizo. The vagueness of his family history was undoubtedly facilitated by the fact that his roots lay in Tamalameque, some 800 kilometers to the north of La Palma and thus fairly inaccessible to the actors in this drama. Other mestizos were not so fortunate. In 1577 Juan de Céspedes, son of the prominent conquistador Captain Juan de Céspedes, as well as a conquistador in his own right, inserted the following question into the interrogatorio that would guide deponents in the report of his services to the Crown, a document that he hoped would earn him a royal pension.

> Item, if they know that being a free bachelor at that time,
> Captain Juan de Cespedes had for many years in his house and
> in his service Ysabel Christian Indian, born in the provinces of
> Peru, herself also an unmarried and free woman, with whom
> Captain Juan de Cespedes had and procreated Juan de Ces-
> pedes, his hijo natural, and he was acknowledged as and com-
> monly reputed to be his son and the son of Ysabel.[52]

Céspedes asked witnesses testifying in his favor to state whether or not his father had recognized him as his son in his will.[53] He possessed, as he noted in the heavily leading questionnaire he placed before his deponents, all the qualities of a man of honor: "Item, if they know that Juan de Cespedes is of high rank [persona prinçipal] and of quality [calidad], calm and peaceful, of good manner and conversation and obedient to the justice of Your Majesty and very zealous in his royal service, and wherever he has been he has lived and lives without slight from any person."[54] Nevertheless, Céspedes never benefited from his service, nor was he awarded an encomienda as were his fellow expeditioners. We know little about this mestizo conquistador who, according to eyewitnesses, lived alongside his Spanish brothers in the paternal household in the barrio of Santa Bárbara in Santafé and was the spitting image (*muestrasello*) of his father in both his deeds and his person.[55]

Juan de Céspedes, like many elite mestizo men in the late sixteenth century, had nowhere to turn. Despite his assertion that Captain Juan de Céspedes had recognized his paternity in his will, the old warrior's midcentury service and merit report did not acknowledge his illegitimate mestizo son's existence, naming only Lope de Céspedes and Antonio de Céspedes, his sons by marriage with the Spanish noblewoman Isabel Romero.[56] Nor does Juan de Céspedes appear in Flórez's genealogical compendium, in which his father not only merits his own family tree but is granted an exceptionally high standing in the hierarchy of Santafé grandees (as the sixth genealogy in the volume) and is accorded a lengthy biography of his feats in conquest and his services to the Crown.[57]

Juan de Céspedes's failure to transcend his mixed ancestry mirrors the experience of most sixteenth-century elite mestizos in Santafé. Juan de Penagos's sons were also unsuccessful in achieving the noble privileges that accrued to conquistadors. One of them, named after his father, took an indigenous concubine in lieu of a Spanish wife, although he successfully married one of his daughters, Úrsula, to a royal notary who was the illegitimate son of an Audiencia official.[58] Another son, Pedro de Penagos, was able to negotiate marriage to a Spaniard, although her artisan family was of lesser status than those of his brothers-in-law.[59] He is the only mestizo son of a conquistador of Santafé I found in the historical records who was able to marry a Spaniard. However, unlike his sisters and nieces, who slipped imperceptibly into Spanish family life, Pedro de Penagos's mestizo condition came back to haunt him when the Audiencia denied him the right to inherit his father's encomienda, despite his lucky match with a European wife, because he was of mixed parentage. In the official letter of denial, the royal magistrate Francisco Auncibay y Bohórquez declared, "In this kingdom there are many mestizos with encomiendas of Indians, and they are cruel and bad Christians, and it would be advisable and convenient if Your Majesty occupied them in other things [and] that those Indians be granted to worthy persons because truly, if there befalls any harm in these lands, it comes from the mestizos."[60]

It was not until the following generation that Pedro de Penagos was able to successfully erase the stain of mestizaje, via his son Juan, who was granted the title of receptor (a kind of judicial notary) of the Royal

Chancellery of Santafé and married the noblewoman doña Francisca de Ontiberos.[61] For the second century of colonization there are a few records of mestizo men who achieved Spanish standing for themselves or for their descendants, but such social mobility was not available in the sixteenth century.[62] Elite mestizos suffered constant snubs from well-placed Spaniards, particularly those not immediately connected to their family circles. And great barriers were erected to prevent these second-class members of powerful lineages from reproducing their fathers' patrilines after the paternal generation had consolidated marriages with Spanish women and produced legitimate heirs.

Juan de Lara, a royal interpreter (lengua) who served as a linguistic intermediary in numerous censuses and official inquiries into the treatment of Santafé's native people, was the son of the Spaniard Juan de Lara and Catalina, an india from Quito.[63] Lara's last will and testament indicates that the mestizo interpreter routinely did business with the Santafé elite, some of whom entered into financial transactions with him. He came under the aegis of Captain Juan de Céspedes, who served as executor of his will and who controlled—functioning in himself almost like a political faction—the Santa Bárbara quarter, where Lara owned property.[64] Despite his broad contacts with high society, Lara took as his partner Ysabel, an indigenous woman from Cáqueza, suggesting that what was really at stake for mestizo men was their ability (or lack thereof) to shape the character of Spanish lineages.[65] In the face of rejection by prospective Spanish fathers-in-law, many mestizo men sought indigenous or mestiza consorts. Note, nevertheless, that Pedro de Penagos, Juan de Lara, and Juan de Céspedes were sons of native women from distant lands, which may have situated them as a different type of mestizo, one who was only marginally associated with local native communities and could thus range more freely in elite circles in Santafé, even if he was ultimately denied all of the prerogatives enjoyed by Spanish men.

Many mestizo sons of encomenderos from Santafé and Tunja abandoned all prospects of producing legitimate Spanish offspring, choosing instead to enter the Church, as did many of their Spanish half brothers. Mestizos were barred from the priesthood because most of them were of illegitimate birth, which constituted an impediment to ordination, a "stain of birth [that] was believed to be a stain on the sacred ministry."[66] However, in practice numerous mestizo priests ministered to indigenous doctrinal communities because they were among the few nonnatives fluent in the Muisca language; nevertheless, they were not permitted to assume other religious positions and could not receive benefices.[67] Despite the issuance in the last quarter of the sixteenth century of papal bulls permitting mestizo ordination in the Indies, there was intense opposition throughout Spanish America to welcoming mestizos into the priesthood, as they were held to be imperfectly trained in the Christian doctrine—incompletely Christianized—and thus to run the risk of backsliding into idolatry. The harvest sowed by mestizo priests was probably mixed. Some of them were barely literate and were awarded doctrinal posts simply because of their linguistic expertise while others, like Gonzalo García Zorro, amply fulfilled all of the qualifications of the priesthood.[68]

THE MESTIZO MINISTRY

The son of Captain Gonzalo García Zorro and Margarita, a native woman, Father Gonzalo García Zorro was a loyal member of the priesthood. A servant of the Church since childhood—he became an altar boy at the age of nine and a sacristan at the age of twelve—Fr. Gonzalo studied liturgical music and became the choirmaster of the Cathedral of Santafé several years before his ordination in 1574. He attests to having had a hand in training numerous generations of boys, some of them future priests, in plain chant and basic literacy. He was fluent in the Muisca language and served in the less prestigious position of doctrinal priest in the native communities of Tunjuelo, Facatativá, Ubaque, and Zipacón, where unlike other priests, he was able to hear the confessions of the indigenous faithful—some six hundred, according to witnesses—in the vernacular.[69] He was repeatedly denied his request to be named to a benefice (an endowed church office with an attached income), which he began to seek in 1575 as a means of ensuring his subsistence. The mestizo priest thus lagged behind his former students, who climbed the ecclesiastical ladder and received benefices years before he did. His application was denied on several occasions despite rulings in his favor emanating from Madrid and Spain, although in 1590 he finally achieved his objective and was awarded a canonry.[70]

Sabine Hyland cogently demonstrates that the stain of illegitimacy was the most effective tool used by opponents of mestizo ordination to block the entry of men of mixed parentage into the Church, so it is not surprising that Fr. Gonzalo emphasized in his report on his services to the Crown that his father had officially legitimized him.[71] But he was unable to hide from the authorities that his mother was native. At the end of one of his two reports, in which he makes no mention of his background, the following note is scribbled: "Gonzalo García Zorro, priest, son of Captain Zorro who was a conquistador of this Kingdom and of an india . . . seeks for Your Majesty to grant him a canonry in [the Church in Santafé] and a benefice in this Kingdom, and in the matter of the canonry, it is not convenient at this moment."[72] It was not illegitimacy that was at stake, but Fr. Gonzalo's mestizo condition.

Fr. Gonzalo García Zorro, like Juana de Penagos, skillfully navigated the social terrain in which he lived, remaining an active member of the highest stratum of Santafereño society and leaving a significant paper trail, despite the fact that as a mestizo priest he was perceived as a threat by those he sought to enlist as his peers. We know that much. But if we are to understand the position occupied by elite mestizo men, then we also need to see Fr. Gonzalo as a person who lived, breathed, owned property, and established close relationships with other people. Unfortunately, the imprints he left on Santafé's memory reveal little about how he negotiated his mixed ancestry on a daily basis. Fortunately, the documented experience of Fr. Gonzalo's brother, Diego García Zorro, opens an unusual window onto elite mestizo existence in the early colonial Nuevo Reino de Granada.

THE ORDEAL OF DIEGO GARCÍA ZORRO

Felipe Guaman Poma de Ayala's line drawing of Santafé's central plaza displays a massive church, government buildings, and the homes of elite Spanish families framed by foliage, reminding his viewers of the exuberant greenery of the northern Andes. The plaza imagined by the indigenous Peruvian author is almost empty, with a few pedestrians and two men on horseback.[73] But on 18 August 1603, it was bursting with people excitedly anticipating the bullfights that marked the feast of San Jacinto, one of almost fifty days of religious celebration that took place in the city each year.[74] Francisco de Reyna, a carpenter— presumably, a low-status Spaniard or the American-born descendant of Europeans, or perhaps even a mestizo who was able to set aside his identity (which is unmarked except by profession in his complaint)— was strolling through the square when he was brought up short by Diego García Zorro, a city alderman (regidor), who was a stately sixty years of age. As Reyna affirms in his complaint,

[I was standing in] the main street [*calle real*], at the entrance
to the plaza, safe and secure, without committing or saying
anything wrong nor expecting any harm, when Diego García
Zorro approached me and said, "Why don't you doff your hat to
a man like me?" And that said, he punched me in the nose, at
which point I struck him, and having committed that offense
against me, he passed me by and entered the cemetery of the
Holy Church, and I, carrying no arms, could not obtain redress,
and there were many people present when Diego García Zorro
committed [that] crime, [which is] worthy of correction and
punishment.[75]

Reyna was then confronted by García Zorro's son-in-law, Esteban de
Rivas, who was "shouting in fury, tearing his hair out [*tirándose de las
barbas*], that I would pay and that he ought to beat me."[76] Witnesses
substantiated Reyna's allegations, adding that Rivas (who was a blacksmith, an unlikely profession for a regidor's son) picked up a rock to
wield against the carpenter before passers-by broke up the brawl.[77] A
few months later, at the Romero family's tile-ovens in the Santa Bárbara quarter, the witness Diego de Salas saw Rivas remove his cape
and ready his sword, preparing to resume his contest with Francisco
de Reyna.[78] Diego García Zorro was arrested on 23 February 1604, six
months after his initial encounter on the plaza and remained in prison
for twelve days before posting bail.[79]

García Zorro was infuriated by Francisco de Reyna's failure to doff
his hat to him because it represented an affront to his honor by a man
who was clearly his social subordinate. Taking one's hat off in the presence of a social superior constituted recognition of that person's status (*honor*) and his virtue (*honra*). One was born with status: in Spain,
honor accrued to the 2 to 4 percent of the population that claimed nobility; in the Americas, most conquistadors acquired noble status by
virtue of their service, although socioracial barriers complicated the
calculation of the honor of those of mixed ancestry. Honra, in contrast,
could be accumulated or lost over a lifetime.[80] Gestures of deference,
such as the doffing of a hat, were centered on the head, which was
considered the place of honor in the human body.[81] García Zorro was
therefore angry because he believed he deserved public recognition by
virtue of his position, yet a lowly carpenter had publicly slighted him
by withholding the appropriate gesture.

The legal documentation raises certain troubling questions. Why did Reyna refuse to doff his hat to García Zorro, if this was an accepted practice routinely performed for regidores by their social inferiors? After all, the document refers to no blemish on García Zorro's social status that might lead Reyna to display such a radical attitude toward his social superior. Furthermore, how did a regidor of the city council of the most important urban center in the Nuevo Reino end up with a son-in-law who was a blacksmith, a person of "vile occupation"? Weren't regidores *gente decente*, individuals worthy of honor, who did not work with their hands? In order to decipher these contradictions, we must follow the archival paper trail left by García Zorro, because it at first appears that the regidor was a prominent Spaniard who may have overreacted to the Reyna's affront, but who nonetheless deserved due recognition and more polite treatment—yet the inconsistencies suggest a more complex scenario.

DISCRIMINATION AND SOCIAL CLIMBING

Like Fr. Gonzalo García Zorro, Diego García Zorro was the son of Captain Gonzalo García Zorro, "a well-known gentleman and hidalgo [caballero hijodalgo notorio]" who was "one of the first conquistadors and discoverers of this kingdom [uno de los primeros descubridores y conquistadores deste reyno]." Flórez de Ocáriz dedicates an entire chapter of his *Genealogías del Nuevo Reino de Granada* to Captain García Zorro. A considerable portion of the genealogy enumerates his collateral relatives (the conquistador's cousins) and affines (the family of his wife, with whom he had no children).[82] In contrast to the effort that Flórez de Ocáriz expends on the Spaniards surrounding the García Zorro family, he pays little attention to the conquistador's own children, all of whom were mestizos: Diego and Fr. Gonzalo García Zorro were full brothers, but there was another half sister, Francisca García Zorro, whose mother was Luisa India. Diego was haunted throughout his life by the stain his legacy left on his name. The archival record notes various occasions on which he was slighted for being of mixed ancestry, not only by his peers but by social inferiors like the carpenter Francisco de Reyna.

In an incident that took place in 1583, for example, one of García Zorro's slaves escaped, triggering incredulous commentaries from his Spanish peers, for García Zorro was reputed to be a fair and reasonable master. The slave, Cristóbal, stated that he had fled his owner because he feared punishment for having lost a saddle. But in a brief but illuminating deposition, which appears near the end of the legal record, the tailor Miguel Francisco identified the predicament faced by the slave owner: "This witness believes [that] black [man] to be arrogant and a scoundrel [soberbio e vellaco] because he has heard Juan de Céspedes say that when he spoke roughly to the black, the black told him that he did not want to serve, nor did he have to serve Diego García Zorro, because he was a mestizo, and [the witness] has heard the same about Diego García Zorro, since it had been told to Luis de Salas Cubides and Lope de Céspedes."[83]

Diego García Zorro purchased the office of regidor from the Crown in 1587 and received his title in 1588, paying the hefty sum of 1,800 gold pesos for the privilege. The royal decree granting him the position cites the Crown's need to raise revenue to offset costs associated with the marriage of King Philip's daughter, Catalina.[84] García Zorro presented the authorities in Madrid with an account of his services to the Crown, as well as those of his conquistador father, identifying himself as "Diego García Zorro, vecino of the city of Santa Fe."[85] In none of these papers is there mention of his mixed ancestry, which was successfully occluded from the record. Nevertheless, it took seven years for García Zorro to achieve admission into the exclusive circle of the cabildo. When they received confirmation of his appointment in 1588, the other regidores ceremonially obeyed the royal decree granting García Zorro office by kissing the document bearing the king's seal and placing it on their heads, but they refused to comply with it—a common legal tactic at the time, known as "obedezco pero no cumplo."[86]

Many of the regidores stated they were otherwise occupied and could not attend personally to García Zorro's formal request to be invested in his office: Captain Juan de Otálora was in Tunja; Pedro Suárez de Villena had traveled to Susa; the chief constable, Juan Cotrina, was at his hacienda, as was Nicolas de Sepúlveda; Luis Gutiérrez was busy supervising work on a bridge under orders of the Audiencia. But their justification for ritually obeying but not in practice following up on an order received from Madrid indicates another layer to their prevarications: they state that it would be impossible for the city fathers to comply with the decree because "it would be optimal if all of them were present to consider an issue so novel as the current one and to this day, the King our Lord has not, in any part of the Indies, conferred the office of regidor on a mestizo."[87] When the cabildo finally found an opportunity to deliberate over García Zorro's appointment, they determined that he was not "qualified for it and [was] a young man with little experience [no ser sufiçiente para ello y hombre moço y poco es-perimentado]."[88] They demanded that the Crown deny mestizos the right to govern. Nevertheless, the king ordered García Zorro be in-stated as regidor, or the cabildo would be fined five hundred pesos. The president of the Audiencia, Antonio González, also pressed the cabildo to comply with the order. And thus, in 1590, the mestizo son of Captain Gonzalo García Zorro finally took his seat on the cabildo of Santafé.[89]

It now becomes clear why Reyna the carpenter refused to doff his hat to Diego García Zorro. Not only had the city fathers spurned the mestizo regidor, but so, too, had their slaves—therefore, why not a carpenter? García Zorro had been deemed unworthy of the honor of being offered public acts of deference. This led to violent outbursts, as occurred on the Day of San Jacinto and again at the Romero tile-works. Cheryl English Martin has compared the verbal theatricality of public insults in seventeenth- and eighteenth-century Paris with the violent confrontations that routinely erupted in colonial Mexico, suggesting that "northern Mexicans differed from Parisians in their style of argument not because they lacked creativity in verbal repartee but because the considerations of calidad often complicated the role of their audience."[90] It was, she remarks, easier to bridge class differences through courteous repartee than it was to resolve socioracial inequal-ities peaceably. Such exchanges were particularly awkward for elite mestizos, who associated with Spaniards as equals but minimized the fact that they were not Spaniards themselves.

THE SOCIAL NETWORKS OF ELITE MESTIZOS

Diego García Zorro and his brother, Fr. Gonzalo, were hiding in plain sight at the heart of the most privileged social circles in Santafé, some of whose members agreed to overlook the stain of their parentage, while others exploited it to their detriment. Richard Boyer's assertion that ethnic labels can be best understood as speech-acts embedded within social relationships is useful here for making sense of the lab-yrinthine social fabric of Santafé, with its tiny Spanish population.[91] The García Zorro brothers were mestizos under certain circumstances and unmarked in others. Most of the interactions in which they were tagged as mestizos unfolded against the backdrop of their personal struggles to acquire positions not generally awarded to individuals of mixed parentage, such as regidor or *canónigo*. Whenever possible, they quietly refrained from pointing out their ancestry, in particular in the legal petitions that were an essential feature of the colonial administration, but also in their public behavior. They endeavored to confront their colleagues as equals by eliding their mestizo condition, but were spurned by those who refused to accept them as peers because of their mixed parentage.

Being mestizo clearly had its disadvantages, a more pressing concern for the García Zorros than for someone like Juan de Salazar, the Quiteño shoemaker arrested in Fontibón for allegedly biting off his friend's nose. Salazar's craft could be practiced regardless of his identification as an indio ladino or as a mestizo, his social circle was not circumscribed by his calidad, and it is not clear that his socior(racial) designation played any influence in his sentencing. For the García Zorros, in contrast, the "mestizo" moniker erected significant barriers to their professional advancement. In a word, they had more to lose, which explains why the legal documents carefully drafted by both brothers are silent about their ethnicity. Instead, both men emphasize that they were legitimized by their father, in attempts to deflect attention from their mestizo condition and to curtail any accusations that as mestizos they were automatically of illegitimate birth.[92]

These elite mestizo brothers sought some kind of fixity, desired to be taken for someone other than who they were, despite their opponents' conscious efforts to "other" them. They could not alter their calidad through legal petition, although their father attempted to erase the stain of illegitimacy on their personas by obtaining royal legitimation decrees. They were not unquestioningly accepted as Spanish, as was Isabel de Sotelo before the unfortunate discovery of her affair with Juan Birves. As much as the two García Zorro brothers strove to relegate the blemish of "mestizo" to the back burner, they found it impossible to erase entirely. Perhaps the challenge was greater for Regidor García Zorro than for Father García Zorro. The mestizo priest eventually surmounted the impediment to his advancement in the Church, although he continued to work with indigenous people in settings in which, for instance, his unusual linguistic abilities were at a premium. The alderman, in contrast, aspired to conducting his public life in a political milieu where there was no advantage to being identified as mestizo, yet he could not pass as a Spaniard in the narrow social world in which he sought acceptance; he was therefore able to transcend only partially the social obstacles that inhibited his progress. More specifically, he could only achieve limited acceptance as an unmarked person.

Just as examining the social milieus in which Lázaro Mulato, Juana

Galván, and Manuel Rodríguez fashioned their respective identities provides an explanation of how "mestizo" was enacted in multiple ways in plebeian society, tracing the García Zorros' social networks reveals how limited their efforts at ethnic refashioning really were. They achieved unmarked status only among a narrow slice of Santafé's elite society and only under particular circumstances; the rest of the time they had no choice but to resign themselves to mestizo status. And even in those limited contexts in which their mestizo condition went unremarked, they lived in constant danger of being "outed" by people like the carpenter Francisco de Reyna.

Both the García Zorro brothers' allies and enemies were members of a narrow social circle: highly placed churchmen, encomenderos, Audiencia officials. What distinguished their supporters from their detractors was the extent to which social distance was ameliorated by everyday contact. Diego García Zorro and his brother Gonzalo appear repeatedly in the notarial record—Fr. Gonzalo more often than Diego—in brief entries documenting sales of land and slaves, agreements over debts originating in the purchase of luxury goods (velvet, wine, etc.) and everyday necessities (soap, buttons, and wax, for instance), and contracts with men who agreed to serve as their legal representatives. The two brothers also engaged in disputes, passed property on to heirs, and served as witnesses and deponents. Certain individuals, such as the encomendero Lope de Céspedes and his brother Juan, as well as the Audiencia lawyer Lope de Rioja, testified in favor of Fr. Gonzalo in his informaciones de méritos y servicios or served as witnesses in favor of Diego García Zorro's legal disputes. They were also involved in more quotidian dealings with the two brothers, as buyers or sellers of property, as witnesses at the signing of their wills, and as their neighbors.[93] Other men they dealt with on a routine basis included their father's associates. For instance, Lope de Céspedes's father, Captain Juan de Céspedes, testified in favor of Captain García Zorro in his report on his services to the Crown as well as in support of his mestizo sons.[94] Everyday exchanges, conducted on the basis of equality of status, led these men to set aside their knowledge of the brothers' mestizo condition and to view them instead as peers, even if, as in the case of Captain Juan de Céspedes, they didn't extend the same courtesies to their own mestizo sons.

However, encomenderos, Crown officials, and other elite Spaniards made up only one of the social networks in which Diego and Gonzalo García Zorro habitually moved. Fr. Gonzalo was, for a time, a doctrinal priest in a series of native communities, as well as in the predominantly Muisca barrio of Las Nieves in Santafé, where his day-to-day dealings were with indigenous tributaries, mestizos, mulattos, and Spanish plebeians. An india ladina, María, who was his servant and a member of his household, also appears in documents relating to his personal affairs. In 1596 Fr. Gonzalo ceded two plots of urban land to María's daughter, Gerónima; he probably called her his *criada*, a word that today refers to a domestic servant, but in the sixteenth century denoted a fictive kin tie that today would best be equated with adoption, but that did not involve all of the rights and privileges accorded to modern adoptees, instead combining paternalism with servitude.[95] Fr. Gonzalo's relationship to Gerónima was similar to that of many Spaniards, both noble and plebeian, who raised servants-cum-sons or criadas-cum-daughters in their households, frequently leaving them small bequests in their wills.[96] Fr. Gonzalo García Zorro's paper trail provides no indication that his relationship with indigenous people and mestizos was anything other than that of a superior to his social subordinates.

Diego García Zorro presents a different story. Why, again, did such a well-placed man have a blacksmith as a son-in-law? The answer lies in the regidor's will and that of his consort, Juana Sangrelinda, an india ladina. The two testaments open a window into the regidor's personal life and the parallel social networks within which he moved as a mestizo, on the one hand, and as a regidor, on the other. Honor was a public virtue, more social than individual in character.[97] In colonial usage, "public" (*público*) denoted that which was "notorious, obvious, and known to all [notorio, patente y que lo saben todos]," whereas "private" (*privado*) denoted "that which was executed under the gaze of few, in the family and domestically, and without any formality or ceremony [lo que se executa à vista de pocos, familiar y domésticamente, y sin formalidad ni ceremonia alguna]."[98] In terms of his performance of honor, García Zorro's personal life unfolded off-stage, whereas he was obligated to defend his position in public. The difference between the two spaces is evident in his last will and testament.

Diego García Zorro begins his will, as did most testament writers in the period, by invoking the Holy Trinity, establishing his parentage and his claim to his position as regidor, and professing his Catholic faith.[99] Like other mestizos, García Zorro cannot hide the fact that his mother was native, but he draws attention away from her and toward the accomplishments of his father, whom he highlights as "one of the first discoverers and conquistadors of this kingdom." As befits the son of a conquistador—even a mestizo son—he requests to be interred in the Cathedral of Santafé, in the burial chapel of his father.[100]

In the first half of the will García Zorro enumerates his properties and goods, those to whom he is in debt, and those who owe him. Here, his Spanish identity is personified, as it is in the other legal papers. Perpetuating a colonial relationship with the native community of Fusagasugá, of which his father was encomendero, García Zorro (who as a mestizo did not inherit the encomienda) stipulates that eight Masses be said by its doctrinal priest for the souls of Indians in purgatory.[101] He declares ownership of a house with a tile roof in the prestigious Cathedral quarter in Santafé, as well as of a cattle ranch in nearby Bosa, the latter housing seven hundred sheep and eight oxen purchased in common with Fr. Gonzalo with money they inherited from their father. In addition to claiming ownership of three black slaves, he lists "a Pijao Indian named Luisa, who cost me seventy pesos and I bought her from Captain Juan de Rozas."[102] Prominent Spaniards—many of them captains, but also one who had founded the Carmelite convent—and the cacique of Fontibón are recorded as owing him money for various purchases, loans, and other obligations. Indeed, Diego García Zorro was a man who moved in well-heeled, influential circles.

It is only in the second half of the will, where he distributes his property and names his heirs, that we encounter the other networks that Diego García Zorro frequented on a daily basis, the private spaces in which his mestizo condition was tacitly acknowledged and where he made no pretensions to unmarked status. Here, he distributes all his property, including agricultural lands, sheep, and slaves, to his consort and to his illegitimate sons and their offspring.[103] This reflects Diego García Zorro's everyday social universe: all of his legatees are mestizos or natives, and all of them belong to his immediate family, with the exception of María Banegas, the daughter of Juana Sangrelinda by another man, who also receives a plot of land.[104] According to Flórez de Ocáriz's genealogical compendium, many of García Zorro's grandchildren married individuals with Spanish surnames; however, we cannot be sure that they were Spaniards, since many native people living in urban areas adopted Spanish surnames in the seventeenth century.[105]

The vast majority of the Spaniards who appear in the archives had illegitimate sons and daughters, some of them mestizos, and concubinage was widespread (although it was considered an offense), so the simple fact that Diego García Zorro had an indigenous partner and mestizo children does not necessarily indicate that he was part of a plebeian social sphere.[106] Illegitimacy rates were considerably higher in colonial Latin America than in the Europe of the period—in seventeenth-century Mexico, up to 50 percent of births were out of wedlock—and only some of these children were formally or informally recognized by their fathers.[107] The fact that García Zorro's entire estate went to his illegitimate children and his partner (as well as to his soul) indicates, nonetheless, that Juana was not a casual liaison, but that she and the children she bore him (whom he recognized as his hijos naturales) played a significant role in his private life. He even provided a hefty dowry to his daughter, Catalina, who married the blacksmith Esteban de Rivas, including a piece of land on which to grow crops and raise sheep.[108] There is good reason why his son-in-law, Rivas, came to his defense on the public square on the day of San Jacinto: there was a solid bond between the two men.

García Zorro's life was divided between his public Spanish persona and his private mestizo family circle. However, the two worlds were not separate; they overlapped in many people's lives, superimposed through relationships of servitude and concubinage, debts and sales, *compadrazgo* (ritual godparenthood). The very fact that the grounds (*solar*) of a colonial elite house were dotted by thatched huts inhabited by servants and slaves belies any impression of insularity.[109] What is notable about Diego García Zorro is how he parsed these relationships: his political dealings and his economic transactions with elite Spaniards, his affect and the transmission of property to his plebeian mestizo kin. It is almost as though he strove in his public life to be an ethnically unmarked person, but when at home with his family, he let his hair down, so to speak, and felt free to acknowledge his mixed parentage.

Diego García Zorro's negotiation of his social world contrasts with the network that emerges from the will of his companion Juana, an india ladina, or what we can piece together for Fr. Gonzalo García Zorro. The life of a priest implied a detachment from everyday life, likely requiring that—and we have no evidence to the contrary—he forgo the intimacy with indigenous women and mestizas that his brother enjoyed in his own family. Juana Sangrelinda, Diego's consort, inhabited a largely indigenous or mestizo plebeian world. Her debts were all to close kin—sister, sister-in-law, brother-in-law—or to local urban artisans.[110] Like many women of her period, whether elite or commoner, her will contained a list of articles of clothing and jewelry, but in Juana's case most of the items noted were native women's garments, including skirts called *anacos* and *líquidas* (a hispanization of the Quechua word "lliclla"), the painted cotton mantles that were customarily worn by Muisca women but were sometimes confected out of European materials, such as Spanish linen or cloth from Holland.[111] Juana probably walked the streets of Santafé in distinctive native garb.[112]

If Diego García Zorro spent his years in the public eye trying to draw attention away from the appropriateness of the soubriquet "mestizo," his family life unfolded in a native and mestizo environment. Ultimately, Diego García Zorro experienced downward mobility, perhaps not in his life span, but in that of his offspring, who could not aspire to the dignified company that he had kept in the cabildo. His experience was opposed to that of the mestiza daughters of the Penagos and the Tafurs, and to that of the granddaughter of the cacique of Ubaque, whose offspring were ultimately absorbed into the Spanish elite. The question of whether a person was a mestizo or a mestiza thus had unexpected implications in colonial Santafé.

CONCLUSION

Early colonial mestizaje is considerably more nuanced than can be captured by merely describing the fluid ascription of socioracial categories or by asserting that these classifications were assigned differentially to men and women. The permeability of categories like "mestizo" and "mulatto," but also of categories like "Indian" and "Spaniard," owed to their intersection with other forms of identification, as well as to the nature of the social groups in which people participated. Language use, place of origin, and occupation transected with attributions of parentage, generating myriad social networks within which the people we would identify today as "mixed" fashioned their self-images. "Mestizo" should be understood, then, not as a sociological group, but as a starting point from which people of mixed parentage constructed their diverse social worlds, sometimes inserting themselves into indigenous families or associating with other nonnative people living at the margins of small-town society, or else melting into the plebeian substratum of colonial cities. In the process of observing the performance of mestizaje, however, it also becomes evident that despite the corporate nature of indigenous communities or the rights and obligations that accrued to those who were called "Indians," their identity was also permeable—that is, it was also defined in relation to the others with whom Indians interacted, including those they married.

In the present chapter I have taken a similar approach, problematizing those who called themselves (or aspired to call themselves) "Spaniards." I have been principally concerned with individuals of mixed parentage who, due to their elite status, were born into polite society and, by marriage, occupation, or family connections, were able to project themselves as ethnically unmarked, sometimes only temporarily or in limited circumstances, sometimes more permanently. While all mestizaje—as well as all Indianness and all Spanishness—was gendered, in this chapter I chose to study the gendering of mestizaje through an examination of the mestizo elite of Santafé, interpreting their strategies of self-identification to generate new questions, inquiries that lead beyond the usual tropes of permeability and flux. Here, we observe the coddled daughters of conquistadors, women who were never recognized as mestizas, the conditions of their birth obscured under the label "hijas naturales." As Isabel de Sotelo's experiences persuasively demonstrate, it was possible for such women not only to marry into Spanishness, but to live their whole lives as Spaniards— unless, of course, they committed an indiscretion, as Isabel did when her affair with Juan Birves was exposed, leading to accusations regarding who was really a mestizo and who was a Spaniard. At that moment, Isabel and her family were suddenly forced to acknowledge origins that they had spent their lives repudiating or, more likely, blatantly disregarding. Isabel de Sotelo was not passing: she was not like the closeted Morisco, Diego Romero, or the mulatto Francisco Suárez, who hid behind his lofty missives. She was not dissimulating, nor was she hiding from her "true" origins. Instead, she was, in the parlance of the period, a Spaniard by reputation.

Negotiating identity was not as easy for elite mestizo men. Honor originated in lineage, which was preserved by the male head of a family, who maintained his own reputation and that of his dependents. It was therefore virtually impossible for a man like Diego García Zorro to produce an honorable family line. While he was able to deflect bigotry in many of his public dealings, due to the support of family friends and, in the last instance, of the Crown, he could not claim the honor he felt was his due as regidor of the Santafé's cabildo in his most intimate family circle, which was peopled by Indians and mestizos, artisans and laborers, many of them born out of wedlock. He could walk the public square as a Spaniard, but he went home as a mestizo. His desire for the kind of ethnic fixity that Pedro de Sotelo thought he had ensured for his daughter Isabel was out of reach.

If these life stories trace the precarious status of mestizos, depicting the routes by which they disappear as members of a social category, they tell us little about how such individuals perceived themselves. What did being mestizo mean to them? Was it a condition they always avoided? Did they fashion their self-images according to the values of the dominant society, which denigrated them, or did they value their bifurcated heritage in some way? How mestizos imagined themselves will be explored in the next chapter through the words and actions of two unusually eloquent and prolific sixteenth-century mestizo caciques: don Alonso de Silva and don Diego de Torres.

4. Good Blood and Spanish Habits

The Making of a Mestizo Cacique

M ost elite mestizos in Santafé de Bogotá struggled, with varying degrees of success, to melt into the woodwork of privileged society. Encomenderos maneuvered their mestiza daughters into carefully planned marriages with Spaniards so that they and their children would be remembered for posterity as Europeans, in the belief that over the course of several generations indigenous blood would be entirely diluted—"redeemed"—by Spanish blood.[1] Mestizo men did not find it as simple to ensure elite membership for their offspring, because as progenitors of lineages they could sully family genealogies. Many of the first-generation mestizo sons of conquistadors for whom there is documentation joined the priesthood, while others managed to penetrate their fathers' social circles to conduct business dealings, although they frequently spent their more intimate moments in plebeian milieus. But it was certainly not common for the mestizo scions of Santafé's better families to seek out native status. Instead, they habitually refused to acknowledge their mixed ancestry in public contexts, hiding in plain sight, as did Diego García Zorro.

For this reason, the lives of don Diego de Torres, cacique of the Muisca pueblo of Turmequé, and don Alonso de Silva, cacique of Tibasosa, men who in the 1570s aspired to positions in the indigenous political hierarchy, present a significant contrast to that of their mestizo brethren. They left voluminous records in Bogotá and in Seville, in the wake of their struggle to defend their rights to their cacicazgos against their encomenderos, who effectively blocked them from taking office.[2] Both men had conquistador fathers and descended on the maternal side from chiefly lines, permitting them to vie for cacicazgos, which were inherited matrilineally among the Muisca. The two mestizos competed against other native pretenders, some of whom had served as regents before the two reached legal age and who enjoyed the support of the local encomenderos. Torres and Silva consistently imagined themselves to be superior candidates for chiefly status precisely because they were mestizos: they repeatedly accentuated the auspicious concurrence between their Christian ancestry and their noble native lineages, echoing the celebration of noble hybridity made by the Inca Garcilaso. That is, they self-consciously projected themselves as a very privileged kind of mestizo, one who could best serve his native community because he was lettered and cosmopolitan, at once versed in the intricacies of the colonial legal system, fluent in both Spanish and Muisca, a legitimate successor to the caciques who came before him, and a pious Catholic.

This was a gendered choice, as were Fr. Gonzalo García Zorro's successful bid for the priesthood and the failed exit strategy of his brother, the regidor Diego García Zorro. The only mestizo caciques I have found in the colonial record for the Nuevo Reino were men, perhaps because, on the one hand, elite mestizas already had a more attractive escape hatch in their ability to embrace Spanishness in their youth, while on the other, the position of cacique appears to have been granted only to men in this period (at least, in Muisca pueblos).[3] At any rate, only a very limited number of mestizos could avail themselves of such an opportunity, because they were required to demonstrate descent from the previous cacique. In the cases of Silva and Torres, however, the two men also devised alternatives which they hoped would allow them to maintain their connections with elite circles: Silva was a notarial assistant in Santafé, while Torres married a Spanish woman while living in Madrid and had Spanish children. Both options were gendered and highly dependent on circumstance: only a literate man with the wherewithal to land an apprenticeship could aspire to work in a notarial office; only in Spain might a sixteenth-century American mestizo find a Christian woman willing to marry him. Before briefly engaging the issue of gender, however, I will dedicate this chapter to exploring what being mestizo meant to these two men.

INTRODUCING ALONSO DE SILVA AND DIEGO DE TORRES

Don Alonso de Silva was the illegitimate son of the Portuguese conquistador Francisco González de Silva and of doña Juana Sirita, the eldest sister of the cacique of Tibasosa (fig. 4.1).[4] Silva was described by Cristóbal Montaño, a vecino from nearby Mariquita, as "very straight-

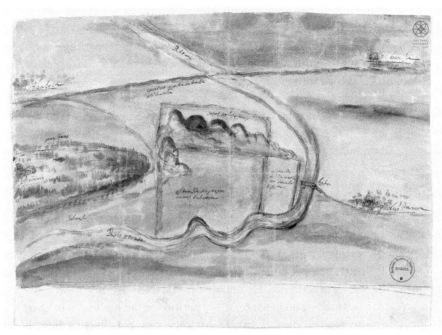

Figure 4.1. *Magdalena Valley, between Sogamoso, Duitama, and Tibasosa, 1653. Archivo General de la Nación, Mapas y Planos, Mapoteca 4, ref. 477-A. Courtesy of Archivo General de la Nación, Bogotá.*

forward and noble . . . a young man who is very well disposed and agreeable [muy llano e noble], with much virtue [allegado a mucha virtud]," a series of adjectives that Spaniards of the period rarely used to describe indigenous subjects (CI 61/3, 270r). Montaño visited Silva's house, a residence where the cacique is reported to have received frequent guests and where he kept two horses and a clavichord (CI 61/3, 270v). The pretender to the cacicazgo of Tibasosa was said to have been an unassuming man who did not subscribe to the martial trappings of the Santafé nobility and whose weapon of choice was the quill pen (CI 61/3, 277v).

The heir to the cacicazgo of Tibasosa was sent by his father at a very young age to Santafé, the administrative seat of the Audiencia, where he probably learned the notarial craft as an apprentice, sleeping on the floor and spending his time on menial duties, like sharpening quills. He ultimately rose to the position of secretary (*oficial*) to the notary Diego de Robles, drawing up the contracts, testaments, and other legal papers to which Robles would affix his notarial signature and rubric, thus coming into contact with a broad swathe of the colonial elite who would later come in useful in his legal crusade (CI 61/3, 303r).[5] Silva was a member of Santafé's "lettered city," rendered by Angel Rama as a baroque edifice dedicated to the civilizing mission, in which architectural, administrative, political, and social practices were consolidated and ordered in relation to an ideology grounded in the primacy of the written word and the power of the pen wielded in the service of empire.[6] The embattled cacique of Tibasosa remained in the colonial bureaucracy for the duration of the dispute over his chiefly position, for this was his livelihood. Nevertheless, his day job interfered with his continued management of the documentation issuing from his lawsuit and that of Diego de Torres: there are some thousand folios in the Bogotá archives alone. Silva attempted unsuccessfully in 1584 to purchase the office of one of the notaries under whom he labored; he was never granted the position because he had no evidence that his birth had been legitimized.[7] Almost nothing is known of Alonso de Silva's private life. He married in the early 1570s—to whom is not documented—and unsuccessfully petitioned the Audiencia to grant his future son the right to inherit his cacicazgo patrilineally (which, he pointed out, was more in keeping with Christianity).[8]

Silva's comrade-in-arms, don Diego de Torres, was the son of Spanish conquistador Juan de Torres and doña Catalina de Moyachoque, the eldest sister of the cacique of Turmequé.[9] Don Diego's father was a member of the minor nobility, an hijodalgo whose family crest bore the image of a tower and a black eagle.[10] Torres was brought up by both his parents in his paternal home in Tunja, where he studied in a school for the mestizo sons of highly placed Spaniards and later took classes in religion, morals, and grammar in the city's Dominican convent.[11] If the former was anything like the schools set up for sons of caciques, it provided training in devotional exercise, good reading habits, Christian doctrine, arithmetic, and music.[12] Torres's studies in morals and grammar were more the province of the Spanish elite than the indigenous nobility, however, for the colonial administration feared that these fields of study would lead native people to heresy.[13]

Like his Peruvian counterpart, Garcilaso Inca de la Vega, Torres was reportedly a fluent speaker of his mother's tongue, in this case, Muisca (CI 37, 255v–256r). He maintained a residence in Turmequé, although it is unclear how often he lived there, given that the lawsuits began shortly after he reached majority and was granted chiefly title. He was ultimately prohibited from visiting Turmequé, and his compound there was dismantled. An experienced archer, jouster, and horseman—a true caballero—Torres was perhaps more familiar with the dinner tables of the Santafé elite than with everyday life in a pueblo de indios, a man who undoubtedly spent more time writing in educated Spanish and reading the important books of his time than conversing in his mother's language. The legal record paints a vivid picture of don Diego as a Europeanized and well-connected member of the most privileged circles of Santafé.

Only in his mid-twenties when he traveled to Spain to press his claims after losing his legal battle in Santafé, don Diego moved in a select milieu of indigenous noble expatriates resident in Madrid, including a grandson of Atahualpa, the last Inca, for whom Torres served as executor of his last will and testament.[14] Torres married Juana de Oropesa, a Spaniard, during his second trip to the Peninsula and died there in 1590, leaving three children (of whose fate we know nothing).[15]

MESTIZO PLAYERS IN A COLONIAL SYSTEM

Torres and Silva were vociferous opponents of the encomienda system and decried the numerous abuses committed by the encomenderos of Tunja, who extracted exorbitant payments from a population base that had been decimated by smallpox and maintained a corps of mestizos, mulattos, and indios ladinos who intimidated indigenous tributaries. The caciques denounced the continuing exploitation of natives as sources of labor for Santafé's and Tunja's encomenderos, the lack of effective doctrinal instruction in indigenous communities, the continuous and disturbing presence of nonindigenous overseers and slaves in native pueblos, and the encroachment of encomendero haciendas onto indigenous lands. They decried the massive frauds in tribute-collection benefiting encomenderos that forced caciques to pay taxes for subjects who were no longer resident in their communities. They complained about the alliance of Spaniards with indios ladinos, who were partners in the plunder of indigenous subjects. They alerted the king to the forced recruitment of native women as wet nurses, which left their own infants without maternal care.[16]

The two caciques confronted a two-pronged challenge in the course of their two-decades-long struggle. On the one hand, they were at pains to expose the unconscionable abuses of the encomenderos of Tunja. On the other, they were compelled as a result of these condemnations to defend their legality as hereditary lords against their encomenderos' charges that presumed they were illegitimate, as much in birth as in the chiefly succession, because they were of mixed descent. Don Diego and don Alonso's legal challenge was met by the Turmequé encomendero Pedro de Torres (don Diego's half brother, born in Spain before his father joined Jiménez de Quesada in the conquest of Santa Marta and the Nuevo Reino) and the Tibasosa encomendero Miguel Holguín (who had succeeded don Alonso's father, Francisco González de Silva, in that position). The two encomenderos joined forces, summoning a series of European and native witnesses to expose the dangers of allowing mestizos to occupy chiefly positions in native communities. They hoped to silence the two caciques by characterizing them as treacherous mestizo outsiders who, because they were also lettered, thus presented multiple threats to the integrity of the native community. Juan de Leuro, a witness and vecino of the nearby city of Ibagué, offered the following line of reasoning against Silva and Torres: "In the opinion of this witness mestizos are not suited to be caciques in this kingdom. . . . When the caciques are Indians, they will understand better what is in the interests of the Indians, they will obey him more than any mestizo, and also because they would treat them better and they would not be as literate as mestizos [e no ternan tantas letras como los mestizos]" (CI 61/4, 552r–v). What was dangerous about lettered mestizos (or lettered Indians, for that matter) was the fact that they had greater access to the law and could better defend themselves, which is precisely what Silva and Torres did.[17]

Don Alonso and don Diego were not the only mestizo caciques of indigenous communities in the early colonial Nuevo Reino. I have found various others in the archival record, although there were undoubtedly many more.[18] These men were eligible to occupy chiefly positions and were generally accepted by both their subjects and the Spanish authorities because cacicazgos were inherited matrilineally among the Muisca, the position passing from the officeholder to the son of his eldest sister. Most cases of mixed ancestry involved a Spanish father and a native mother, so as a consequence, the majority of mestizo caciques could establish a clear succession to chiefly office through the maternal line. This was the genealogical claim made by don Alonso and don Diego. However, it was not their mestizo condition per se, but their strident condemnations of the abuses committed by their encomenderos that led the grandees of Tunja to oppose their assumption of chiefly office, notwithstanding the fact that both caciques had received confirmation of their status in royal decrees emanating from Spain.

Mixed descent offered a useful argument against the two men, whose pressure on the encomenderos was public, vigorous, and infuriating. In particular, the encomenderos painted mestizos as having the power to persuade and to corrupt, as being incomplete Christians always in danger of backsliding into idolatry, and as being of illegitimate birth. "Mestizo" stood in for these dangerous qualities. While all mestizos were seen as inferior in these respects and as a danger to supposedly innocent indigenous tributaries, caciques, who wielded power in the colonial system, presented a greater threat than did common mestizos, particularly such articulate and well-connected caciques as the hereditary lords of Tibasosa and Turmequé: they were viewed as treacherous, not simply as lesser humans.

The stories of don Diego and don Alonso are acutely compelling, in part because there is so much information on the two men, much of it in their own words, thanks to their education and to Silva's notarial experience. Like other mestizos in Mexico and Peru who could claim elite status on both their mother's and father's sides, Torres and Silva effectively moved between identities, depending on the context in which they found themselves. The Peruvian literary critic Antonio Cornejo Polar says the same for the author and son of Inca royalty, Garcilaso Inca de la Vega: "I would even affirm that Garcilaso himself lived his mestizaje in many diverse ways: sometimes as a double legitimation of his noble status and sometimes as a form of social marginalization that he shared with the Indians, the mestizos, and the creoles despised by peninsular Spaniards; sometimes as an almost-hymnic fulfillment of neoplatonic harmony, and sometimes as incurable tragedy."[19] Juan Bautista Pomar, a sixteenth-century mestizo descendant of the Tezcoco dynasty of central Mexico, oscillated between the category of Spaniard and heir to Nezahualpilli, depending on his sphere of action. In those legal cases in which he appeared as a witness allied with Spanish vecinos, his identity was unmarked, but when he collaborated with the indigenous elite, he emphasized his native noble ancestry.[20]

When we encounter don Alonso de Silva sitting at his scribal desk, his mixed ancestry goes unmentioned in the documentation, whereas in the dispute over the legitimacy of his chiefly title, his dual claims to nobility come to the fore. In a racial regime, he might have been accused of passing, although the conditions under which Silva negotiated his identity were quite different from those of Francisco Suárez, Diego Romero, and Isabel Tafur. Silva occupied a more powerful position than did Suárez or Tafur; in this sense, he had the latitude to manipulate his identity much as Diego Romero did. As Judith Butler underscores in her interpretation of the African American author Nella Larsen's novel *Passing*, the act of crossing from one identity to another is grounded in much more than phenotype. Like Larsen's main character, Clare, a black woman passing for white, it was not so much that Silva "looked" the part, but that he refused to make his mestizaje a public issue in his everyday life, thus "withhold[ing] the conversational marker which would counter the hegemonic presumption" that he was Spanish.[21] Of course, colonial Santafé was a much smaller space than Clare's modern, urban, North American world, and Silva was identified as mestizo not so much by his aspect as by his parentage, which was common knowledge in the social circles he inhabited. He could not pass, as could Clare. In fact, there is no evidence that he ever identified himself as a Spaniard. But in professional contexts Silva appears to have taken care to not introduce his mixed heritage into the legal record, and his classification as a mestizo was politely ignored in the documentation—although we cannot know whether it was similarly disregarded in everyday social interaction in the notarial office or in the Audiencia; we have only to recall the travails of Diego García Zorro, the mestizo regidor, to bear in mind the painful fact that many of these men suffered snubs and insults on a regular basis.

But the choice faced by the two caciques was not simply between "mestizo" and "unmarked," and this is precisely what makes colonial mestizaje so fascinating. There were multiple avenues along which Silva, Torres, and their opponents could deploy the label "mestizo," confounding our twenty-first-century interpretations of the meaning of the term (whether the iconic definition pointing to a mixture of Spanish and Indian or the more diffuse modern concept of mestizo nationalism). The caciques' case records display the usual vilifications of mestizos as dishonest and as products of illegitimate unions, affronts that were to be expected from the encomendero elite. But these slurs were met with novel vindications by the two chiefly pretenders, who never acceded to the label "mestizo," but found other ways to describe their mixed ancestry. In particular, in their briefs they draw attention away from their indigenous mothers and toward their Spanish parentage by identifying themselves as "hijos de españoles" (sons of Spaniards) and by engaging the synecdoche of a Christian bloodline to reposition their mixed backgrounds to their advantage. Their encomendero opponents also deploy Christian symbols to denigrate the chiefly pretenders, making use of (clearly fictitious) references to their use of indigenous ritual and ceremonial forms of bodily adornment in efforts to paint don Diego and don Alonso as idolaters.

What defined a mestizo in the early colonial period? Parentage, color, attire, cultural practices, and language all came into play in self-presentation and in representations by others. In the sixteenth-century rural context, the vast majority of the population was composed of indios chontales who did not speak or understand Spanish; in Silva's and Torres's era many of them had not yet converted to Christianity. In their midst lived indios ladinos, some of them the children of local native families but many of them forasteros in the service of the encomenderos, hailing from other towns in the region or even from as far as Nicaragua and Peru, brought to the New Kingdom of Granada at the time of the Spanish invasion.[22] There was also a small number of mestizos and mulattos, as attested by the stories of Manuel Rodríguez and Lázaro Mulato. On the periphery of the native community—sometimes called the *repartimiento*, alluding to the inhabitants' status as tributaries to the Crown—lived mestizo and mulatto hired hands (laborers, cowboys, overseers) and African slaves toiling on Spanish estates. Over the course of their dispute, don Diego and don Alonso came to be at loggerheads with local indios ladinos, singling them out as guilty of overworking, stealing from, and physically abusing the native workforce. Certainly, the urbane, Spanish-speaking caciques ran a risk by singling out other, lower-status hispanophones who shared the landscape with the indigenous tributaries of Tibasosa and Turmequé, since it was their own bilingualism and adherence to European custom that, the two men argued, made them perfect candidates for the post of cacique.

Borrowing from (and paraphrasing) Judith Butler's recommendations for how to approach the process of "coming out," we might ask the following of don Diego de Torres and don Alonso de Silva: "For whom is [the label of mestizo] a historically available and affordable option? Is there an unmarked class character to ["outing" oneself as a mestizo]? Who is represented by *which* . . . term and who is excluded? For whom does [mestizo] present an impossible conflict between racial, ethnic, or religious affiliation and sexual politics? What kinds of policies are enabled by what kinds of usages and which are backgrounded or erased from view?"[23] Obviously, don Diego's and don Alonso's strategies of identification were highly dissimilar to those of gay people today, but the notion of coming out provides a useful angle for conceptualizing their bold foregrounding of their mestizo identity. Few mestizos enjoyed the freedom of expression and movement evinced by the two caciques, or their wealth of powerful political contacts in the capital of the Audiencia. For this reason, Butler's questions assist in scrutinizing with greater precision the rationales Silva and Torres employed to justify their impossible position in the colonial power structure.

The ambivalences and ironies of elite mestizo status in the early colonial period crystallize in the lives of don Alonso and don Diego, particularly in their command of the written word, which is where they argued the benefits of their mestizo condition. Like so many of their brethren, the two caciques are figures who are difficult to pin down. Their actions cannot be interpreted as those of indigenous actors, given their Spanish upbringing and their classification as mestizos, although they certainly spoke in the name of native people and were familiar with Muisca culture. While they belonged to the prosperous world of the encomenderos, as children of mixed parentage they were not entirely welcome there either, particularly among the encomenderos of Tunja. Luis Fernando Restrepo insists that don Diego frequently distanced himself from his subjects at the same time that he sought to protect them, referring to them in the third person as "miserable Indians" (*indios miserables*), a common trope of the time. But sometimes, Restrepo observes, Torres includes himself as one of the "miserables," using the first-person plural form of "nosotros," which would make him into an "indio."[24] This ambivalence must be further problematized by the fact that neither Silva nor Torres—nor any cacique, for that matter—would consider himself a humble indio, because as a noble he was of a higher social status, a grander calidad than were his subjects, who would never be his equals. Notably, the first-person plural usage cited by Restrepo appears more frequently in the documentation produced in the late 1570s and the 1580s, when Torres was in Spain, with a vast ocean separating him from the encomenderos, the Audiencia, and his subjects. The Bogotá record, dating from the early 1570s, unfolded on a smaller local scale, in a setting in which the caciques were at greater pains to distinguish more closely among the diverse actors, leading them to distance themselves more meticulously from the indigenous masses.[25] The ambivalence of mestizaje played out differently in distinct scenarios.

The challenge faced by the two caciques was how they were to negotiate the neither-nor status they occupied, how they might draw attention toward their more desirable qualities and encourage those surrounding them to forget the more common stereotypes associated with mestizos. They were obliged to set themselves apart from their subjects by emphasizing their own noble status, but were simultaneously forced to distance themselves, delicately, from nonindigenous commoners, whether mestizo or Spanish. This left them essentially placeless in the colonial world, because their claim to both European and Muisca nobility was highly precarious. Their unrootedness turned them into "inappropriate Others," who could not be clearly situated in any single ethnic camp; they refused to limit themselves to a single identity, thus placing their authenticity at risk when their cacicazgos were threatened.[26] This chameleon-like strategy necessitated, however, that the two men ally themselves firmly to powerful political factions, both in Spanish and indigenous circles. Unlike the mestizos whose everyday lives unfolded in restricted milieus, Silva and Torres were obligated to move across social scenarios, aligning themselves with multiple elites and claiming membership in various groups. In this sense, they were also different from Diego García Zorro, who enjoyed access to only one center of power, thanks to his position as regidor and his entrées into polite society through his father's associates; his private life, with his Indian wife and mestizo children, consigned him to the social spheres of the powerless. The mestizo caciques, in contrast, were intimately associated with the chiefly strata of their respective communities and of neighboring ones, as well as with the Spanish elite.

SITUATING THE MESTIZO CACIQUES: STRUGGLES FOR REFORM IN THE NUEVO REINO DE GRANADA

The legal battles of don Alonso de Silva and don Diego de Torres took place against a backdrop of intense factional struggle in the Nuevo Reino, erupting on the heels of the New Laws, issued in 1542, that sought to reform the worst abuses of the encomienda system, bringing it under Crown control. Royal attempts to wrest power from the encomenderos came to a head across Spanish America in the 1560s with the appointment of viceroys in Mexico and Lima who were to institutionalize colonial administration. Before the founding of these viceroyalties, Spain's colonial possessions in the Americas were characterized by an anarchy in which personal interest was paramount and rival factions of conquistadors warred with one another. While the Crown's power effectively weakened the reach of local powerholders in Lima and New

Spain, the process took considerably longer in the Nuevo Reino. When Andrés Venero de Leiva, the first president of the Audiencia of Santafé, assumed office, in 1564, he confiscated encomiendas from abusive encomenderos and redistributed tribute grants to those individuals he felt were most worthy; he also convened the religious and secular leadership of the Audiencia to legislate the just deployment of indigenous labor. However, it was not until the 1570s that these measures actually came into effect.[27]

Venero met strident opposition from the grandees of Santafé and Tunja, who sent a constant stream of slanderous grievances to Madrid, prompting the appointment in 1569 of the visitador Lope de Armendáriz, who was to conduct an investigation of the administrative workings of the Audiencia. After Armendáriz arrived, Venero ordered a series of inspections, which documented the abuse of indigenous labor in the goldmines, the mistreatment of native tributaries in Tunja, and the apathetic teaching of the Christian doctrine in the repartimientos. One of Venero's subordinates, Iñigo de Aranza, uncovered the theft from the royal treasury of a considerable sum by Audiencia officials. Clearly, public administration was in shambles in Santafé. Armendáriz singled out Venero, accusing him of a wide range of improprieties, including shady economic dealings, incomplete prosecutions of alleged mestizo rebels, and the persecution of Alonso de la Torre, the prosecutor of the Audiencia and one its president's most determined critics. Venero was removed from office in 1572 without having achieved the reforms he had hoped to implement.

Not surprisingly, the prosecutor Alonso de la Torre figured as one of the principal challengers of the petitions of don Diego de Torres and don Alonso de Silva. The mestizo caciques, whose own condemnations of the encomienda system echoed those of Venero, were intimately associated with some of the president's closest confidants. Most notably, they were allies of Aranza, a candidate for the position of notary after Silva's supervisor Diego de Robles vacated the post; Aranza came from a family line of notaries belonging to the minor nobility in Guipúzcoa, in the Basque country.[28] Aranza served as Silva's representative during the process of securing his chiefly title, and Silva lived for a time in Aranza's Santafé house.[29] The Basque noble also interceded on behalf of the cacique of Turmequé, pressing the Crown to cover the costs of Torres's funeral and burial when he died in Spain, in 1590.[30]

The appointment, in 1578, of Juan Bautista de Monzón, then a royal judge (*oidor*) in Lima, to conduct a far-ranging inspection in Santafé and Tunja set in motion a sequence of events that resurrected local opposition to Venero de Leiva's reform agenda a decade earlier, this time directed against Monzón. Monzón enjoyed only limited collaboration from Audiencia officials, whose foot-dragging forced him to dismiss a number of oidores. His investigations into the manipulation of treasury funds provoked a rebellion by the encomenderos of Tunja and Mariquita. He was accused of complicity with prominent mestizos, such as don Diego de Torres, who was charged with organizing an armed uprising.[31] The visitador was ultimately imprisoned, in 1581, along with the cacique of Turmequé. A second visitador, Juan Prieto de Orellana, assumed Monzón's duties, uncovering the theft of objects and the mistreatment of caciques during the Audiencia's campaign to extirpate idolatries by rooting out *santuarios* (indigenous ritual spaces) containing gold offerings.[32] Prieto de Orellana concluded that the orders contained in previous visitas had not been implemented, especially those concerning payments to indios for their services. He ordered a halt to encomendero occupations of indigenous lands, advocated reducing the presence of Spaniards in native communities, and barred priests from charging exorbitant fees for administering holy sacraments.[33] Diego de Torres stood in the eye of this hurricane, the instigator of Monzón's inspection, his crucial ally and co-conspirator against the Audiencia.

Venero's interrupted presidency and the witch-hunt against Monzón are not simply the historical backdrop to the story of the two mestizo caciques. Torres and Silva were intimately embroiled in the factional struggles taking place in Santafé. They were not innocent bystanders, but full-blown political actors, their activities impacting directly on the exercise of authority and the administration of native communities, as well as exacerbating the problematic relationship between the Audiencia and the Crown. In this sense, we cannot portray them in the timeworn framework of an iconic struggle between "indigenous victims" and "Spanish overlords," nor can we cast their allegations as a heroic native defense against malicious colonialists seeking to deprive them of their birthright. To the contrary, don Diego de Torres and don Alonso de Silva must be understood as consummate insiders, as it were, welcome in the halls of power in Santafé but castigated in the noble households of Tunja, at the same time that they maintained close relationships with some of their indigenous followers.[34] The question thus becomes: what kind of insiders were they? A look at the momentous transformations that Muisca cacicazgos underwent in the late sixteenth century offers a partial answer to this query.

At the time of the Spanish invasion, Muisca cacicazgos were pyramidal structures in which local territorial and kinship groups called utas nested into larger political units, called *sybyn* in Muisca (sybyn are referred to more commonly in the documentation by the Spanish term *capitanía*) and led by a capitán (which I translate as "captain") who inherited his position matrilineally from his mother's brother.[35] The capitanías, in turn, came together under the authority of rulers that the Spaniards called "caciques," bundling into a single term the *psihipcua*, who presided over groups of capitanías, and the *uzaques* or *bacatás*, who occupied a superior level in the chiefly social structure.[36] The hereditary lords of each level were hierarchically organized, following the model of a sibling group in which elder brothers occupied positions superior to younger ones. Thus, the ruler of a lesser capitanía occupied the position of the younger sibling in relation to the capitán of a hierarchically superior capitanía, the latter also possibly assuming the role of cacique over both units.[37] By the time of the arrival of the Spaniards, a number of caciques had consolidated power over groups of cacicazgos, including the caciques of Bogotá (called the *Zipa* in the chronicles) and Tunja (the *Zaque*), but also the caciques of Duitama and Sogamoso. All Muisca political units, ranging from the local utas to the regional cacicazgos, were anchored by communal ancestors and shrines.[38] Caciques were carried on litters, practiced polygamy, and had access to certain luxury goods (like gold and venison); their subjects were not permitted to look them in the face.[39] Their houses were surrounded by elaborate palisades (*cercados*) constructed with the labor of their subjects.[40]

After coming under Spanish rule the most powerful caciques ceded control over their vast territories and their authority was reduced to that of local capitanías and cacicazgos, although they did continue to exert informal influence over the vast territories they once ruled. This is evident in the dispute over the cacicazgo of Tibasosa, whose hereditary lord's appointment was subject to approval by the cacique of Sogamoso (CI 37, 460r). Although capitanías were assigned to individual encomenderos, the colonial administration did not appear to comprehend entirely what constituted a cacicazgo, how Muisca political hierarchies functioned, or which captains were subject to a given cacique. As a result, colonial capitanías came to be unmoored from their cacicazgos, resulting in numerous disputes over the affiliation of tributaries, a predicament that was compounded by population loss due to disease and a highly mobile indigenous population.[41] Over time, many caciques converted to Christianity and the elite-centered ancestor cult no longer anchored chiefly rule, although it was not until the latter part of the sixteenth century that friars had any success at all in converting native commoners; this is evident in the testimonies of witness upon witness in the Torres-Silva cases, most of whom were not baptized.[42]

Santiago Muñoz offers a novel interpretation of how cacicazgos in the Muisca area morphed over the course of the sixteenth century. He contends that we would do better to interpret the early colonial encomienda not exclusively as a vehicle for European exploitation of native peoples (which, of course, it certainly was), but also as a symbiotic arrangement through which caciques and encomenderos entered into reciprocal relations of production and exchange that were not entirely embedded in the colonial monetary economy and which were legitimized by the performance of autochthonous rituals acknowledging chiefly authority.[43] Muñoz bases his interpretation on the 1563 trial of the cacique of Ubaque, who had gathered hereditary lords from far and wide to accompany him in his funerary rites (he was ill, but still alive). Don Ubaque's encomendero, Juan de Céspedes—the father of the mestizo Juan de Céspedes—witnessed this ceremony, called a *biohote*, which is described in the documentation as an occasion for remembering history and looking toward the future; five or six thousand people attended the ritual, according to eyewitnesses.[44] Muñoz reasons that the biohote was a scenario in which the cacique's power was legitimized through a ritualized rejection of Christianity taking place under the acquiescing eye of the encomendero.[45]

By the 1580s, however, such rituals were harshly repressed, and a growing indigenous population began to embrace Christianity, or, at least, consented to the waters and oil of baptism. A new cacique appeared in Ubaque, don Francisco, a "good Christian" married to a mestiza (she is called an *"hija de español"* or "daughter of a Spaniard," as are Silva and Torres). Don Francisco was fluent in Spanish and was literate. He lived in a house decorated in the European fashion, slept in a European bed, ate at a European table, and dressed "in Spanish habit" (en ábito de español): "He has all of his appurtenances and costume, as

Figure 4.2. *Mural with the portrait of a hispanized cacique, Church of San Juan Bautista, artist unknown, ca. 1620, Sutatausa, Cundinamarca. Courtesy of Diana Murcia.*

much in his clothing as his household and table and customs, as any Spanish gentleman, and he always maintains arms and a horse and can provide all that is necessary in the service of Your Majesty" (fig. 4.2).[46]

Muñoz notes a particular usage that comes up repeatedly in witnesses' testimony: "Don Francisco, cacique of Ubaque, *although an Indian* [avnque yndio], is a man of great honor and his behavior is that of a Spanish Christian with much order [*policía*]," which he likens to a kind of positive or beneficial "passing" by the cacique, a brand of colonial mimicry by a subject who was no longer indigenous but not yet Spanish.[47] He widens our appreciation of don Francisco's mission to redefine the nature of chiefly office, describing how the cacique sought to destroy indigenous shrines instead of hosting biohotes and to sell off communal lands.[48] Don Alonso de Silva and don Diego de Torres were also part of this brave new world of hispanized, cosmopolitan, and fiercely Christian caciques, and their efforts to be recognized by their subjects were perhaps thwarted by local native reactions to these transformations in the nature of chiefly office.

CRAFTING A NARRATIVE OF CHIEFLY SUCCESSION

Urbane, educated, and hispanized, the two mestizo caciques were at pains first of all to legalize themselves as heirs to the cacicazgos of Tibasosa and Turmequé. Becoming a cacique meant verifying and legitimizing one's position in a noble matriline. Both don Diego and don Alonso were too young to occupy chiefly office when their maternal uncles died: they were not mature enough to sit on the *tiyana*, the stool occupied by the cacique during his installation, nor could they receive gifts of mantles from neighboring hereditary lords present at the ceremony.[49] Their duties were assumed by regents, in both cases their maternal uncles, who enjoyed the support of their encomenderos. Consequently, one of don Alonso de Silva's fundamental objectives was to prove that don Martín Cuyqui, his mother's younger brother and a regent, had no legitimate claim to the office. Silva argued that Nomensira, the cacique of Tibasosa at the time of the Spanish invasion, died without an heir, his title passing to his close relative Sugunmox and in turn to his sister's son, Guyaguaychara. At Guyaguaychara's death, the position was to be transmitted through his sister, doña Juana Sirita, to don Alonso de Silva, after a period of regency by don Martín (fig. 4.3). In order to substantiate this claim, Silva compiled a set of questions—an interrogatorio—to guide the depositions of members of the Tibasosa nobility and knowledgeable Spaniards, taking care to balance the specificities of his chiefly genealogy against the generalities of Muisca "uses and customs" (CI 61/3, 253r–v). As a notarial secretary, he knew the formulas for composing interrogatorios and the proper form that the depositions—the compilation of evidence was called a *probanza*—should take.

Silva substantiated his succession narrative with appeals to both Muisca and Spanish law. He emphasized that don Martín, as the *younger* brother of Guyaguaychara and doña Juana Sirita, was inferior to him in the line of succession (CI 61/3, 70r). In his interrogatorio he inquires into the hierarchy of Tibasosa's noble lineages, in effect drawing a road map for determining degrees of nobility among native authorities.

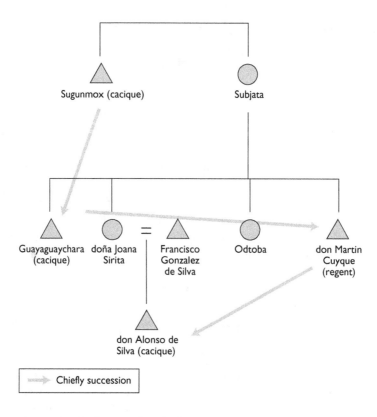

Figure 4.3. *Chiefly succession of Tibasosa, according to Alonso de Silva.*

Item, if [the witnesses] know that the caciques Sugunmox and Guyaguaychara, uncles of don Alonso de Silva, and doña Joana Sirita, his mother, and don Martin Cuyqui and his entire group of descendants and kin never were nor are they captains or *pregoneros* in the pueblo of Tibasosa, but they were and are of the very ancient generation and caste, that since time immemorial has inherited and been elected caciques, and they are the caciques of the pueblo of Tibasosa, and for this reason, in the language of the Indians themselves, they are called and named and have been called and named caymusi and çipascogi, which means caste and descendants eligible to be caciques and of caciques. (CI 37, 455v)[50]

In this seemingly irrelevant ethnographic detour, Silva draws on his knowledge of the Muisca language to explore the categories of kin groups that structured Tibasosa's nobility, focusing on captains and pregoneros, in order to establish the fact that his ancestors—who he alleges were caciques—belonged to a hierarchically superior line. The pregoneros mentioned by Silva were not town criers, as a Spanish gloss would suggest, but were those who inhabited a position called *guaysiga*, which was held by men who bore extensive genealogical knowledge, were empowered to represent caciques to outsiders, and could serve as regents in the absence of a chiefly title-holder (CI 37, 17r, 407v).[51] Silva makes these distinctions in an effort to contradict his opponents—not don Martín (who was his close kin), but others who were also clamoring for chiefly recognition.

Silva was aware that his status as the illegitimate son of a Portuguese soldier would interfere with his claim in the ambiguous space in which Muisca and Spanish law intersected, so he carefully outlined some of the differences between the two legal systems by questioning the relevance of Spanish notions of legitimacy to pre-Columbian uses and customs.

> Item, if [the witnesses] know that said law and custom has been and is customary and preserved by said order and in such a way that if one is the son of the sister of the cacique, in order to inherit the cacicazgo it has been and is only necessary that he be the son of the sister of the cacique, even if distantly, and although not legitimate, because among the Indians no one can be called legitimate, nor do they exist because they do not marry, nor do they have marriages, because the Indians have many women and they leave them when they wish. State what you know. (CI 61/3, 253r–v)[52]

Silva prodded his witnesses to explain that legitimacy was not at issue in a society that had never known the institution of Christian marriage. Those who testified in his favor argued that legitimacy was even more irrelevant for women of noble lineage, like don Alonso's mother: the royal interpreter, mestizo Juan de Lara, asserted that the sisters of caciques were "privileged and protected from the cacique's control [preuilegiadas e reserbadas de no estar subjetas al caçique]" and could "go where their fancy took them [andan por su albedro por do quieren]," adding that in any case, caciques had so many wives that there was no such thing as legitimate offspring (CI 61/3, 280v). Nevertheless, at the end of the interrogatorio, Silva reveals that his father, the conquistador Francisco González de Silva, had officially legitimized him, but that the papers authenticating this change in status had been lost (CI 61/3, 259r). That is, he struggled to reconcile two simultaneous and contradictory appeals to Muisca and European law, although perhaps Silva's attempts to square the circle by superimposing two distinct legal systems weakened his claims to the chiefship of Tibasosa, because by making these contradictory arguments he effectively hints at the fact that he might not have been the maternal nephew of the cacique but a more distant relative.

Don Alonso was a shrewd operator, as befitted a notarial secretary serving the phalanx of lawyers attached to the Audiencia. Both he and don Diego de Torres were careful to examine their witnesses in the safe haven of Santafé, distant from the maelstrom of Tunja, where too many conflicting interests were at play. They were strategic in the witnesses they interviewed, choosing only those who belonged to their own political faction.[53] Their strategy backfired, however. A stream of antagonistic testimony already collected from what appears to be a marginal bloc of the native nobility substantiated an alternative narrative of succession that locked don Alonso (and don Martín) entirely out of the chiefship.

A pretender by the name of don Laureano emerged from obscurity early on in the dispute, offering testimony through interpreters, for he and almost all of his supporters were chontales (they did not speak Spanish). In a series of startling statements, they asserted that cacique Nomensira did die without an heir, but they identified Sugunmox, his successor, as a member of the corps of pregoneros—lesser indigenous nobility—and hence, as a regent, not a title-holder (which is why Silva distinguished so carefully between different levels of native nobility in his ethnographic digression). Sugunmox was said to have been subsequently removed from office and his replacements—also pregoneros— died, one by one, of smallpox, forcing the assumption of the cacicazgo by yet another pregonero and regent, don Martín Cuyqui. In the interim, Nomensira's sister gave birth to a son, don Laureano, who had now stepped up to challenge don Alonso de Silva (CI 37, 398r–452v) (fig. 4.4).[54]

We will never know which of the three pretenders—don Martín Cuyqui, don Laureano, or don Alonso de Silva—was the rightful cacique of Tibasosa, despite don Alonso's popularity among many modern-day historians. The genealogy presented by Silva sidesteps the troubling gap between the conquest-era cacique and his successor, a chasm that don Laureano neatly fills with his genealogy. Nor will we be able

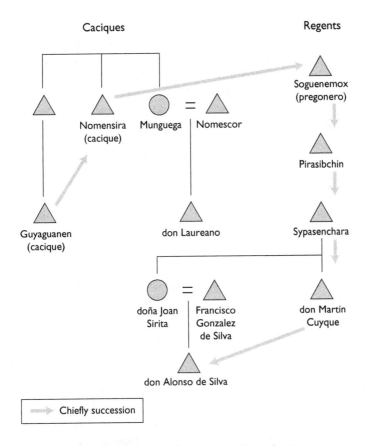

Caciques   Regents

Soguenemox
(pregonero)

Nomensira   Munguega   Nomescor
(cacique)

Pirasibchin

Guyaguanen   don Laureano   Sypasenchara
(cacique)

doña Joan   Francisco   don Martin
Sirita   Gonzalez   Cuyque
             de Silva

don Alonso de Silva

⟶ Chiefly succession

Figure 4.4. *Chiefly succession of Tibasosa, according to don Laureano.*

to decipher the particulars of the intense factionalism that encouraged
such heated conflicts, which quite likely emerged out of the massive
transformations in Muisca cacicazgos in the 1570s. We might imagine
don Laureano as representing an earlier brand of cacique, unfamil-
iar with Spanish custom or language and exercising an authority that
drew on the sort of hybrid colonial rituals recorded for Ubaque, perhaps performed with the collusion of encomenderos like Miguel Holguín. We might also speculate as to the fears that chontales like don
Laureano might have felt toward a devoutly Christian mestizo cacique
who could, potentially, promote the Audiencia's policy of extirpation
of idolatries, as did don Francisco in Ubaque. Don Martín states that
the people of Tibasosa were afraid that don Alonso de Silva "would
mistreat them, being, as he is, a Christian [que les trataria mal por ser

como es cristiano]" (CI 37, 430r). Don Martín was himself a Christian, although he was not the son of Christians, as was Silva. It is not simply Christian faith that is at stake in this statement, but the unwelcome and possibly disruptive intrusion of an alien European bloodline and set of cultural mores into the leadership of Tibasosa.

The presence of Spanish ancestors in a Muisca chiefly line did not appear to pose a threat to Silva's followers, although it did to the proponents of his adversaries. Robert Haskett reports that in seventeenth-century Cuernavaca, ruling families acknowledged being mestizos, even calling themselves Spaniards.[55] Certainly, other mestizo caciques in the Santafé-Tunja region were embraced unproblematically by their subjects. What is clear from the dispute over the cacicazgo of Tibasosa is that this was an internecine struggle over which model of chiefly authority would prevail. In this sense, perhaps the more pertinent question arising from the documentation is not who was the rightful cacique of Tibasosa, but who was the most *appropriate* one, and for whom. Haskett infers that Mexican mestizo rulers and their indigenous subjects expanded their notion of what constituted "Indian," so that it not only referred to the children of native men and women from a specific community, but had become a category defined in relation to the dominant Hispanic society: "Instead of viewing outsiders of any ethnicity as foreigners, they were coming to comprehend the existence of a broader group of 'Indians' with shared cultural traits and interests that were different from those of Hispanic society."[56] This shift in worldview enabled the acceptance of mestizos in positions of authority. It is not clear that this was the situation in Tibasosa and Turmequé, whose mestizo caciques rarely identified themselves as "indios" or even "indios caciques," preferring to simply call themselves "caciques," without referring at all to their socioracial classification. Instead, Silva and Torres offered what to Spaniards was an unlikely argument: that their mixed parentage—the very attribute the encomenderos and don Martín held to be unacceptable—made them the most suitable candidates for chiefly office.

GOOD BLOOD

What is remarkable about the documents penned by don Alonso and don Diego is how they strove to legitimize themselves as mestizos, even as their opponents maligned their mestizo condition. The Inca Garcilaso conveys the ambivalences of being called a mestizo in the following oft-quoted passage: "The children of Spaniards by Indians are called mestizos, meaning that we are a mixture of the two races. The word was applied by the first Spaniards who had children by Indian women, and because it was used by our fathers, as well as on account of its meaning, I call myself by it in public and am proud of it, though in the Indies, if a person is told: 'You're a mestizo,' or 'He's a mestizo,' it is taken as an insult."[57] Like Garcilaso, the two Colombian hereditary lords used their dual birthrights as sons of conquistadors and maternal nephews of caciques to confirm their legitimacy. They claimed that their suitability for office originated not only in their descent from previous caciques, but also in their Iberian genealogies (and their descent from the grandees of Tunja, the city in the Nuevo Reino with the largest number of nobles, whose coats of arms still grace the portals of their stately houses).[58] Diego de Torres was explicit about the connection between his mestizo status and his capacity to govern Turmequé.

> You will understand that by virtue of being the son of a Spaniard and a Christian, the President and Judges take my cacicazgo from me, and that it would have benefitted me more to be the son of an idolatrous Indian and not of a Christian [me uviera valido mas ser hijo de yndio ydolatra y no de crisptiano], understanding that as son of a Spaniard and Christian, as I am, I should have a stronger case because I am of such good blood, flowing from Spaniards and Christians [tan buena sangre proçedida de españoles y crisptianos], which is why all the caciques of this kingdom love me [me quieren y aman]. (Enc 21, 409r)

This is a clear statement of the conviction that mestizaje was a process through which Spanish blood "redeemed" native blood.[59] It also conveys Torres's keen sense of the extent of his power: the reference to love at the end of this passage, which is also repeated in some of the missives exchanged between Silva and his encomendero, should be interpreted in its early modern political context, in which it referred to allegiance to a sovereign, not to the romantic or social emotion.[60] In Torres's opinion, neighboring caciques exhibited love to him because of the overwhelming legitimacy and potency of his dual bloodline.

However much don Diego's glorification of his family tree showcased his Muisca descent alongside his European roots, he drew on his parallel genealogies in different and unequal ways. Descent from his maternal uncle, the previous cacique of Turmequé, provided him

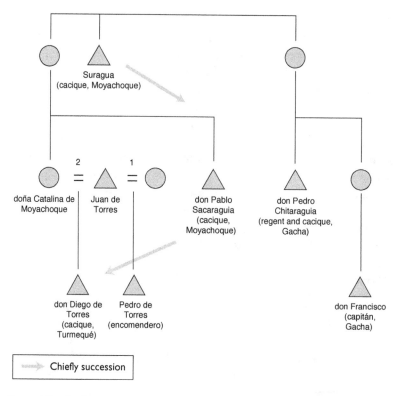

Figure 4.5. *Chiefly succession of Turmequé, according to don Diego de Torres.*

with the legal legitimacy he needed to occupy the cacicazgo, which he could not have inherited otherwise (fig. 4.5). However, he supported his genealogical claim with a Christian moral framework that justified why he, a mestizo, would be preferable to the various other indigenous pretenders to the same title. This involved an appeal to his essential Christian nature, which was constituted not simply by his profession of belief in the Christian doctrine, but by the very Christian blood he carried in his veins. As much as he appealed to his noble Muisca forebears, don Diego de Torres had no choice but to privilege his European roots in the late sixteenth-century political context.

Jean-Paul Zuñiga cogently argues that the principles inherent to both the notion of purity of blood and the concept of mestizaje in the early modern Spanish world lie in what he calls a "moral economy of blood," which distinguished commoners from aristocrats, as well as lesser noble lineages from their superiors. Mixing was thought to inexorably taint the reputation of descent lines. It was not so much that one became "half Jewish" or "half Indian" as a result of intermarriage, but that the standing of one's lineage as a whole was altered.[61] Mixing could potentially stain lineages and condemn their members to ignominy, such as when Jewish, Muslim, or heretic ancestors were discovered in bloodlines. But, as Zuñiga notes with a reference to Fray Benito de Peñalosa y Mondragón's *Libro de las cinco excelencias del español* (Book of the Five Excellences of the Spaniard), noble blood was also like mercury insofar as it purified other, baser bloods, just as mercury purifies silver.[62] Peñalosa y Mondragón directs readers' attention to the Visigoths and Arabs on the Iberian Peninsula, whose lineages, he argues, were improved by mixture with the first inhabitants (whom he calls the Tubalos), just as mestizos were an improvement on American natives.

> And if the nations that in ancient times peopled Spain . . .
> were without doubt so warlike and brave, much of their valor
> came not only from their good land and the heavens, but they
> also had the mixture of Spanish blood from the first Tubalos,
> retaining always their family tree [*tronco*] and purity in the
> mountains. Today we have experienced the same in the Indies,
> where the pure natives are very inferior to Spaniards, but in
> mixing their blood with them, they are capable of more, as are
> the mestizos born of Spaniard and india.[63]

Don Diego de Torres stood on firm ground when he extolled the merits of his Spanish ancestry and celebrated how it enhanced his Muisca bloodline. Nonetheless, in the combative worldview of the encomenderos of Tunja, his noble Iberian family tree would still have been judged as having received the taint of his Muisca mother's blood.

AN "INAPPROPRIATE" CACIQUE

Mestizos were legally barred from residing in indigenous repartimientos because of the moral and economic harm they presumably caused there. This forced the mestizo caciques to distance themselves from undesirable mestizo commoners and play up their noble heritage, which Silva accomplishes in the following quotation.

> It is not an impediment . . . that your judges who have visited
> these lands ordered that mestizos not live in repartimientos,

because this does not apply to those who are the rightful successors to cacicazgos, as I am, nor are they to be understood in the aforementioned orders. Instead, they refer to those mestizos, and even Spaniards, who idly roam this land without any employment or privileges to support them, because one must presume that by being in the communities they will mistreat the natives, and this will come to an end with caciques like me, who have the right, [and] it is to be presumed, no one will better attain the health and conservation of his subjects and vassals than their lord or cacique. (CI 61/3, 117v)

In other words, while he believed the commonly held assumption that mestizos endangered native communities, he felt it could not possibly hold for men like Silva, in whose veins flowed noble Muisca blood.

Nevertheless, being of chiefly blood did not protect Silva and Torres from the accusation made against all mestizos: that they were of illegitimate birth. Don Diego's half brother Pedro luridly made this case against the cacique of Turmequé, deploying a time-worn and venomous stereotype: "A spurious mestizo born of the questionable copulating adultery of a married man and a common Indian woman, and not a descendant of the legitimate caciques" (Enc 21, 404r).[64] Pedro de Torres thus accused don Diego not of being an hijo natural, a natural son born out of wedlock to two unencumbered parents, but of being a *bastardo*, born of an illicit relationship in which one of the parties was already married; the latter status could not be as easily assuaged by legal sleight-of-hand, such as recognition of paternity or formal legitimization, as could the former.[65] Don Diego countered his half brother by maintaining that he was the child of a legitimate Catholic marriage, his father's second, since Juan de Torres had already been married once in Spain.

Alonso de Silva was also accused of being a bastard: "He is not only an hijo natural, but is also a spurious child of adultery, born of a man who at the time of his conception and birth was married in the kingdoms of Spain, as has been verified" (CI 61/3, 370r).[66] Note the formulaic nature of encomendero Miguel Holguín's accusation, which mirrors the words of Pedro de Torres. Juan de Orozco, one of Holguín's witnesses, embellished the accusation with a convoluted narrative of sexual license by Silva's father.

[After] Francisco de Silva was in this city and kingdom, more or less twenty years ago he went to the kingdoms of Spain where

it was said that he was married and had his wife, and they said
that when the aforementioned went to the kingdoms of Spain,
he went there for his wife, and when he went to the town to
get her and bring her here, he found her married to a mulatto
and black ironsmith [mulato e negro herrero] and that she hid
herself so as to not come back with him, and he found her there
with the children by the blacksmith, and seeing that he left her
and returned to this kingdom and brought with him a woman
called "La Basquez" who is a midwife [and] whom Francisco
de Silva wanted to marry. And when the ecclesiastical judge
Matamoros found out . . . he impeded it and made sure that the
marriage did not take place. And this witness does not remember if Alonso de Silva was born at that time, and if Alonso de
Silva was born in any of those times, with the wife of Francisco de Silva alive, it is notorious he is born of a married man.
(CI 61/3, 222r–v)

The evidence that Silva was a bastard, and not just an hijo natural, was
damning. The argument he so cogently articulated—that legitimacy
was not an issue in the Muisca system of chiefly succession because
there was no Christian marriage—began to unravel with this assertion, for if Silva hoped to appeal simultaneously to his Muisca and
Spanish noble roots, his legitimacy would also be subject to European
scrutiny, and not only was his father, reportedly, not just an adulterer,
but his European wife was consorting with a mulatto of questionable
descent. What Silva and Torres needed was to steer clear of the label of
mestizo, with the perilous stains it carried.

Juan Felipe Hoyos observes that don Diego de Torres was careful
in the early stages of his lawsuit to avoid the appellation "mestizo"
and to speak, instead, of being the "son of Spaniard and Christian"—a
phrase also used to describe the mestiza wife of don Francisco of
Ubaque.[67] "Sons of Spaniards" were mestizos who adopted Spanish
culture, counterposed to rural mestizos, who were perceived as illegitimate.[68] In fact, Fray Francisco de Gaviria, a Franciscan from Tunja,
said of the mestizo caciques: "They are more Spaniard than Indian
[son mas españoles que yndios]" (CI 61/3, 241v). By employing "hijo de
español"—a usage that predates "mestizo"—Torres effectively skewed
his genealogy toward his father's side, ignoring his mother's.[69] But by
taking this tack he also weakens his claim to a Muisca noble lineage.
Ultimately, like the Métis interpreter Andrew Montour, of eighteenth-

century Pennsylvania, whose facial paint clashed with his European clothing and provoked puzzled reactions from observers, Torres was to some degree "handicapped by [his] own ambiguity."[70]

Torres was particularly irritated with the indios ladinos who lived alongside his subjects and consistently abused them: "In said repartimiento there is an indio ladino named Luisico, in the service of Partearroyo, vecino of the city of Tunja, who disturbs the Indians, directing the blacks in the pueblo to take away their mantles so that they weed and plow the land for the farms of the aforementioned blacks and [the] indio ladino [Luisico], three leagues distant from the repartimiento" (CI 61/4, 470r). Note that Torres identifies Luisico as a man in the service of Partearroyo, a vecino of Tunja, describing him as doing his bidding. The encomendero Diego de Partearroyo had a mestizo son who inherited the encomienda grant from his father in the early 1580s, so it is possible that Luisico's master was of mixed parentage himself.[71]

The mestizo commoners and indios ladinos from whom Torres and Silva sought to distance themselves posed a threat to the colonial order because their behavior was offensive to Europeans. As remarked Duarte Núñez, a witness from Tunja testifying on behalf of Miguel Holguín, "Said mestizos are very independent and impudent [muy libres e atrevidos], and every day they go on multiplying, as much in their numbers as in their vices" (CI 61/3, 230r). Mestizos introduced natives to "many evils and treacheries and other defects that could redound in bad examples for the natives, with their bad customs [mal biuir]," warned Martín de Rojas, a lifetime member of the city council of Tunja (CI 61/3, 245v).

What was truly offensive was the fact that it was so difficult to pinpoint with any precision who was an indio ladino and who was a mestizo, since in rural areas many people belonging to both categories behaved like Spaniards. Juan Anacona, a Nicaraguan indio ladino attached to the encomendero Pedro de Torres was described as "a Christian indio ladino who was like a Spaniard [un yndio ladigno y cristiano que era como español]" (Enc 21, 440r). The corps of indios ladinos in Turmequé kept itself separate from the other natives. Alonso, who testified on behalf of Pedro de Torres, responded to a question about non-Christian rites taking place in Turmequé: "He has not seen what the question says because he is an indio ladino and he does not want to live among the chontales" (Enc 21, 556r). Don Diego de Torres condemned these outsiders for their laziness, which he attributed to the fact that they did not operate under the supervision of the native authorities. He went on to describe how the indios ladinos of Turmequé passed their time: "There were many gamblers, as much in card games as in bowls, that those indios forasteros set up for the chontales, a very common way to rob them" (Enc 21, 411v).[72]

The untrustworthiness of the indio ladino mirrored that of the mestizo. The very broadness of the definition of who was an indio ladino caught mestizos in its snare, particularly given the fact that there were many mestizos living in the countryside, dressed in the native costume of their mothers.[73] The bilingualism of don Diego de Torres and don Alonso de Silva propelled them into serving as intermediaries between the largely chontal populations of their repartimientos and their encomenderos or Crown officials; however, like lettered, bilingual caciques throughout the Americas, they were also perceived as being dangerous, even more so than were mestizo commoners or indios ladinos, because not only could they communicate with the natives, but their political legitimacy brought them to the fore as skilled and charismatic organizers.[74] The caciques' repeated efforts at quelling abuses of chontales by indios ladinos, mestizos, and mulattos turned these unaffiliated rural denizens against them and into the hands of their employers, the encomenderos. Tibasosa and Turmequé present a palimpsest: an internal power struggle within Tibasosa's and Turmequé's indigenous elite, overlain by a contest between local mestizos, ladinos, and urban caciques for the hearts and minds of the indios chontales, which was, in turn, encased in a third rivalry between mestizo and Spanish members of the urban elite, itself ultimately framed by the efforts of the encomenderos to put the brakes on Crown reforms of the colonial economic and political system.

LITERACY AND MESTIZO REBELLION

Silva's and Torres's literacy—understood in the sense not only of their command of written Spanish, but, even more so, of their command of the Spanish legal system and its notarial conventions—brought them into the foreground of these three overlapping disputes, to which they contributed thousands of pages of legal petitions now housed in Colombian and Spanish archives. Literacy bound Silva and Torres to their encomenderos in multiple ways. In the years before the suit, don Alonso de Silva and the encomendero Miguel Holguín maintained not only a cordial relationship, but an affectionate one, as evinced by a series of letters between the two men regarding everyday matters. Holguín routinely addressed the cacique as "the very magnificent señor, my son [muy magnifico señor hijo]" and in one of the missives told Silva, "I received your letter and was very content, understanding the love you have for me [entendydo tengo el amor que me teneis] and sure that you are not deceived, that all my life I will hold you as a son [toda mi vida vos terne por hijo]" (CI 61/3, 162r).[75] While such forms of address and protestations of affection are clearly formulaic, they suggest, at the least, a relationship of mutual respect and recognition (which is the reason Silva included them as evidence to support his case). They also constitute discursive modes of mutually recognizing the legitimacy and power of the two correspondents, as expressions of love were integral to forms of rule in the early modern world.[76] However, the condemnations made by the two caciques over the abusive treatment their encomenderos meted out to their subjects soured this relationship, and in this way literacy also fueled conflict.

The enmity that emerged between the caciques and their encomenderos, and the slurs hurled against Silva and Torres by their opponents, betray global events that extended far beyond their personal relationships with Miguel Holguín and Pedro de Torres. As Kathryn Burns observes, "The making of 'mestizos' was a politically charged, historical process." Throughout Spain's American possessions, mestizos came at midcentury to be seen as a potential threat, "as a group of frustrated, armed, and dangerous aspirants to the legacies of their Spanish fathers" who might rise up, as had the converted Muslims in the Alpujarras revolt in Spain in the late 1560s.[77] Indeed, the fear of elite mestizos like Torres and Silva was pervasive in sixteenth-century Santafé and Tunja. Anxieties over the possibilities of a mestizo-indigenous alliance peaked after Diego de Torres took his lawsuit to Madrid and allied himself with Juan Bautista de Monzón, the visitador sent by the Crown to investigate abuses in the encomienda system. Alarmed by revolts that had erupted in Quito, the Audiencia worried that Torres would spread such sentiments to Santafé, as revealed by a missive the Santafé authorities sent to the Crown in 1583.

> [Regarding] what happened in Quito, Your Majesty will understand the mistreatment by these mestizos and the danger in which we live with them, and Your Majesty should believe that the justice done by Licenciate Pedro Vanegas de Cañaveral, your magistrate, has been a very good idea, and if he continues his proceedings we will discover the mother lode that leads to this

region. Because it has already arrived in Anserma and Cartago, where three mestizos guilty of conspiracy were arrested, and they say that one is the brother of Diego Machado, a comrade of don Diego de Torre, the mestizo from Turmequé, and another, Marcos de Ayala, a conceited man and a great friend of don Diego's and of all the mestizos of these lands, who, when taken prisoner, escaped. It is clear that don Diego corresponded and communicated with those in Quito, and if we take care we can verify this. And now, we have news in missives from the mayor [*alcalde ordinario*] and other people in Anserma, written to a Florencia Serrano and Melchor Vázquez Campusano and others who are in this city [Santafé], to the effect that on the very day of Corpus those in Quito had arranged for the mestizos from Anserma to kill the judicial authorities and the Spaniards and rise up.[78]

Of particular note is the fact that Spanish anxieties revolved around mestizo literacy. The pen was understood to be a potent and deadly instrument when wielded by individuals of mixed descent.

According to his opponents, the cacique of Turmequé courted his subjects by promising to write petitions in their favor, which, indeed, he did (CI 61, 213r–v). But literacy was also believed to constitute a tool of violent subversion. The Audiencia magistrate Francisco Auncibay y Bohórquez accused Diego de Torres of organizing neighboring caciques by post from Spain:

We have been informed that while on the road [Torres] wrote some letters to the caciques of the Indians, especially to the [cacique] of Bogotá, calling himself the head of all the Indians, the lord of the valleys of Turmequé, and promising them liberty and other nonsense. We realize that with the confidence that they place in him, if he returns [from Spain] to these parts, he will go to the Llanos [the plains to the east of Santafé], where he can organize all the Indians and mestizos of this kingdom.[79]

In early 1580 there was great alarm in Tunja over a possible attack to be led by Diego de Torres, which would purportedly involve theft of the royal seal, the ultimate symbol of the Spanish "lettered city."[80] Whether there really were plans afoot for a general indigenous-mestizo rebellion is doubtful, although the extensive contacts that Torres and

Silva had with the majority of the powerful caciques of the altiplano is substantiated by the roster of witnesses who testified in their support.[81]

The meaning of "mestizo" in these letters is focused, precise. It centers not so much on the shortcomings of the caciques' sociracial classification, as on the threats inherent to a particular type of mixed-blood individual: a man of letters, a chiefly indio ladino-cum-mestizo operating simultaneously out of his urban notarial perch and his palisade in the repartimiento, an agitator who could potentially cause a legal mess for the powers that be.[82] But presumably, this was not enough for the encomenderos of Tunja, who pursued all possible leads in their efforts to defame the two chiefly pretenders, even when their smears contradicted one another. At the same time that the encomendero Pedro de Torres accused don Diego of being the sophisticated and worldly leader of a mestizo rebellion, he pursued a parallel strategy that demonized his half brother by targeting him as an idolater—another slur commonly hurled against mestizo commoners and indios ladinos living in rural areas, who were thought to be imperfectly Christianized. It was also an effective insult against don Diego de Torres, depriving him of the claim that his "good blood" made him a better cacique than the other pretenders to the hereditary lordship of Turmequé. Finally, the way in which Pedro de Torres accused his mestizo brother painted him as occupying the status of a woman.

CHRISTIAN MESTIZOS AND IDOLATROUS NATIVES

Don Diego de Torres was maligned as a subversive because of his versatility in written Spanish, while at the same time he was excoriated as a heathen (who, presumably, would remain aloof from the trappings of European culture). His encomendero identified him as the leader of offensive rites and ceremonies ostensibly taking place in Turmequé. In particular, Pedro de Torres declared that his half brother was guilty of the following transgressions: "Aggravating even more his iniquities, he has stripped himself of his Spanish habits at the drunken orgies [borracheras] and dances and put on Indian mantles and dressed in that habit, he has stood before the Indians of the repartimiento and with his own hands painted their skin red in offense of God" (Enc 21, 404r). It appears astonishing that the encomendero could equate the hispanized and devoutly Catholic mestizo with such activities, but it was, in fact, a common trope of the time.[83]

Pedro de Torres metaphorically cloaked his half brother Diego in native costume, insinuating that he was a particular type of "mestizo in Indian habit" by accusing him of cross-dressing in a native ritual context. Ares Queija argues that Peruvian mestizos hiding from the authorities disguised themselves in indigenous costume.[84] This was certainly a preoccupation voiced by a colonial administration confronted by mestizo rebels hiding under cover of the costume of their native relatives. But almost no mestizos clad in Muisca mantles surface in the documentary record for Santafé and Tunja, and the mestiza women who dressed in native clothing were more confusing than intimidating to Spanish observers. In fact, throughout the Spanish colonial world, indigenous men wearing *European* garb were considerably more threatening than were mestizas in Indian habits, particularly urbane and literate caciques who defended their subjects against the depredations of the encomenderos.[85] It was not only the Spaniards who found ethnic cross-dressing mortifying, an act that turned the world upside down. Witness Felipe Guaman Poma de Ayala's declaration on the proper costume to be worn in native communities: "How good each one looks in his own costume, the principal cacique dressed as a principal cacique, the Indian like an Indian, the female nobility [*la principala*] as a lady, and the Indian woman like an Indian woman, so that they will all be recognized and respected and honored."[86]

Outside of the repartimientos, where perhaps mestizos as well as mestizas may have worn the same clothing as the rest of the population, the option of dressing in native garments was resolutely gendered. One might spy female cross-dressers sporting native cotton mantles over linen blouses and underskirts of European confection on the streets of sixteenth-century Bogotá and Tunja, but all men wore some version, however humble, of European dress. The mestiza in Indian habit was among the most marginal of mestizas, so it is telling that Pedro de Torres equated his cosmopolitan brother with the lowest class of servants—female servants, at that—as a way of taking him down a notch, or several notches. By cloaking don Diego in Indian habit, Pedro de Torres did not seek to transform his half brother into an indio (just as indigenous dress did not make a mestiza in Indian habit into an india). Don Diego, like any hereditary lord, self-consciously distanced himself from his subjects by his behavior, his language, and his attire, just as did don Francisco in Ubaque, costume being one of the ways he constructed such distance. Nor was Pedro de Torres seeking to feminize the cacique. Instead, he was playing on the common stereotype of mestizos as backsliders who only partially embraced Christianity, a trope that don Diego and don Alonso also employ in their depositions of witnesses and their condemnations of the excesses of their encomenderos. Pedro de Torres meant to imply not that the cacique *dressed* like an Indian, but that he *acted* like one, just as did many of the indios ladinos and mestizos who plagued the tributaries of Turmequé. What the encomendero intended when he accused his brother of dressing in Indian habit was to recast don Diego as a mestizo commoner, perhaps the most disparaging portrayal he could have possibly uttered about his opponent.

Pedro de Torres's accusation of cross-dressing opens other unanticipated windows into don Diego de Torres's performance of his identity, further complicating our understanding of his predicament. During one of his incarcerations, Diego, an experienced jouster,

> [was] set free from the prison where he was held, and your
> prosecutor, who today accuses him, and licenciado Zorrilla,
> your oidor, gave him their horses so he could ride them . . . and
> ordered him to teach their sons, kinsmen, and followers to use
> a lance and a shield on horseback. And they persuaded him to
> play, as he did, with lance and shield, in jousting competitions
> at the doors of the royal buildings in the presence of your pres-
> ident and judges and prosecutor, on their own horses, in public
> view.[87]

The *juego de cañas*, a distinctively Spanish form of jousting, came originally from North Africa. Its players rode on saddles with short stirrups and high seats, carrying rounded shields called *adargas* and light canes different from those common to the northern European form of the sport. Players wore characteristically Moorish clothing, including cloth wrapped around their heads in a style that suggested a turban (fig. 4.6). Barbara Fuchs makes a convincing case that the borrowing of Moorishness in a ceremonial and chivalric setting was part of an "Andalusi habitus," an appropriation of North African lifeways that was no longer self-conscious but had come to merge so intimately with Christian Iberian culture as to no longer be considered exotic by Spaniards (although foreign observers did see it as patently Islamic).[88]

Diego de Torres is, in fact, portrayed in this manner in chapter 14 of Rodríguez Freile's *El carnero*. He has just broken out of prison through a large hole in the window, after having been served a meat pie (an *empanada*) that contained two knives for cutting his chains and a sheet of paper with instructions. A witness spies him in a field owned by

Figure 4.6. The Game of Canes, *1538, Jan Cornelisz Vermeyen, private collection. Courtesy of Photographic Survey, The Courtauld Institute of Art, London.*

"Zorro" (perhaps one of the García Zorros?): "I saw a man come out on a good horse, with a lance and an adarga, and he made straight for Zorro's lodgings."[89]

Imagine, then, a young mestizo pretender to the cacicazgo of Turmequé, his Spanish father an hijodalgo, plucked out of prison where he has been languishing as a dangerous rebel and deposited on the plaza's playing field before a huge and cheering crowd. Quite possibly, he was dressed in a Moorish-style cloak, perhaps with his head encased in a turban, carrying a round shield, amusing the spectators with his equestrian prowess. No longer a "mestizo in Indian habit," Diego de Torres is transformed into a "mestizo in Moorish habit." In this guise he might be considered equally (but differently) threatening, carrying a similar (but distinct) tinge of the non-Christian. Yet Torres in Moorish habit embodies all that is Iberian in his mestizo body: a crossdresser, passing simultaneously for Moor and Iberian noble, and resolutely masculine. For the moment, the treacherous rebel, armed and on horseback, is no longer threatening to his Spanish audience: he has briefly appropriated Spanish masculinity as his own.

Notably, this scenario was not singled out by Torres's enemies, because, living in the New World, they did not perceive any danger in

Moorish garb. Despite the fear sown by converts from Islam in the Morisco rebellions taking place on the Iberian Peninsula in the late sixteenth century, in the American context Torres was more easily equated with the Alpujarras Rebellion in his role as an idolatrous mestizo in Indian habit than when he donned respectable Moorish garments (respectable, at least, in the context of the juego de cañas). Don Diego is at his most Iberian when he is on horseback. It is at this moment that mestizo gives way to Spanish, and the utter impossibility of painting him with a single brush as "indio" or even as "mestizo" becomes apparent. Don Diego de Torres is clearly a more complicated figure than that.

CONCLUSION

Antonio Cornejo Polar writes of Garcilaso Inca de la Vega that it is difficult to separate the Inca and the Spanish strands of his experience because each of them constituted the grounds on which the other was predicated.

> What I want to say is that it will be necessary to know with more certainty the extent to which Garcilaso was able to articulate an indigenous consciousness . . . with the classical and Renaissance conscience, or how he instrumentalized it to resolve his own problems; or how his insertion into Western culture erased the memory of that indigenous consciousness, which was for many reasons indecisive. In other words, I don't know now if Garcilaso appropriated European culture or if European culture appropriated him.[90]

Cornejo Polar's quandary is mirrored in the tale of the two mestizo caciques from Tunja. Don Diego de Torres and don Alonso de Silva were "insiders-outside," in the parlance of the African American feminist theorist Patricia Hill Collins, and they straddled multiple and conflicting identities.[91] But what constitutes the "inside" for them as mestizos is difficult to determine: were they insiders because their indigenous mothers were the sisters of caciques or because their Spanish fathers were among the "first conquistadors of the Nuevo Reino de Granada"—or possibly because of both? Were they outsiders because they defended their Christian blood in order to lead a community that was largely non-Christian? Did their descent from Old Christians only confirm their (in)appropriateness as late sixteenth-century caciques?

What did they share with their mestizo commoner brethren or their Spanish half siblings, both of whom occupied a discernible position in colonial society? The quandary that the two mestizo caciques faced exemplifies the challenges presented by efforts to define what mestizo signified in early colonial Tunja and Santafé.

5. "Asi lo Paresçe por su Aspeto"

Physiognomy and the Construction
of Difference in Colonial Santafé

In mapping the predicaments of individual mestizos and mulattos—
the sometimes ambivalent and frequently painful choices they were
forced to make as they fashioned their identities, as they contested or
eluded those made by Crown officials, and as they forged bonds with
people they recognized as belonging to their peer group—I have addressed a certain set of questions: under what circumstances do these
individual mestizos live? How do they drop in and out of the mestizo
slot? Why and in what situations would someone come out as a mestizo
or be outed by others? A twenty-first-century mindset would question
why physical appearance is not at the center of my vignettes. To be
sure, in some of the examples I have analyzed, skin color is mentioned
as a possible identifying feature of mestizos, for example, in the case of
Isabel de Sotelo, who was said to "look like" a mestiza, but only after
she was accused of being one. The documentary record is surprisingly
bereft of arguments centering on racial physiognomy, although some
of the documents contain brief descriptions of what these individuals
were reported to look like. This chapter will explain why this should
be the case.

Catalina Acero de Vargas claimed that Francisco Suárez's appearance and diction betrayed his calidad, although she doesn't provide
any particulars, indicating that she read important cues from his
aspect, which she may have found difficult to define. In other documents I found more precise descriptions. Witnesses testified that Diego
Romero had brown skin, curly hair, and a facial tic that caused one
eye to open and close with frequency; his associates in Spain thought
he looked like a Moorish slave, but no one in Santafé had questioned
his appearance until he was brought up on charges of being a New

Christian.[1] Fr. Gonzalo García Zorro's description could have been that of any dark-complexioned Spaniard: "brown of face [moreno de rostro], black beard that is growing out [barbinegro que le apuntan]."[2] Likewise, don Diego de Torres's distinguishing characteristics do not necessarily mark him as a mestizo: "a good-sized man [hombre de buen cuerpo], not very tall [no muy alto], robust [robusto], a bit cross-eyed [un poco visco de los ojos], and with scant beard [de pocas barbas]."[3] García Zorro and Torres could be easily confused with many Spaniards in the Nuevo Reino. Their physical descriptions do not differ, for example, from that of Romero, who was from Spain. What made them "mestizo" was not how they looked, but how observers, allies, and opponents identified them; this depended on their bearing, clothing, speech, behavior, and peer group, in addition to their physical characteristics.

The juxtaposition of aspect (appearance) and calidad (socioracial category) can be explored through ethnographic case studies, but a wide-angle view is also necessary, in order to make sense of how adjectives used to describe physical appearance intermeshed with the broad socioracial categories that actors negotiated on the ground. Illuminating in this context is the visual practice of bureaucrats, who in the course of their labors were required to describe the appearance of those who came before them as petitioners, tributaries, or prisoners. While Crown officials were more likely to embrace the very classificatory schemes that actors on the ground thought of as negotiable, they did not possess the vocabulary necessary to make sense of the diversity that lay before them in the New World; the descriptive adjectives at their disposal did not effectively differentiate mestizos from indios, nor did they facilitate distinguishing among the different residents of a native pueblo. In effect, a wide-angle examination of how bureaucrats observed people in the flesh further strengthens the contention that "mestizo," "mulatto," "indio," "negro," and "español" operated not as stable categories akin to racial groupings that can be identified physically but as floating signifiers that can only be interpreted situationally.

I have thus far taken a largely ethnographic approach, producing "thick descriptions" by exploring in depth the experiences of particular individuals and by extracting from the documentary record an interpretation of the contradictions generated in the process of socioracial classification. I now shift my ethnographic imagination to focus on the general process of classification, and thus recruit documentation of a different nature. The physical descriptions contained in the historical record are brief, frequently one or two sentences long, appearing primarily in certificates granting travel permission or in lists of tributaries or taxpayers. There is little in these documents about the lives of the people inscribed in them. They record procedures that are exceedingly routine and repetitive, with cursory descriptions of individuals as tall or short, bearded or clean-shaven, brown-skinned or pale. It is such repetition and the use of the same adjectives across documents, sometimes replicated under apparently contradictory circumstances, that interest me. Such documents certainly help to construct an ethnographic scenario, but this is primarily due to their quotidian redundancies and their formulaic nature, rather than to the striking images and pointed language they might contain.

My ethnographic vignettes have clearly demonstrated that classificatory practices were not entirely premised on physical appearance, but were considerably more complex. Only after comprehending that "Spaniard," "Indian," and "mestizo" were not self-evident categories arising out of the natural process of human reproduction, only after appreciating that the meanings of these terms were not stable across time or space, and only after recognizing that the classificatory process was not dependent on a set of rigidly circumscribed physical attributes can we begin to problematize visual practices. Indeed, colonial vision was a multifaceted process of identification, not a verification of stable identities.

MULATTO OR INDIAN?

One day in early 1627, Juan Mulato, a young slave in the city of Santafé, was marched by his master, Juan de Segura, into the workshop of the silversmith Juan de Otálora, who branded his cheeks with a rebus containing the letter S and an image of a nail (*clavo*)—spelling out "*esclavo*" or "slave"—to ensure that he would not run off, as he had done many times before.[4] Otálora's testimony to the Audiencia revealed that he had been deeply troubled by the hideous task and had postponed it for a month before relenting and marking the child, who was only five years old. Juan Mulato's ordeal was brought to the attention of the colonial authorities by a merchant, Diego de León, who told a neighbor that he was "horrified, that not in Barbary nor in Turkey would what Juan de Segura did occur, which is to brand a little mulatto, the son of a Pijao, being that all of the Pijao Indians are free."[5]

What horrified Diego de León was not so much the fact that a five-year-old child had been branded on the face, but rather that the boy should not have been branded because he was a free Indian, not a slave. The crux of the Crown's case against Segura revolved around the assertion that little Juan Mulato was free because he was the son of Catalina, a Pijao woman purchased in Mariquita, a mining center on the Magdalena River. The Pijaos had resisted Spanish incursions throughout the sixteenth century, and many of them were sold into slavery in an effort to stem their insurgency. The enslavement of recalcitrant native groups was permitted for limited periods, despite the fact that indigenous slavery was abolished in 1542 under the New Laws. After the Spanish forces won the war against the Pijao in the early seventeenth century, the Crown decreed an end to their enslavement. In the wake of these events unfolding on the larger colonial stage, Crown prosecutors endeavored to prove that Juan was Pijao like his mother and hence not subject to slavery.[6]

Despite the Crown's central argument concerning his Pijao identity, Juan is consistently described as *looking like* a mixed-race person, "in appearance, half Indian and mulatto [al pareçer medio yndio y mulato]"; moreover, he is identified by calidad through the use of the surname-like soubriquet "Mulato," as were many non-Spaniards belonging to subordinated categories (73r). Of course, Juan's mulatto appearance and his rights as a free person were not necessarily in contradiction, since there were free mulattos in Santafé. This is conveyed by another label in which he is called "Juan free mulatto [Juan mulato libre]" (104r). Neither the prosecutor nor Juan de Segura claimed that Juan's slave status owed to his mixed parentage. Rather, the fact of his black father was incidental to the dispute over his status as a free person, which derived from his Pijao mother. However, the documentation is ambiguous with regard to Juan's identity: some officials describe him as a mulatto with a native mother, while others identify him as an "Indian of the Pijao nation [vn yndio muchacho de nacion pixaguo]" (71r), suggesting that they did not agree on his classification but nevertheless concurred over his free status.[7] The simultaneous appeal to Juan's physical appearance, which associated him with one category, and his genealogy, which connected him to another, provides a telling example of the frequently disregarded fact that terms like "mulatto" or "mestizo" carried specific but ambiguous meanings in early colonial Santafé. In the legal domain they identified particular permutations of mixed parentage, constructing legal truths that determined how people were to lead their lives.[8] But at the same time, they frequently overlapped or contradicted other labels, equally legal in nature, that were assigned to specific individuals. Juan's dual identification suggests, moreover, that the early colonial sociracial hierarchy cannot be understood simply as a "pigmentocracy" in which "people were classified in accordance with the color of their skin," but that the categories they either willingly inhabited or were forced into were considerably more convoluted than that.[9]

In the early colonial period "mulatto" could refer to those individuals born of a range of combinations of mixed parentage: indigenous-African or European-African in the Americas, but also European-North African in Spain. However, the same term could also indicate a skin color, which might be used for individuals belonging to various categories. Today, the categories of "indigenous" and "mulatto" are deployed in everyday practice in distinct speech-acts, so that Juan would probably not be both in the same utterance, although he might identify himself as one or the other in different social situations. However, in modern Colombia color is sometimes compared to the sociracial label with which an individual identifies. This was also true in the colonial period, as Richard Boyer demonstrates in his interpretation of the appearance of Christóbal del Toro, an early seventeenth-century Spanish mulatto: del Toro was described as "a *mulato* although white," where "mulatto" does not refer to his appearance but to his classification. Boyer points out that "the 'although' here is crucial. It signals that the categorization of del Toro as *mulato*, a reference to his *calidad*, overrides his phenotype. Reality and appearance, in other words, did not coincide."[10] Likewise, appearance and descent could be calculated independently of one another in a single legal procedure in early colonial Santafé. The particular nature of the juxtaposition of these two means of gauging Juan Mulato's identity provides an intriguing entrée into the problem of the intersection of vision and race in colonial Spanish America, as the boy's mulatto appearance (*aspecto*)—what observers saw when they looked at him, or, in the language of the period, "In the man, it is what he visibly offers [en el hombre es lo que se ofréce à la vista]"—did not easily conform to his rights as a free indio or as the descendant of an Indian mother.[11]

VISION AND CALIDAD

The relationship between perception and classification in the early colonial Nuevo Reino cannot be taken at face value. In sixteenth- and seventeenth-century Santafé, the appellations "indio," "mestizo," "mulatto," "negro," and "Spaniard" interacted in a complex relationship with observers' reactions to the physiognomy of the individuals who bore these labels.[12] The fluidity of classification—the possibility that people could move between categories or be identified by observers as belonging to a category other than the one into which they were born—derived in part from the interpretation by actors of visual cues. That is to say, vision both reinforced and subverted the classificatory system.[13]

In the example of Juan Mulato, physiognomy and ethnic classification were not perceived as necessarily contradictory by those seventeenth-century observers who declared the boy was Pijao but described his appearance as mulatto. Instead, they furnished parallel sets of cues for determining his status, multiple axes for plotting his calidad. However, not all cases were as intricate as Juan Mulato's. Individuals were frequently identified without ambiguity as members of a particular category by virtue of their physical attributes, as in the case of the indio Juan Zamorano, who was "taken as an Indian by birth [lo tienen por indio de naçion]" because "this is how he appears according to his aspect [porque asi lo paresçe por su aspeto]."[14] In other instances, however, individuals were seen and depicted in certain ways *because of* the label they carried, so that prejudices engendered by designations of calidad led observers to see people in particular ways. Diego Romero, the encomendero who was accused of disguising his identity as a Muslim slave, was described by witnesses as though his condition were natural for a man of his phenotype: "Diego, *as he was a slave*, was brown-skinned and curly-headed [el dicho Diego *como hera esclauo* hera moreno e crespo]."[15] Sight at once constituted and was constituted by the process of classification, visual cues forming part of a colonial habitus through which categories of calidad were continuously reinterpreted, depending on social context.

If we pay closer attention to the connection between appearance and calidad in the early colonial era, a new series of problems is opened up by the documentary record. We discover that the physiognomy of an Indian or a mestizo, for instance, was described differently depending on the context of enunciation: whether the year was 1570 or 1685; whether the person being described was a man or a woman; whether the observer was a local-level town official in Spain drawing up a travel document, a Crown-appointed visitador charged with investigating the administration of a native community in the Nuevo

Reino, or an eyewitness to a crime in Santafé. In other words, the physical features that were determined to be salient—the kinds of adjectives used to describe the person's aspect—were contingent on the time and place of observation, as well as on who was speaking. There was nothing natural about what observers reported seeing, just as the physical manifestations of "race" in the twenty-first century are not self-evident but learned.

An examination of how aspect was constructed over time reveals subtle shifts in the construction by early colonial officials of categories such as "Indian," "mestizo," and "mulatto," which were in formation in this period. In sixteenth-century Santafé, Spanish observers from various walks of life had trouble differentiating mestizas in Indian habit (like Catalina Tafur) from native women, suggesting that their physical dissimilarities were not entirely obvious and that the distinctions between Indian and mestiza women resided more in their clothing than in their physiques. Notwithstanding the ambiguities inherent in identification by phenotype, the kinds of descriptors observers used to verify physical appearance indicate an attentiveness to detail that echoes the medieval discourse of physiognomy, which sought to read the inner qualities of individuals by interpreting their external characteristics.[16] As a result, features such as skin color, for example, frequently overflow the boundaries of discrete socioracial categories, cautioning the modern reader away from interpreting their meaning in the narrow context of racial hierarchy. As the art historian Magali Carrera puts it for eighteenth-century (but still preracial) New Spain,

> Generally absent from critical discussions of race is the recognition that, like other cultural practices, seeing is a culturally-located practice. Depicting individuals with diverse skin colors, hair textures, etc. does not universally constitute racial imagery. Rather, the viewer constructs meaning/s for such images. As a result, while the twenty-first-century viewer may "see" categories of twenty-first-century "race" when, for example, looking at an eighteenth-century painting of the peoples of New Spain, an eighteenth-century viewer could not because such category formation did not underlie eighteenth-century looking.[17]

Instead, we must focus in, as Carrera does, on "historically specific practices of seeing" in order to comprehend what led to the identification of a person as a mestizo or an Indian in the early modern period, because such an act was not as clear-cut as we might imagine. Not only were such categories in flux, but what observers chose to see might not conform to our own sensibilities, because the attributes selected frequently originated in physiognomic conventions that are no longer relevant; the end result did not necessarily fit neatly in what have since become accepted as racial markers. We must also take the classifications that accompany physical descriptions with a grain of salt, as it was not difficult for people to shift categories of calidad according to the situations in which they found themselves, thus altering the framework through which they were looked at. In short, while calidad and appearance entered continuously into interaction, the terms on which their relationship was based were always shifting.

Nor did the European physiognomic descriptors available to colonial observers easily conform to the categories that sprang up on American soil. The ambiguous use of adjectives denoting color and hair or beard quality, which were commonly among the most essential characteristics used in physical descriptions on the Peninsula, betray the obstacles that sixteenth-century visitadores encountered for discriminating among indigenous individuals: they were hampered by a limited color palette and the fact that, in contrast to the range of hirsuteness in Iberian men, most of the natives of the Nuevo Reino were beardless. While beards functioned in Spain primarily as generational markers, in Santafé they served as both generational and ethnic indicators. Later, in an effort to distinguish between individuals, royal census-takers came to describe the physiognomy of Indians through comparison to commonly accepted characteristics of mestizos and mulattos. That is to say, descriptions played off individual appearance against populational characteristics in novel ways that departed from physiognomic conventions, suggesting that in certain historical and geopolitical contexts, an incipient socioracial hierarchy was acquiring heightened significance.

VISUALIZING DIVERSITY

We do not have for early colonial Santafé, as we do for late colonial Mexico and Peru, an extensive set of visual documents that could alert us to how people of various calidades were thought to appear—in the parlance of the time, their "aspect."[18] What we do have is a corpus of narrative conventions, originating in medieval Europe, for identifying individuals. In the documentation of the sale of slaves, censuses of indigenous tributaries, lists of native people sent to work in the mines, criminal cases, and, above all, applications for permission to travel from Spain to the New World, physical descriptions of people are ubiquitous, meant to serve as does a photograph on an identity document: to identify the bearer.[19] Coupled with classifications of individuals as "Indian," "mestizo," "mulatto," "black," or the frequently unmarked category of "Spaniard," these descriptions highlight specific traits—such as stature, skin color, beards, noteworthy features like scars and moles—and other types of information, such as language use and religion, which could assist authorities in recognizing an individual by sight. Such descriptions also appear in the archival documentation for the Nuevo Reino, especially for the high plateau where the imperial cities of Santafé and Tunja—the principal destinations of travelers to the region—are located.

These narrative portraits are generally contained in a sentence or two and are highly formulaic. For example, Andrés Martín—presumably of Spanish descent, as he is identified as a "vecino" of Santafé—sought to return home in 1615, after a sojourn in Spain, producing a petition that includes his physical description, along with those of the slaves accompanying him: "Andres Martin is of good stature [de buen cuerpo] with a ruddy face [cara colorada], the sign of a wound on his forehead, of some thirty-two years [of age] and Catalina would be of some twenty-five years, strong and tall, of green-black color [color lora], with an infant at her breast = and Nycolas, of more or less thirty-five years, tall, mulatto in color [de color mulata], with a white mole at his hairline."[20] Juan Meléndez, a mestizo from the emerald-mining town of Muzo, identified as the son of a Spaniard and a native woman, was, in 1601, "of the age of more or less eighteen years, of small stature, brown of face [moreno de rostro], a slightly protruding tooth in the upper part [of his mouth], who in his color likewise appears mestizo [que en su color ansimismo pareze mestiço]."[21]

Physical descriptions originating in other legal contexts are similarly structured. A 1586 census of native tributaries in the indigenous villages of Cucunubá and Simijaca describes don Hernando, hereditary lord of Bobotá, as "a ladino Indian and Christian [yndio ladigno y cristiano]" and "of tall stature, bearded on his upper lip [alto de cuerpo barbado en el boço]."[22] Note the combination of physiognomic and cultural features, such as language and religion, the latter two providing a decisive identification of the individual. Outside of legal settings, other nonphenotypical characteristics might be added to a description, combining with those used in the standard format. Take, for instance, how Pedro Pizarro portrayed the conqueror of Peru, Francisco Pizarro, who was his relative: "A tall man, easily agitated [seco], of good countenance, the beard thin [la barba rala], a valiant man by personality and courageous, a man of truth."[23] While the first four descriptors can be found in legal documents, the qualitative personality judgments are less common in legal discourse and indicate that this narrative description was offered in a different setting and for a distinct purpose than the others I have quoted.

These portraits are of individuals, detailing their personal characteristics in order to identify them, not of populations or groups of people. Some of the terminology they employ, however, echoes that used in generic characterizations of ethnic types, such as Columbus's description of the natives of Guanahaní, where he made first landfall: "They are very well formed, with handsome bodies and good faces. Their hair is coarse—almost like the tail of a horse—and short. They wear their hair down over their eyebrows except for a little in the back which they wear long and never cut. Some of them paint themselves with black, and they are the color of the Canarians, neither black nor white, and some of them with red, and some of them with whatever they find."[24] Narrative portraits sometimes appear to make value judgments on body type, as Columbus does, but this is due to the use of what were in reality standard descriptors—Diego de Torres being a "good-sized man," for example. Columbus is not concerned with identifying individuals, but in conveying his appreciation of the appearance of an entire population. He does not name persons, but rather describes a group in the third-person plural, and he depicts members of the group as visually homogeneous. Columbus evinces a great concern for detailing cultural traits (hairstyles, body paint) as opposed to physical features. The well-developed physiognomic terminology used for determining skin color gives way in Columbus's description to less precise comparisons of one population against another ("They are the color of the Canarians, neither black nor white"). While he employs some of the same adjectives as physical descriptions in legal discourse, Columbus's observations are more akin to the socioracial classifications we find in the legal record than they are to the narrative portraits that sometimes accompany them. Valentin Groebner proposes that Columbus's depictions of the people he encountered were not actual descriptions of individual appearances but "Petrarchian metaphors" based on literary models.[25]

An extensive series of certificates of purity of blood (*limpieza de sangre*) prepared in Spain contain physical descriptions. Over the course of the first four decades of the sixteenth century, new Christians—converts from Islam or Judaism—were barred from traveling to the Indies (which is what Diego Romero's lawsuit challenged).[26] Certificates of limpieza detailed the applicant's genealogy by recording the testimony of the town's leading citizens, who traced back the individual's ancestry two generations on both the mother's and father's sides. These documents functioned as vouchers for the applicant's good standing and facilitated screening by the House of Trade (Casa de la Contratación), the institution that controlled the movement of people and cargo across the Atlantic.[27] The certificates, which I will call travel papers, included narrative portraits of the travelers, which served to identify them to the authorities much as a photo would today. Applicants were generally also classified in these documents by calidad or as vecinos of a given place (in the case of Spaniards, American-born individuals of Iberian parentage, and other unmarked people), providing modern readers with a means of deducing how early modern observers might have visualized different socioracial categories.

Imagine, then, an office presided over by a local judge—a "licentiate," a man with a university degree—surrounded by scribes and a notary. Before him stands the applicant. One by one, witnesses, most of them prominent men in the community, enter the room to deliver their testimony, which is recorded by a scribe and validated by the notary. The judge, perhaps in consultation with the notary, peruses the applicant, noting his build, the quality and hue of his beard, the color of his skin, inspecting him closely for scars and moles, which might be found behind his ears or under his hairline. The judge might decide to note that the man is a stutterer or that he has a twitch in his eye. If the applicant is a nobleman, he (or his lawyer) might provide his own narrative portrait to the assembled officials. If he is an indio, the officials might sort through their visual memories to recall what some of the indigenous slaves in their town look like to gain some purchase on how to describe him.[28]

Alternately, imagine a public square in a native town near Tunja. The caciques have assembled their subjects, who wait in a long queue to be examined by officials charged with compiling a list of laborers to be sent to work in the silver mines. At a table sits the oidor, an Audiencia magistrate, surrounded by soldiers. The doctrinal priest stands behind him, notary and clerks at the magistrate's side, busy scribbling down the sometimes untranscribable Muisca names that have been conveyed to them by the interpreter (a local mestizo or mulatto, quite possibly, or an indio ladino who arrogantly scrutinizes the interminable line of men, all of whom he sees as his social inferiors) (fig. 5.1). The assembled functionaries strive to make sense of what distinguishes one man from another (for their own prejudices would persuade them that all of the natives look the same). Each of the cacique's subjects is asked to respond via the interpreter to the magistrate's questions, who then instructs the scribe to record whether or not the respondent is a ladino or a chontal. The priest also confirms whether he has been baptized. All of this data will be noted in the final document and signed by the notary.[29]

Some of the narrative portraits I examined are phrased in the first person and composed by the applicants themselves, particularly those of men of wealth or position, while others were made by local authorities or the witnesses attesting to the travelers' blood purity. It is not clear from the documents how officials arrived at applicants' socioracial classifications, although it is possible that they were provided by the applicants themselves; the fact that the mestizo priest Gonzalo García Zorro's travel papers do not identify him as a mestizo, for example, suggests that he was responsible for identifying his own calidad when he met with local officials in Spain before returning to the Nuevo Reino. Nor is it possible to decipher the extent to which applicants' self-identification by ethnic category influenced the nature of the physical description drawn up by government functionaries, as it did in the testimony describing Diego Romero's appearance. All that is available is the final recorded result of the transaction. Nonetheless, narrative portraits do provide a glimpse of what well-placed and educated male Spaniards and Americans of Spanish descent thought they saw when they observed an person who was self-described as a member of a particular category (or, at least, the portraits reveal what these men thought was worth describing with pen and ink). Travel papers indicate little about how members of lower social strata or women viewed themselves, however, since information on their appearance was routinely provided by the men they accompanied.

Most of these visual narratives are about Spaniards. All of them were produced by observers of Iberian descent, whether Crown officials or the upper-crust Spanish applicants themselves. I collected roughly 200 descriptions of Spanish men and women whose certificates were approved by the House of Trade in Seville, but only 27 of

Figure 5.1. *"El notario de cabildo recibe cohecho de un indio tributario,"* Felipe Guaman Poma de Ayala, Nueva corónica y buen gobierno, *1515, 521 [525]. Courtesy of Royal Danish Library, Copenhagen.*

mestizos (the vast majority male), 14 of blacks (including only one woman), and a handful of mulattos, mulattas, and male Indians (none of indias).[30] Ultimately, my corpus does not reflect how *all* colonial observers described individuals pertaining to *all* categories of calidad. Instead, the formulaic character of these narratives likely provides evidence of the existence of a set of widely accepted conventions for describing appearance or "aspect," conventions that were conspicuous throughout the Spanish world, not just in the Nuevo Reino.

THE PHYSIOGNOMICAL EYE

Colonial-era formulas for describing aspect derive from Galenic medicine, which read such features as skin color and facial hair with an eye to determining the inner humors of the person, classified according to the four poles of warm, cold, humid, and dry. Galenic conventions were based on a model that was largely confined to European physiques and was concerned with the identification of individuals, not of groups. From this model originates the early modern and medieval use of the word "complexion," which refers not only to color but also to those inner qualities. Complexion was thus more than a simple external manifestation, it was part of what Martin Porter calls a "physiognomical eye," a way of seeing the world that was widespread across Europe, including Spain. Physiognomy was not limited to the erudite science depicted in numerous manuals published in the early modern period, as folk physiognomists circulated across Europe, along with their fellow travelers, the diviners, astrologers, and doctors who tended to the medical needs of the poor. In other words, physiognomy was a set of observational and classificatory practices that was integral at many levels to the early modern era.[31] It thus provides clues to the foundations of early modern bureaucratic descriptions of physical appearance.

To get a sense of how physiognomic discourse filtered into the Spanish American psyche, it suffices to take a brief look at how the Andean author Felipe Guaman Poma de Ayala equates body and facial type with character: "And the middle-sized men and women of good figure and visage [buen talle y rostro], large eyes, spirited, wise, and lettered, always serve God and Your Majesty and gentlemen with their judgment. These govern the world and are charitable workers, righteous, of good works. He should have a thin beard [pocas barbas] and the woman, large eyes and a small mouth, an insole of four points [a cobbler's measure], an ant's waist [cintura de hormiga]."[32]

But however widely physiognomic conventions spread throughout colonial society, the bureaucrats who composed the descriptions contained in travel documents exercised what could be called a kind of "skilled vision," which Cristina Grasseni explains as "an embodied, skilled, trained sense," an "apprenticeship of the eye" that was acquired through both formal education and informal means, such as play. This was an "institutionalized and formalized" way of looking.[33] Charles Goodwin offers some concrete examples.

An archaeologist and a farmer see quite different phenomena in the same patch of dirt (for example, soil that will support particular kinds of crops versus stains, features, and artifacts that provide evidence for earlier human activity at this spot). An event being seen, a relevant *object of knowledge*, emerges through the interplay between a *domain of scrutiny* (a patch of dirt, the images made available by the [Rodney] King video-tape, etc.) and a set of *discursive practices* (dividing the domain of scrutiny by highlighting a figure against a ground, applying specific coding schemes for the constitution and interpretation of relevant events, etc.) being deployed within a *specific activity* (arguing a legal case, mapping a site, planting crops, etc.).[34]

We might imagine Crown officials learning to read the signs on the human face in the course of their grammar-school education, where they read classical and medieval authors, like Petrarch, whose works contained models of this discourse.[35] They were also exposed to these conventions in printed portrait-books that contained narrative descriptions and portraits of prominent people of their time and of ancients, such as Giovanni Battista Della Porta's *Della fisionomia dell'uomo*.[36] But men of letters were not the sole authors of these portraits in words; narrative descriptions also emerged out of collaborative working relationships established between bureaucrats and scribes, and between town officials and witnesses, all of whom contributed to the production of legal documents, thereby condensing the multiple practices of skilled vision that underlay their production: while officials may have learned these conventions in grammar school, scribes and notaries knew how to record them in the proper legal discourse, which they had acquired through years of experience.

Notwithstanding its pervasive influence, the science of physiognomy was probably not at the forefront of the minds of local officials charged with drawing up these papers. More likely, physiognomic conventions were habitual and standardized in their daily practice, following legal templates that diverged from the discourses they assimilated in the course of their education. Valentin Groebner indicates that physiognomic discourses became increasingly formulaic in the passage from the medieval to the early modern period, moving toward an insistence on stable descriptors of appearance and revolving less around the determination of the inner humors of individuals, which were based on the examination of ever-changing external attributes.[37] The formulaic nature of the narrative portraits in the certificates issued to travelers to Santafé and Tunja provides evidence of this trend toward stable models for registering appearance. This trend is also conspicuous in the narrative portraits that I was able to locate in a less systematic fashion in the archives in Bogotá, where a handful of censuses describe native tributaries and a few narrative portraits are inserted into judicial records. The descriptions composed in the Nuevo Reino, however limited in number, provide hints as to the limits of applicability of the physiognomic model. What is notable is not how broadly physiognomy was applied, but why, in those instances in which it was attempted, physiognomic discourse did not work in the Americas. Crown officials found it impossible to effectively distinguish among native people or between them and mestizos using conventions meant to highlight features of importance to Europeans. The American examples I discuss can best be appreciated, not as a means by which to derive general rules used in Santafé for observing native people, but as instances in which bureaucrats struggle to make sense of a new human landscape using an unsatisfactory European measure.

PHYSIGNOMIC PORTRAITURE

Conventional European narrative portraits were highly stylized, consisting of a series of brief and formulaic statements of the age, size and build, skin color (generally expressed as the color of the face), quality of facial hair, and individual markers such as moles, warts, missing teeth, or scars. Many of these descriptors direct attention toward the head and the face, which constituted the index of humanity in the period; the few animal descriptions I uncovered in the archives did not privilege the face to the same extent as did those of human beings.[38] The order and nature of these descriptors goes back to the medieval period and can be found not only in legal documents but in literary texts such as the *Libro de buen amor*.[39] A human being can be recognized by reference to hundreds of characteristics, ranging from the shape of the head and eye color or hair color, to paunchiness and foot size. However, the narrative portraits I collected tend to draw attention to particular characteristics, only a few of which receive sustained attention. By focusing on two of these—face color and quality of beard—we can begin to discern the ways in which classifications of calidad were generated through speech-acts informed by visual cues.

The following descriptions portray sixteenth- and seventeenth-century Spaniards who applied to travel to Santafé and Tunja.

[Jerónimo Vicente Colomer is of] the age of at least twenty-four years and his face is ruddy [rostro bermejo] and his beard red [barua roja] and he has a very small mark on the nose on the right side.[40]

Alonso del Pulgar would be more or less thirty-eight years of age, of good stature, thin, with a black beard [baruinegro], and he has a scar from a wound on the finger of the hinge of the left hand, and Alonso del Pulgar, his son, of more or less eighteen years, of good stature . . . who is beginning to grow a beard [que comiença a baruar].⁴¹

Juan Garcia, of more or less twenty-three years of age, of good stature and his beard is growing in [le apunta la uarua], and Simon Perez, of twenty years, of good stature and he is beginning to grow a beard [comiença a baruar].⁴²

[Magdalena Diaz Rodríguez] is a girl, small of stature and brown of face [moreno de rostro], and she has two moles, one next to the nose by the left cheek and the other smaller on the nose, toward the same side as the other, and she is more or less of twenty-two years of age.⁴³

Toribia Sanchez is a young unmarried woman and is of the age of twenty-four years, more or less, not subject to matrimony or religion, in whom there is no defect that would prevent her from going to the Indies, and she is a middle-sized woman, her face pockmarked by smallpox, her eyebrows joined [at the middle], with a small mole behind her right ear.⁴⁴

Surprisingly, there is little difference in the nature of these narrative portraits and that of the following narrative renderings of the features of mestizos, whose descriptions are more abbreviated in part because they appear in conjunction with those of the higher-status travelers whom they accompanied, but possibly also because the officials describing them lacked the proper vocabulary to render their appearance in prose.⁴⁵

This witness knows that the aforementioned girl [Juana de Albornóz] is a mestiza and native [natural] of the province, and this witness takes her and she is perceived and taken for a mestiza [por tal mestiza este testigo la tiene y es auida y tenida]. . . . She is of the age of nine or ten years and [has] a freckled face [rostro pecoso].⁴⁶

[Gabriel Sánchez] is a young man, brown [moreno], mestizo by birth [mestiço de su naçion], with a scar from a wound above his left eyebrow next to the hairline and another scar from a wound at the edge of his right eyebrow, next to the eye, who is beginning to grow a beard [comiença a barbar] [and who] from his aspect [por su aspecto], appears to be twenty-two years old, more or less.[47]

Note that in the narrative portrait of the mestiza Juana de Albornóz, in particular, classification is not a foregone conclusion but the observer's individualized act of recognition of her social persona: "She is *perceived and taken for* a mestiza." These descriptions are specific to the legal (and literate) context in which they were produced and cannot be construed to exemplify a broad and general visual experience. Although everyday usage probably retained many of the features that appear in legal documentation, it was most likely not as stylized or constrained; to a greater degree, it probably juxtaposed physical features to other characteristics, such as clothing, language use, or bearing; it was never as specific, as is evident in Catalina Acero de Vargas's ambiguous description of Francisco Suárez.

Two particularly notable elements in the legal descriptions of Spaniards and mestizos are the significance of facial hair and references to color of the face, especially to the color brown, both of which open important windows into how descriptions of non-European individuals were forced into the framework of physiognomic conventions. Notwithstanding the preferred physiognomic template, however, these descriptors both overflow the bounds of calidad and at the same time are constitutive of it.

BEARDS, MASCULINITY, AND CALIDAD

Among the most striking attributes of these narrative portraits is the almost obsessive attention functionaries give to beards: dark or light in color, thick or sparse, mature or just growing in. This was a mark of the times. Sebastián de Covarrubias dedicates almost two pages of his dictionary to the word "beard," in comparison to relatively brief glosses of the terms "mestizo" and "mulatto." The seventeenth-century lexicographer calls the beard one of the fundamental symbols of masculinity, denoting virility and strength, and he associates it with prudence and reliability, all of these being qualities that in the period distinguished mature men from youth and from women.[48] The lexicographer also makes recourse to classical antiquity: "When Diogenes was asked why he had such a long beard, he responded: So that at all times I am reminded that I am a man."[49] The association of beards with masculinity has a long history in the Iberian Peninsula. We have only to remember the medieval poem of the Cid, whose hero refuses to trim his beard, which stands in for his masculine honor.[50]

The Spanish physiognomer Jerónimo Cortés, echoing Covarrubias, also connects beardedness with masculinity, inserting a distinct, but equally gendered evocation of its meanings.

> Those who have a well-formed [bien compuesta] and thick [espesa] beard are naturally of good nature and mild condition; and the contrary, for those who have it poorly formed [mal compuesta]. The woman who has many hairs on the jaw and near the chin is of a strong nature and a terrible condition, and is exceedingly warm: for which reason she is very lustful, and of a manly condition. The woman who is completely naked and free of hairs, principally around the mouth, is naturally of good temperament, timid, shameful, meek, pacific, and obedient.[51]

Cortés brings to mind Juan Sánchez Cotán's *La Barbuda de Peñaranda* (1590), a portrait of Brígida del Río, and José de Ribera's *La mujer barbuda* (1631), an image of another bearded woman.[52] In both portraits we see an individual dressed in the attire of a female member of the elite, but with a long and thick beard. Ribera depicts the woman carrying an infant, accentuating the incongruity of the representation and forcing the viewer to confront the overwhelming significance of facial hair in defining the attributes of Iberian men (and women) and in constituting salient sexual characteristics.

Narrative portraits associated with requests for permission to cross the Atlantic demonstrate a tremendous preoccupation with beards, whether in their presence (in Spanish men) or their absence (explicitly noted in young Spanish men and generally unmentioned for mestizos, mulattos, Africans, and, of course, women), as well as with their color: black, blonde, brown, red, and vermilion. Young men are continually compared with their elders in these applications, particularly by reference to their scant beards (poca barba), which are only beginning to grow in ("comiença a barbar" or "le apunta la barba"). What the modern observer might consider an inconsequential distinguishing feature—the stage of the growth of facial hair—was a significant component of the calidad of an early modern person, marking his age and therefore his status.

Will Fisher points out that in early modern England the process of determining an individual's sex did not involve distinctions between primary and secondary sexual characteristics—that is, between genitalia and features like facial hair—nor between sexual characteristics and gender attributes like clothing.[53] Instead, the beard distinguished not only men from women, but also bearded from unbearded men, who were seen as differently sexed. As Joan Cadden appropriately puts it, the beard differentiated the masculine from the nonmasculine, the latter including women, immature males, and castrati.[54] Douglas Biow cogently explains how the early modern beard set mature men off from everyone else.

> Beards, like testicles, signal manliness. Hence, beards adorn men's faces to differentiate them all the more from women and, by extension, not only boys but also young men who are on the verge of becoming full-fledged adults. Beards consequently highlight the "virtue" of adult men *as* men, with emphasis on the first syllable *vir*. The stages by which hairs grow on the human form indeed conventionally marked a natural break between adolescence and manhood, between the time when the boy has just smooth peach-fuzz on his cheeks and chin and seems effeminate, and the time when the mature man can instead grow a robust, virile beard and beget children. . . . A beard, in short, signaled an aggressive, rigorous, virtuous, and thus adult manly mind.[55]

This was as much the case in the Middle Eastern cultures as in Europe. As Afsaneh Najmabadi elucidates, eighteenth-century Persians distinguished beardless adolescent boys from bearded grown men, the passage from the first phase to the second marking "the beginning of the end of [a young man's] status as object of desire for adult men and his own movement into adult manhood." At the same time, she cautions that, in Persia, the beard was more a generational marker than a feature distinguishing men from women.[56] In many respects, European and Middle Eastern cultural forms were fused in the Iberian Peninsula into what Barbara Fuchs has called an "Andalusi habitus" (as with don Diego de Torres's jousting costume).[57]

In light of the cultural mores surrounding facial hair in early modern Europe, it is not surprising that beard growth is highlighted as a significant distinguishing feature in Alonso de Sandobal's license to travel from his home in Cáceres, Spain, to the Nuevo Reino.[58] Sandobal first petitioned for a travel permit in 1616, at age twenty-five, when he was described as "tall of body, brown face [moreno de rostro] and scant beard and black [de poca barba y negra] and with a robust face."[59] But he did not make the crossing at that time and was compelled to file a second request four years later, in 1620. In his second application he explicitly recognizes that his beard has grown in since his first petition: "When the first license was granted, he had scant beard, and now that three years have passed it has grown in and is thicker [mas poblada] and black [negra]."[60]

The salience of the stages of beard growth was also preserved on the other side of the Atlantic. In the kidnapping of a mestizo child in Santafé in 1621, the culprit, Jorge Baca Moscoso, was identified through a lineup (reconocimiento) in which the witness (a black slave named Antonio) was asked to examine a group of men, many of them state functionaries, and to choose from among them the kidnapper, whom he had observed in the course of committing the crime. Antonio identified Baca Moscoso by his beard, but only after first mistakenly choosing an innocent man (by the name of Algarate):

> He pointed out Martin de Algarate and said, "This is the man who took the mestizo." And he repeated it twice and then I, the investigating officer, asked him if he was sure that the man whom he pointed out was the one he said had taken the boy. And he returned his gaze to the face of Algarate and said that he was not the one, because the one who had taken the boy was beginning to grow a beard [le empeçauan a salir las barbas].[61]

The investigating officer was unclear as to why Antonio should have first singled out Algarate, so he inquired into the confusion of identities: "Pedro Gomes de Miranda told me that Martin de Algarate had put on the cape of Jorge Baca and that Jorge Baca [put on] Algarate's, and for this reason the negro [the witness, who was black] must have thought that Algarate was Jorge Baca, since he named him first and after taking a good look, pointed to Jorge Baca."[62] Baca Moscoso's cape, a piece of clothing whose use was limited to Spaniards, must have been recognizably part of his persona, if Antonio picked it out in a room of similarly attired men. After being challenged, the witness correctly identified Baca Moscoso, highlighting the incipient nature of his beard.[63]

Beards took on new meanings on American soil. Facial hair constituted a crucial feature for distinguishing Spaniards from Native Americans, furnishing a portal through which we can observe the incongruities in early modern New World physiognomic discourse. The seventeenth-century author Gregorio García dedicates a good portion of his *Origen de los indios del Nuevo Mundo e Indias Occidentales* (Origin of the Indians of the New World and West Indies) to argue why native people of the Americas do not have beards. He reasons that the natives of the Americas originated in Carthage, where they were bearded, but that exposure to the American climate caused their descendants to become beardless. According to García, the descendants of Spaniards who resettled in the New World kept their beards because Spain was more temperate than Carthage and therefore the American climate affected Iberians to a lesser extent than it did the ancestors of American natives.[64]

Chantal Caillavet reasons that in the Americas the beard came to symbolically mark the difference between Spaniards and native people, the latter occupying a feminine position vis-à-vis the masculinity of Europeans.[65] Guaman Poma, taking the native point of view, privileges socioracial category over gender as the most significant feature denoted by facial hair, when he stipulates that caciques should not wear beards, lest they look like mestizos: "And if he has the beard of a cooked shrimp, he will look like a mestizo, a cholo, of bad caste [mala casta], a mulatto, a zanbahigo." At the same time, he chides a clean-shaven Spaniard for looking like an "old whore" or "puta bieja."[66] Guaman Poma does not equate the lack of facial hair among native Andean men with femininity, although he certainly does so when he refers to unbearded Spaniards. In other words, his value judgments take on different accents, depending on the object of his invectives. But from a Spanish perspective, beardedness unquestionably signified manliness in ways unavailable to many indigenous men, a distinction that appears to have been extended to other low-status categories. Travel permits display few references to the facial hair of mestizos, mulattos, or blacks, even though many of them probably had beards, perhaps in an effort to refrain from accentuating their virility in comparison to that of the Spaniards whom they were accompanying.[67]

In spite of the dearth of bearded indigenous faces, the centrality of facial hair to the Iberian imagination and its prominent place in conventions of physiognomic description led Crown investigators to distinguish among natives in the Nuevo Reino according to the same criteria that regulated their identification of Europeans. In a 1586 census of indigenous tributaries of Simijaca, man after man is described as having a scant beard (poca barba), notwithstanding the fact that this descriptor is not relevant for identifying individuals in a population whose men are only infrequently bearded.[68] A century later, in 1687, the census takers in a series of towns near Santafé were more careful to detail beard color and thickness, their descriptions echoing the narrative portraits of Spaniards produced a century before in the travel permits.[69] However, even in these documents, beardedness continues to be an elusive mode of identification, since so few tributaries were bearded, and hirsuteness was even less useful a tool for distinguishing among their wives, who were also listed in the census.[70] Although facial hair was central to Iberian forms of self-identification and to strategies for differentiating Spaniards from indigenous people, the nature of the narrative portrait—which identified an individual, not a group—could not successfully distinguish among non-European individuals, although the features it contained, such as the beard, were deployed to differentiate Europeans as a group from others. In other words, the physiognomic conventions based on a European template available to early colonial record keepers and judicial officials in Santafé were not suited to the kinds of distinctions that they needed to draw to control an ethnically diverse, non-European population.

PHYSIOGNOMY AND THE CLASSIFICATION OF SKIN COLOR

One of the colors mentioned with greatest prevalence in the requests for permission to travel to America was "moreno" (which I have translated as "brown"), which was used routinely to describe indigenous people, mestizos, some mulattos, and even Spaniards.[71] The lexicographer Sebastián de Covarrubias defined "moreno" as "a color, that which is not completely black, as in that of the Moors, from whence it took its name, or of blackberry."[72] North Africans were the ground against which individuals of this color were compared, although it would be simplistic if we were to immediately equate a term used to describe a swarthy complexion with subordinate status. A broad range of individuals was perceived as being "moreno"; the descriptor did not function in travel permits as an identifier of membership in a single category but was used across almost all the groups to identify individuals, irrespective of whether they were Spaniard, indigenous, mulatto, or mestizo.[73] Until the last quarter of the sixteenth century, when a small number of Spaniards began to be identified as having "white faces" (*rostros blancos*), even many Old Christians and members of the Iberian nobility were described as "moreno" in color.[74] Groebner affirms that "brown" was frequently employed in the Middle Ages to characterize Europeans, denoting not so much their skin color as their physiognomic complexion, that is, their inner qualities.[75] Edward Behrend-Martínez notes that brown signified masculinity, while the eighteenth-century Spanish physiognomist Gerónimo Cortés calls brown a "good complexion" (*buena complexión*).[76] "Moreno" thus carried a range of meanings, suggesting that perhaps what early modern observers meant when they described someone as brown was different from what a modern-day usage of "brown" would mean.

Nonetheless, the meaning of "moreno" shifted in the Americas in reaction to the process of mixing that was occurring there. A Spaniard identified as "moreno" in Mexico City, Santafé, or Lima was at risk of being associated with mixed populations of low prestige. Thomas de Rizo, a Spaniard from the Canary Islands resident in Mexico in the 1620s, was denied the right to bear arms, his darker complexion leading to confusion with his mestizo and mulatto neighbors.[77] This suggests that in the context of New World population mixing, the meaning of "moreno" morphed from one that carried dual connotations—on the one hand being associated with non-Christian congregations, on the other being used to identify a panoply of admirable individuals—to one that classified American "others" by virtue of their color.

At the same time, "white," which in the Middle Ages denoted lethargy and dull-wittedness, begins to appear in the seventeenth century in physical descriptions of travelers to the Nuevo Reino as a quality equated with Europeanness; only Spaniards were described as "white in color" in the travel documents I examined.[78] As more individuals came to be identified as white-skinned, a slippage occurred between white as the color of individuals and white as a potential category. For example, a witness to a civil suit in Santafé in the 1630s "said she was a quarteroon and is a white woman [dijo ser quarterona y es muger blanca]."[79] However, "white" was not reserved exclusively for Europeans. A 1628 list of indigenous laborers identifies some of them as white in color, suggesting that "white" was not a stable (racial) category, but continued to function as a descriptor for a wide variety of individuals.[80]

The Galenic typology that associated complexion with the inner humors of the person coexisted with an "ethnogeographic" system inherited from antiquity, which classified populations by superimposing color onto the world map and attributing different skin tones to climate or to the absence or presence of strong sunlight. The two systems of color classification, physiognomic and geographic, could not entirely be reconciled with one another, particularly given population movements in the early modern period. That is to say, people did not change color when they moved from Europe to America, although, perhaps, they did change complexion.[81] But even the ethnogeographic system—which was discriminatory in the sense that it imputed moral value to skin color, creating others by comparing darker to lighter skins—saw color as mutable.

The Jesuit Alonso de Sandoval, writing in 1647 from Cartagena de Indias on the Caribbean coast of the Nuevo Reino, disputes the ethnogeographic system of color classification in *De instauranda aethiopum salute*, his treatise on Africans, by acknowledging that climate does not affect the color of individuals who move from one continent to another: "If temperature did it or climate caused it, Spaniards who live in the land of blacks [negros], married to Spanish women, would beget blacks; and to the contrary in our Europe, blacks [morenos] would beget whites, of which experience disabuses us."[82] Instead, he points to the power of the imagination in determining the color of human beings. Drawing on classical sources, he argues that if a European mother were to look at the image of an Ethiopian during pregnancy, her child could be born black.

> And Celio Rodiginio, discussing the dominion the imagination
> has over the actions of the body, recounts to us how a noble ma-
> tron gave birth to a child who was black in color, like those of
> Ethiopia, and who (says Fabio, referring to the self-same Celio)
> was accused before judges of adultery, and just when she was
> about to be punished, as such an atrocious and obvious crime
> required, Hippocrates says (referred to by the self-same Celio)
> he saved her from such a fate by informing the judges that it was
> necessary to make an examination and see if by chance in the
> room where it was understood she had conceived, there was a
> portrait of an Ethiopian child. And finding that, he said that was

the cause of such an unusual occurrence: with which the judges, satisfied, declared her free of guilt.[83]

Sandoval then attributes to the transformative forces of the imagination a series of cases from Cartagena and nearby Mompox, where seemingly white children were born to black slaves.

> What I saw with my own eyes in this city of Cartagena de Indias, was a child named Francisco, seven years of age, of Angola nation, native of the town of Quilimbo, whose parents were burnt-black negros [negros atezados], but he was incomparably white, exceedingly white, blonde, and with shockingly Spanish features, so that he was a marvel to the whole city, who held him as a marvelous thing. His eyes were brown and he was very short-sighted: he only showed his Negro nation in his nose, which was flat [roma], and his hair, which although it was golden, was very curly.[84]

The child Francisco sounds very much like an albino, particularly given that he is described as having weak eyesight. But what is significant here is not so much the validity of Sandoval's observations as the prominence of a narrative of the possibilities of color change, a discourse with classical and medieval epistemological foundations that attributes a mutable character to skin color.[85] This suggests that color and calidad existed in the early modern imagination in a fluid relationship to one another.

"Mulatto," "mestizo," "black," and "Indian" are terms whose usage moves almost imperceptibly between color categories and ascriptions of calidad in the travel documents. The categories "mestizo" and "mulatto" were coined not in the Americas but in Spain, the product of centuries of Islamic dominance and the circulation of slaves from north and sub-Saharan Africa to the Iberian Peninsula. Jack Forbes reveals a complex constellation of color terms used in early modern Spain to differentiate among its myriad inhabitants: "*blanco mulato*" (white mulatto), "*color membrillo*" (quince color), and "*membrillo cocho*" (cooked quince), for example, were among the terms employed to denote mixing of Iberians with North Africans.[86] Slave populations themselves were classified simultaneously by religion (Moor), territory (Berber), and skin color (black).[87]

These Old World categories—which acquired new meanings on

American soil—as well as new ones, like "Indian," that emerged in the Americas simultaneously distinguished individuals by their calidad and referred to their skin color. In other words, "mulatto," "mestizo," and "indio" not only were categories of people but were also colors, as evident in an aforementioned narrative portrait: "Nycolas, of more or less thirty-five years, tall, mulatto in color, with a white mole at his hairline." Similarly, Juan de León was described as being "mestizo in color [color mestizo]."[88] Pedro de Cabrera Bohórquez, a Indian from the Nuevo Reino seeking return to his homeland, was identified by Captain Pedro Núñez, who originally took him to Spain, as "twenty years of age, Indian in color [del color yndio]."[89] The category "black" was frequently qualified with color descriptors, such as "burnt black" (atezado) or "green-black" (loro), because "black" was an early modern term that signified "slave" regardless of the skin color of the individual.[90] "Mulatto," "mestizo," "Indian," and "black" were thus simultaneously nouns (categories) and adjectives (color terms). It is telling that the only terms in these papers that functioned at once as categories and as colors in this period referred to subaltern groups; "white" did not exist as a category, although it came into use as a color term to describe primarily (but not exclusively) European faces.[91] The sixteenth- and seventeenth-century Iberian colonial imagination needed to consolidate the classification of subordinate groups, both to make sense of them and to control them (particularly through taxation), while on the other hand it allowed European appearance to go unmarked as "normal." Travel permits illustrate the origins of appearance as a means by which to create categories that merge color terms and socioracial categories.

Early modern travelers to the Nuevo Reino consciously distinguished between calidad and color (as in the case of Juan Mulato), suggesting that a degree of uncertainty was inherent to their classifying practice. Officials were forced to jog between classification and aspect, describing individuals not only by their bodily or facial features, but also, in those cases in which phenotype was an insufficient or ambiguous marker of category, by their clothing and behavior. Juan Zamorano, a late sixteenth-century returnee to his native land, substantiated his identification as an Indian with testimony that emphasized not his category, but his aspect: "He is taken as an Indian [indio de naçion] because this is how he appears according to his aspect [asi lo paresçe por su aspeto], and in addition to this when this witness made his acquaintance in Cartagena he was dressed in the clothing of an

Indian [benia en abito de indio], and he was held and taken for and called as such [era auido e tenido e nombrado por tal]."[92] That is, he "looked like" an Indian, in addition to seeking to be "classified" as one.

But what did an Indian "look like"? Don Juan, the cacique of Cunucubá, a native town near the colonial urban center of Vélez, was accused of being mestizo by his encomendera, who sought to remove him from office by supplying descriptions of his aspect as evidence that he was not an indio. A native authority who testified in the encomendera's favor declared, "This witness thinks that don Juan is a mestizo because he has a different manner of color from the Indians [tiene la color de otra manera que los yndios], and it is their custom that mestizos not be caciques because they do [the Indians] harm."[93] What, precisely, was meant by "a different manner of color" was never explained in the legal record, just as Catalina de Vargas never clarified her first impression of Francisco Suárez. It was this very ambiguity that made the category of mestizo so malleable. Such markers were, nonetheless, insufficient in the eyes of the cacique's opponents, who also latched onto nonphenotypical attributes, arguing that he must be a mestizo because he was fluent in Spanish (muy ladino) and because his children wore European dress (bestidos en trajes despañoles).[94] The degree of care don Juan's opponents took in describing his children's clothing, as compared to witnesses' vagueness in specifying the cacique's skin color, illuminates the challenges that both natives and Spaniards faced when they attempted to talk about phenotype. The difference between "he has a different manner of color from the Indians" and the considerably more meticulous catalog of don Juan's daughters' clothing is dramatic: "Doña Maria de Salaçar [don Juan's daughter] wears the habit of a Spaniard, and when she hears mass she customarily goes covered in a silk cloak, and the other daughters of the cacique wear underskirts of well-made flannel [paño] and a ruff [jergueta] and when they go out of the house they cover themselves with native mantles [liquidas] and shawls and the sons of said cacique ordinarily wear Spanish habits [abito de españoles]."[95] It was much more straightforward to distinguish among members of the lower orders by their clothing and habits than to do so by their color or facial features.

PHYSICAL DESCRIPTION IN THE AMERICAN SCENARIO

At the same time that European observers were registering in travel documents the heterogeneity of appearance among subordinated social categories, revealing the obstacles they encountered in distinguishing between individuals by deploying color terms, a series of social, political, and discursive transformations were occurring in Santafé. Elite members of intermediate groups, especially mestizos, begin to experience a loss of status in the late sixteenth and the seventeenth centuries and were forced into a single "mestizo" category shared with plebeians of mixed parentage. In the mid-sixteenth century the mestizo sons of conquistadors or Spanish nobles had enjoyed access to positions of relative power (including those of city council aldermen, priests, and even caciques), but by the end of that century and the beginning of the seventeenth, they were being socially excluded and relegated to marginal positions similar to those of their poorer cousins, a development that originated as a fear response to mid- to late sixteenth-century rebellions among the indigenous and mestizos in the New World and among Moriscos in Spain, but then probably transformed into a more generalized form of discrimination. "Mestizo" began to solidify as a subordinated social category, coming to function as more than a vague form of genealogical sorting. This was likely the phenomenon at play when Diego García Zorro was repeatedly snubbed at the beginning of the seventeenth century (as opposed to don Diego de Torres twenty-five years earlier, who was feared to some degree).

In the course of this transformation and in a departure from physiognomic conventions, enumerations of native tributaries began to include socioracial types as descriptors, reflecting efforts to more precisely identify individuals. What is notable is that officials began to use adjectives that did not correspond to the group to which the tributaries belonged (such as, for example, "Indian color" or "color indio" for native people). The new terminology instead summoned comparisons across categories. A 1628 inventory of indigenous conscripts to be sent to work the mines of Las Lajas and Santa Ana, for example, included the following narrative portrait: "Diego Tentesuca Varriga of thirty-four years, of good stature, his hair mulatto-like [cauello amulatado]."[96] A 1687 census of a series of Muisca communities followed a similar pattern of usage, comparing indigenous tributaries to mulattos and to mestizos: "Don Silbestre, governor, of thirty-six years, mulatto-like [amulatado], curly-haired" and "Salvador Aogado of twenty-four years, of good stature and face, with large eyes and lips, somewhat mestizo-like [amestisado], his wife Marcela, of good build and a mestizo-like face [cara amestisada] and of the same age."[97] In a dispute that began in 1699, the governor of the native town of Ubatoque was accused of being mestizo because of his light skin; he and his supporters defended his classification by arguing that his mother was of a "mestizo-like color" (color amestizada) but was nevertheless an Indian.[98] Similarly, a 1664 list of free mulattas in the city of Vélez included a description in which the physical appearance of a mulatta was conflated with that of Indians: "Ysavel de Angulo, an Indian-like mulatta [mulata ayndiada], tall, pock-marked."[99]

Such usages bring to mind late sixteenth-century literary evocations of the *chacona*, a popular dance genre characterized by animated music and bawdy lyrics. The words of some chaconas revolved around attractive mulattas or dark-skinned women, as, for example, in Miguel de Cervantes's 1613 "La ilustre fregona" (The Illustrious Scullery Maid):

> Esta indiana amulatada,
> de quien la fama pregona
> que ha hecho más sacrilegios
> e insultos que hizo Aroba.

> This mulatto-like *indiana,*
> of whom her fame proclaims
> has committed more sacrileges
> and insults than did Aroba.[100]

An *indiano* (or indiana) was a criollo who returned to the Iberian Peninsula from America bearing great wealth, an early modern specimen of the nouveau riche. By alluding to a returnee carrying the stain of miscegenation on her skin, Cervantes's chacona compares members of one group with those of another that is different in aspect. This may have been an insult hurled at a group of individuals who were disliked for their newly acquired wealth and whom Cervantes knew were of Spanish descent, or it might have referred to the slave of an indiana.[101] Whatever the intention may have been, the chacona's comparison echoes the pairing of sociracial categories in the lists of seventeenth-century indigenous laborers and mulatto tributaries in the Nuevo Reino: color is superimposed on category through comparisons of native individuals with the classes of "mestizo" and "mulatto" (or of mulattas with the class of "Indians") by indexing hair texture or skin color, representing a move toward categorizing individuals by reference to group types. These narrative portraits obey the structure of physiognomic descriptions but with a twist: the slippages they evince indicate that the boundaries between "Indian," "mestizo," and "mulatto" could not be determined by visual observation, even by those possessing "skilled vision."

The contrasts between the nature of descriptions in travel documents produced in Spain and that of other forms of documentation in the Nuevo Reino complicate modern appreciation of the fit between physical appearance and calidad in the early modern Atlantic world, where observers were frequently uncertain about how to classify individuals. Such differences force us to pay closer attention to the place of enunciation of such utterances. Travel documents were prepared in Iberian towns by local officials, who drew on testimony collected from local witnesses, most of whom had never ventured beyond the Peninsula and had come into only sporadic contact with the American natives, mulattos, mestizos, and African slaves who lived in their midst. The interests of these Iberian functionaries more properly revolved around distinctions between Old and New Christians, one of the fundamental differentiators of social status in Spain at that time. The demarcation of the boundary between converts and their descendants, on the one hand, and lineages deemed to be "pure," on the other, was central to the objectives of this documentary genre, whose purpose was to corroborate the Old Christian status of the applicant.

The goals of the American census taker were very different. His objective was to identify and catalog indigenous tributaries, who were taxed in products, labor, and money by the Crown. In this context, the axis along which diversity was organized was distinctly socioracial. While the distinction between Christians and the unconverted was, indeed, influential in the ecclesiastical administration of native people in the Nuevo Reino, the difference between Indian and non-Indian was of utmost significance in the collection of tribute, as members of different categories made distinct types of payments to the Crown. Over time, the identification of indigenous tributaries was complicated by the growing presence of mestizos and mulattos in native communities, who increasingly intermarried with the indigenous inhabitants. As demonstrated by the examples of Juana Galván in Chitaraque and of Lázaro Mulato's children, who were identified as tributaries in Chocontá although their father was not, indios could not be isolated by deploying genealogical information. The process was much messier than that. Visitadores relied on the self-identifications supplied by their informants; they "eyeballed" tributaries to estimate their classification; or they followed the recommendations of encomenderos. The growing presence of "outsiders-within" forced colonial administrators to seek new techniques for making sense of who was indigenous and who was not, leading to new framings of timeworn physiognomic formulas. Most notably, they were compelled to compare native bodies, not to their own European ones, as Eurocentric physiognomic conventions would dictate, but to precisely the mixed groups who threatened to interfere most directly with their supervision of native people. At the same time, all non-Spaniards, both Indians and people of mixed parentage (as well as foreigners), were increasingly denied rights to citizenship (*vecindad*) in towns and cities, a practice that locked into place a colonial power system that was less imbalanced on the Peninsula, where members of the groups excluded in the New World could claim rights as vecinos in Spanish towns.[102]

Colonial and early modern conventions of ascription of the sort observed here for the Nuevo Reino involved a complex balancing of various physical and nonphysical forms of identification with socioracial taxonomies, deployed in differing combinations in distinct contexts, a kind of "ethnophysiognomic eye" engendered by colonialism. Combining various features of appearance—including lineage and religion, color, hirsuteness, age, costume, language, and a range of other markers—people used appearance to move in and out of categories of calidad, dedicating considerable effort to debating and thwarting the classification of themselves and others. At the same time, aspect served to distinguish among individuals within a category, a process that unfolded in different ways in Santafé and in Spanish towns, but which drew on a common language of identification. The origins of this descriptive idiom lay in classical and medieval physiognomic discourses. However, when these tools for recognizing individual differences were relocated to the Nuevo Reino, where the colonial bureaucracy was charged with managing a profusion of new categories, they interfered with the drawing of relevant distinctions within these populations. Such moments of uncertainty are evident in how officials manipulated forms of physical description on both sides of the Atlantic, although these practices manifested in distinct ways in Spain and in Santafé.

In order to make sense of the epistemological grounds on which these compromises took place, we not only need to examine the unusual instances in which classification is unclear or disputed, which comprise the majority of those cases studied by historians, but we also must turn our focus toward more common situations in which categories are agreed on, where what is at stake are the multifarious attributes juggled by observers and the observed: the tributary who is indisputably Indian but who has "mulatto-like hair," which does not make him less Indian but does serve to identify him in contrast to his neighbors; the Castilian man whose beard has grown in since his travel papers were drawn up and who therefore enters a new category of European maleness, while at the same time he remains a Spaniard. In other words, we must transcend conceptual models that posit a stable hierarchy of socioracial categories and instead focus in on calidad as a broader set of practices within which these categories function. This can only be accomplished effectively if we begin to deconstruct the significance of socioracial terms across Spanish America with an eye to comprehending how they are deployed differently in distinct geographical and documentary settings. Only then can we begin to visualize what Crown officials saw when they beheld Juan Mulato and undertook to determine where he belonged in Santafé's social matrix.

6. The Problem of Caste

In 1665, Pablos de Orejuela, a sixty-year-old mestizo laborer from Usaquén—today a tony northern suburb of Bogotá, but in Orejuela's days a sleepy pueblo de indios—was detained by the Inquisition and called to appear before the Holy Office in Cartagena de Indias to be tried for heresy.[1] Jokingly labeled an "old mestizo philosopher" by a sympathetic neighbor, Orejuela was denounced by an anonymous informer for declaring that souls in hell did not experience torment because they did not have bodies, and that the only anguish they felt originated in their inability to see God. Various of his acquaintances— all of them mestizo and mulatto artisans, all of them identified by Orejuela as his enemies—testified to his heretical behavior at a secret trial, as was common Inquisitorial practice. Orejuela was tortured and ultimately punished with exile; he was also forced to wear a *sanbenito*, a tunic that publicly marked him as a heretic.[2]

Orejuela was the grandson of Juan Ruiz de Orejuela, a conquistador and encomendero from Córdoba, in southern Spain. The mestizo laborer had a series of well-placed Spanish uncles, half-brothers, cousins, and nephews who occupied positions in the civil and ecclesiastical administration in Santafé, including friars in the major religious orders and Crown attorneys charged with providing legal representation to native communities (*protectores de indios*), whose names and positions he relates in some detail in his testimony to the inquisitors. Orejuela also recalled the women into whose families they had married, some of whom carried the noble title of doña. In contrast, all he could say about his indigenous family was that his mother's name was Luysa Baroso.[3] Orejuela's lack of familiarity with his maternal relatives insinuates that he probably grew up at some distance from them and in close proximity to his Spanish family (so he was more like the children of Juana Galván than like those of Lázaro Mulato). This does not mean, however, that the Orejuelas recognized Pablos de Orejuela as an equal, just as Juana Galván's presence in her father's household in Vélez did not guarantee that she would enjoy the same privileges as her half siblings and cousins.

One of the advantages of Inquisition records is that the accused was required to narrate his life story, which provides a window into the wanderings of a Santafé mestizo in the first half of the seventeenth century.

> Asked his life story he said, as he has already stated, that he was born in the city of Santafé, where he was brought up in his parents' house, serving their every need without leaving the city, until at seventeen [years of age] his father died and he went to work on a cattle farm three leagues from the city, where he spent more than twelve years running it and amusing himself by hunting deer and going to hear mass every Sunday and on feast days in the pueblo of Usaquén, on occasion going in that period to Santafé. And when the farm was sold he went with his brothers to work on a ranch they owned, where he stayed for ten or eleven years. After that time he went as a tithe collector [*diezmero*] to a pueblo in Tunja Province called Sátiva where he was for two years, and then he went to do the same job in the pueblo of Chita for two or three years, and another five or six years spent in collecting tithes in various pueblos in the jurisdiction of Tunja, and at the end of that he returned to his ranch where he raised pigs for two years and then came to Santafé, where he opened a dry-goods store on the main street, which he had for five or six years. And then he went to live in a house a brother had mortgaged, and there he mounted a *barras* game from which he earned his living and fed his wife and children and grandchildren, and he declares that he married his wife when he was running the herd of cattle he has already mentioned. Some fourteen months ago don Antonio de Bergara detained him in the royal jail and he was there for about a year. A brother of his named Francisco de Orejuela posted bail so that he could present himself to this tribunal as, in effect, he has, and near Honda he met Father Pedro de Achuri, whom he told that he was coming to this tribunal, and he came with him to this Inquisition, where he arrived four days ago.[4]

Pablos de Orejuela was brought up by Spaniards, not as a son but as a servant. He narrates his life as a series of moves from one rural site to another, where he worked as a farm manager and a tithe collector. In his younger days he had seen the wrong side of the law, having been accused of having sexual relations with a young indigenous servant on a farm in Usaquén.[5] Finally, he established his independence as the proprietor of a small dry-goods store in Santafé and as the manager of a popular urban gaming site, where plebeian men congregated to play, drink, and socialize. While he was familiar with his Spanish relatives, some of whom had hired him as a laborer or lent him real estate to mount his small business, he was not welcome in the circles in which they socialized or in the private spaces where they lived. Like Juana Galván, he came of age at a time when conquistador fathers were no longer anxious to recognize their mestizo offspring or to marry their mestiza daughters to eligible Spaniards. Ultimately, their criollo sons married Spanish women and privileged their legitimate, Spanish progeny. In turn, the legitimate sons and daughters of the conquistadors marginalized their mestizo siblings.

Pablos de Orejuela was similar to Manuel Rodríguez, the mulatto from Soatá, in the sense that both moved on the edge of the rural indigenous communities in which they resided, seeking employment on haciendas, with urban merchants, or with the Church, jobs that led them to occupy the position of intermediary between powerful institutions and their indigenous neighbors. The relationships Orejuela enumerates in his testimony are largely with other mestizos and mulattos, as was the case with Rodríguez (although their relationships with Spaniards were quite different, since Orejuela was brought up in a Spanish household). However, the countryside looked different in Orejuela's time, a half-century after Rodríguez's mishaps in Soatá. Now, in the mid-seventeenth century, there were more mestizos and fewer Indians in the hinterlands of Santafé and Tunja. People of mixed parentage had not yet overtaken the indigenous population in terms of numbers, but would do so in the next hundred years; the presence of mestizos and mulattos was already transforming the nature of rural life. For many scholars, this would be the moment at which we should begin to speak of "caste," of a hardening of socioracial classifications emerging out of an ever-more heterogeneous population.

Historians of New Spain who study the mid- to late seventeenth century routinely refer to people like Pablos de Orejuela as "castas," a term that in the sixteenth century signified lineage, in particular, a noble lineage free of Jewish or Muslim ancestors (and sometimes, of mulatto ancestors)—as Covarrubias succinctly states, "Means noble lineage."[6] But by the mid-seventeenth century, when separate parish registers appear in Mexico City, "casta" had begun to refer more specifically to categories of admixture or to the universe of mixed categories.[7] There were potentially up to forty caste groups, although R. Douglas Cope points to seven constants: Spaniards, castizos, Moriscos, mestizos, mulattos, Indians, and blacks, with castizos and Moriscos being variants of indigenous-European mixes. Cope, like most other Mexicanists, calls caste a *system*, which he describes as a hierarchical ordering of racial groups classified according to their relative proportions of Spanish blood.[8] "Casta" was not employed in this sense in the documentation I consulted for the Nuevo Reino during the first century and a half of Spanish domination, nor does this particular usage appear in the published literature of the era or in most legal usage in the Caribbean and Peru, although it does emerge in administrative reports in eighteenth-century Nueva Granada (as the Nuevo Reino came to be called when it was elevated to the status of viceroyalty in the early eighteenth century).[9] Casta coexisted in Nueva Granada with another more localized scheme, in which people who were not Spaniards, Indians, or slaves were assigned to the category *"libres de todos los colores"* (free men of all colors) which identified them as free of tribute, bondage, or other similar obligations.[10]

The casta model used by historians of New Spain lends a certain conceptual fixity to a set of practices that was fluid in Mexico, the Nuevo Reino, and other regions of Spanish America, where the contours of classificatory practice were continuously shaped by context and overlapped with other means of categorizing individuals. The apparent stability of casta categories in the colonial documentation—particularly in the visual record, as exemplified by the illusory fixity of socioracial categories in eighteenth-century Mexican castas paintings—and their articulation by scholars into a "system" has led historians to focus on cases of mistaken or ambiguous identity as a characteristic of casta as an epistemological formation: an emphasis on "mistakes" in classification implies the existence of a system that governs the "correct" use of socioracial labels.[11] However, by privileging a set of practices that bestow primacy on what we would today call "race," we lose sight of the other ways in which diversity was managed and negotiated in the colonial period.[12] We also tend to ignore how different practices of distinguishing one individual from another came into play in concrete situations. That is, we end up labeling as "race" something that was much more multifaceted.

Landmark studies of casta in late colonial Mexico, such as the work of John Chance in Oaxaca, hint that the Mexican casta model might not have been quite so iconic in eighteenth-century New Spain either. Chance submits that other systems that distinguished between tributaries and nontributaries, between *gente de razón* ("rational" people, i.e., Spaniards or Christians) and Indians, or between gente decente ("decent" folk, i.e., persons who accrued honor) and plebeians were as decisive as casta in regulating social intercourse and self-identification, and were relevant to a broader array of social contexts. He points out that caste designations were germane only to marriage records, Inquisition trials, and certain censuses; they were largely eclipsed by other social typologies in the vast range of administrative and judicial proceedings.[13] More recently, Jake Frederick has demonstrated that in eighteenth-century eastern Mexico "marriage . . . was very often the first time that an individual could be said to have entered into the sistema de castas, through the logging of a racial identity in the legal documentation," a moment at which "casta identity was not merely a matter of recorded genealogical origins but was also conferred by public consent."[14] While the casta hierarchy appears to have been a significant feature of late colonial Mexican society, we cannot read New Spain exclusively through caste, much as such an approach appeals to modern academic proclivities toward critical race theory.

Consequently, it behooves us to examine classificatory practices such as caste and ask whether they are, indeed, relevant as conceptual frameworks for scholarly interpretation beyond the documentary contexts in which they appear. Chance questions the status of the caste system when he makes the thought-provoking assertion that caste was a "folk model" of the Spanish elite; Cope also suggests that the casta system, understood as a complex hierarchy determined by genealogy, was largely confined to the Mexican elite, whereas plebeian determination of socioracial classification was much looser.[15] In this sense, caste in Mexico was a culturally, geographically, and historically specific discourse employed by members of the upper reaches of society.

In this sense, it is certainly amenable to ethnographic interpretation. But was it an overarching system that governed people's lives as modern historians have imagined? Should we transport it wholesale as an imperial model to other parts of Spanish America and to time periods other than the eighteenth century? Should we assume that it was equally relevant to all members of society? These and several other questions are pertinent to any inquiry into the centrality of caste in colonial Spanish America. In framing them, I refrain from using the word "casta" and instead continue to use "calidad": did colonial worldviews privilege color over other social diacritics? Did early moderns understand calidad as pertaining to individuals or to groups? Was it stable across the life cycle, or was it transitory?

Early colonial Santafereños did not negotiate their social worlds through the lens of a full-blown caste system or even a through a looser array of stable soci{racial categories, but instead disputed what constituted a mestizo or a mulatto—as well as a Spaniard or an Indian—not only because people's individual statuses were at stake, but also because these categories were not entirely clear to anyone, and uncertainty as to who might belong to them prevailed. Indeed, it remains in question whether such classes of mixed persons constituted sociological groups at all. Identity, even physical appearance (including color), was not believed to be fixed or stable, but was seen as highly malleable, subject to transformations generated by behavior, by the simple process of aging, by official decree, and by the force of the imagination. Processes of identification certainly revolved around aspect or parentage, but they also were grounded in conflicting strategies for determining birthright, which only partially involved parentage and, when they did, were primarily concerned with issues of honor and nobility.

Some historians of New Spain have argued that the fluidity of caste characteristic of the early colonial period "hardened" in the eighteenth century, taking on aspects that would later develop into a racial discourse characterized by exclusion from privilege.[16] By tracing transformations in the demography of the central highlands of the Santafé and Tunja Provinces during the seventeenth and eighteenth centuries, I explore whether such a hardening did indeed take place in late colonial Nueva Granada. While the following interpretation of seventeenth-century demographics is based on a combination of primary and secondary sources, my treatment of the eighteenth century is largely confined to the secondary literature, permitting me to engage in speculation, as opposed to the presentation of historical evidence.

A CENTURY OF MESTIZOS

By the time of Pablos de Orejuela's adulthood in the mid-seventeenth century, the indigenous population registered in censuses of the provinces of Tunja and Santafé had dropped precipitously, a casualty of disease and flight from tribute and mita obligations. The fluid and ever-diminishing population of the pueblos de indios was also a product of the peripatetic character of Muisca society, whose members moved from their communities of birth to the pueblos where they had married, or from their fathers' villages to their mothers', posing a challenge to Spanish census-takers obliged to pinpoint the whereabouts of tributaries.[17] Working with census data from Tunja, Germán Colmenares computes a 69 percent decline in the native population over the sixteenth century, which had mounted to 84 percent by 1636.[18] Juan Friede calculates the combined population loss for Santafé and Tunja provinces at two-thirds, with numbers declining from 34,914 in 1565 to 10,295 in 1636.[19] The disparity in the two historians' figures can be explained by the fact that native demographic decline was not as steep in seventeenth-century Santafé as it was in Tunja, where the encomienda system was more consolidated and brutal.

Eventually, the demographic space left by the declining indigenous population was filled by mestizos, mulattos, and others—many of them, perhaps, natives who were not registered on the tribute rolls. Those who came to inhabit villages like Usaquén were frequently peripatetic men like Pablos de Orejuela, whose ties to native communities were precarious and who moved where their work took them. When they eventually settled down, as Orejuela ultimately did in Usaquén, the relationships they established did not necessarily draw them closer to indigenous people, unless they married local women.

Those mestizos who married native women or mestizas who had grown up in indigenous households quite likely raised their children in a native milieu. This complicates how we might delimit the scope of the "native world" in mid- and late colonial Santafé and Tunja. The extent of indio intermarriage with mestizos, blacks, mulattos, and poor Spaniards in the seventeenth century is unclear from the available documents, which were more concerned with enumerating the number of native tributaries than counting the mestizos living in indigenous communities. Visitadores found it challenging to identify with any precision the size of the nonindigenous population in the pueblos de indios. Whether or not a local mestizo was investigated by colonial officials depended to a great extent on the willingness of local witnesses to testify to his or her presence; those mestizos who were family members of indigenous officials probably passed under the radar of many a visitador, while those who allowed their pigs to graze on native lands would have their names brought to the authorities. However, a perusal of the indices of visita holdings in the Archivo General de la Nación in Bogotá reveals that there were very few censuses of indigenous communities in the central Andean region of the Nuevo Reino from the mid-seventeenth to the mid-eighteenth century, the last major visita being Juan de Valcárcel's, in 1636.

Mestizaje was an emergent fact of life in the seventeenth-century hinterlands of Santafé and Tunja, as Valcárcel discovered in his investigation of the status of the pueblos de indios of Sogamoso in Tunja Province, including Mongua, Monguí, Sogamoso, Tópaga, and Tutasá. Valcárcel commenced his visita by declaring to the assembled Indians "that he had come to expel the mestizos, mulattos, blacks, zambaigos, indios ladinos, and other persons who cause them harm and offense, and to order that [the Indians] live in and frequent their towns, [settling] as a group [juntos] in town centers [poblados], so that they are most easily taught the Christian doctrine and have enough lands for their labors and for raising their cattle."[20] Valcárcel's objective was to isolate the indigenous community from pernicious external influences, which involved not only shutting off native people and their lands from outsiders, but also containing them in an easily managed and centralized pueblo (a strategy that was not entirely successful). Valcárcel's interrogations of local Spanish officials and indigenous nobles uncovered a significant group of mestizos renting lands and living within the confines of the pueblos de indios. The parcels they had acquired were part of the collective estates called resguardos, a system of protective segregation instituted in the late sixteenth century as a means of isolating native people from non-indios; the assignation of resguardo lands also had the collateral effect of freeing up some 95 percent of the surrounding territory for exploitation by other sectors, principally by large haciendas, although there were also smallholders living legally on the outskirts of resguardos and sometimes illegally on resguardo lands themselves.[21]

Spanish authorities of Valcárcel's time exhibited certainty as to who was a forastero (an "outsider") in the native communities they surveyed: nonindigenous smallholders inhabiting the pueblos de indios, even those who were married to native women, even their mestizo children. A visitador would not have considered mestizos, mulattos, and Spaniards living beyond the resguardo boundaries as outsiders, because they were not breaking the law by inhabiting those spaces, which were not legally segregated. Note, therefore, that the systems of settlement and land tenure did not completely isolate native people from other inhabitants of the countryside. A mestizo living on a privately owned plot outside the pueblo and resguardo boundaries could legally continue to reside there and pursue various sorts of economic and social relationships with his indigenous neighbors. Valcárcel was concerned with those who lived on resguardo property.

The men Valcárcel identified as interlopers in Sogamoso included Pedro Mendo, a mestizo who farmed pigs on resguardo lands. He had been denounced on a previous occasion by indigenous officials for allowing his animals to overrun indigenous plantings and had therefore been forcibly evicted and imprisoned, but he had eventually returned to Sogamoso (323r–v, 339v–340r, 444r). Diego Pacheco, another mestizo, grew wheat on a plot left vacant by the cacique. He supported himself by purchasing even more wheat from his neighbors, operating mule trains, fueled by indigenous labor, that circulated throughout the region and supplied him with the raw material for his flour mill (324r, 325v–326r). While Pedro Mendo's pig-headed relationship with his indigenous neighbors would have also made him an outsider to the native community, it is less certain that local merchant Diego Pacheco stood in an adversarial relationship to his indigenous suppliers. Pacheco probably paid rent for the plot he farmed, and his commercial activities would have brought cash into the community.

There were others living in Sogamoso who were not naturales, in the sense of formally belonging to the community, but who were nevertheless indigenous. Francisco Pongota, an indio ladino from Quito—like the clandestine suitor Francisco Suárez, Pongota was a huauqui—ran a dry-goods store, a *pulpería*, that supplied the native population with foodstuffs,

With respect to the charge that I have sold wine by barter to
the Indians of this pueblo, and soap, honey, and candles and
other items contained in the aforementioned accusation, I am

innocent because I have kept in my house the aforementioned merchandise, and I have very comfortably sold it in exchange for money to the Indians without having given wine in exchange for wheat, because it never happened. In contrast, I should be rewarded for having in my house the merchandise included in the accusation, because in the time of the plague [peste general] and smallpox in this pueblo the Indians had comfortable access in my house to whatever they needed, and moreover, the profit I have earned has paid my tribute to His Majesty and supported my wife and my four children, in the absence of any other way of supporting myself, since I have no lands on which to plant. (447r)[22]

Indios ladinos living in Muisca communities were frequently disposed to fraternize largely with other forasteros; the fact that they were also "indios" did not necessarily draw them into social circles frequented by native tributaries. "Indian" was certainly a legal identity, but "Sogamoso" aroused sentiments of shared affinity from which indios ladinos like Francisco Pongota were excluded. He was in a position similar to that of the cobbler Juan de Salazar, who was sometimes identified as an Indian and sometimes as a mestizo, given his ambiguous relationship as a huauqui to the tributaries of Fontibón.

Some people residing in the vicinity of Sogamoso fervently denied any attachment, genealogical or otherwise, to the pueblos de indios. Juan López de La Cruz stated,

I am not a mestizo, as I have been charged, but a quarteroon, the legitimate son of Juan López de la Cruz, who lives in the Chocontá Valley and María de Carrión, my parents, and I was raised by Juan de Torres Contreros with the upbringing that a man of his virtues could give me, and today I am in his household, taken as an honorable man and not as a mestizo, and it is public and notorious that I have committed no offenses against any Indians or any other people. (464r)

López de la Cruz distanced himself from the indios by emphasizing his attachment to a European household, just as Juana Galván did in her lawsuit. Whether his identification as a quarteroon was based strictly on his parentage or if it was grounded in the Spanish social networks in which he had been raised cannot be determined. Unlike Pablos de

Orejuela, López de la Cruz apparently enjoyed a close relationship with his Spanish employer, and his service to his adopted family was not as a menial laborer, given that he identified himself as "honorable," although what that relationship involved remains unknown.

But there were also many mestizos in Sogamoso who had built close attachments to the pueblos de indios: men like Pascual Sánchez (323v–324r), Pedro de Torres (325r), and the blacksmiths Blas Martín and Francisco Pérez (325r), who had all married local indigenous women. The children of these unions remained in the pueblos de indios, tilling resguardo soil and marrying local indias or mestizas (325v, 341r). The relationships they established with the local indigenous elite ran deep. Pedro Rodríguez Mendo testified, "For more than thirty years I have lived in this valley and have been married to the sister, now deceased, of don Juan Yrcansas, cacique of this pueblo, and my second marriage is to a noble india from there, and I have lived quietly and peacefully, and I have had many children, and at present there are seven who are alive, from both marriages" (444r).[23] Rodríguez Mendo claimed he had in his possession an order, obtained by local caciques from the president of the Audiencia, that permitted him and his children to remain in the community. In fact, one of his sons was, at the time of his testimony, the captain of Tópaga, one of the capitanías of Sogamoso (444r).

By 1668, three decades after Valcárcel's visit to Sogamoso, there were some eighty mestizos and other outsiders identified in the Audiencia's records—still a relatively small number, but growing.[24] The historian Víctor Álvarez calls the seventeenth century "the century of the mestizo," because this is the era in which the mestizo population of the Nuevo Reino began to consolidate, despite the fact that mestizos were still not in the majority.[25] The men who appear in the 1636 visit to Sogamoso had little in common with don Diego de Torres or don Alonso de Silva, who claimed descent from chiefly lines, or with the García Zorro brothers and Isabel de Sotelo, who moved comfortably in polite society. The "century of mestizos" was, instead, populated by people like Juana Galván, Lázaro Mulato, Pablos de Orejuela, and the mestizos of Sogamoso: still in the minority, living on the edge, moving in plebeian urban circles, eking out a living on rented lands or shrewdly making ends meet through petty commerce, artisanal labor, or mule trains. These were men and women who, one way or another, were compelled to establish productive and sometimes affective relationships with the Indians who surrounded them.

There were only 3,378 mestizos in the hinterlands of Santafé Province at the dawn of the eighteenth century according to what were unquestionably incomplete census data, although the mestizo population would grow eightfold in subsequent decades.[26] While the seventeenth-century central highlands are described by some historians as a bipolar society, largely comprising Spaniards and Indians, acceptance of mestizos in the countryside was fostered by a low population density and a level of interethnic conflict that was relatively muted in comparison to the fears of Indian and mestizo rebellion that had characterized the sixteenth century.[27] Mestizos living in rural areas were called "outsiders" by Spanish officials, who concerned themselves with preserving the ethnic purity of the pueblos de indios, but this does not mean that in fact these people existed entirely outside an imagined autonomous indigenous community, particularly when many of them were the children of native women or were their spouses.

THE CULTURAL ENVIRONMENT OF RURAL MESTIZOS

We know nothing of the cultural matrix that these mestizos drew on in their efforts at coexistence with their indigenous neighbors. None of them enjoyed a Spanish education or entrée into elite social networks, nor did they share the prerogatives of the descendants of Muisca nobility, so that unlike elite mestizos, these individuals did not leave significant paper trails of the sort that might provide palpable cues for describing their cultural ethos. As was true for both Juana Galván and Pablos de Orejuela, the private lives of some seventeenth-century mestizos unfolded in a plebeian milieu, where their daily activities led them to interact with mestizo, mulatto, and ladino artisans as friends, with tributary Indians as clients, and with indios ladinos as political allies or mates. But there were also men, like Lázaro Mulato, who were immersed in a web of largely indigenous relationships, despite their classification as people of mixed parentage. Although the Spanish administration was alarmed by the pernicious effect these mestizos and mulattos might have on indigenous communities, it is just as likely that their own quotidian habits—agricultural techniques, culinary practices, relations of respect, the local lexicon their spoken Spanish drew on—were colored by Muisca lifeways, as they continue to be in modern-day Boyacá and Cundinamarca. Certainly, some of these mestizos and mulattos spoke the Muisca language, as Manuel Rodríguez probably did. A number of them, particularly the women, wore native costume and were called "mestizas in Indian habit" when they migrated to the cities.

We might speak of certain mestizos, especially those who grew up in pueblos de indios with their native mothers, as "deindianized." Guillermo Bonfíl Batalla defines deindianization as a process through which communities or individuals shed their indigenous identity but continue to maintain indigenous lifeways.[28] According to colonial policy, the mestizos of the Nuevo Reino were not recognized as Indians in the first place, so it is perhaps a stretch to use this term. However, as Juana Galván's efforts at removing herself from the tribute rolls implies, acknowledgment of Indian identity did not necessarily mean that one's ancestors were exclusively Muisca: being an indio was an act of enunciation by an individual who recognized him- or herself as carrying that label and fulfilling the obligations it entailed, or by colonial officials who sought to impose that classification. It is therefore likely that many of the mestizos living in the hinterlands in the early seventeenth century moved in and out of the Indian slot. Furthermore, the notion of deindianization most clearly conveys the cultural tensions and ambiguous allegiances experienced by mestizos raised in pueblos de indios; it underlines the fact that although such mestizos were not recognized as Indians by the administration, they might very well have self-identified as such, as certainly did the son of Pedro Rodríguez Mendo, the capitán of Tópaga.

At the same time that these settlers were immersed in Muisca cultural practices, native tributaries increasingly became Spanish-speakers and intermarried with mestizos, fostering a transculturative effect in the indigenous population that brought them closer to their mestizo neighbors.[29] In his now classic 1957 article on the creation of the resguardos, Orlando Fals Borda dwells on Andrés Berdugo y Oquendo's 1755 visita of the pueblo of Soatá—where the mulatto Manuel Rodríguez lived a century and a half earlier—and notes that the visitador had trouble defining which inhabitants were Indians and therefore counted mestizos as Indians.[30] Don Francisco Silvestre, secretary of the viceroyalty of Nueva Granada, reported in 1789 that "the Indians have not become a minority where they had been, but have been hispanized, and have passed into other castes [los Yndios no se han minorado donde los havia, sino que se han ido españolizando, y pasando a otras castas]."[31] In other words, census-takers found it difficult to distinguish between Indians and non-Indians, suggesting that native pueblos in the latter half of the colonial period should be understood as increasingly open, instead of imagined as closed corporate communities.[32]

DEMOGRAPHIC SUBSTITUTION IN THE EIGHTEENTH CENTURY

While the experiences of Pablos de Orejuela and the mestizos of Sogamoso fit neatly into the dynamic process of early colonial social classification, a demographic sea change took place in the eighteenth century. Because there were so few visitas in the early part of the century, it is difficult to gauge the process of population substitution that unfolded, but by the mid-eighteenth century mestizos and other people of mixed parentage reportedly comprised a majority in both the countryside and in the city of Santafé. The visitador Andrés Berdugo y Oquendo counted 26,123 Indians and 44,566 nonindigenous inhabitants in the province of Tunja in 1755. He tallied 28,721 indios and 23,303 non-Indians for the province of Santafé, with some localities that once were homes to vast native populations—Guatavita, Zipaquirá, and Ubaté, for example—having become 62.6 percent nonindigenous, while in others the native population held its own. In summary, Berdugo discovered that only a third of the population of the central highland provinces of Nueva Granada was indigenous.[33] Twenty years later, in the 1770s, Francisco Antonio Moreno y Escandón encountered a population distribution in Tunja that roughly mirrored Berdugo's figures, with 48,459 vecinos and 28,735 Indians. He also reported a notable increase in the vecino population of the province of Santafé, which rose to 42,798 vecinos, as opposed to 29,442 Indians. If those figures are accurate, the vecino population of Santafé doubled in two decades.[34]

A large proportion of the late colonial rural populace was made up of mestizos, mulattos, and individuals who self-identified as Spaniards, all of whom were called by the collective name "vecinos," expanding the early colonial concept of citizen so that it included a much broader swath of the population than it had previously. Many vecinos were poor, living hand-to-mouth on rented lands, although among them there emerged a small-town elite, the *orejones*, who inhabited the urban periphery and, along with the surviving indigenous nobility, exerted control over the institutions of these localities.[35] Some vecinos were deeply enmeshed in indigenous social networks, while others may have considered themselves to be the social superiors of the indios, interacting with them only in formal contexts, like business deals, religious activities, or in the marketplace. However, occupying a higher social position in a rural pueblo did not mean that the vecinos were of equal status to the urban elite: the vecinos of Chiquiza, for example, were all illiterate.[36]

While we know that there were many non-Indians in the late colonial pueblos de indios of Santafé and Tunja, it is difficult to take the population figures contained in the visitas at face value. Censuses, like all administrative procedures, were permeated by the ideology of the official charged with compiling them; eighteenth-century visitadores systematized their collection of demographic facts in accordance with their own political objectives. One of the central debates that consumed mid- and late eighteenth-century administrators concerned the early colonial policy of segregating the indigenous into nucleated settlements and delimiting communal resguardo lands in an effort to restrain encroachment by "outsiders." Joaquín de Aróstegui y Escoto, a visitador working the central highland region in the same period as Berdugo y Oquendo, defended the segregation policy in his 1758–60 visita, blaming the disintegration of native communities on the presence of mestizos, whom he sought to remove from the pueblos and resguardos. In contrast, Berdugo sought to reverse the protectionist agenda that was crystallized in the resguardo system, which he contended was inhibiting vecinos from obtaining the resources they needed to make a living at a time when nonindigenous smallholders exerted so much pressure on lands in rural districts. Aróstegui found that 62 percent of the population of the forty-five pueblos of the province of Santafé was indigenous and only 38 percent mestiza, while Berdugo's survey of Santafé, Tunja, and Vélez counted a population that was 32.4 percent native and 67.6 percent white or mestizo.[37]

These discrepancies can be partially explained by the diverse demographic panoramas of the three provinces. There was a considerably higher proportion of Indians in Santafé than in Tunja, and there were also notable differences in population distribution in the various *corregimientos* (subprovincial jurisdictions) of the three provinces.[38] But the divergent findings of the two inspections can also be attributed to what their visitadores were looking for. Aróstegui, for example, found himself correcting the lists of tributaries that had been compiled by priests in advance of the census, deleting mestizos and reconciling the correct number of Indians in each pueblo.[39] As Alfonso Múnera infers, there might well have been more Indians in the countryside than colonial officials reported.[40] This can be surmised by the sudden appearance of a substantial indigenous contingent in the Comunero Rebellion of 1781, which in the Santafé and Tunja area took the form of a native struggle to restore communal resguardo lands that had been auctioned in the wake of the visitas.[41] The continued presence of native people, despite the insistence by visitadores that they no longer existed, attests to the persistence of indigenous identity in the late colonial period. However, visitas not only counted people; they also set into motion processes of land redistribution that gutted the resguardos, fostering further deindianization. The consequences would permanently alter the socioracial identity of the rural population, as well as the nature of land tenure in the altiplano for centuries to come.[42]

LIBRES DE TODOS LOS COLORES

What distinguishes viceregal Nueva Granada from eighteenth-century Mexico, apart from a paucity of classificatory terminology in comparison to its profusion in New Spain, is the extraordinarily sweeping replacement of the indigenous population of the central highlands by mestizos. This process bred an environment in which it became increasingly difficult to distinguish among individuals by their calidad. A second system of categorization emerged that distinguished between Indians, whites, slaves, and "free men of all colors" or "libres de todos los colores," the latter making up almost half of the population in the second half of the eighteenth century. Margarita Garrido has called the category "libre" a response to a situation in which classification based on mixture—of the sort we imagine when we think of the casta system—had become impossible. "Libre," notes Garrido, "signified independence from a cacique, a slaveowner, or a lord, autonomy to leave the town, to labor in different places, or to support oneself by one's own industry. Recognition as free men or women signified an inclusion among non-Indians and nonslaves, although the qualification 'of color' alluded to a stain, which justified exclusion from whites."[43] Thus, the category "libre" was at once a kind of socioracial classification and a condition demarcated by the scope of one's freedom of movement. It was both inclusive, distinguishing the indigenous tributary and the slave from the "free man," who was not subject to the same obligations, and exclusive, premising the separation into categories on the basis of color.[44]

Individuals identified by calidad were also described in terms of their complexion, specifically the color of their faces; indeed, the two forms of identification interacted with one another. With the exception of blacks, whose moniker served both to classify by calidad and to indicate their complexion, other color terms, such as "white" (blanca) and "brown" (morena), were used in the sixteenth and seventeenth centuries to signify not classes of people, but the color of individual faces (their complexions). In fact, terms of calidad like "mestizo" or "mulatto" become color terms in the documentation, indicating a degree of uncertainty in applying physiognomic conventions to non-European bodies. Sebastián de Covarrubias defines "blanca" as a color, but not as a class of persons; "morena" receives a similar treatment from the lexicographer, whereas "negro" is defined as "the Ethiopian of black color."[45] Note that Covarrubias's entries for "white" and "brown" are in the feminine—"blanca" and "morena"—since they refer exclusively to color, which in the period was a feminine noun; the entry for "black" (negro), which Covarrubias defines as both a color and a class of people, is in the masculine, which suggests that in this case classificatory group takes precedence over color.

In contrast, the eighteenth-century *Diccionario de autoridades* does refer to "blanco" as a class of persons, including in its definition noticeable value judgments regarding socioracial categories other than "white."

> Hombre *blanco* [white man] Muger *blanca* [white woman]. The same as honorable person, noble, of known calidad: because the blacks, mulattos, Berbers, and other peoples who among us are taken as insignificant and abject normally lack the white color, which Europeans almost always have: to be a white man, or a white woman, is taken as a prerogative of nature, which marks as well-born those who have it: and for this reason it is said, "That is not done among white men," to signify that an action is bad, common only among despicable people.[46]

Ann Twinam observes that "color" was an important word in late colonial documentation, where "whiteness" became a key characteristic of those seeking certificates of purity of blood. *"Pardo,"* another word for "brown," also became a term used to indicate a class of people in the eighteenth century, denoting free blacks but also a baser nature.[47]

"Libre" was a form of classification used in Nueva Granada that combined color with degree of autonomy from the established authorities, and it operated side by side with calidad. Marta Herrera hypothesizes that context determined which classificatory scheme took precedence over the other, affording the colonial state the space to simultaneously globalize and particularize.[48] Thus, for example, in civil disputes and in suits over inheritance, individuals are labeled as "vecinos" with no attention paid to calidad. A look at this documentation would lead the reader to assume that the only socioracial epithets in use in the period were "indio" and "negro," because everyone else is assigned to the "vecino" slot; however, designations of calidad were ubiquitous in the criminal record, in which the accused was always identified by socioracial category. This suggests that judicial authorities perceived certain classes of people to be more prone to criminal activity than were others or, perhaps, in an effort to more easily recognize offenders, whereas in civil disputes between landowners, to take one example, calidad was immaterial. People were also identified by calidad in marriage registers, although, as Guiomar Dueñas points out, marriage was practiced largely by the Spanish elite (and by Indians living in pueblos where there were doctrinal priests), with the "Spanish" designation encompassing not only those born in Spain but also American-born creoles and mestizos able to integrate into Spanish society. Libres, in contrast, produced an exceptionally high number of illegitimate births, accentuating a bipolar divide that distinguished an amorphous group of (illegitimate and honorless) people of color from (legitimate and honorable) people who were either genealogically or culturally European.[49]

It would be erroneous, however, to assume that the assignment of individuals to the category of libre was entirely grounded in color or calidad. Bonil Gómez's examination of population lists (*padrones*) from Mariquita suggests that indios were distinguished from their nonindigenous neighbors according to a series of criteria, some of which transcended color or calidad. Non-indios living in the countryside were called "blancos" or "*gentes de color*" (people of color), which distinguished them by color; "vecino" or "libre," which pointed to their lack of tributary status; "*arrendatario*" (renter), which highlighted the temporary nature of their access to land; "*feligrés*" (faithful), emphasizing their membership in parishes, as opposed to the doctrinal churches attended by Indians; and "*cosechero*" (harvester), which was used to identify individuals by occupation in tobacco-growing regions.[50]

Balancing the classification of individuals by calidad with the tributary-libre oppositional pair involved an intricate series of juxtapositions of color, occupation, and place of residence that drew a precarious dividing line between "libres" and "Spaniards," which some historians have argued, was largely based on the degree of honor accruing to individuals. In plebeian barrios like Las Nieves in Santafé, where Spanish laborers and artisans shared a common economic and occupational status with their mestizo neighbors and there was a great deal of intermarriage, it would be difficult to delimit Spaniard from mestizo genealogically, and it was not easy to differentiate people by color. Such blurring of calidad's boundaries was less conspicuous in neighborhoods characterized by economic diversity, like La Catedral, a barrio whose Spaniards were differentiated from libres by their economic status.[51] But sometimes, even in largely plebeian social spaces like Las Nieves, mestizos angled for a more prestigious label. López Bejarano registered the categories assigned at baptism to the children of a single extended family in that barrio. Some were labeled in the church records as mulattos and mestizos, while others, whose parents shared the same occupations as other family members and presumably were of similar appearance, were recorded as "white." López Bejarano attributes this to the fact that they lived along the main street (the Calle Real), occupying a higher-status location than did their relatives.[52]

Mestizos were further distinguished from Spaniards by the degree of honor that adhered to their occupations. López Bejarano refers to "mestizo work" as the series of baser forms of employment that were once the province of Indians and were now carried out by the libres who had supplanted the indigenous population of Santafé. Some of these occupations, such as blacksmith, tailor, cobbler, and carpenter, were deemed to be "honorable" by official edict in the late eighteenth century, a kind of escape hatch out of libre status.[53] In other instances, individuals were forced to defend the honor of their work through convoluted legal argumentation that reclassified their trades as honorable. López recounts the intriguing case of a nobleman whose family opposed his marriage to a mestiza. The woman lived in one of the plebeian quarters of the city, where she sold corn beer (chicha). Her future in-laws contended that her occupation as a *chichera* (chicha-seller) was "mestiza" and hence not honorable. The couple argued in her defense that she was not a chichera, but instead operated a small store in her place of residence, where she also sold bread, candles, and firewood, thus making her employment less vile (*infame*): she was a tradeswoman (*comerciante*), working honorably in the private sphere. This explanation of her livelihood was meant to make her more acceptable to the nobleman's family, although when the couple eventually married, it was with the consent of their local parish priest, not of the young man's parents.[54]

CONCLUSION: CASTE AND CLASSIFICATION IN EIGHTEENTH-CENTURY NUEVA GRANADA

The early colonial period was a time when the rural landscape of the central highlands was more consistently native, boasting a gradually declining population of indigenous tributaries and a handful of mestizos who coexisted with their native neighbors in the pueblos de indios. The cities of Santafé, Tunja, and Vélez were also largely indigenous, although mestizos, mulattos, blacks, and Spaniards are ubiquitous in the early colonial documentary record, and their stories illuminate what it meant to dwell in and toggle between the loosely defined categories of the period. My early colonial documentary research, combined with secondary readings on the eighteenth century, convinces me that we must discard the one-size-fits-all model of a stable caste system in our efforts to comprehend how diversity was managed, lived, and contested by early colonial people. A quick peek at the eighteenth century dispels any impression that the hardening of socioracial categories or the emergence of a full-blown casta system was the rule across Spanish America, even if it was true for New Spain.

The early colonial set of fluid classificatory practices gave way in eighteenth-century Nueva Granada to the use of the umbrella term "casta" to refer to all who were not Spaniards, Indians, or slaves; the concept presumably provided a way to make sense of an increasingly mixed population, particularly via those administrative procedures that counted and classified broad swathes of the populace, and which sought to redistribute resguardo lands into non-Indian hands. However, the usage of "casta" appears to be looser than in Mexico and confined to administrative documents like visitas.[55] I find no "system" in the legal record, and there are no visual documents, like the Mexican casta paintings, which would suggest that the process of classification was conceived in a systematic way. Moreover, socioracial designations were juxtaposed to other means of distinguishing among the population on the basis of the rights and obligations that different classes of people enjoyed; in fact, "libre" seems to refer to the same population as does "casta."

I don't engage in this exercise with the limited objective of demonstrating that a case study from a peripheral region like the Nuevo Reino can "disprove" the Mexican model. Nonetheless, it is significant that evidence for a complex and possibly systematic casta hierarchy can only be found in the Mexican historical literature, just as casta paintings appear to be almost exclusively a Mexican genre.[56] In a review of recent major publications on casta paintings, the art historian Tom Cummins points out the error of treating casta paintings "as an element of a universal Spanish colonial culture." Instead, he urges scholars to investigate "the particularities and the conditions of possibilities by which the casta paintings were produced."[57] The same could be said for the casta system in general. What conditions led to its emergence in certain legal contexts (or documentary genres) and among specific elite social sectors in late colonial New Spain, but not in Nueva Granada or in Peru? As a corollary, we might also think about what makes casta so appealing to us as scholars: which of our concerns are most easily satisfied by adhering to a model that can potentially stand in as an empire-wide prototype? Perhaps we assume there is a coherence to the Spanish colonial world because we as academics treat "Latin America" as a region that is susceptible to study as a unit, when, in fact, there was tremendous variation across colonial Spanish America in demographic, cultural, economic, and political terms. More important, the casta prototype seems to me to stand for "race" in its modern epistemological configuration; it is as though we have been unwilling to look at a world in which race was not a relevant discourse. We might do better to investigate other parts of the Spanish empire without submitting to the straitjacket of caste, at the same time that we attempt, in general, to decouple "casta" from "race."

Am I throwing out the baby with the bathwater? Does my rejection of the casta model leave scholars without an interpretive framework for making sense of colonial difference? I don't think so. Instead, I believe, it can help focus attention on alternative entrées into our material by opening a series of questions. First, what terminologies did people use in the period we are studying? Did they employ the word "casta," or were other terms like "género" or "calidad" more common? If "casta" appears in some documents, did it refer to a particular social group or category, or to a broad segment of the population? Or was it an alternative term for "lineage"? Who used it and under what circumstances? What was the purpose of classifying people using this particular terminology? If other terms were more frequently employed, what did they refer to and how broad were they in scope? How did they interface with "casta"? Is it possible to identify the documentary or legal scenarios in which the different terminologies were employed in order to further decipher their meanings and functions? How did the usage and performance of these terminologies change over time? In other words, by cross-examining the vocabulary we encounter in the documentation, terminologies we normally accept as transparent—and that we sometimes import unquestioningly from the secondary literature—we might open new windows into their operation as social practices in the colonial world.

Second, we need to question whether or not the use of "casta," or any of the other terminologies encountered in the documentation, implies the existence of a system. Clearly, there was some systematicity to casta in late colonial Mexico, particularly in its use in pictorial representation, where it appears as a hierarchical series of images, as well as in marriage registries, but this does not imply that the notion of system can be translated to other contexts, regions, and time periods. One of the dangers inherent to interpreting casta as a monolithic imperial system is that it exposes us to the risk of assuming that it was central to the colonial psyche, more so than other forms of stratification, such as gender, occupation, religion, geographic origin, or noble status, all of which were as significant as socioracial differentiation in generating hierarchical relationships. In fact, when we examine concrete ethnographic scenarios, we find that most frequently the various forms of social distinction operated in combination.

In short, I urge readers to consider why we might do best to approach our research not with preformulated model, but instead by engaging historical evidence more fully to construct explanations that emerge out of the documentation instead of imposing frameworks on it. If we commence our reading of the historical record with the casta system in mind, we will always find evidence that fits the model, as well as some exceptions to the rule. But we will also remain prisoners of an epistemological framework—the idea that there was a stable and coherent "system"—that limits and skews our interpretation of what we discover in the archives.

Conclusion

My central concern in this book has been to determine how mestizos and mulattos in the Nuevo Reino de Granada navigated their social worlds in the sixteenth and seventeenth centuries: who they thought they were and how they were viewed by others; what they felt it meant to be a person of mixed parentage; whom they associated with, and how their social networks shaped their processes of identification; how they moved in and out of the mestizo slot. I responded to these questions by constructing ethnographic scenarios based on close readings of the archival documentation. These vignettes feature a small number of individuals whose stories elucidate the textured nature of early colonial mestizaje. As I immersed myself in the lives of these individuals, I discovered that their indeterminate status and the far-ranging heterogeneity that characterized early colonial society unsettle our impression of a stable, systematic, and clearly delineated socioracial hierarchy in the provinces of Santafé and Tunja. That is to say, my research revealed that it would be a misnomer to speak of a "casta system" in early colonial Nuevo Reino. If we wish to comprehend how difference was negotiated by colonial people, we must be willing to set aside predetermined models and, instead, interpret their experience in context.

Unlike most scholars of race in colonial Spanish America, who provide a bird's-eye view of how hierarchy and difference were negotiated across a given region—the vast majority of these authors focusing on New Spain, with its rich documentation and extensive corpus of historical writing—I have chosen instead to write an ethnographic history. I dwell in considerable depth on a small number of historical actors, following their paper trails when possible and endeavoring to construct detailed ethnographic interpretations of key life moments in which they were forced to classify themselves in one way or another.

The ethnographic approach allows me to balance the multiple ways in which these people negotiated their identities, instead of focusing exclusively on socioracial categories; in other words, through ethnography I have been able to document processes of identification in place of concentrating on the labels—which are situational, temporary—that are the final results of this process. My scenarios are not strictly exemplars, but function as spaces of interpretation from which I have been able to tease out the complexities and ambivalences of identity production: the contexts in which one socioracial label is chosen over others, the power plays that inform these choices, the ideologies that inform them.

Diego de Torres's experience is a case in point. He is reticent in the documentation to call himself a mestizo, preferring, alternately, to frame his status as "cacique of Turmequé" (without tacking "indio" onto the title) or as "son of a Spaniard," both being genealogical appeals to his legitimate noble standing in distinct social circles, neither being, properly speaking, a socioracial label. His opponents, however, routinely refer to him as "mestizo," as well as calling him "illegitimate" or even a "bastard," sometimes even alluding to his allegedly idolatrous nature. They are much more willing to ignore Torres's genealogical pretensions and to disregard his solidly Christian credentials— both in terms of his stated beliefs and the Christian blood running in his veins—in favor of a characterization that accentuates his negative character traits, which they attribute to his being a mestizo. This is not a simple case of racial labeling, but a complicated series of actions and reactions that are ultimately intertwined in the course of an adversarial legal proceeding, whose nature can be teased out through ethnographic interpretation.

I offer my interpretations with a full awareness that the region I have chosen to examine is not as thoroughly documented by historians as are the core regions of Mexico and Peru; nor is the early colonial period I have looked at as broadly or deeply studied as is the eighteenth century. The archival corpus at my disposal is, without doubt, less rich than are the documentary repositories of the core areas, both of which functioned as major administrative and economic centers in the colonial period and still constitute the most popular locations for North American and European scholarship. My earlier research into colonial-era indigenous literacy in the northern Andes, as well as in my work on twentieth-century Colombian indigenous historical memory, concentrated on places located in what could be called the scholarly periphery in relation to the "Andean core" of Peru and Bolivia, on which most Andeanist scholars have concentrated. I found that distance from the core enabled me to question what "Andean" meant in different contexts. This book will, I hope, contribute in a similar way to a questioning of processes of socioracial identification in colonial Spanish America by focusing on a period in which the seemingly stable categories of caste never took hold and a region in which racial mixing was both more wide-ranging and resulted in a more ambiguous application of terminologies used in other colonial locations. The contrast may help us to question the models we bring with us to our readings of the archival record.

CLASSIFYING THE UNCLASSIFIABLE

The people who populate my ethnographic vignettes are not easily classifiable. They move between identities in myriad ways. Sometimes these individuals are identified as mestizos; at other times they project an unmarked identity that slips imperceptibly into the Spanish slot. Some of them are described physically as mulattos but classed as Indians; others are said to "look like" mestizos, whereas they demand recognition of Indian status; and still others do not appear to conform physiognomically to a single category. At times they opt for identification according to occupation instead of calidad. Their indeterminacy is precisely what makes them mestizos. Catalina Tafur, whose defiant and desperate act of donning native garb was condemned by her family as impertinent and self-destructive, is at some moments in her life the unmarked daughter of a conquistador and at others a "mestiza in Indian habit," a marginal woman whose status is closer to "Indian" than to "mestiza." Diego García Zorro, a man whose private life unfolded amid native and mestizo plebeians, strove to be a well-placed member of the Spanish elite despite the fact that many felt he was not owed the respect due an honorable member of Santafé's cabildo. The only wish of Lázaro Mulatto, formerly a soldier in the war against the Pijaos, was to peacefully live out his remaining years with his indigenous family in Chocontá, all of them registered native tributaries although he was a mulatto. Alonso de Silva was a figure who was so cosmopolitan, well connected, and legally savvy that it was inconceivable to the encomenderos of Tunja that he be trusted to speak for a downtrodden native community; they were forced to argue over his birthright and exclude him as a bastard unsuited to the position of cacique. None of these individuals was immediately recognizable as a mestizo or mulatto, but neither was he or she unmistakably a Spaniard, an Indian, or a black.

It is this neither-nor persona who takes center-stage here, instead of what seem to be the more stable identities of Indian, Spaniard, and African, which have occupied the epicenter of most studies of race in Spanish America. I have opted to follow the paper trails left by mestizos and mulattos, expressly because colonial practices of identification and classification permitted them to emerge in public in some circumstances and disappear into the shadows in others. This chameleon-like quality led me to pose the question of *when* they were mestizos—why they chose to "come out" as mestizos—as opposed to asking what made them mestizos or why they were correctly or incorrectly classified as such. It is not only that the colonial categories of mestizo and mulatto were permeable or fluid (which they certainly were), but that they did not operate as stable categories. There was no defined type into which a mestizo in colonial Santafé could be fitted: no clearly delineated set of attributes that distinguished him from others, whether in his physical aspect, costume, or behavior. That is why we encounter such ambiguous descriptions in the documents, informing us what color mestizos are *not*, as opposed to what they color are—don Juan, cacique of Cunucubá, "had a different manner of color from the Indians"—or relegating them to a vague, intermediate color category, such as "mestizo in color" or "mestizo-like color."

But if mestizo was such a volatile label, we may also be in error when we speak of the categories of Spaniard, African, and Indian as entirely stable themselves. In fact, these three classes, which are generally taken to be the supports of the colonial socioracial hierarchy, were themselves highly permeable. Mestizos and mulattos—those who were unclassifiable—moved in and out of the "pure" categories, thereby expanding their membership. Hence, the space of mixture functions as a site from which we can question the ostensibly more predictable and pure labels. Take again, for example, Catalina Tafur, who in reaction to the death of her father replaced her "Spanish habit," which marked her as a member of the colonial urban elite, with an "Indian habit," then later readopting European costume and marrying a Spaniard. Catalina, whom we would call a mestiza, because she had an Iberian father and an indigenous mother, spent her life moving between native and Spanish identities, but she never publicly inhabited the mestizo slot. "Indian" and "Spanish" thus acquire new meanings when viewed through the lens of the experiences of a mestiza.

The unclassifiability of mestizos was gendered in nature. Isabel de Sotelo could easily live as a Spaniard because women were Spanish only in an informal sense, which made it less challenging for her to occupy that status than it was for her lover, Juan Birves, who, as a man with a public life, had to be formally classified. It was only when Sotelo was discovered in bed with Birves that she was labeled a mestiza, an epithet that shadowed her in later years. Birves's identity was also ambiguous: he was tagged as a mestizo, but managed to acquire two encomiendas, royal grants that were only meant for Spaniards. Nevertheless, Birves started out his life as a mestizo, while Sotelo did not. She was Spanish by default, while he had to prove his Spanishness, and like so many other elite mestizo men, he encountered closed doors along the way.

There were, moreover, other identities in Santafé and Tunja that overlapped uncomfortably with the category "mestizo." Take, for example, the "huauquis" of Santafé and Fontibón. Francisco Suárez, the devious pretender to the hand of doña Catalina Acero de Vargas, was at times called an "indio" and at others a "zambo," his native Quiteño origins baffling those who sought to label him as one or the other. The same was true of Juan Salazar of Fontibón, another "huauqui" who was alternately called an "indio" and a "mestizo." Did it matter to Suárez and Salazar that colonial officials and even their peers could not pinpoint who they were? We cannot know whether they found that confusion to be problematic. Perhaps Salazar's plebeian network trumped his identification as a huauqui or an indio. Suárez's pretensions to noble Limeño status would be equally flawed regardless of whether he was classified an Indian or a zambo. In other cases, elite standing could potentially mitigate conflicting ethnoracial labels. The mestiza daughters of conquistador fathers and native women from Quito, Popayán, and Lima quietly moved into the unmarked category. This was the story of Juana de Penagos, whose mother was the daughter of the cacique of Cali, who married a wealthy Spaniard and owned several haciendas in the Santafé hinterlands. Nonetheless, Juan de Céspedes, a conquistador whose mother was a native Peruvian servant, was never able to move out of the mestizo slot; for him, gender trumped social status and geographic origin, locking him out of a substantial inheritance and access to a royal pension in recognition of his military exploits.

Finally, one's calidad was only at issue in certain social or legal scenarios, on those administrative and judicial occasions when one might be labeled a mestizo. People were free to pass as unmarked in other instances, particularly when they were affluent and educated enough to function in polite society. Thus, Alonso de Silva is a mestizo in the documentation of his struggle to legitimize his chiefly status, but he is unmarked in the writs he pens as secretary to a notary; in the notarial office, his literacy, his costume, and his command of educated Spanish all trump the color of his skin. Nor was Diego de Torres a mestizo when he took up his shield, donned his turban, and mounted his horse in the game of canes; at that moment he represented the epitome of Spanishness. However, this escape hatch was available only to those whose social status was sufficient to gain access to elite circles of urban society, where one could work as a notarial secretary or demonstrate one's horsemanship, the latter activity being reserved for a narrow slice of the elite. The rural mestizos and mulattos were more permanently and unproblematically categorized according to their mixed parentage; they did not as often dispute their calidad.

Were all of these people "really" mestizos and only temporarily "passing" as members of another category? This is what is suggested by many studies of legal cases in which individuals' calidad was in dispute, in which historians closely follow the arguments in favor of one attribution or another. Perhaps, in contrast, it would be more appropriate to say that circumstances permitted individuals to assume multiple calidades. If we focus on the circumstances of identification, as opposed to an imagined socioracial essence, we move into more thought-provoking territory. "Mestizo" constituted a strategy of identification that was more "actual"—more circumstantial—than "real": in Spanish, *actualmente* means not "actually," but "right now."[1] In many instances, being an artisan, a cacique, or the "wife of," constituted an identity that supplanted that of "mestizo," while in other cases, people had little choice concerning their classification. Returning to the Tunja adulteress Inés de Hinojosa, I suggest that the question of whether or not she was "really" a mestiza does not help us to explain early colonial processes of socioracial identification. Inés was not seen by colonial observers as half-white and half-Indian. Her mixedness disappeared into calculated but ill-fated marriages with Spaniards, and the lack of emphasis on the specificities of her birth blurred her classification. Ultimately, her identity as "murderous adulteress" was significantly more definitive than was the label "mestiza" or even "Spaniard," since the former was the label under which she was executed by hanging.

Despite the fluid movement between ethnoracial identities, the lack of stability or fixity to the categories that presumably anchored the socioracial hierarchy, and the importance of other kinds of social markers, such as gender, geographic origin, marital status, and occupation, colonial mestizos and mulattos did not necessarily envision themselves as occupying ambiguous positions in the milieus they inhabited. The world in which they lived was not as strictly delimited as we might imagine. A brief contrast with North American scholarship demonstrates this. In recounting the travails of don Alonso de Silva and don Diego de Torres, I made brief reference to the experience of Andrew Montour, a mid-eighteenth-century Oneida-French métis interpreter on the Pennsylvania frontier, the son of a genteel Frenchwoman and an Oneida warrior. The historian James H. Merrell describes Montour as a man who puzzled people because they could not place him in a single, unambiguous identity: this multilingual man, who had five names—part-European, part-Native American—which he used interchangeably, this fellow who displayed a heterogeneous aspect that mixed European garments, indigenous ear pendants, and facial paint did not fit neatly into the colonial world that Merrell identifies as "bifurcated," in which Indians inhabited "the woods" and colonists lived in towns.[2]

The mestizos and mulattos of the Nuevo Reino de Granada whose archival traces I have uncovered were not as hard to place as Montour. The world they inhabited was not a frontier society; it could perhaps be understood as more interstitial than bifurcated. While the early colonial central highlands of the Nuevo Reino exhibited a bipolar character in the sense that its dominant populations were Muisca and Spanish, the two poles did not constitute entirely distinct social and cultural worlds. Mestizos and mulattos, even plebeian Spaniards, who melted into the rural indigenous milieu inhabited pueblos with a recognizable European urban structure—even if the indigenous residents assigned to them successfully avoided living there—and prayed alongside Indians under the supervision of the Catholic Church; they ate the same foods as their native neighbors, many of them speaking or at least understanding the Muisca language. As for the Indians, their economic activities were managed by hispanized caciques with a vested interest in acquiescing to the colonial system. Over time, many natives became fluent in Spanish and, at least publicly, most professed to being devout

Christians. They spent a considerable portion of their working lives amassing the tribute they owed their Spanish overlords, paid in woven mantles or hard cash. They served as laborers on nearby haciendas or as muleteers for local vecinos. Many of those who paid their mita obligations permanently relocated with their families to urban centers, living in huts on the grounds of Spanish-style houses or on the city's fringes, serving in European households or plying the various trades—cobbler, tailor, carpenter, tanner, blacksmith—that the conquerors brought with them from the Iberian Peninsula. They were the bricklayers and ditch-diggers who built Santafé's public buildings. Their wives and daughters were the housemaids of the elite and, frequently, the mothers of mestizo children by their masters.

Nor would it be appropriate to speak of the space inhabited by mestizos and mulattos as an intermediate step between European and Muisca settlements. Mestizos and mulattos were, in many ways, legal outsiders, in relation both to the indigenous community and to Spanish social milieus. These classifications were, in fact, ambiguous, and they deprived their holders of many rights in colonial society. But the fact that mestizos and mulattos were not a group, but a loose class of people, explains why so many people of mixed parentage were absorbed in the early period into indigenous or Spanish social circles, which demonstrates how they acquired "insider" status. Institutions like the tribute system, under which administrators were prone to enumerate mestizos as Indians, facilitated such transformations of personal identity, while the heterogeneity and fluidity of the urban centers enabled movement from one socioracial designation to another. A case in point is the experience of Juana Galván, whose petition to be recognized as a mestiza conformed more to her urban plebeian social network than to the Muisca pueblo of Chitaraque, where her mother was born. The transculturative pressures under which everyone lived drew Spaniards and Muiscas into an increasingly shared culture that bore distinct accents depending on one's ethnic or linguistic identity, social status, occupation, economic possibilities, and gender, as well as on the nature of the bonds of servitude that tied a person to a slave master or a cacique. Transculturation is obvious in the documents that describe the integration of mestizos and Spaniards into the social life of seventeenth-century Sogamoso, for instance, where the son of a mestizo could unproblematically occupy the chiefly status of capitán.

This was probably not as true of other regions of the Nuevo Reino, like Popayán, where native people like the Nasa successfully maintained a greater degree of autonomy from the dominant society, escaping the encomienda system until the eighteenth century by waging war on the Spaniards, and after that, by refashioning the resguardo on their own terms so that it legitimized extensive native landholdings and cemented indigenous authority.[3] In the central highlands, in contrast, the resguardo, which was originally intended to shield natives from external influences, effectively integrated the Muisca into colonial society during the first hundred years of European domination and ceded the bulk of native lands to nonnatives. The mita drew the inhabitants of the pueblos de indios into European economic circuits and ultimately deposited many of them in migrant barrios like Las Nieves in Santafé. Likewise, the relatively small population of African slaves in Tunja and Santafé gave way increasingly to a burgeoning group of mulattos. Those who did not pay tribute as did Indians and mulattos, or cleave to other forms of solidarity as did urban artisans, and those who were not subject to servitude, could be said to lie "outside" of the colonial system: their lack of formal rights and obligations made these mestizos placeless. But in another sense, in their very unclassifiability mestizos were perfect candidates for playing the system.

Nor do we find mestizos (or after the 1570s, even indios) exhibiting the kind of cultural alterity that Merrell paints in his portrait of Montour. To be sure, recognition of the cultural differences that marked mestizos as a dangerous part of the Indian fold did surface occasionally in Spanish circles, especially in the last quarter of the sixteenth century, when the fear of rebellion dominated the imagination of the elites of Santafé and Tunja. But despite the circulation of such threatening fantasies, early colonial mestizos endeavored to fashion themselves in the image of their conquerors. Don Diego de Torres, for example, appeals his case to the Crown by emphasizing his noble lineage and his Christian blood. Don Francisco, cacique of Ubaque in the same period, sports Spanish dress, dines at a Spanish table, slumbers in a Spanish bed, and weds a woman who is called not "mestiza" but "daughter of a Spaniard."

What is characteristic of these individuals is that they don't really look or act differently from those who surround them. This tendency to adopt markers other than those we would today associate with "race" or "ethnicity" makes the elite mestizos of the Nuevo Reino so ambiguous to us and, therefore, so fascinating: like the indios ladinos unmasked by Pedro de Quiroga, they might not be recognized at all. This is what led me to think of them as "disappearing," not only because so many of them were able to modify their identities circumstantially, but because socioracial labels were not the only means by which colonial self-fashioning took place. Perhaps we are missing the point when we dwell persistently on the racial dimension of calidad, without paying attention to the multiple modalities out of which calidad was constructed. This is not to say that this book minimizes the impact of race in colonial society; however, gender, social status, and occupation could be equally limiting—indeed, equally devastating—to colonial lives, and frequently operated in concert with socioracial designations.

Over time, elite mestizos like Alonso de Silva, Diego de Torres, Isabel de Sotelo, and Diego García Zorro drop out of the picture. A new layer of the Spanish elite emerged in the seventeenth century, disinheriting the early mestizo sons and daughters of conquistadors and to some degree homogenizing the category. Mestizos came to look much more like Juana Galván, who moved in a plebeian milieu in which her socioracial label provided her and her children with a convenient path for escaping tribute obligations, but where the heterogeneity of her social contacts perhaps led her peers and her social superiors to identify her more by class than by ethnicity. As the mestizo population of the central plateau grew, little by little overtaking majority status from the natives who inhabited the resguardos in the countryside and populated urban census rolls, the sense of ambiguity associated with mestizos diminished, although never entirely. The mestizos of eighteenth-century Nueva Granada were increasingly enveloped into a new worldview that distinguished them as "not-Spanish" and "not-white," but that also paid less heed to the specific nature of their parentage. Rural vecinos were not necessarily an elite; they were no less disadvantaged than Manuel Rodríguez had been in Soatá, or the mestizo smallholders in Sogamoso. Perhaps the permutations of their mixed parentage appeared on baptismal certificates or in the marriage registry (depending on whether the parish priest recorded their stated identities or chose to label them using his own criteria), or perhaps they were identified as mestizos when they were detained in a criminal proceeding. But the meaning of mixed descent lost significance, given that a significant plurality of the inhabitants of late colonial Nueva Granada were mestizo or mulatto in some way. In this scenario, mestizos were differentiated from Spaniards by their lower social and economic status and by their "not-whiteness," unless, of course, they were able to reclassify themselves through a writ of gracias al sacar or to achieve informal Spanish status through clothing, occupation, place of residence, or legal sleight of hand. As the mestizo population increased, mestizos disappeared from the landscape. It is the very invisibility of the mestizo in the midst of great numbers of people who could potentially be classified as such that makes mestizaje such an expedient handle for revising our notions of race in the colonial period.

Hinojosa, Inés de: A sixteenth-century Tunja adulteress who murdered several husbands and was ultimately hanged for her crimes. Hinojosa is a racially unmarked fictional character in Juan Rodríguez Freile's seventeenth-century satire *El carnero,* but is identified by the twentieth-century novelist Próspero Morales Pradilla as a mestiza.

CHAPTER 1

Acero de Vargas, doña Catalina: A sixteen-year-old Spanish noblewoman living in Santafé who is seduced by an "indio zambo" from Quito, Francisco Suárez, under the pretense that he is a nobleman from Lima. Her brother, Juan de Vargas, who is raising Catalina in his household, brings criminal charges against Suárez in 1675 for wounding the family honor.

Romero, Diego: Also known as Diego Hurtado. A conquistador and encomendero in Santafé, allegedly from Oran, who is accused in the 1550s of being a Muslim convert and having escaped Spain after murdering a woman. Romero lives in the barrio of Santa Bárbara, where he owns a tileworks. The father of both Spanish and mestizo children, several of whom go on to become priests, he is described as "a tall man with a large body, brown-skinned [and] curly-headed, and with scant beard, with an eye that opens and closes frequently."

Suárez, Francisco: The late seventeenth-century suitor of doña Catalina Acero de Vargas. Suárez, who was from Quito and was identified both as an indio and a zambo, passed as a noble from Lima in his missives to doña Catalina.

Tafur, Catalina: The mestiza daughter of the conquistador Juan Tafur. She was brought up in seclusion (recogida) in sixteenth-century Santafé to ensure she would grow up to be a lady, but after her father's death she escapes from her stepmother, Antonia Manuel de Hoyos, to live as a mestiza in Indian habit. Although she attempts in this way to assuage her placelessness after the death of her father, Catalina eventually marries a Spaniard.

CHAPTER 2

Galván, Juana: The mestiza daughter of the former encomendero of Chitaraque, near the city of Vélez, and of an indigenous woman who later married the cacique of the town. Galván petitions the authorities in 1645 to be stricken from the tribute rolls on the grounds that she is a mestiza and not an Indian. Raised in the paternal household in Vélez, probably as a servant to the family, she is married to Juan Malasmaños, an Indian, and has two cuarterón children by a priest.

Mulato, Lázaro: A sixty-year-old mulatto, former soldier in the war against the Pijaos, and the grandson, son, and husband of native women from Chocontá. He finds himself ensnared in the grip of colonial authorities during the 1639 visita of his community, when he is ordered to leave Chocontá because he is a mulatto. Lázaro convinces the authorities that he is a "natural" of Chocontá, with children who are listed as indigenous tributaries, and that he has nowhere to go, so he is permitted to remain but must pay a fine to the Crown.

Rodríguez, Manuel: A mulatto living in late sixteenth-century Soatá, to the northeast of Tunja, who is accused of inciting a rebellion, along with a group of indios ladinos and mestizo artisans based in Soatá and surrounding communities. A muleteer by occupation and blind in one eye, twenty-four-year-old Rodríguez hauls loads of meat from Tunja to buyers in Mariquita and Riohacha. He has been accused of raping local women and assaulting native men, and appears to be complicit in a conspiracy to replace Soatá's cacique with an indio ladino.

Salazar, Juan de: A Fontibón shoemaker who, in 1650, is jailed for having bitten the nose off the tanner and indio ladino Juan de Medina at a party hosted by the local cacique, after Medina called him an insulting nickname. Salazar, who is alternately identified as a mestizo and as an indio ladino, is originally from Quito and, like Francisco Suárez in chapter 1, would have been called a huauqui.

CHAPTER 3

Birves, Juan: A late sixteenth-century mestizo from Tamalameque, living in La Palma. Birves is an encomendero whose sexual relationship with Isabel de Sotelo is discovered, and he is pressured to marry her, which he refuses to do.

Céspedes, Juan de: The mestizo son of the conquistador Juan de Céspedes and of Isabel, an indigenous woman from Peru working as a servant in the Céspedes household in the Santa Bárbara quarter of Santafé. The younger Juan de Céspedes is a conquistador and is said to be the spitting image of his father, who nevertheless refuses to recognize him. He has two brothers, Lope de Céspedes and Antonio de Céspedes, who are the legitimate sons of his father by a Spanish noblewoman. In 1577 Juan de Céspedes, who goes unmentioned in his father's report of services to the Crown, submits his own record of his contributions to the conquest of the Nuevo Reino in an effort to obtain a pension.

García Zorro, Diego: An alderman (regidor) on the city council of Santafé in the first years of the seventeenth century. He is the son of the conquistador Gonzalo García Zorro and of Margarita India, as well as the brother of Fr. Gonzalo García Zorro. Although he holds an important post, García Zorro suffers from constant slights because he is a mestizo. His experiences are particularly interesting because he appears to lead a double life: as a regidor, moving in polite Spanish society, and as a mestizo, inhabiting a plebeian milieu where he has several illegitimate mestizo children by his native partner, Juana Sangrelinda. One of his daughters is married to a blacksmith, an unlikely match for the daughter of a regidor.

García Zorro, Fr. Gonzalo: Son of the conquistador Captain Gonzalo García Zorro and of Margarita India, Fr. Gonzalo is the choirmaster of the Cathedral of Santafé, having served as a doctrinal priest in Facatativá, Tunjuelo, Ubaque, and Zipacón during the second half of the sixteenth century. He spends decades trying to obtain a benefice, but is continually slighted because he is a mestizo. He is the brother of Diego García Zorro and is described as follows: "Gonçalo Garcia would be of more than forty years, of middling stature, brown of face, black beard that is growing out."

Penagos, Juana de: Mestiza daughter of the conquistador Juan de Penagos and an indigenous noblewoman from Cali, married to the Spaniard Alonso Valero de Tapia. Penagos has successfully integrated into sixteenth-century Spanish elite society, owning haciendas near Santafé and marrying her daughter to a well-placed Spanish official.

Sotelo, Isabel de: The daughter of the conquistador Pedro del Acebo Sotelo, who is a lawyer for the Real Audiencia in Santafé, and the widow of the Spanish shipbuilder Lorenzo Núñez. In 1577 she is discovered in her home in La Palma in bed with Juan Birves, an encomendero from Tamalameque. Birves has given her his word of betrothal, but reneges on his promise when confronted by members of Isabel's household. Her father brings suit against Birves for wounding his honor. Both Birves and Isabel de Sotelo are accused of being mestizos, although she appears to live her early life, unproblematically for the most part, as a Spaniard.

Ubaque, don Francisco de: A late sixteenth-century cacique of Ubaque. Highly hispanized and married to a mestiza, don Francisco exemplifies the profound transformations that Muisca cacicazgos underwent during the first century of Spanish domination.

CHAPTER 4

Silva, don Alonso de: The illegitimate son of the Portuguese conquistador Francisco González de Silva and of doña Juana Sirita, the eldest sister of the cacique of Tibasosa. He is in line to assume the cacicazgo of Tibasosa, in the province of Tunja. He is also secretary to a Santafé notary, working in the legal world of the capital of the Audiencia. In the 1570s Tibasosa's encomendero, Miguel Holguín, disputes don Alonso's right to the cacicazgo on the grounds that he is a mestizo and the son of an illicit union involving a man who was already married; this leads to a lengthy legal battle in which Silva allies himself with don Diego de Torres, the cacique of Turmequé (see below), with the Audiencia's first president, Venero de Leiva, and with the visitador Juan Bautista de Monzón.

Torres, don Diego de: The son of the conquistador Juan de Torres and of doña Catalina de Moyachoque, the eldest sister of the cacique of Turmequé, pueblo de indios in the Province of Tunja. Raised in the paternal household and educated by Dominicans, don Diego is urbane and cosmopolitan. In line to assume the cacicazgo of Turmequé, he vehemently denounces abuses by the encomendero class of Tunja, who in turn oppose his assumption of the cacicazgo on the grounds that he is a mestizo, illegitimate, and an idolater. His principal opponent is his encomendero, Pedro de Torres, a Spaniard and his half brother. Like don Alonso de Silva (see above), who is his ally, Diego de Torres is associated with powerholders in the Audiencia in Santafé, who are locked in struggle with the encomenderos of Tunja. Torres defends his mestizo condition, arguing that he would make the best cacique because of the strength of his Spanish blood and calling himself the "son of a Spaniard." He was "a good-sized man, not very tall, robust, a bit cross-eyed, and with scant beard." Married to Juana de Oropesa during his stay in Madrid, Torres dies in Spain.

CHAPTER 5

Cunucubá, don Juan: A seventeenth-century cacique of Cunucubá, in the province of Vélez. He is accused by his encomendera of being a mestizo on the basis of his color, hirsuteness, mestiza wife, and facility with Spanish.

Mulato, Juan: The son of a Pijao slave woman and an African slave. In the 1620s he is branded by his master, Juan de Segura, an act denounced to the authorities of Santafé. The legal case that ensues revolves around whether or not Juan, as the son of a Pijao woman, is indigenous himself and thus not subject to slavery. However, he is continuously identified in the documentary record as being of mulatto appearance.

CHAPTER 6

Orejuela, Pablos de: A sixty-year-old mestizo laborer from Usaquén. The son of an encomendero father and an indigenous commoner mother, Orejuela is brought before the Inquisition in Cartagena in 1665 on charges of heresy. His autobiography, which is recorded in the trial records, depicts the peripatetic life of a man who works as a laborer, a tithe collector, and a shopkeeper.

1. Rodríguez Freile, *El carnero*, chap. 10. *El carnero*'s original title was *Conquista y descubrimiento del Nuevo Reino de Granada* (Conquest and Discovery of the New Kingdom of Granada). It is an unpublished work that only appeared in print in 1859, based on eighteenth-century copies of the original manuscript. Susan Herman details the history of the manuscript in the introduction to her unpublished doctoral dissertation and inquires into the multiple meanings of the word "carnero," which might have referred to an ancient chronicle or the place where old manuscripts like Freile's were archived, a kind of "morgue" for antiquated documents. See Herman, "The Conquista y Descubrimiento del Nuevo Reino de Granada, Otherwise Known as El Carnero." Some of the most illuminating commentaries on the story of Inés de Hinojosa can be found in a volume edited by Rodríguez Vergara, *Inés de Hinojosa* (1999).

   In the remainder of this book, I refer to colonial Bogotá as Santafé, which was the name used in the period; its inhabitants were called Santafereños. Santafé was the capital of the Nuevo Reino de Granada (New Kingdom of Granada), one of the Audiencias or royal courts of the Spanish colonial empire, which I henceforth refer to as the Nuevo Reino. Some authors call the jurisdiction by its eighteenth-century name, Nueva Granada (New Granada), which it received when it became a viceregal seat in 1717, but I refer to it by its early colonial name, except in chapter 6 when I enter the viceregal period, where I refer to it as Nueva Granada. Tunja was the wealthier major city in the Nuevo Reino, although since the colonial period it has declined in status and is now the provincial capital of the modern department of Boyacá.

2. Colmenares, *La Provincia de Tunja en el Nuevo Reino de Granada*; Francis, "The *Resguardo*, the *Mita*, and the *Alquiler General*"; Villamarin, "Encomenderos and Indians in the Formation of Colonial Society in the Sabana de Bogotá Colombia."

3. Herman, "La encomienda de Chivatá."
4. Porro Gutiérrez, *Venero de Leiva*.
5. Glave, "Sociedad colonial, discurso literario e imaginario colectivo," 45.
6. For readers who do not speak Spanish: "mestiza" is the feminine of "mestizo," that is, a "female mestizo"; likewise, "india" is the feminine of "indio," and "mulatta" is the feminine of "mulatto" (note that I am using the English spelling of mulatta and mulatto which, in Spanish, have a single "t"). I will pay close attention to gendered forms in my use of Spanish terms, as gender is a fundamental component of colonial socioracial systems of classification.
7. Morales Pradilla, *Los pecados de Inés de Hinojosa*, 19–20. All translations are mine, unless otherwise specified. Isabel Rodríguez Vergara reads the purpose of the shift from *criolla* to mestiza in Morales's text as one that converts Inés into a bridge between two worlds. Rodríguez Vergara, "Mujeres transgresoras (criollas, indias y brujas) en la Colonia," 83.
8. Mercedes López interprets Morales Pradilla's imaginings of the mestiza Inés de Hinojosa as owing to her *Venezuelan* origins. For López, Morales's Inés is not so much a bridge between the "Spanish world" and the "indigenous world" of the central highlands, as she is a link between the Spanish manhood of her husbands or lovers and the female sensuality of the coast, a racially hybrid space that lies outside of the confines of "white" central Colombia. Alternately, Inés could represent a reminder of the distant colonial past, when there "really" were mestizos in Tunja (Mercedes López, personal communication). Colombian national imaginings differ from the more familiar Mexican ones, where the mestizo came to represent the nation, reimagined as a "cosmic race." See Stepan, *"The Hour of Eugenics"*; Vasconcelos, *The Cosmic Race*. Early twentieth-century Colombia was more fervently Hispanist, the nation embodied in the unmixed descendants of Spaniards, who spoke a "pure" variety of Spanish—*un español castizo*; only the popular classes (the vast majority of the population, of course) were called mestizos, and racial categories came to be seen as rooted in the country's broken geography, recast as regional traits. Later in the century, however, Colombian elites and intellectuals came to embrace the "myth of the three races," the vision of the nation as the harmonious melding of Europeans, Africans, and indigenous people. See Appelbaum, *Muddied Waters*; Fals Borda, *Mompox y Loba*; Wade, *Music, Race, and Nation*. Since 1991 minority groups in Colombia—native peoples, Afro-Colombians, the English-speaking Afro-Caribbean inhabitants of the islands of San Andrés and Providencia, the Rom (Roma, or gypsies)—have been afforded a special status in a new "multicultural and pluriethnic" Colombia that embodies ethnic diversity but is overwhelmingly mestizo. But still, no one identifies him- or herself as

mestizo. On nineteenth-century mestizaje, see López Rodríguez, "Ficciones raciales"; on twentieth-century mestizaje, see Figueroa Muñoz and San Miguel, ¿*Mestizo yo?*; Ospina, "Lo que le falta a Colombia."

9. "Mestizaje" is a twentieth-century word that signifies the process of racial mixing. Although "mestizo" was used in the colonial era to classify individuals, "mestizaje" did not exist in the colonial lexicon.

10. I use the word "Indian" as a translation of the term "indio" to refer to the colonial category, just as I use "Spaniard" as a translation of the category of "español." In all other instances in which I speak about native people, I employ less racially charged terminologies as a means of disentangling the colonial category from any notion of cultural or ethnic essence.

11. Katzew, *Casta Painting*. These paintings were largely Mexican in origin, and a good deal later—by more than a century—than the period with which I am concerned. They should not be taken as an empirical model for how individuals were identified in early colonial Santafé or even in sixteenth-century Mexico, for that matter.

12. For recent examples, see Fisher and O'Hara's *Imperial Subjects* for studies of casta in Mexico, as well as O'Toole's *Bound Lives* on the use of these designations in coastal Peru.

13. I am indebted to Boyer's "Respect and Identity" for the conceptualization of socioracial classification as a speech-act. Boyer writes about eighteenth-century Mexico, but his conclusions are equally valid for sixteenth-century Santafé.

14. Brubaker and Cooper, "Beyond 'Identity.'"

15. On the fruitfulness of conceptualizing medieval hierarchical systems in terms of race, see Nirenberg, "Race and the Middle Ages." On the problems of conceptualizing the connections and lacunae between racism and race in colonial Spanish America, see Sweet, "The Iberian Roots of American Racist Thought." The Portuguese term *"qualidade"* was employed until the 1980s as a euphemism for race. See Delaney, "Understanding *Qualidade*." I examine "calidad" and "raza" in chapter 1, and turn to "casta" in chapter 6.

16. Readers will notice that I speak only tangentially of blacks, whether slaves or freedmen, in this book. The documentary record from the Bogotá region contains very little information pertinent to my research questions, although there is a lengthy section of the Archivo General de la Nación called "Negros y Esclavos" that catalogs the sales of slaves and disputes over slave ownership. Had I chosen as my region of study either Antioquia to the west or Popayán to the south, blacks would have been more prominent in my research.

17. Herzog, *Defining Nations*. The nature of "vecino" expanded to encompass non-elite elements later in the early modern period. Herzog, "Early Modern Spanish Citizenship." By the eighteenth century, even mestizo townspeople in the hinterlands of Santafé and Tunja were

called vecinos, reversing its restricted early colonial sense. Herrera Ángel, *Ordenar para controlar.*

18. Earle, "'Two Pairs of Pink Satin Shoes!!'"

19. That this could become an onerous obligation, not just an honor, is evident in the refusal of don Pedro de Aldana, a member of the city council (*cabildo*) of the emerald-mining town Muzo, to participate in the 1677 Good Friday procession. Although he had joined the procession the previous three years, he did not intend to do so in 1677, which brought him to the attention of the authorities. "Incidente causado por el regidor de Muzo, don Pedro de Aldana, al resistirse a llevar la vara de palio, por encargo del cabildo, durante la procesión del Viernes Santo en que se venerarían la virgen de la Soledad y el Santo Sepulcro, con asistencia de todos sus cofrades," Muzo, 1677, AGN/B, MC 78, doc. 23, 638–42.

20. On how socioracial terminologies like "indio" also operated as legal locations in the colonial period, see O'Toole, *Bound Lives*, chap. 3.

21. Baber, "Categories, Self-Representation and the Construction of the *Indios.*"

22. On violent encounters between Iberian nationalities in Potosí, Bolivia, see Arzáns de Orsúa y Vela, *Historia de la villa imperial de Potosí.* For a gendered reading of the category "Spaniard," see Almorza Hidalgo, "Género, emigración y movilidad social en la expansión Atlántica," 168.

23. Rachel O'Toole reminds us, however, that these collective names for African nationalities did not accurately reflect many slaves' origins. In Africa new identities and polities were constantly emerging, and individuals who were sold into slavery manipulated these identities in their efforts to engage African rivalries in the American setting. See O'Toole, "From the Rivers of Guinea to the Valleys of Peru"; see also O'Toole, *Bound Lives.*

24. For example, "Padron de los negros [*sic*] libres y mulatos [*sic*] que hay en la ciudad de Velez para la cobranza de los requintos," 1664, AGN/B, MC 54, doc. 16.

25. Almorza Hidalgo, "Género, emigración y movilidad social en la expansión Atlántica," 168. I thank Nancy van Deusen for pointing this out to me.

26. For demographic projections, see Herrera Ángel, *Poder local,* chap. 2.

27. The lack of a formal mestizo classification remains in place to this day. The category of mestizo does not appear in the Colombian national census, which lists various other minority ethnic groups, including indigenous, Rom (Roma), *raizal* (natives of the English-speaking Caribbean islands of San Andrés and Providencia), *palenquero* (descendants of maroon communities), black, mulatto, and African descendant; mestizos and whites are classified as "none of the above." See

República de Colombia, *Colombia una nación multicultural*, 37–38, accessed 1 August 2013, http://www.dane.gov.co/files/censo2005/etnia/sys/colombia_nacion.pdf. However, even before Colombia's 1991 constitution recognized the rights of ethnic and racial minorities, the post-independence category of mestizo never amounted to a distinguishable group. See López Rodríguez, "Ficciones raciales."

28. See Zúñiga, *Espagnols d'outre-mer*, chap. 8, on the difficulties in identifying mestizos by phenotype, customs, or language in colonial Santiago de Chile. A Duke University Press reader of this manuscript expressed surprise at the use in the seventeenth-century documentation of cuarterón to refer to a kind of mestizo. I do not know if this usage was unique to the Nuevo Reino or if it was more generalized in the Andean region; given that most scholars of race focus on Indians and blacks, as opposed to mestizos, I have not seen it mentioned in the literature.

29. Graubart, "The Creolization of the New World."

30. Barth, *Ethnic Groups and Boundaries.*

31. Schwartz and Salomon, "New Peoples and New Kinds of People," 478. See also Graubart, "Hybrid Thinking," in which mestizos are described as "placeless" in the colonial order.

32. Schwartz and Salomon, "New Peoples," 444. Ruth Hill observes that the meaning of mestizo was not formalized until the late colonial period ("Casta as Culture and the *Sociedad de Castas* as Literature," 234).

33. Álvarez M., Melo, Meisel, and Tovar, "La relevancia de la historia colonial en el mundo de hoy," 183.

34. Cobo Gutiérrez, *Mestizos heraldos de Dios*; Hyland, "Illegitimacy and Racial Hierarchy in the Peruvian Priesthood"; López Rodríguez, *Tiempos para rezar y tiempos para trabajar* (henceforth, *Tiempos para rezar*); Olaechea, *El mestizaje como gesta*; Toquica, *A falta de oro*, 34–37, 255–60.

35. "Expediente de la ciudad de Santa Fe, por su procurador Alonso de S. Miguel, solicitando no se haga efectiva la merced que hizo SM a Juan Sarabia de una escribanía pública de dicha ciudad, que este a su vez renunció en el mestizo Juan Sánchez," 1563, AGI/S, SF 60, n.14.

36. Spanish women were entitled, as were men, to encomienda grants, so there were encomenderas as well as encomenderos.

37. "Don Juan, cacique de los indios de Cunucubá," AGN/B, CI 11, doc. 6, 189–561. I describe don Juan de Cunucubá in more detail in chapter 5. Note that "color" was a feminine noun in early modern Castilian Spanish. Note, also, that Cunucubá was an indigenous pueblo near the city of Vélez, and is not the same town as the more well-known Cucunubá, near Santafé.

38. See chapter 4 for an in-depth consideration of what mestizaje meant to these two men, whose defense of their chiefly positions is recorded in

thousands of pages of legal documentation held in Bogotá and Seville. A summary of the documentation can be found in Rojas, *El cacique de Turmequé y su época*.

39. I further document Isabel Sotelo's experiences in chapter 3.

40. Ares Queija, "'Un borracho de chicha y vino.'"

41. Burns, "Unfixing Race."

42. In chapter 4 I discuss in greater detail the alliance between the Crown and the mestizo caciques Silva and Torres.

43. Nirenberg, "Figures of Thought and Figures of Flesh," 402, 418.

44. In chapter 2, I explore in more detail the phenomenon of mestizos being born in native communities.

45. Covarrubias Orozco, *Tesoro de la lengua castellana o española*, 751.

46. Real Academia Española, *Diccionario de autoridades*, 2:556. In this definition "casta" is used in its general sense to denote both lineage (in the case of human beings or animals) and classes of inanimate things (*Diccionario de autoridades* points, for example, to "castas" of pears or peaches [2:219–20]).

47. "El hombre, casándose con una mitaya yndia, es mestizo sus hijos y sus desendientes," Guaman Poma de Ayala, *Primer nueva corónica y buen gobierno*, 788 [802] (henceforth, Guaman Poma, *Nueva corónica*). I have tried to retain the ambiguity of Guaman Poma's construction in my English translation of this quotation. In English this phrasing is grammatically incorrect: It is the cacique, not the cacique's children and descendants, who marries the yndia mitaya. However, it is equally incorrect in the Spanish original. See also de la Cadena, "Are *Mestizos* Hybrids?," 264.

48. This usage may derive from Inca distinctions between their own descent-lines and those of non-Incas. Julien, *Reading Inca History*, 43. However, as in so many New World examples in which it is difficult to distinguish between pre-Columbian and European antecedents, similar usages can be found in Europe.

49. Zúñiga, "La voix du sang." See also Feerick, *Strangers in Blood*, introduction.

50. In chapter 1, I discuss "raza" as "lineage" in greater detail.

51. Aubert, "'The Blood of France,'" 445–48.

52. Feerick, *Strangers in Blood*, 10.

53. Some Spanish theologians also subscribed to the notion that the child's condition followed that of his or her mother ("el parto sigue al vientre"), and this viewpoint crops up in the documentary record, as Margarita González reminds her readers in her treatment of the eighteenth century in *El resguardo en el Nuevo Reino de Granada* (114). However, early colonial documents are hardly consistent in this respect. Most of the mestizos in the hinterlands of Tunja and Santafé were the children of native women, yet they were often considered to be mestizos by the Spanish authorities. I use "doctrinal town" to refer to the nucleated

settlements set up to ensure that the indigenous population was effectively taught the Christian doctrine; in Spanish these settlements were sometimes called *doctrinas*.

54. Herrera Ángel, "'Libres de todos los colores,'" 259.
55. Hill, "Casta as Culture and the *Sociedad de Castas* as Literature," 234–36.
56. I examine this belief in greater detail in chapter 5.
57. Guaman Poma, *Nueva corónica*, 539 [553].
58. Lizárraga, *Descripción breve de toda la tierra del Perú, Tucumán y Río de la Plata*, 101.
59. Bergmann, "Milking the Poor," 92–93. See also "Constituciones Sinodales del obispo seguntino Fernando de Luján," 1455, Archivo Catedral de Sigüenza, signatura 105 mod., 67v–68v, accessed 9 September 2012, www.histgueb.net/expositos/nodrizas.htm.
60. Pech, "L'influence des nourrices sur la formation physique et morales des enfants," 494.
61. María Elena Martínez, *Genealogical Fictions*, 55.
62. "Cacicazgo de Tibasosa: Títulos de Alonso de Silva en la sucesión en dicho cacicazgo; su pleito con Miguel Holguín, encomendero, quien se oponía a esa sucesión," 1571–76, AGN/B, CI 61, doc. 3, 258r-v.
63. "Testamento de doña Maria Manuela de Avila, hija legitima de don Juan, cacique de Guatavita," 1616, AGN/B, N2, t. 17, 88r.
64. "Casa de Expósitos: Su fundación en Santa Fe, documentos sobre la organización de ella, sus reglamentos, su situación fiscal," 1641–65, AGN/B, Pol 3, doc. 8, 106–242. See also María Himelda Ramírez, *De la caridad barroca a la caridad ilustrada*, chap. 4.
65. Many European historians, most prominent among them being Serge Gruzinski, speak of mestizaje in a cultural sense, as in the creation of a hybrid culture. See Gruzinski, *The Mestizo Mind*. Although to some extent I inquire into the cultural matrix of the mestizos whose lives I detail in the following pages, I focus more properly on the category "mestizo" than on cultural hybridity.
66. "Francisco Antonio de Colmenares, se querella criminalmente, por haberle seducido y sacado de su casa una muchacha, de Jacinto de Padilla," AGN/B, JCC 46, 54–69. Specific page references will be supplied in parentheses in the body of the text.
67. I draw on John and Jean Comaroff's *Ethnography and the Historical Imagination*, chap. 1, for my critique of social history. The Comaroffs criticize social history for being insufficiently theorized, in comparison to ethnography.
68. Dening, *History's Anthropology*, 99.
69. Ibid. Dening contrasts this with history as what "really" happened, which he fears comprises the fitting of historical referents into preexisting models.
70. Dean, "Beyond Prescription," 295.

71. Trouillot, *Silencing the Past*.
72. Dumont, *The Headman and I*.
73. De Certeau, *The Writing of History*.
74. Of course, you don't have to be an anthropologist to do this. *Into the Archive*, a book by the historian Kathryn Burns, is equally ethnographic.
75. The poet also suggested I look at one of her own books, a history of her family's house, which alternates between a portrayal of the former owners and a narrative of her own experiences while living there. See Messer, *Red House*.
76. Each protagonist is actually a historical person, not a fictional "character," as one of the readers of my manuscript noted, although they clearly function as actors in dramas of mestizaje.
77. Such as, for example, Fisher and O'Hara, *Imperial Subjects*.
78. Lewis, *Hall of Mirrors*, chap. 7.

1. MISCHIEVOUS LOVERS, HIDDEN MOORS, AND CROSS-DRESSERS

1. "Causa seguida a Francisco Suarez, en virtud de denuncio de Juan Acero de Vargas, de haber seducido y desflorado a Catalina Acero de Vargas, su hermana," 1667, AGN/B, JC 93, doc. 12, 902r–906v. Further quotations from this document will be cited in parentheses in the text.
2. For an introduction to the notion of honor in the colonial Nuevo Reino, see Garrido, "Entre el honor y la obediencia"; Rodríguez, *En busca de lo cotidiano*, 188–96.
3. "Huauqui" means "brother" in Quechua. Other documents also identify native Andeans from Quito as "huauquis," which suggests this was a descriptive term used for indigenous Quiteño migrants in the Nuevo Reino. See "Documentos referentes a la visita que practicara el Oidor Juan de Valcárcel en las encomiendas indígenas de Sogamoso, Monguí, Tópaga, Tutasá y Mongua," 1636, AGN/B, VB 8, 341r, 447r. I read Juan de Vargas's statement as implying that he uncertain as to whether Francisco Suárez was an Indian from Quito or a zambo.
4. Rappaport and Cummins, *Beyond the Lettered City*; Seed, *Ceremonies of Possession in Europe's Conquest of the New World, 1492–1640*, chap. 3.
5. As I will explain later in this chapter, Old Christians were individuals who could trace their Christian ancestry back at least two generations; New Christians were converts to Christianity, or the children or grandchildren of converts.
6. R. Douglas Cope argues that racial passing between the major categories of Indian, black, and Spanish was not commonplace in colonial Mexico City, although there was mobility across the intermediate mixed categories (*The Limits of Racial Domination*, chap. 4).
7. A good introduction to the concept of calidad can be found in Carrera,

Imagining Identity in New Spain, 4–5, as well as in Boyer, "Negotiating *Calidad.*"

8. Twinam, "Racial Passing," 255. By "private," Twinam means the domestic context, which was, of course, legally dominated by men like Juan de Vargas, who ruled his wife and children in the interests of maintaining his own honor and status by policing their behavior; this understanding of the term reflects the formal definition of "privado" in the Real Academia Española's *Diccionario de autoridades* of 1726 (386). However, we can also interpret "private" in a more intimate sense, that of the relationship between Spanish men and the female indigenous slaves or servants with whom they engaged in sexual relations, a site in which gender and calidad played off one another in complex ways. See van Deusen, "The Intimacies of Bondage."

9. Twinam, "Racial Passing."

10. Zúñiga, *Espagnols d'outre-mer,* 203. In chapters 3 and 4 I introduce several elite mestizos whose legitimization by their Spanish fathers was key to their calidad.

11. Ahmed, "She'll Wake Up One of These Days and Find She's Turned into a Nigger,'" 92, 94. Of course, Ahmed is referring to modern Anglophone notions of racial passing, which assume that identities are somehow connected to innate biological realities. What people recognize or misrecognize, what they project knowingly or unknowingly, depends on a historically specific discourse that governs what the observer chooses—or is compelled—to see. This discourse does not make racial identity any less fluid than other forms of identification, as Marisol de la Cadena so eloquently captures in *Indigenous Mestizos,* her ethnography of the complex negotiation of racial categories among plebeians and elites in twentieth-century Cuzco, Peru.

12. Flórez de Ocáriz, *Genealogías del Nuevo Reino de Granada,* 2:488. Those conquistadors and their associates who were of noble Iberian extraction are identified as such in Flórez's two-volume work.

13. Gamboa, *Encomienda, identidad y poder,* 25–31.

14. Ibid.; Luis Fernando Restrepo, *Un Nuevo Reino imaginado,* 110–19.

15. Castro-Gómez, *La hybris del punto cero,* chap. 2; Rojas, *Escudos de armas e inscripciones antiguas de la ciudad de Tunja.*

16. Hill, "Between Black and White," 276–77.

17. Guaman Poma, *Nueva corónica,* 506 [510].

18. To give a sense of how individual blunders could blemish entire extended families, we might look at the late seventeenth-century case of Pablos de Orejuela, a mestizo accused and convicted of heresy by the Inquisition in Cartagena. While Orejuela appears to have occupied an inferior position in his father's family, he traced his descent to a noble lineage whose members occupied positions in the Church and the colonial administration. In his defense he expressed deep concern that his

conviction would damage the reputation of his well-placed relatives and their children (although this did not sway the tribunal). "Proceso de fe de Pablos de Orejuela, natural de Santa Fé (Granada [sic]), vecino de Santa Fé de Bogotá (Colombia), mestizo, labrador, seguido en el Tribunal de la Inquisición de Cartagena de Indias, por herejía," AHN/M, ICI, 1621, exp.12, 128v–133v. I will come back to Orejuela's case in chapter 6.

19. Rodríguez, *Seducción, amancebamiento y abandono en la Colonia*, 56. Suits over marriage proposals are an excellent site for examining the intersection of gender, status, and race in the colonial period. I will come back to this topic and to Pablo Rodríguez's work in chapter 3.

20. Ibid., 54.

21. Van Deusen, *Between the Sacred and the Worldly*, 17–22.

22. Vives, *Instruccion de la muger christiana*, 128–29.

23. Van Deusen, *Between the Sacred and the Worldly*, chap. 5.

24. Ibid., 76–77.

25. Perhaps this is why the family is given short shrift by Flórez de Ocáriz, who was their contemporary. On the late colonial population of Santafé, see Vargas Lesmes, "Santafé a la luz de sus padrones (1778–1806)," 22–23.

26. Vargas Lesmes, "La mita urbana."

27. Colmenares, *La Provincia de Tunja en el Nuevo Reino de Granada*, 66–70; Francis, "Población, enfermedad y cambio demográfico," 62–63; Jaramillo Uribe, *Ensayos sobre historia social colombiana*, 169. As these authors demonstrate, the mid-1600s constituted the lowest point in the demographic curve of the native population, which had sunk in Tunja to only 10 percent of its conquest-era numbers.

28. Gamboa, *Encomienda, identidad y poder*, 25–31.

29. Douglas Cope argues in *The Limits of Racial Domination*, chap. 4, that racial passing between the major categories of Indian, black, and Spanish was not commonplace in colonial Mexico City, although there was mobility across the intermediate mixed categories.

30. Sandoval, *De instauranda aetiopum salute*, 10. I will return to a more extended discussion of this issue in chapter 5.

31. Seth, *Europe's Indians*, chap. 4.

32. Müller-Wille, "Figures of Inheritance, 1650–1850," 186.

33. See Nirenberg, "Race and the Middle Ages," and Zúñiga, "La voix du sang," on descent and lineage in Europe. See Zúñiga, *Espagnols d'outremer*, chap. 7, on descent and lineage in Chile. For a similar treatment of race in Renaissance England, see Feerick, *Strangers in Blood*, introduction. The differences we read into these distinct forms of thought must also be gauged through comparison to contemporary Latin American racial discourses, which differ in many respects from northern racial regimes that normally provide the ground against which such contrasts

are drawn by many authors. See Bourdieu and Wacquant, "On the Cunning of Imperialist Reason," 44–46. In particular, we might note how cultural characteristics, as opposed to phenotype, drive modern racial discourse across the Southern Hemisphere, making Latin American racial discourse a more malleable system than we generally would admit to in the North American context. De la Cadena, *Indigenous Mestizos*. Maité Yié, a Colombian historian who read this book in manuscript form, noted that she had difficulty identifying with the concept of race as it is articulated in North America, pointing out that her own notion was more "hybrid and ambiguous." The concept of "passing" is equally problematic in the fluid racial landscape of Colombia, as it is difficult to dissimulate a racial identity in a context in which race is muted while racism is ever-present. However much practices of establishing difference in modern Colombia are permeable and flexible, they still constitute a racial discourse that assigns members of the population to three main racial classes that function on the basis of a synchronic biological metaphor, in this sense differing significantly from the genealogically based classificatory practices of the colonial period. For more on nineteenth- and twentieth-century notions of race in Colombia, see Appelbaum, *Muddied Waters*; Múnera, *Fronteras imaginadas*; Safford, "Race, Integration, and Progress"; and Wade, *Music, Race, and Nation*. Nonetheless, Anglo-Northern European racial discourse may itself not conform to our stereotypes. In chapter 6 of *Sorting Things Out*, Geoffrey C. Bowker and Susan Leigh Star make a convincing case for the interaction of multiple parameters in the process of racial classification under the South African apartheid regime, which was without doubt the most inflexible system of racial discrimination in the modern world; I thank Ilana Gershon for bringing this fascinating study to my attention. I hesitate to move race, or the more diffuse notion of "racial thinking," back to the sixteenth or seventeenth centuries, as have some authors, such as Cañizares-Esguerra, *Nature, Empire, and Nation*, chap. 4, and Silverblatt, *Modern Inquisitions*. Following Vanita Seth's advice, I prefer to view its early modern manifestation as a distinct epistemological formation, as does Ruth Hill, in *Hierarchy, Commerce, and Fraud in Bourbon Spanish America*, chap. 5.

34. Real Academia Española, *Diccionario de autoridades*, 1:67.
35. "Guayana, Juan, Capitán del pueblo de Suta, encomienda de don Nicolás de Guzmán; sus títulos de tal," 1643–49, AGN/B, CI 54, doc. 31, 533v. Emphasis added.
36. "Don Diego de Torres, caciques, capitanes e indios de Turmequé contra Pedro de Torres su encomendero, sobre delitos," 1574–75, AGN/B, Encomiendas 21, doc. 9, 409r. I will examine this quotation in detail in chapter 4.
37. María Elena Martínez, *Genealogical Fictions*.

38. Peñalosa y Mondragón, *Libro de las cinco excelencias del español*, 99r.

39. Schwaller, "Defining Difference in Early New Spain," 52; Schwaller, "'For Honor and Defence,'" 242–43.

40. "Que no deben ser ordenados los mestizos," AGI/S, SF 528, 32r.

41. "Causa seguida a Juan Virues, en virtud de acusacion de Pedro de Sotelo, padre de Isabel de Sotelo, viuda de Lorenzo Nuñez, de haberla forzado en su propia casa," 1577, AGN/B, JC 91, doc. 2, 498v. I develop an ethnographic portrait of Virves and Isabel de Sotelo in chapter 3.

42. "Cacicazgo de Turmequé: Pleito de Diego de Torres con Pedro de Torres, su encomendero, en dicho cacicazgo," 1571–76, AGN/B, CI 61, doc. 4, 442r; "Cacicazgo de Tibasosa: Títulos de Alonso de Silva en la sucesión en dicho cacicazgo; su pleito con Miguel Holguín, encomendero, quien se oponía a esa sucesión," 1571–76, AGN/B, CI 61, doc. 3, 326v.

43. "Diaz Hernando y Leonor, su consorte, indios ladinos, se querellan criminalmente de los alguaciles de Santafé, Angulo y González, por hablerlos golpeado y herido," 1582, AGN/B, CI 26, doc. 10, 282v.

44. "Informaciones de la visita del Lic. Francisco de Monzón (30/03/1580)," AGI/S, SF 16, r.24, n.99, C2, 3v.

45. Mörner, "Las comunidades de indígenas y la legislación segregacionista en el Nuevo Reino de Granada," 65–66.

46. Covarrubias Orozco, *Tesoro de la lengua castellana o española*, 586. Note that the Spanish "género" encapsulates distinctions made by two terms, "genre" and "gender," in English. See also Rappaport and Cummins, *Beyond the Lettered City*, chap. 2.

47. A fuzziness marks the border between preracial and racial thinking in Latin America, where colonial memories are still embedded in modern usages. See de la Cadena, "Are *Mestizos* Hybrids?"

48. Rivas, *Los fundadores de Bogotá*, 2:256. For the Anuncibay quotation, see ibid., 255. Romero's requests for office can be found in "Informaciones de los méritos y servicios de Diego Romero," 1561–66, AGI/S, Pat 154, n.3, r.1, c.1–4; "Informaciones de oficio y parte: Diego Romero, encomendero de Santa Fe, vecino de Santa Fe," 1561–72, AGI/S, SF 122, n.32.

49. "El fiscal contra Diego Romero, vecino de Santa Fe, por haber pasado a Indias sin licencia siendo cristiano nuevo e hijo de moro," 1550–78, AGI/S, Just 509, n.1, 21r. All subsequent references to this document will be cited in parentheses in the body of the text.

50. Rivas, *Los fundadores de Bogotá*, 2:252–53.

51. Luis Fernando Restrepo, *Un Nuevo Reino imaginado*, 76–83; Zúñiga, *Espagnols d'outre-mer*, chap 7.

52. See, for example, "Emplazamiento a Diego Romero," 1554, AGI/S, Pat 282, n.2, r.4; "Romero Diego, encomendero de los indios de Bosa, en pleito con Andres Lopez de Galarza, quien le adujera una escritura de renuncia a la encomienda," 1557, AGN/B, Enc 20, doc. 15, 744–56; "Indios de Sisativa, encomienda de don Hernan Perez, ensayador: De-

manda de éste contra los indios de Tibagoya, de la encomienda de don Diego Romero, por su intromision en las tierras de sus resguardos," 1563, AGN/B, CI 30, doc. 60, 723–48; "Juan de Céspedes, vecino de la ciudad de Santa Fe, contra Diego Romero, de la misma vecindad, sobre la restitución del cacique Unicipa y sus sujetos en el valle de Ubaque," 1563–70, AGI/S, Just 502, n.2, r.1; "Sentencias y autos originales pronunciados en el Consejo en los pleitos seguidos entre partes y por el fiscal de S.M.: Dos sentencias, Juan de Céspedes con Diego Romero sobre indios," 1571, AGI/S, Esc 952; "Diego Romero, vecino de la ciudad de Santa Fe, contra María Salazar, de la misma vecindad, sobre la posesión de la encomienda de Machetá," 1572–76, AGI/S, Just 505, n.3, r.2. Romero was continually in debt, facing suits, imprisonment, and penury for shirking financial obligations. See "Ejecucion por suma de pesos, seguida por Alvaro de Zebreros a Diego Romero, como fiador de Domingo Gonzales," 1566, AGN/B, JCC 21, 742–854; "Ejecucion por suma de pesos, seguido por Alonso Coronado y otros acreedores a Diego Romero de Aguilar y su hijo," 1583, AGN/B, JCC 29, 893–980.

53. Karoline P. Cook summarizes this case in "Forbidden Crossings," 222–30.

54. "La casta de caballos castizos, a los cuales señalan con hierro para que sean conocidos. 2. Raza en el paño, la hilaza que diferencia de los demás hilos de la trama. . . . Raza, en los linajes se toma en mala parte, como tener alguna raza de moro o judío" (Covarrubias Orozco, *Tesoro de la lengua castellana o española*, 851).

55. Nirenberg, "Race and the Middle Ages."

56. Sicroff, *Los estatutos de limpieza de sangre.*

57. Nirenberg, "Figures of Thought and Figures of Flesh."

58. Ray, *The Sephardic Frontier*, 156–64; Root, "Speaking Christian," 132.

59. Woolard, "Bernardo de Aldrete and the Morisco Problem," 457.

60. Rivas, *Los fundadores de Bogotá*, 2:251.

61. Ray, *The Sephardic Frontier*, 156–64.

62. Pardo Tomás, "Physicians' and Inquisitors' Stories?"; Vincent, "The Moriscos and Circumcision."

63. Ehlers, *Between Christians and Moriscos*, 95.

64. His legitimate son and successor, Diego Romero de Aguilar, was a prominent encomendero. See "Testamento de Diego Romero de Aguilar, encomendero," 1630, AGN/B, N3, t. 26, 42r–44r; also Flórez de Ocáriz, *Genealogías del Nuevo Reino de Granada*, 2:67 (henceforth, *Genealogías*); Rivas, *Los fundadores de Bogotá*, 2:256. His two daughters, doña Francisca de Mendoza y Aguilar and Isabel Romero (an illegitimate daughter whose identity is unmarked, so her mother might have been Spanish or perhaps mestiza), married wealthy men. See "Testamento de Isabel Romero, viuda de Alonso de Coronado," 1619, AGN/B, N3, t. 9, 396r–401r; also see Flórez de Ocáriz, *Genealogías*, 2:67–68. His legitimate son, Melchor Romero de Aguilar, was a doctrinal priest

in Tenjo. See "Romero Melchor y Gabriel López de la Cruz sus nombramientos como curas de Facatativá y sus anexos, y, Tenjo y sus anexos respectivamente," 1608, AGN/B, CO 28, doc. 4, 34r–v; also see Flórez de Ocáriz, *Genealogías*, 2:67. His illegitimate mestizo sons, Andrés Romero and Alonso Romero, were also priests; Andrés was named to the parish of Nuestra Señora de las Nieves, one of the largely indigenous quarters of Santafé. See "Bermúdez Gonzalo y Romero Andrés, su postulación para parroquial de las Nieves de Santa Fé," 1586, AGN/B, CO 9, doc. 143, 239r–v; also see Flórez de Ocáriz, *Genealogías*, 2:67–68. Romero was not unique in having endured a court case defaming his character. Almost all of the prominent Spaniards of the period I encountered in the archives suffered legal smears of one sort or another from time to time.

65. Hill, "Towards an Eighteenth-Century Transatlantic Critical Race Theory," 57–58. One American witness denies that this is the case, stating that Romero was the son of two Muslim parents (296v), while yet another attempted to resolve this quandary on a visit to Spain but did not find an answer to his question (298v). While their testimony questions Romero's mulatto background, it does indicate that the accusations of mixed parentage leveled against him were of concern to his peers in Santafé.

66. "Expediente de información y licencia de pasajero a Indias de Juan García, criado de Jerónimo de León, natural de Sevilla, hijo de Pedro García y de Ana Díez, al Nuevo Reino de Granada," 1605, AGI/S, Ct 5287, n.11.

67. María Elena Martínez, *Genealogical Fictions*; Martínez, "Interrogating Blood Lines." In a different but related vein, Kathryn Burns reasons that in early colonial Peru the imposition of categories like "indio," "mestizo," and "mulatto" must be considered an outgrowth of the concept "raza," in the sense that, like the Moriscos, people thus categorized, or their children, were recent converts and hence carried idolatry in their blood ("Unfixing Race," 191).

68. Cook, "Forbidden Crossings," 218–22.

69. See, for example, among numerous others, "Proceso de fe de Pedro López, natural de Castelo Branco (Portugal), y vecino de Zaragoza (Colombia), tratante, seguido en el Tribunal de la Inquisición de Cartagena de Indias, por judaizante: Recibió tormento y fue condenado a relajación, pero murió en la cárcel," 1625–28, AHN/M, ICI, 1620, exp. 6; "Proceso de fe de Luis Franco, natural de Lisboa (Portugal), vecino de Zaragoza (Colombia), tratante, seguido en el Tribunal de la Inquisición de Cartagena de Indias, por judaizante," 1624–49, AHN/M, ICI, 1620, exp. 5. See also Navarrete, "Judeo-conversos en la Audiencia del Nuevo Reino de Granada," 62. Muslim and Jewish antecedents were more significant in larger and wealthier colonial settings, like Lima, where

Jewish converts of Portuguese nationality were persecuted and discredited by the Inquisition in the seventeenth century. See Silverblatt, *Modern Inquisitions*.

70. "Hernandez Tejero, Pedro, su causa de expulsion, por ser moro," 1553–57, AGN/B, Neg 4, 1–23. Hornachos was the most important Mudéjar center in Castile, with Muslims making up a majority of the population in 1502, when the Crown decreed the conversion and expulsion of the Moors. See Dedieu, "Entre religión y política," 68; Molénat, "Hornachos fin XVe–début XVIe siècles."

71. Cobo Betancourt, *Mestizos heraldos de Dios*; Lee López, *Clero indígena en el Arzobispado de Santa Fé*, 29–32, 50; López Rodríguez, *Tiempos para rezar y tiempos para trabajar*. I will come back to this issue in chapter 3.

72. Sicroff, *Los estatutos de limpieza de sangre*; Zuñiga, "La voix du sang." The fact that the descendants of heretics could not demonstrate purity of blood suggests that it is not mixing that is at stake, but the transmission through the blood of an undesirable trait.

73. Londoño, "Mantas muiscas una tipología colonial." On the appropriation of European and Asian textiles, see the wills transcribed in Rodríguez Jiménez, *Testamentos indígenas de Santafé de Bogotá*, and the very thoughtful critique of the notion of hybridity by Dean and Leibsohn, "Hybridity and Its Discontents." On urban indigenous costume in Santafé, see Vargas Lesmes and Zambrano, "La población indígena de Santafé," 61.

74. Carrera, *Imagining Identity in New Spain*, chap. 2; Graubart, "Hybrid Thinking"; Graubart, *With Our Labor and Sweat*, chap. 4. The extent to which attire was policed among all calidades or genres of people in the Nuevo Reino is apparent in a 1606 criminal suit against Luis Fernández de Valdivia, a knight of the habit of Saint George and *corregidor* (magistrate) of Tunja. Fernández was accused of using the insignia of another order, Calatrava, instead of the order he rightfully belonged to. The lawsuit against him contains detailed descriptions (and even an image) of the cross he wore on a chain around his neck, comparing it to those on the habits of knights of Calatrava and Saint George. "Juicio que le siguio al corregidor de Tunja, a Luis Fernandez de Valdivia, caballero del habito de San Jorge, por usar insignias ajenas a su orden," 1606, AGN/B, JC 75, doc. 2, 166–401.

75. "Causa seguida a Juan Marquez, por tentativa de estupro a Bernardina Villabona, hija de Catalina Villabona," 1628, AGN/B, JC 107, doc. 25, 333r; "Sumario instruido a Maria de Useche, por amancebamiento con Juan Diaz, y con un eclesiastico," 1610, AGN/B, JC 137, doc. 11, 499–551.

76. "Causa seguida a Cristobal de Henriquez e Ines Ortiz, por amancebamiento," 1619, AGN/B, JC 14, doc. 8, 434r.

77. "Causa seguida a Juan Ramirez, por rapto," 1636, AGN/B, JC 107, doc.

36, 741r. What the official saw when he looked at Ana—what led him to determine that she was a mestiza—is not stated. How colonial people recognized calidad visually will be taken up in chapter 5.

78. In some cases, language was more trustworthy than costume. David Tavárez describes how the Inquisition determined the identity of a woman whose parentage and appearance were mulatto, but who wore indigenous dress and was monolingual in the indigenous Chocho language. (Tavárez does not mention whether she was called a "mulata in Indian habit.") She was ultimately identified as an Indian, privileging her upbringing and culture over her lineage. See Tavárez, "Legally Indian," 90–93.

79. On Latin America, see Ares Queija, "*Mestizos en hábito de indios*"; Graubart, "Hybrid Thinking." On Europe, see Groebner, *Who Are You?*, chap. 3. See also a Popayán lawsuit, in which a Spanish man was accused of adopting Indian dress while in Peru. "Con don Sebastián de Belalcázar, vecino de Popayán, sobre la culpa que contra éste resulta de haberse querido alzar con la gobernación de dicha provincia de Popayán," 1559, AGI/S, Just 1118b, n.5, r.2, librillo 4. I thank Santiago Muñoz for bringing this document to my attention.

80. In part, migratory movements were stimulated by the labor levies that brought thousands of native men and their families to participate in construction projects in Santafé and Tunja. Vargas Lesmes, "La mita urbana." Indigenous men also fled their communities to avoid paying tribute. But, as J. Michael Francis observes in "The *Resguardo*, the *Mita*, and the *Alquiler General*," absenteeism from native communities was more massive than can be accounted for by these explanations. Francis suggests that even before the Spaniards arrived in the region, there was substantial migratory movement among the Muisca, leading in the colonial period to large numbers of *ausentes*, tributaries who had abandoned their communities.

81. Alaperrine-Bouyer, "Comment 'policer' les nobles indigènes," 206–7; Jones and Stallybrass, *Renaissance Clothing and the Materials of Memory*, 2–11.

82. Powers, "The Battle for Bodies and Souls in the Colonial North Andes," 36.

83. Mangan, "A Market of Identities," 73.

84. Cope, *The Limits of Racial Domination*, 16.

85. Mangan, "A Market of Identities," 71–76. Kimberly Gauderman's perceptive study of marketwomen in Quito mentions the existence of mestizas in Indian habit and their alliance with indigenous market vendors, but she does not dwell on these cross-dressers in any detail (*Women's Lives in Colonial Quito*, 85).

86. Poloni-Simard, *La mosaïque indienne*, 120–22.

87. I did find one census of tributaries in which a native authority responded to the question of whether or not there were mestizos in the

community by telling the authorities that there were no mestizos in Indian habit there. He was undoubtedly referring to mestizo men in Indian habit, not to the more ubiquitous mestizas dressed like their native mothers. Note that the holder of the encomienda in question is Diego Romero. "Documentos judiciales de lo actuado en las encomiendas indigenas de Tibaguyes de Diego Romero y Juan de Guzman en la visita practicada por el oidor Diego Gomez de Mena," 1603, AGN/B, VC 7, doc. 19, 997v.

88. Powers, "The Battle for Bodies and Souls in the Colonial North Andes," 39–42.

89. "Demanda de Catalina Tafur contra Luis Bermúdez, vecino de Tunja," 1596, AGN/B, TB 3, 993–1005. All citations from this document will appear in parentheses in the body of the text. Note that many first names—such as Inés or Catalina—appear repeatedly in the documentation. What distinguishes Catalina Tafur from doña Catalina Acero de Vargas, whose story opens this chapter, is her lack of the noble title of "doña."

90. Flórez de Ocáriz, *Genealogías*, 2:333–35; Rivas, *Los fundadores de Bogotá*, 2:374–84.

91. "Catalina y Maria Ordoñez, hermanas, hijas naturales de Juan Ordoñez; su demanda de libertad contra Isabel Rodriguez, viuda del dicho progenitor, quien las mantenia en la esclavitud," 1578, AGN/B, NEC 3, doc. 1, 60r–v. I will come back to Fr. García Zorro in chapter 3.

92. Flórez de Ocáriz, *Genealogías*, 2:335.

93. Burns, "Gender and the Politics of Mestizaje"; van Deusen, *Between the Sacred and the Worldly.*

94. Toquica, *A falta de oro*, 34, 206–8, 255–60.

95. Cummins, "Three Gentlemen from Esmeraldas." See also Dana Leibsohn's commentary on this painting at World History Sources, http://chnm.gmu.edu/worldhistorysources/analyzing/mcimages/mcimgsq5.html, accessed 7 February 2006.

96. Dean, *Inka Bodies and the Body of Christ.*

97. Fuchs, *Mimesis and Empire*, 2.

98. Fuchs, *Exotic Nation*, 3.

99. Fuchs, *Mimesis and Empire*, 1–2; Espinosa, "Colonial Visions."

100. Zambrano Escovar, *Trabajadores, villanos y amantes*, chap. 6. However, don Diego de Torres, the mestizo cacique of Turmequé, was falsely accused by his opponents of assuming Indian habits, which, in this case, did not imply cross-dressing; instead, it invoked the fear of idolatry. I will consider this at length in chapter 4.

101. However, well into the late eighteenth century there were mestizo men living with their native mothers in the indigenous communities of the Audiencia de Quito. These men wore native costume until the moment at which they petitioned to be recognized as mestizos in order to escape from tribute and labor obligations. Whether or not they

were called "mestizos en hábito de indios" is not mentioned in the secondary literature. See Ibarra Dávila, *Estrategias del mestizaje*, 59.

102. Fuchs, *Mimesis and Empire*, 5.

103. I am thinking in particular of Ella Larsen's 1929 novel, *Passing*, and Colson Whitehead's recent *The Intuitionist*, both of which depict light-skinned African Americans who pass for white as a long-term option.

2. MESTIZO NETWORKS

1. Israel, *Race, Class and Politics in Colonial Mexico*, 63.

2. I thank Marta Herrera Ángel for alerting me to this possibility.

3. Loveman, "Is 'Race' Essential?," 891–93. I thank Jean-Paul Zúniga for pointing me to this article and for prodding me to think more about the fit between category and group.

4. I consider the issue of why mestizos became countable in the late colonial period in the last chapter of this book.

5. "D. Juan de Borja, encomendero del pueblo de Ochica, jurisdiccion de Tunja, por medio de apoderado solicita provision real para que los espanoles, mestizos y mulatos sean expulsados por los danos y agravios que causan a los indios," 1635, AGN/B, MC 82, doc. 74, 738–39.

6. "Mestizos del Pueblo de Valegra, agregado a Servitá," 1637, AGN/B, CI 32, doc. 37, 312–19. Marta Herrera Ángel cautions that historians do not sufficiently distinguish between the nucleated settlements—the pueblos de indios—where Indians were supposed to reside, the resguardo lands set aside for their agricultural labor, and other rural localities that non-Indians could legally inhabit. As a result, many assertions about the early colonial mestizo presence in the countryside, particularly for the seventeenth century, do not take adequate account of the territorial, spatial, and social organization of the rural population. See Herrera Ángel, *Poder local, población y ordenamiento territorial en la Nueva Granada*, 54–55 (henceforth, *Poder local*); and Herrera Ángel and Bonnett Vélez, "Ordenamiento espacial y territorial colonial en la 'región central' neogranadina, siglo XVIII," 12–22.

7. Tavárez, "Legally Indian," 86–90. Another, more extended description is Noble David Cook's "The Mysterious Catalina."

8. "Salazar, Juan, mestizo, zapatero, causa que se le siguió por haber desnarigado de un mordisco a Juan Medina, indio de Fontibón," 1650–51, AGN/B, CI 24, doc. 2, 124–47.

9. "Letras annuas de la vice provincia de Quito y el Nueuo Reyno de los años de mil y seyscientos y ocho y seycientos y nuebe," 1608–09, AGC-G/R, NRQ, Historia 12-I, 51v–52v.

10. One of these celebrations included one hundred natives on horseback, dressed as "savages" and as wild animals. "Letras annuas de la Prouinçia del Nueuo Reyno del año de 1611 y 612," 1611–12, AGCG/R, NRQ, Historia 12-I, 71r.

11. AGCG/R, NRQ, Historia 12-I, 79v.

12. Vargas Lesmes, "La mita urbana."

13. AGCG/R, NRQ, Historia 12-I, 68v–69r.

14. "Salazar, Juan, mestizo, zapatero, causa que se le siguió por haber desnarigado de un mordisco a Juan Medina, indio de Fontibón," 1650–51, AGN/B, CI 24, doc. 2, 124–47. All further citations for this document will be parenthetical.

15. According to Diego González Holguín, "yaya" in Quechua translates as "Padre, amo Señor" (Father, Lord master) (*Vocabulario de la lengua general de todo el Peru llamada lengua qquichua o del inca*, 366). The nickname thus mocked Salazar by jokingly referring to him as a man of high status while acknowledging his Quito origins.

16. Boyer, "Respect and Identity."

17. In the variety of Quichua that Salazar might have spoken, "*wawki*" is the term used for "brother" when the speaker is a man, while a woman would call her brother "*turi*"; the same sort of gendered usage characterizes the terminology for "sister." Can we read any sort of gendered analysis into the Santafereño use of "huauqui"? Could "huauquis" only be men? The subtleties of Quichua kin terminology as they are expressed in Quito were unlikely to have caught the attention of Spanish monolinguals in the Nuevo Reino. I encountered no female huauquis in the documentation. I thank Tom Abercrombie for prodding me to think about this issue.

18. Nancy van Deusen urges readers to pay more heed to the multiplicity of types of intimate relationships experienced by indigenous slaves under Spanish colonialism, in "Diasporas, Bondage, and Intimacy in Lima, 1535 to 1555" and "The Intimacies of Bondage."

19. Simón, *Noticias historiales de las conquistas de Tierra Firme en las Indias Occidentales*, 4:527; cited in Herrera Ángel, *Poder local*, 55.

20. Herrera Ángel, *Poder local*, 55–56, 63–64. When the nonindigenous population grew large enough, separate parishes were set up for them.

21. Colmenares, *La Provincia de Tunja en el Nuevo Reino de Granada*, 68–70.

22. Non-Indians were not permitted to encroach on the resguardos, although in practice large landholders rented out resguardo lands. Herrera Ángel, *Poder local*, 64. On the process of creating these indigenous collective estates and their impact on indigenous communities, see Fals Borda, "Indian Congregations in the New Kingdom of Granada"; González, *El resguardo en el Nuevo Reino de Granada*.

23. Herrera Ángel, *Ordenar para controlar*, 173–75.

24. Herrera Ángel, *Poder local*, 176–77.

25. That is, contact impacted in both directions (as opposed to the unidirectional notion of acculturation). On transculturation, see Ortiz, *Cuban Counterpoint*.

26. White, *The Middle Ground*. I am, perhaps, extending the notion of the

middle ground much further than White meant it to go. While my attention is drawn toward a colonial situation in which native peoples had been forced to convert to Christianity and to live in European-style towns, their interethnic contacts being largely with mestizos and mulattos whose mothers or grandmothers might have been local indigenous women, White is concerned with a frontier society in which interethnic contact was predicated on trade between more autonomous native communities and French fur-trappers.

27. Therrien and Jaramillo Pacheco, *"Mi casa no es tu casa,"* 96–118. R. Douglas Cope gives emphasis to such an interethnic milieu in mid-colonial Mexico City (*The Limits of Racial Domination,* chaps. 2–3). However, he is dealing with a later period than I am, when mixing was considerably more advanced and the nature of the socioracial hierarchy that emerged from this process appears to have been more well defined, at least in Mexico.

28. On the significance of gender, see Kuznesof, "Ethnic and Gender Influences on 'Spanish' Creole Society in Colonial Spanish America."

29. Boyer, "Negotiating *Calidad.*"

30. See, for example, "Indios de Simijaca, encomienda de don Gonzalo de León Venero; su censo de población, formado por el Corregidor don Juan Guemez de Ceballos," 1660, AGN/B, CI 32, doc. 16, 154–64.

31. Alternately, I might hope to locate such information in baptismal and marriage registries, which could provide detailed evidence of the socioracial categories used to classify people. Such statistical information has provided historians with invaluable data for constructing models of social hierarchy in mid- and late colonial society. See, for example, Cope, *The Limits of Racial Domination;* Dueñas Vargas, *Los hijos del pecado.* However, such registries do not exist in the Nuevo Reino for the early colonial period that I am concerned with, and the complex systems of nomenclature reported by scholars do not appear in the documentation to which I have access.

32. "Sanabria Luis, mestizo de Paipa, su solicitud de relevación de la presentación de seruicios," 1659, AGN/B, CI 18, doc. 41, 300–301; "Galán Diego, mestizo, natural de Servitá, jurisdicción de Pamplona; su memorial sobre exención del pago de tributos," 1669, AGN/B, CI 32, doc. 53, 472–73. Only infrequently were these individuals awarded mestizo status and relieved of their tribute obligations. See "Martín Bartolomé, natural del pueblo de Susa; su negativa a pagar tributos por ser mestizo," 1670, AGN/B, CI 23, doc. 46, 504–9.

33. Guevara-Gil and Salomon, "A 'Personal Visit.'"

34. "Descripción de los indios de Chocontá," 1639, AGN/B, MC 8, doc. 18, 559–767. Further citations of this document will appear in parenthetical notes.

35. Note that the authorities also expressed their concerns over the pres-

ence of indios ladinos, who posed a threat as harmful barriers between the monolingual Muisca-speakers and the doctrinal priest and other functionaries. This turned out to be a moot point, when a Dominican priest, Brother Miguel García, testified that the majority of the natives were ladinos themselves (609v). See chap. 4 in this volume, on the equating of indios ladinos with mestizos.

36. On the meaning of the term "uta," see Villamarin and Villamarin, "Kinship and Inheritance among the Sabana de Bogotá Chibcha at the Time of the Spanish Conquest."

37. When "mulato" takes on the function of a quasi-surname I will use the Spanish spelling, as opposed to the English "mulatto."

38. "El protector de indígenas contra Francisco de Vargas Figueroa, encomendero de los aborígenes de Chitaraquem, por haber incluido éste en el censo de indígenas, a Juana Galbán y sus hijos," 1642, AGN/B, JC 97, doc. 17, 747r. All further citations of this document will appear in parenthetical notes.

39. It was not all that uncommon for clergy to father and recognize their children, who were called *hijos sacrílegos* (children of sacrilege), as opposed to hijos naturales (natural children), the latter being the children of a union between two unmarried individuals. See Twinam, *Public Lives, Private Secrets*, 129, for an explanation of the various categories of illegitimacy in colonial Latin America and early modern Spain.

40. "Cuarterón" was used in the Nuevo Reino to refer to the children of unions between mestizos and Spaniards; in the same period in Mexico the term "castizo" was employed, according to Cope, *The Limits of Racial Domination*, 24. The fact that we commonly think of "cuarterón" as a term denoting mixture of Europeans with Africans, rather than with native people, and my intimation that "cuarterón" was more a self-ascription than an official class of persons, leads me to conclude that the caste categories analyzed by Cope and others were not employed in the same way in the mid-colonial Nuevo Reino as they were in Mexico.

41. Unfortunately, like many other documents, this legal brief has no conclusion, and we never discover how the colonial state ultimately decided to classify Juana Galván.

42. Herrera Ángel, *Ordenar para controlar*, 177–80. I will return to the expansion of the base of vecinos in rural towns in chapter 6.

43. "Causa seguida a Manuel Rodríguez, mulato, por heridas y otros delitos," 1596–97, AGN/B, JC, 162, doc. 4, 617–708. Subsequent citations of this document will be parenthetical.

44. Note how the priest refers to all of these men in the diminutive, using the suffix *-illo*.

45. "Letras annuas de la vice provincia de Quito y el Nueuo Reyno de los años de mil y seyscientos y ocho y seycientos y nuebe (por el padre

Gonçalo de Lopez)," 1608–9, AGCG/R, NRQ, Historia 12-I, 50v. For a discussion of the spatial organization of doctrinal instruction, see Rappaport and Cummins, *Beyond the Lettered City*, chap. 6.

46. For example, in the pueblo de indios of Guatavita there were a number of religious confraternities (cofradías), some with an indigenous membership and others for outsiders. Juan Lázaro Zapago, a mestizo, was the treasurer of the cofradía of Las Ánimas, which had an indigenous membership, as well as holding office in two others in town. See "Testamento de Juan Láçaro Zapago, de Guatavita, hijo de español y de Catalina, india," 1656, AGN/B, n.3, t. 62, 423v. Cofradías furnished the institutional link by which the church exerted its influence over the population through the organization of church rituals, feast days, and funerals. See Graff, "Spanish Parishes in Colonial New Granada," 341–42.

47. The most extensive early colonial treatment I have found concerning the presence of outsiders in Muisca pueblos is the visita of Juan de Valcárcel in 1636: "Documentos referentes a la visita que practicara el Oidor Juan de Valcárcel en las encomiendas indígenas de Sogamoso, Monguí, Tópaga, Tutasá y Mongua," 1636, AGN/B, VB 8, 216–725. I examine this visita in chapter 6.

48. Lee López, *Clero indígena*, 13–24.

49. Pedro de Quiroga, *Coloquios de la verdad*, 65.

50. On the interpenetration of mestizaje and *ladinaje*, see Adorno, "Images of *Indios Ladinos* in Early Colonial Peru"; Charles, *Allies at Odds*; Gruzinski, *The Mestizo Mind*. On the legal separation of ladinos from other Indians in the Nuevo Reino, see Mörner, *La corona española y los foráneos en los pueblos de indios de América*, 109–11. One of the readers of an earlier version of this chapter asked whether ladinos were pretending to be something that they were not, if they were passing, like the individuals whose lives I consider in the previous chapter. I think that in Spanish circles there was deep-seated fear of ladinos, a sense that they might always be "passing," as the Quiroga quote suggests, but I have no indication that the ladinos in Soatá were engaged in any sort of subterfuge that would depend on a misreading of their calidad; their maneuvers were, clearly, much more transparent.

51. Saints Crispin and Crispinian are the patron saints of shoemakers, the guild that sponsored the fiesta.

52. "Cacicazgo de Tibasosa. Títulos de Alonso de Silva a la sucesión en dicho cacicazgo; su pleito con Miguel Holguín, encomendero, quien se oponía a esa sucesión," AGN/B, CI 61, doc. 3, 215v. On mulatto and mestizo bilinguals in early colonial Mexico, see Schwaller, "The Importance of Mestizos and Mulatos as Bilingual Intermediaries in Sixteenth-Century New Spain."

53. Cope observes that this was a general rule for mid-colonial Mexico City as well (*The Limits of Racial Domination*, chap. 4).

54. Colmenares, *La Provincia de Tunja en el Nuevo Reino de Granada*, 16–25.

55. Bonnett Vélez, "Entre el interés personal y el establecimiento colonial"; Villamarín, "Encomenderos and Indians in the Formation of Colonial Society in the Sabana de Bogotá, Colombia," 48.

56. Colmenares, *La Provincia de Tunja en el Nuevo Reino de Granada*, 67–68. Abuses committed by these employees in collusion with their encomenderos will be discussed in further detail in chapter 4. There is ample evidence that some of these interlopers disrupted indigenous plantings and livelihoods by setting their animals loose in cornfields, and that they maltreated tributaries through forced labor and physical abuse. There is abundant documentation of such abuses in most colonial archives. For Santafé and Tunja, see, for example, "Ayala, Francisco, mestizo; juicio que se le siguió por haber sacado a la fuerza y contra la voluntad de ellos indios de Guatavita, encomienda del Capitán Hernán Venegas," 1562–63, AGN/B, CI 69, doc. 6, 137–81; "Pedro Peña Ludueña, alcalde mayor de Turmequé, sumario que le instruyó a un negro, llamado Diego, por el mal trato que daba a los indios del lugar, y por otras causas," 1573, AGN/B, NEC 9, doc. 19, 412–16; "Diego y Beatríz, su consorte, indios de Siachoque, su solicitud de amparo para vivir en dicho pueblo y entrega de Felipa, su hija, que está en poder del encomendero," 1591–98, AGN/B, CI 26, doc. 5, 98–103; "Queja de los indios de Tequia contra el mestizo Joan de Castro, por los daños que les causan en sus sementeras las yeguas y mulas de ese vecino," 1649, AGN/B, MC 120, doc. 74, 935r–v; "El protector de naturales se querella criminalmente del mulato Pedro Hernández, vecino de Chocontá, por agravios que hacía a los indios," 1656, AGN/B, MC 110, doc. 7, 116–18; "Indios de Bosa, investigación sobre los malos tratamientos que les daban con motivo de la extracción de oro en el Corregimiento de Fontibón, de la Real Corona," n.d., AGN/B, CI 10, doc. 11, 61–71.

57. Flórez de Ocáriz, *Genealogías*, 2:416.

58. Cope, *The Limits of Racial Domination*, 32–34, 53–57. Nonetheless, Cope also determines that there was a degree of casta endogamy, particularly among castes with sizable populations, that provided a substantial base of possible mates, such as was the case among Mexico City's mestizos (see chap. 4).

3. HIDING IN PLAIN SIGHT

1. There are no extant baptismal or marriage records from the early colonial period of the Nuevo Reino that are coded by casta, as there are for Mexico. In *The Limits of Racial Domination* Cope works extensively with such records.

2. Cope dedicates a chapter to elite mestizos and castizos (ibid., chap. 6).

3. See Simard, "Problèmes et tentatives d'identification des métis à travers la documentation coloniale," for a discussion of the invisibility

of mestizos in the seventeenth-century archives of Cuenca, Ecuador. I thank Kathryn Burns for sharing with me her acute observations regarding the differing applications of socioracial classification across colonial legal genres. Historians of eighteenth-century Mexico note that these classifications appear more frequently in church records than in secular documentation and were more prominent in marriage registries than in baptismal books. See Chance, *Race and Class in Colonial Oaxaca*, 129–32; Frederick, "Without Impediment," 591–93.

4. "Cacicazgo de Tibasosa: Títulos de Alonso de Silva en la sucesión en dicho cacicazgo; su pleito con Miguel Holguín, encomendero, quien se oponía a esa sucesión," 1571–76, AGN/B, CI 61, 270r.

5. Ibid., 270v.

6. "Testamento de Alonso Valero y Juana de Penagos," 1626, AGN/B, N3, t. 18, 412r–417v.

7. See Pagden, "Identity Formation in Spanish America," for a description of the changing colonial strategies employed by criollos to assert their ascendancy in the colonial social hierarchy.

8. Almorza Hidalgo, "Género, emigración y movilidad social en la expansión Atlántica," 168–69. Almorza notes that some of these women were distinguished as "criollas," starting in the late sixteenth century (174).

9. Lockhart, *Spanish Peru*, 153.

10. Ibid., chap. 9; Mannarelli, *Private Passions and Public Sins*, 10–11; Powers, *Women in the Crucible of Conquest*, chap. 3.

11. In sixteenth-century Dutch Indonesia, elite Eurasian women also acquired European status when they married well-placed Dutch immigrants, assumed Dutch names, and adopted European clothing and lifeways. Unlike in Spanish America, however, Eurasian men could also come to identify as Europeans through employment and migration to the Netherlands. See Taylor, *The Social World of Batavia*, 42–45.

12. See, for example, among many others, Dueñas Vargas, *Los hijos del pecado*; Gauderman, *Women's Lives in Colonial Quito*; Mannarelli, *Private Passions and Public Sins*; Powers, *Women in the Crucible of Conquest*; Stolcke, "Invaded Women"; and Zambrano Escovar, *Trabajadores, villanos y amantes*.

13. The idea of tracing mestizo social networks comes from Poloni-Simard, *La mosaïque indienne*, chap. 6, although my treatment will be more ethnographic than that of the French historian, whose work privileges breadth.

14. Bloch, *The Historian's Craft*, 46. Flórez de Ocáriz occasionally identifies the mestizo offspring of his grandees, but not always. The purpose of his compendium is to foreground what he considers to be the local aristocracy descended from the original conquistadors, which is why he includes in his preface—he calls it a "Preludio"—a treatise on nobility. Flórez de Ocáriz, *Genealogías*, 1:1–60. Enumerating mestizo and mulatto children was not central to his lofty objectives, so he does not

always include them; alternately, in those cases in which the children were remembered as Spaniards, he sometimes call them "hijos naturales" (illegitimate children). Flórez de Ocáriz was not trying to hide mestizos; they were simply not germane to his mission. On his notion of nobility, see Villamarín, "El concepto nobleza en la estratificación social de Santa Fé de Bogotá en la época colonial"; Villamarin and Villamarin, "The Concept of Nobility in Colonial Santa Fe de Bogotá"; McFarlane, *Colombia before Independence*, 239–40.

15. Twinam, "Racial Passing." For examples from eighteenth-century Santafé, see López Bejarano, "'Hommes fainéants et indolents, femmes dissolues,'" 204–6.

16. Burns, "Gender and the Politics of Mestizaje." See also Burns's monograph, *Colonial Habits*, as well as Nancy van Deusen's study of the institutionalization of recogimiento, the sheltering of elite women, in colonial Lima, *Between the Sacred and the Worldly*.

17. De la Cadena, "'Las mujeres son más indias'"; Weismantel, *Food, Gender, and Poverty in the Ecuadorian Andes*.

18. Weismantel, *Food, Gender, and Poverty in the Ecuadorian Andes*.

19. Juan Marchena Fernández asserts that in the early years of colonization 60–65 percent of the children of conquistadors were mestizos, and that some 18 percent of conquistadors in New Spain and 14 percent of those in Peru married mestizas, attracted by generous dowries ("Los hijos de la guerra," 366, 374). Only some of the mestizos' mothers were members of the indigenous nobility; according to van Deusen, many were slaves who had been transported from the Caribbean to new Spanish colonies on the mainland ("The Intimacies of Bondage," 13).

20. Flórez de Ocáriz, *Genealogías*, 2:148–49. For a summary of the Mendoza genealogy, see Therrien and Jaramillo Pacheco, *"Mi casa no es tu casa,"* 82–83. Doña María Manuela de Ávila, the mestiza daughter of the cacique of Guatavita, also married a Spaniard, Salvador de Ojeda, who was a royal notary. See "Testamento de doña María Manuela de Ávila, hija legítima de don Juan, cacique de Guatavita," 1616, AGN/B, N2, t. 17, 83v–91v; also see her mother's will, "Testamento de María Vásquez, casada con Juan, cacique de Guatavita, hija natural de Pedro Vásquez y Catalina," 1630, AGN/B, N3, t. 27, 191r–197r. But while doña María Manuela de Ávila married a Spaniard, her mother had taken the opposite route: a mestiza marrying into the indigenous nobility (a strategy I will return to in chapter 4, with reference to the late sixteenth-century cacique of Ubaque, don Francisco, whose wife was the "daughter of a Spaniard").

21. Villamarin and Villamarin, "The Concept of Nobility in Colonial Santa Fe de Bogotá," 131.

22. Ibid., 127, 129–30.

23. "Inventario de los bienes del capitán Juan de Penagos," 1576, AGN/B, TC 35, doc. 2, 292v–293r, 297v.

24. "Carta del cabildo secular de la Trinidad de los Musos sobre los trabajos que han padecido en la conquista de aquella tierra, buen proceder del gobernador Juan de Penagos, descubrimiento de minas de oro plata y esmeraldas, y relación de los indios de aquella provincia," 1564, AGI/S, SF 67, n.38.

25. Flórez de Ocáriz, *Genealogías*, 2:489. Penagos provided in his will for Francisca, the cacica from Popayán and the mother of Pedro, Juan, Isabel, and Catalina, beseeching Pedro and Juan to care for their mother and sisters (AGN/B, TC 35, 194v, 297v).

26. Flórez de Ocáriz, *Genealogías*, 2:489–90.

27. AGN/B, N3, t. 18, 412r.

28. Ibid., 413v–414v.

29. Gutiérrez Ramos, *El mayorazgo de Bogotá y el marquesado de San Jorge.*

30. Zúñiga, "La voix du sang."

31. In *Certezas ante la incertidumbre* Pilar Ponce de Leiva documents these strategies among the Quito elites in the seventeenth century. For the Nuevo Reino, see Castro-Gómez, *La hybris del punto cero*, chap. 2.

32. Burns, "Gender and the Politics of Mestizaje," 6–8.

33. Ruggles, "Mothers of a Hybrid Dynasty."

34. Flórez de Ocáriz, *Genealogías*, 2:335.

35. Rodríguez Freile, *El carnero*, 43.

36. "Causa seguida a Juan Virues, en virtud de acusacion de Pedro de Sotelo, padre de Isabel de Sotelo, viuda de Lorenzo Nuñez, de haberla forzado en su propia casa," 1577, AGN/B, JC 91, doc. 2, 496–636. Further citations to this document will appear in parenthetical notes in the text.

37. A summary of Sotelo's life is provided in Rivas, *Los fundadores de Bogotá*, 2:332–41, culled for the most part from the service reports Sotelo prepared with the objective of acquiring encomiendas and official appointments. See, for example, "Informaciones de oficio y parte: Pedro de Sotelo, procurador de la Audiencia de Santa Fe," 1562–63, AGI/S, SF 123, n.1; "Informaciones de los méritos y servicios de Pedro del Acevo Sotelo," 1564, AGI/S, Pat 156, r.11. A 1587 letter from Sotelo to the Crown describes his struggle to recover his Audiencia position after he was removed from it. See Friede, *Fuentes documentales*, 8: 376–80.

38. Hering Torres, "Color, pureza, raza," 460.

39. Garrido, "La vida cotidiana y pública en las ciudades coloniales," 135. See also Garrido, "Entre el honor y la obediencia." I will return to the subject of honor and the extensive Latin Americanist literature that delves into its nature later in this chapter, when I describe the travails of Diego García Zorro.

40. Dyer, "Seduction by Promise of Marriage," 443–45; Rodríguez, *Seducción, amancebamiento y abandono en la Colonia*, 29–30.

41. Rodríguez, *Seducción, amancebamiento y abandono en la Colonia*, 32–35, 42, 56.

42. Dyer, "Seduction by Promise of Marriage," 447–48.

43. Ibid., 451.

44. I will return to the issue of appearance in chapter 5.

45. "Juan Delgadillo marido de Maria de Ualle hija de Diego de Valle contra Geronimo de Uega, sobre pesos de oro," 1630, AGN/B, TC 12, doc. 5, 571r. I will come back to the significance of jousting in chapter 4.

46. "Esteban, Juan, alcalde de La Palma, demanda que ante el puso Juan Virgues, contra Salvador Perez, por el despojo de unos indios," 1584, AGN, EPC 3, doc. 40, 572–78.

47. "Diligencias practicadas por el Oidor Lesmes de Espinosa Saravia en su visita a las parcialidades indígenas de Terama y Namazguata, de la jurisdicción de La Palma, y a las de Cunucubá y Tiquisoté, de la de Vélez, y cargos que les resultaran a Juan de Virnés [sic], Francisco Rodríguez Hermoso y Francisco de Ovalle, encomenderos que fueron de ellas," 1617, AGN/B, VB 1, 664r–v.

48. Birves did not collect tribute in Terama, where he alleged that the tributaries did not have the means to pay him. Instead, he operated a textile factory (obraje) with indigenous labor, hauling in wool to be carded, spun, and woven into women's garments (ibid., 689v–690r).

49. AGN/B, JC 20, doc. 13, 408v.

50. Bonil Gómez, Gobierno y calidad en el orden colonial, 132–33. In the construction of this argument, Bonil distinguishes between individuals as physical beings and individuals as public social beings, a distinction also made by the art historian Magali Carrera (Imagining Identity in New Spain, 1–6).

51. "Investigacion que practico el corregidor de La Palma, respecto de la tentativa de envenenamiento, con yerbas toxicas hecha por Juan de Trujillo con Ursula Nuñez, su mujer," 1592, AGN/B, JC 20, doc. 13, 408v.

52. "Información de los méritos y servicios del capitán Juan de Cespedes y de su hijo natural," 1577, AGI/S, Pat 160, n.3, r.3, 3r.

53. Ibid.

54. Ibid., 5v.

55. Ibid., 7r–v.

56. "Informaciones de oficio y parte de Juan Céspedes, vecino de Santa Fe," 1556–95, AGI/S, SF 122, n.24, 2v.

57. Flórez de Ocáriz, Genealogías, 2:69–76. If the notary Flórez compiled the Céspedes family tree on the basis of existing documentation, he would not have seen Juan de Céspedes's name associated with his father's in the notarial record.

58. AGN/B, N2, t. 52, 71r–76v; Flórez de Ocáriz, Genealogías, 2:489–90.

59. Flórez de Ocáriz, Genealogías, 2:489–90. After Pedro de Penagos was killed by his brother-in-law, Juan de Soto Collantes, his wife remarried, this time to a Spaniard.

60. "Carta de Francisco Auncibay y Bohórquez, oidor de la Audiencia de Santa Fe (4/2/1577)," 1577, AGI/S, SF 16, r.21, n.73, 2r. See also "Al

Audiencia del Nueuo Reyno de Granada que proua justicia en vn pleito que trata en aquella audiencia con vn hijo mestizo de Joan de Penagos y en bien razon," 1580, AGI/S, SF 528, 57r–v. Auncibay incorrectly labels Penagos as a "bastardo" (born out of wedlock to a parent already married), when he was an "hijo natural" (born out of wedlock to two unmarried parents). I will come back to this distinction in chapter 4.

61. Flórez de Ocáriz, *Genealogías*, 2:489.

62. Take, for example, Juan de Olalla, a resident of Cartago, to the south of Santafé, and the illegitimate son of Governor Antonio de Olalla and Beatriz India. Olalla's 1618 will lists him as married to doña María de la Chica, the daughter of Pedro Fernández de Biedma and doña Ana de Biedma, a woman of noble standing. See "Testamento de Juan de Olalla," 1618, AGN/B, N1, t. 35, 180v–182r; see also Flórez de Ocáriz, *Genealogías*, 2:369. Note, however, that Olalla was a resident of the district of Popayán, where there may have been greater leeway for mestizos to move up the social ladder than there was in the more rigidly stratified Santafé.

63. How the son of a conquistador and a Quiteña native became fluent in Muisca remains a mystery.

64. Therrien, "Indígenas y mercaderes," 192. Céspedes sustained fierce rivalries with Crown officials and with his neighbor, Diego Romero, who accused him of disrespecting Audiencia officials: "Acusacion del licenciado Garcia de Valverde fiscal de la Real Audiencia, contra el capitan Juan de Cespedes por desacatos a los funcionarios de ella," 1558, AGN/B, HC 7, doc. 1, 1–24. For readers familiar with Bogotá: when I speak of Santa Bárbara, I am referring to the colonial quarter anchored by the church of the same name, immediately south of the Palacio de Nariño (the presidential palace), not to the modern barrio in the northern part of the city.

65. "Testamento de Juan de Lara, intérprete de la Real Audiencia," 1617, AGN/B, N2, t. 17, 244v–249r.

66. Hyland, "Illegitimacy and Racial Hierarchy in the Peruvian Priesthood," 441. See also Bouysse-Cassagne, "Etre métis ou ne pas être," 16–20.

67. The first mestizo to be ordained in Santafé was Andrés Romero de Aguilar, the son of Diego Romero (see chap. 1), who served for many years as the parish priest of the Santafé quarter of Las Nieves, where many indigenous migrants lived. See "Bermúdez Gonzalo y Romero Andrés, su postulación para parroquial de las Nieves de Santa Fé," 1586, AGN/B, CO 9, doc. 143, 239r–v.

68. On the battles over the ordination of mestizos that took place in the New Kingdom of Granada, see Cobo, *Mestizos heraldos de Dios*, and Lee López, *Clero indígena en el Arzobispado de Santa Fé en el siglo XVI*, 8–28. López Rodríguez presents a particularly detailed image of the

heterogeneous corps of mestizo doctrinal priests (*Tiempos para rezar y tiempos para trabajar*, 49–60). See also Olaechea, *El mestizaje como gesta*, chap. 7.

69. In the first years of the seventeenth century, the Jesuits made a massive effort to learn the Muisca language and develop an alphabet. See "Carta anua," n.d., AGCG/R, NRQ, Historia, 12-I, 34v–35r; "Letras annuas de la vice provincia de Quito y el Nueuo Reyno de los años de mil y seyscientos y ocho y seycientos y nuebe por el padre Gonçalo de Lopez," 1608–9, AGCG/R, NRQ, Historia 12-I, 45v–46r. However, although Jesuits claimed they were the first to preach in Muisca, sixteenth-century clergymen like García Zorro had already been doing so some two decades earlier. In the early 1580s, a royal decree ordered that chairs be established to teach native languages to priests. "Zapata de Cárdenas Luis, arzobispo del Nuevo Reino de Granada, en pleito con los franciscanos, por la provisión de algunos curatos," 1588, AGN/B, CO 9, doc. 136, 226r–227r. Fr. Gonzalo Bermúdez, a nonnative fluent in Muisca, is on record as examining the linguistic abilities of potential priests later in the decade. "Fernández Antonio y Ramiro Esteban, postulados para el curato de Sogamoso," 1587, AGN/B, CO 9, doc. 145, 245r–v.

70. The life of Fr. García Zorro is documented in Lee López, *Clero indígena en el Arzobispado de Santa Fé en el siglo XVI*, 40–42. See also Cobo Betancourt, *Mestizos heraldos de Dios*, chap. 3; López Rodríguez, *Tiempos para rezar y tiempos para trabajar*, 52–53; Restrepo Posada, *Arquidiócesis de Bogotá*, 35–38. García Zorro's experience as a music teacher and as a Muisca-speaking confessor is included in the interrogatorio that accompanies his información de servicios y méritos. "Información sobre los servicios prestados y méritos alcanzados por Gonzalo García Zorro, en el desempeño de su ministerio sacerdotal, arquidiócesis de Santafé," 1576, AGN/B, HC 15, doc. 14, 519v, 530v, 544v, 557r. There is also documentation of his appointment as doctrinal priest to indigenous communities, including "García Gonzalo, su nombramiento de cura de Facatativá," 1585, AGN/B, CO 9, doc. 58, 110–11; "Zapata de Cárdenas, Luis, arzobispo de Santa Fé, hace nombramientos de curas para los pueblos de Usme, Remedios, Soracá, Trinidad y San Agustín," 1581, AGN/B, CO 9, doc. 11, 41–47.

71. AGN/B, HC 15, doc. 14, 519r; Hyland, "Illegitimacy and Racial Hierarchy in the Peruvian Priesthood."

72. "Informaciones de oficio y parte: Gonzalo García Zorro, clérigo presbítero," AGI/S, SF 124, n.18, 6v.

73. Guaman Poma, *Nueva corónica*, 997.

74. Julián Vargas Lesmes, "Fiestas y celebraciones públicas en Santafé," 303–4.

75. "Demanda de Francisco de Reina, por injurias de palabra y obra, contra Diego Garcia Zorro," 1603, AGN/B, JC 22, doc. 5, 333r.

76. Ibid.

77. Ibid., 336r.

78. Ibid., 337r–v. The social landscape of this case connects protagonists from various chapters of this book: one of the witnesses to García Zorro's attack on Reyna was the grandson of Alonso de Silva (351r), the mestizo pretender to the cacicazgo of Tibasosa (chap. 4); the Romero tile-ovens were established by Diego Romero, the encomendero accused of being a Moor (chap. 1); Santa Bárbara was the command center of the political faction led by Captain Juan de Céspedes and his sons (chap. 3). Santafé was indeed a small town in the seventeenth century. Many of the stories I tell in this book took place in the shadow of the site where the national archive now stands.

79. Ibid., 340v. There is no conclusion to the case in the existing documentation.

80. On honor in colonial Latin America, see Boyer, "Honor among Plebeians"; Burkholder, "Honor and Honors in Colonial Spanish America"; Johnson and Lipsett-Rivera, "Introduction."

81. Lipsett-Rivera, "De Obra y Palabra," 514.

82. Flórez de Ocáriz, Genealogías, 2:58–68. See also Rivas, Los fundadores de Bogotá, 1:245–53.

83. "Pedro Lugo, alguacil de corte de Santa Fe, su informe sobre la aprehension de un negro esclavo llamado Cristobal, de Diego Garcia Zorro, y sumario que le hizo instruir por resistencia a la autoridad," 1583, AGN/B, NEC 6, doc. 4, 266v.

84. "Expediente de confirmación del oficio de regidor de Nueva Granada a Diego García Zorro," Madrid, 1595, AGI/S, SF 146, n.64; see 2r–v for an explanation of the price of the position. To get a sense of how expensive the cabildo seat was, we can look at notarial documents to establish comparative prices. In 1567, Diego García Zorro sold a horse for 300 pesos ("Venta. Diego Garcia el Zorro, vende a Geronima Martin un caballo," 16 August 1567, AGN/B, N1, t. 4, caja 2, 217r) and a slave for 160 pesos ("Obligación. Lope de Rioja debe dinero a Diego García el Zorro," 5 July 1567, AGN/B, N1, t. 4, caja 2, 204v). His brother, Fr. Gonzalo García Zorro, sold carpenter Pedro de Reina (perhaps a relative of the Reyna that Diego attacked) two urban garden plots for seventy pesos ("Venta. El padre Gonzalo García, clérigo presbítero, vende a Pedro de Reina, carpintero, dos huertas en Santafé por 70 pesos de oro corriente," 18 April 1580, AGN/B, N1, t. 11, 560v–561r). So buying the office of regidor was comparatively expensive, although not as costly as the same office in Cusco (2,500 pesos), Lima (5,000 pesos), or Mexico City (6,000 pesos), according to Burkholder ("Honor and Honors in Colonial Spanish America," 32).

85. I have not found Diego García Zorro's service report, which is mentioned in the Crown's confirmation of his appointment (AGI/S, SF 146, n.64, 3r). Two reports by his father are in the archives in Seville: "Informaciones de oficio y parte: Gonzalo García el Zorro," 1542, AGI/S,

SF 122, n.10, c.1–4; "Información de los méritos y servicios del capitán Gonzalo García el Zorro," 1566, AGI/S, Pat 157, n.2, r.1.

86. See Rappaport and Cummins, *Beyond the Lettered City*, chap. 5, for an interpretation of this ritual, which appears frequently in the colonial archive. On the legal practice of obeying but not complying with a royal decree, see González Alonso, "La fórmula 'obedezcase, pero no se cumpla' en el derecho castellano de la baja Edad Media."

87. AGI/S, SF 146, n.64, 4r.

88. Ibid., 5r.

89. Ibid., 5r–6r.

90. Martin, "Popular Speech and Social Order in Northern Mexico," 322.

91. Even at the tail end of the seventeenth century, 80 percent of the population of Santafé was indigenous. Vargas Lesmes and Zambrano, "La población indígena de Santafé," 57.

92. Note, however, that despite the fact that they could not obscure or deny their parentage, being mestizo or mulatto was, indeed, an obstacle to many commoners in the hinterland. Their very presence in the villages in which they lived was threatened because of their calidad, as I describe in chapter 2. Lázaro Mulato had a great deal to lose, for instance, were he to have been barred from living in Chocontá. Various readers of my manuscript suggested I temper my assertion that Crown officials feared all mestizos and mulattos, observing that it was mestizo priests and officials or caciques of mixed parentage who posed a threat to the status quo, while the mestizos and mulattos I described in chapter 2 continued to live their lives peacefully. But Lázaro Mulato was dangerous, although not in the same way as a priest, a cacique, or an official posed a threat; while he was not "uppity" like Diego García Zorro, while he didn't exert power over such sacred acts as the consecration of the host or confession as did Fr. Gonzalo, and while he may not have been accused of fostering rebellion as were don Alonso de Silva and don Diego de Torres, Lázaro was felt to endanger the innocence of the native community of Chocontá by his very presence in the village.

93. AGN/B, MC 23, doc. 18, 618–30; AGN/B, NEC 6, doc. 4; AGN/B, N1, t. 4, caja 2, 204v; "Gonzalo García Zorro, clérigo maese de la capilla de la Iglesia, otorga poder a Lope de Rioja, relator para pleitos, causas y negocios civiles y criminales, y para pedir mercedes," 19 April 1578, AGN/B, N3, t. 1, 252r–v; "Calongia. Dinero sobre el pleito del dean y cabildo de la iglesia de Santafé con Gonzalo García Zorro," 19 May 1585, AGN/B, N1, t. 11a, 345bis.r–v; "Escritura de donación de un solar yermo que otorga el presbítero Gonzalo García Zorro en favor de una niña indigena," 1596, AGN/B, MC 126, doc. 28, 627–34. In Fr. Gonzalo's información de méritos y servicios some of the old encomenderos remembered seeing him as a child in the paternal household (AGN/B, HC 15, doc. 14).

94. AGI/S, Pat 157, n.2, r.1.

95. For Fr. Gonzalo's bequest to Gerónima, see AGN/B, MC 126, doc. 28, 627–34. A wide range of individuals, some of whom were not servants in any strict sense of the word, could be called criados. For instance, Amador de Gorraiz, a young man of noble blood, came to Santafé as the "criado"—which I would translate here as "assistant" or "protegé"—of Audiencia president Francisco de Arbizo. "Expediente de información de licencia de pasajero a indias de Amador de Gorraiz," 1555, AGI/S, Ct 5218, n.27. Gorraiz's circumstances were in no way similar to those of Gerónima, Fr. Gonzalo García Zorro's criada, although the same terminology was employed in both cases.

96. See, for example, "Poder. Isabel india, criada de Diego López, otorga poder a su patrón, para que herede cualquiera de sus bienes," 1556, AGN/B, N1, t. 1, caja 1, 63v. Was Gerónima in reality Fr. Gonzalo's daughter? That we will never know.

97. Mejía Espinosa, "La preocupación por el honor en las causas judiciales seguidas por adulterio en la Nueva Granada entre 1760 y 1837," 12–14.

98. Real Academia Española, *Diccionario de autoridades*, 3:386, 3:421.

99. "Testamento de Diego García Zorro," 17 October 1615, AGN/B, N1, t. 34, 447r.

100. Ibid.

101. Ibid., 447v–448r. See Rivas, *Los fundadores de Bogotá*, 1:247.

102. AGN/B, N1, t. 34, 448v. Into the early seventeenth century, the Pijao waged war against the Spaniards and were thus subject to slavery. See chapter 5 for a discussion of Pijao slaves in Santafé.

103. AGN/B, N1, t. 34, 451r–452v.

104. María Banegas was the illegitimate daughter of don Pedro Vanegas and Juana Sangrelinda. She married Marcos García de la Jara, a vecino of Santafé, once again illustrating the fact that even mestiza commoners, as opposed to mestizos, could successfully marry men of unmarked calidad. She calls García Zorro her "tío," or uncle, in her dowry contract. "Dote de Marcos García de la Jara y María Vanegas," 1619, AGN/B, N2, t. 22, 40r–43r.

105. Flórez de Ocáriz, *Genealogías*, 62; Vargas Lesmes and Zambrano, "La población indígena de Santafé," 59.

106. On concubinage (*amancebamiento*) in colonial Santafé, see Dueñas Vargas, *Los hijos del pecado*; Rodríguez, *Seducción, amancebamiento y abandono en la Colonia*; Tovar Pinzón, *La batalla de los sentidos*; Zambrano Escovar, *Trabajadores, villanos y amantes*.

107. Twinam, *Public Lives, Private Secrets*, 11, 140–42.

108. AGN/B, N1, t. 34, 425r.

109. Therrien and Jaramillo Pacheco, "*Mi casa no es tu casa*," 105.

110. "Testamento de Jhoana yndia ladina," 22 April 1611, AGN/B, N1, t. 32, 85–88, 89v–90r; Juana's will appears transcribed in Rodríguez

Jiménez, *Testamentos indígenas de Santafé de Bogotá, siglos XVI–XVII*, 85–88.

111. Ibid., 90v–91r.
112. Ibid., 91r–v. Juana's property, like García Zorro's (albeit much more limited in scope), went to her children and grandchildren.

4. GOOD BLOOD AND SPANISH HABITS

1. María Elena Martínez, *Genealogical Fictions*, 158–59.
2. See "Cacicazgo de Tibasosa: Títulos de Alonso de Silva en la sucesión en dicho cacicazgo; su pleito con Miguel Holguín, encomendero, quien se oponía a esa sucesión," 1571–76, AGN/B, CI 61, doc. 3, 14r–409r (henceforth, CI 61/3, in parenthetical notes in the body of the text); "Cacicazgo de Turmequé: Pleito de Diego de Torres con Pedro de Torres, su encomendero, en dicho cacicazgo," 1571–76, AGN/B, CI 61, doc. 4, 410r–607r (henceforth, CI 61/4); "Cacicazgos de Turmequé y Tibasosa, encomiendas de don Pedro de Torres y don Miguel de Holguín, respectivamente," 1574–49, AGN/B, CI 37, doc. 8, 251r–506r (henceforth, CI 37); "Don Diego de Torres, caciques, capitanes e indios de Turmequé contra Pedro de Torres su encomendero, sobre delitos," 1574–75, AGN/B, Enc 21, doc. 9, 392r–594r (henceforth, Enc 21); and "Visita del Presidente y oidores de la Audiencia de Santa Fe por Juan Bautista de Monzon; esta visita fue continuada por Juan Prieto de Orellana," 1576, AGI/S, Esc 822A–B, 823A–B, 824A–B, 825C, 826A–B. In this chapter I will focus on the Bogotá documentation, which is earlier, contains the testimony of a larger number of local witnesses, and is more closely concerned with the issue of mestizaje.
3. Information on other mestizo caciques can be found in "Cacicazgo de Chia, solicitud de Eusebio Espinosa hijo del extinto cacique Francisco Cantor, sobre sus derechos a la sucesión en el dicho cacicazgo," 1689, AGN/B, CI 10, doc. 79, 908–19; "Chinchilla, Juan, cacique del pueblo de Bogotá; juicio que se le siguió por haberle raptado la mujer de un indio, amancebándose con ella," 1626, AGN/B, CI 66, doc. 3, 42–49; "Don Lorenzo, cacique de Cáqueza, encomienda de doña Antonia de Cháves, demanda por haberlo herido, a don Bernardino, hijo del cacique de Ubaque," 1614, AGN/B, CI 64, doc. 1, 1–21; "Olalla, Juan de, cacique de los indios de Ubaté," 1618–19, AGN/B, CI 34, doc. 8, 106–237. Most of these men were officially confirmed as caciques. However, in the case of a mid-seventeenth-century suit in Guasca, near Santafé, the aspirant was rejected because although he was able to prove he was the maternal nephew of the previous cacique, both his father and his mother were mestizos, a situation that the colonial authorities found to be unacceptable. "Cacicazgo de Guasca. Título que alegó el mestizo Luis Romero a la sucesión en el cacicazgo de dicho pueblo como sobrino del

finado cacique don Juan," 1643, AGN/B, CI 20, doc. 17, 826–40. There is also archival information on mestizo and even mulatto governors of Muisca communities, even late into the seventeenth century. "Cantor Agustín. Su nombramiento de gobernador de los indios de Ubatoque, pueblo agregado al de Cáqueza," 1699–1705, AGN/B, CI 56, doc. 17, 493–509. See also Gutiérrez de Pineda and Pineda Giraldo, *Miscegenación y cultura en la Colombia colonial*, 1:327–31. For Mexico, see Haskett, *Indigenous Rulers*, 152–58.

4. For a brief biography of Francisco González de Silva, see Rivas, *Los fundadores de Bogotá*, 2:331–32. See also Corradine Mora, *Los fundadores de Tunja*, 2:297–304, where González de Silva is described as a minor conquistador of low status (*baja condición*) and of scant luck and quality (*de poca suerte y calidad*), whose task was to care for the horse of a superior. Nevertheless, González de Silva was awarded a number of encomiendas, among them Tibasosa, which he eventually ceded in exchange for another encomienda, and Tibasosa passed into the hands of Miguel Holguín. See "Probanza por receptoría de orden de la real audiencia a favor del peticionario Miguel Holguín," 1550, Archivo Histórico de Tunja, in Roncancio, *Fuentes documentales del Archivo Regional de Boyacá*, 45. For a biography of don Alonso de Silva, see Palacios Preciado, "El cacique de Tibasosa."

5. For a description of the training of a notarial secretary, see Burns, *Into the Archive*, 70–71.

6. Rama, *The Lettered City*, 17.

7. Silva's professional career is described by witnesses and by Silva himself throughout the record of the dispute over his cacicazgo. See AGN/B, CI 61, 118v. His service as a notarial secretary is documented in "Albiz Juan de, fallecido en el desempeño de la secretaria de camara. Demanda de Alonso de Silva, por sus honorarios, del tiempo que tuvo bajo su cuidado los papeles del extinto secretario," 1582, AGN/B, EPC 29, 394–411. Silva served as secretary to the notary Juan de Albiz after the death of Diego de Robles and attempted to purchase the position Albiz ultimately vacated. See "Alonso de Silva: Fianzas. Alonso de Silva dijo que se remató el oficio de escribano de cámara en Francisco Alava de Villareal, en 9500 pesos de oro de 20 quilates," 1584, AGN/B, N1, vol. 11a, 76v. In 1593, as a private citizen, he assisted the hereditary lords of Guatavita in drawing up legal papers protesting their forced move to a nucleated settlement. "Indios de Guatavita: Piden no ser trasladados," 1593, AGN/B, CI 25, doc. 2, 30r–44v. Silva's notarial paper trail extends to 1598, when he was secretary to the notary Francisco Alvarez de Villarreal. "Alvarez de Villarreal, Francisco, escribano de camara, demanda que le pusiera Juana de Olalla, hija natural del capitan Anton de Olalla, por refundicion de documentos," 1598, AGN/B, EPC 11, 528–49. The Audiencia opposed Silva's ambitions to become

a notary, citing royal decrees barring mestizos from such offices and suggesting that they should not even be employed as secretaries to notaries. See "Carta del doctor don Lope de Armendariz (30/03/1580)," AGI/S, SF 16, r. 24, n.99–1. Solórzano Pereira declares that mestizos born in wedlock were eligible for these posts, but those born of adulterous relationships—who, as, he curtly observes, were the majority of mestizos—were not (*Política indiana*, lib. 2, cap. 30, arts. 20–21). I discuss Silva's attempts to prove his legitimate birth below.

8. "Don Alonso de Silua caçique," 1572, AGI/S, SF 534, l.3, 1, 400v–401r.

9. For a biography of Juan de Torres, see Rivas, *Los fundadores de Bogotá*, 2:392–99. A lengthy biography of don Diego de Torres appears in Rojas, *El cacique de Turmequé y su época*.

10. Flórez de Ocáriz, *Genealogías*, 2:189.

11. On Torres's early life, see AGN/B, CI 37, 276r; Rojas, *El cacique de Turmequé y su época*, 7–8.

12. Charles, *Allies at Odds*, chap. 1; Wood, *"Teach Them Good Customs."*

13. Silva, *Saber, cultura y sociedad en el Nuevo Reino de Granada*. See also Kagan, *Students and Society in Early Modern Spain*.

14. On his friendship with the grandson of Atahualpa, see Rojas, *El cacique de Turmequé y su época*, 484. For an excellent study of the community of expatriate caciques in Madrid, see Puente Luna, "Into the Heart of the Empire." On the transatlantic voyages of Peruvian caciques, see Glave, "Gestiones transatlánticas."

15. Documentation of Torres's marriage is found in "Carta acordada del Consejo a Diego Ruiz Osorio, su receptor, dándole orden de pago de dos ducados por una vez a doña Juana de Oropesa, viuda de D. Diego de la Torre," Madrid, 10 May 1596, AGI/S, Ind 426, 1.28, 242v. One of his children resided with Juana de Oropesa, as a power of attorney signed in Madrid attests. "Poder que da Juana de Oropesa biuda muger que fue de don Diego de la Torre cacique del Nuebo Rreyno de Granada por si y como curadora de Hernando de la Torre su hijo. Madrid, 10 October 1603," AHP/M, Juan de la Cotera, protocolo 1819, 926r–v (I thank José Carlos de la Puente for sharing this document with me). Don Diego also produced as evidence in his Madrid lawsuit the first cartographic documents we know for Colombia. Torres's maps are held in "Plano de la Provincia de Tunja, sus pueblos y jurisdicción," 1584, AGI/S, MP, Panamá 7; "Plano de la Provincia de Santa Fe, sus pueblos y términos," 1584, AGI/S, MP, Panamá 8. The best reproductions of these maps can be found in Acevedo Latorre, *Atlas de los mapas antiguos de Colombia*, 45–46.

16. "Relación sobre el buen gobierno del Nuevo Reino de Granada," 1584, AGI/S, Pat 196, r. 16, has been published in numerous versions, including by Friede, *Fuentes documentales*, 8:236–74, and by Rojas, *El cacique de Turmequé y su época*, 67–69.

17. Bartolomé Álvarez, writing in 1588, was most concerned that educated indios ladinos would turn away from the Christian doctrine. See his *De las costumbres y conversión de los indios del Perú*, 268–29.

18. See chap. 4, note 3.

19. Cornejo Polar, Santa Gadea, Tamayo Vargas, and Tauro del Pino, "Cinco preguntas en torno a Garcilaso," 20.

20. Lesbre, "Un représentant de la première génération métisse face à l'aristocratie acolhua." The same was true for mestizo officials in the indigenous towns of Cuernavaca over the course of the colonial period. Haskett, *Indigenous Rulers*, chap. 5.

21. Butler, *Bodies that Matter*, 171; Larsen, *Passing*.

22. On the displacement of indigenous people from Central America and elsewhere who were brought to the Andean heartland as slaves or permanent servants, see van Deusen, "Diasporas, Bondage, and Intimacy in Lima, 1535 to 1555."

23. Butler, *Bodies that Matter*, 227.

24. Luis Fernando Restrepo, "Narrating Colonial Interventions," 108–11.

25. Hoyos García and Rappaport, "El mestizaje en la época colonial," 313–14.

26. Trinh T. Minh-Ha, *When the Moon Waxes Red*, 74.

27. My summary of Venero de Leiva's presidency is drawn from Porro Gutiérrez, *Venero de Leiva*. On the encomienda in the Santafé-Tunja region, see Colmenares, *La Provincia de Tunja en el Nuevo Reino de Granada*, and Villamarin, "Encomenderos and Indians in the Formation of Colonial Society in the Sabana de Bogotá, Colombia." On the consolidation of a centralized Spanish administration in the Nuevo Reino, see Bonnett Vélez, "Entre el interés personal y el establecimiento colonial," and Friede, "La conquista del territorio y el poblamiento."

28. "Confirmación de oficio: Iñigo de Aranza," 1562, AGI/S, SF 144, n.16. In 1588 he was serving as corregidor of Mariquita and its silver mines. "Confirmación de oficio: Iñigo de Aranza," 1588, AGI/S, SF 145, n.58. By the end of his career, he was named governor of Veragua, which today is the coast of Costa Rica, Nicaragua, and Panama. "Nombramiento de Iñigo de Aranza," 1592, AGI/S, Ct 5792, l.2, 196r–197v.

29. On Aranza's role in procuring Silva's chiefly title, see CI 61/4, 278r. On Silva's living arrangements, see CI 61/3, 269r–270v.

30. Rojas, *El cacique de Turmequé y su época*, 504.

31. Monzón also married his son to the daughter of Antón de Olalla, a local grandee, contravening the rules of behavior for Crown officials, who were supposed to maintain a distance from locals.

32. On the initiation of the campaign to extirpate idolatries among the Muisca, see "Idolatría de los indios: Disposiciones dictadas en Tunja por el Licenciado y Oidor Juan López de Cepeda, para extirpar la idolatría de los indios en aquella provincia," 1569, AGN/B, CI 70, doc. 28, 613–21; Francis, "'La tierra clama por remedio.'" A list of the contents

of one of the santuarios is reproduced in Cortés Alonso, "Visita a los santuarios indígenas de Boyacá en 1577."

33. Gálvez Piñal, *La visita de Monzón y Prieto de Orellana al Nuevo Reino de Granada*.

34. I am beholden to Luis Miguel Glave for pointing this out to me.

35. For a detailed evaluation of the treatment of chiefly succession among the Muisca by chronicle and documentary sources, see Broadbent, *Los chibchas*; Correa Rubio, *El sol del poder*, chap. 7.

36. *Diccionario y gramática chibcha*, 201; Herrera Ángel, "Autoridades indígenas en la provincia de Santafé, siglo XVIII," 12.

37. Marcela Quiroga, "Las unidades sociopolíticas muiscas en el siglo XVI"; Villamarin and Villamarin, "Kinship and Inheritance among the Sabana de Bogotá Chibcha at the Time of Spanish Conquest."

38. Langebaek Rueda, *Noticias de caciques muy mayores*.

39. Don Diego de Torres's subjects and the captains under his rule also would not look at him directly (CI 37, 284v–285r).

40. Anonymous, "Epítome de la conquista del Nuevo Reino de Granada"; Fernández de Piedrahita, *Noticia historial de las conquistas del Nuevo Reino de Granada*, 1:71–72. For an analyses of the chronicle sources on the trappings of hereditary lordship, see Correa, *El sol del poder*. Colonial caciques like Alonso de Silva and Diego de Torres also maintained cercados, although there are no extant descriptions of them, and it is unlikely that they would have been permitted to erect elaborate defensive palisades like those of the pre-Columbian era once the Muiscas came under Spanish rule. We have little idea of how these traditional structures may have been transformed by hispanized mestizos like Silva and Torres. The mid-sixteenth-century cacique of Ubaque, who was not as European in outlook, erected palisades around his compound and adorned them with feather standards, although the structures were associated with a *biohote*, a mourning ceremony that was discovered and halted by the colonial authorities. Out of this cacique's compound door there stretched a ceremonial path that was "ten or twelve paces wide and very long." Casilimas and Londoño L., "El proceso contra el cacique de Ubaque en 1563," 56–57. According to the archaeologists Hope Henderson and Nicholas Ostler, the combination of ceremonial paths and patios with palisades afforded caciques a spatial expression of their religious authority ("Muisca Settlement Organization and Chiefly Authority at Suta, Valle de Leyva, Colombia," 160). They also report a chiefly residential compound in Tunja, described in 1666, with thick wooden walls "in which wooden planks were covered in cane, on both sides, and then covered with daub" (ibid., 156). See also Román, "Necesidades fundacionales e historia indígena imaginada de Cajicá," 290–91.

41. Bernal V., "Relaciones entre caciques y encomenderos en el inicio del período colonial"; Muñoz Arbeláez, "Espacio y autoridad en el valle

de Ubaque, 1550–1600," chap. 1. The indigenous population of Santafé and Tunja fell by two-thirds in the first century of colonization, declining from some 200,000 in the early sixteenth century to less than 50,000 in the mid-seventeenth century. Francis, "Población, enfermedad y cambio demográfico, 1537–1636."

42. Langebaek Rueda, "Resistencia indígena y transformaciones ideológicas entre los muiscas de los siglos XVI y XVII"; López Rodríguez, *Tiempos para rezar y tiempos para trabajar*.

43. Muñoz Arbeláez, "Espacio y autoridad en el valle de Ubaque, 1550–1600," chap. 2.

44. Casilimas and Londoño L., "El proceso contra el cacique de Ubaque en 1563."

45. Muñoz Arbeláez, "Espacio y autoridad en el valle de Ubaque, 1550–1600," chap. 2.

46. The description is transcribed in ibid., 101. The original document from which the quote is taken is a request by don Francisco to recognize his son (and not his sister's son) as heir to his chiefdom. "Informaciones de oficio y parte: don Francisco, cacique de Ubaque," 1583, AGI/S, SF 125, n.10, 3r–v. Karen Graubart describes early colonial Spanish men's dress: "Sixteenth-century Spanish men wore a white shirt, *camisa*, with a waistcoat, *jubón*, over it and often another overgarment, the *ropilla*, which might have an extra set of hanging sleeves or *mangas*. Their legs were covered by *calzas* or stockings, and they wore a short skirt, the *sayo*, around the waist. Over the latter part of the century, stockings were replaced with *calzones*, calf-length breeches, and colored socks. Over all of this went a long, dark cape, the *capa* or *capote*, which covered the body and presented the strong, severe aspect known from colonial artwork" (*With Our Labor and Sweat*, 128). Susan Ramírez reports a similar transition in 1570s Peru, from old-style *curacas* (caciques) who mediated between their subjects and the deities, to new indigenous leaders who acquiesced to the requirements of the colonial administration (see "The *'Dueño de Indios'*" and "*Amores Prohibidos*"). Robert Haskett notes a move to hispanized (and, frequently, mestizo) native authorities in seventeenth-century Cuernavaca, Mexico, and surmises that they were welcomed by their indigenous subjects as useful intermediaries (*Indigenous Rulers*, 157).

47. AGI/S, SF 125, n.10, 3r, emphasis added. Muñoz Arbeláez, "Espacio y autoridad en el valle de Ubaque, 1550–1600," 105–7.

48. Muñoz Arbeláez, "Espacio y autoridad en el valle de Ubaque, 1550–1600," 115, 118.

49. On chiefly installation ceremonies among the colonial Muisca, see Rappaport and Cummins, *Beyond the Lettered City*, chap. 6.

50. I thank Juan Felipe Hoyos for alerting me to the significance of this quotation. Note Silva's use of "casta" as "lineage" in this quotation.

51. Gamboa Mendoza, *El cacicazgo muisca en los años posteriores a la Conquista*, 116–17.

52. Silva's mention of the fact that chiefly succession could be traced "distantly" through the maternal line refers to the practice of tracing descent not only through maternal uncles, but also through maternal great-uncles, that is, by expanding the range of collateral relatives in the line of succession.

53. Pedro de Torres requested, for instance, that witnesses be examined in Tunja to "avoid fraud [evitar fraudes]" (CI 37, 260v–261r). Alonso de Silva added that it would be impossible to question witnesses in Tunja because there were no officials in that city who were not in some way beholden to the group of powerful encomenderos (CI 61/3, 73r).

54. Silva responds to the pretender by arguing that he is an impostor: "He pretends to be don Laurean [se finge ser don Laurean]" (CI 61/3, 383r–v). Titibi, a cacique who testified in don Alonso's favor, opined that don Laureano was born after the cacicazgo passed from Nomensira to Sugunmox, so that he could not be inserted after the fact into the line of succession (ibid., 459v). Michael J. Francis documents several epidemics in this period: smallpox and measles (1558–60) and influenza (1568–69) ("Población, enfermedad y cambio demográfico, 1537–1636," 26).

55. Haskett, *Indigenous Rulers*, 156–57.

56. Ibid.

57. Garcilaso de la Vega, *Royal Commentaries of the Incas,* 607.

58. Almansa Moreno, "Arquitectura doméstica en el Nuevo Reino de Granada," 246; Fernández de Piedrahita, *Noticia historial de las conquistas del Nuevo Reino de Granada,* 1:330–31; Rojas, *Escudos de armas e inscripciones antiguas de la ciudad de Tunja.*

59. María Elena Martínez, "The Black Blood of New Spain," 483–84.

60. Cañeque, "The Emotions of Power."

61. Zúñiga, "La voix du sang," especially 447–48 on the "moral economy of blood [économie des vertus du sang]."

62. Ibid., 449.

63. Peñalosa y Mondragón, *Libro de las cinco excelencias del español,* 80r–v. I learned of this source from Zúñiga's excellent article, "La voix du sang," 448.

64. "Mestizo espurio nacido de pugnable e concubito adulterino de hombre casado e de una yndia comun e no descendiente de los ligitimos caciques."

65. See Twinam, *Public Lives, Private Secrets,* 26.

66. "No solo es natural pero avn spurio adulterino nasçido de hombre que al tiempo de su procreaçion e nasçimiento era casado en los reynos de España como esta aberiguado."

67. Hoyos García, "El lenguaje y la escritura como herramientas coloniales," 142.

68. Van Deusen, *Between the Sacred and the Worldly,* 40.

69. Ares Queija, "El papel de mediadores," 42.

70. Merrell, *Into the American Woods,* 75.

71. "Carta de Alonso Pérez de Salazar, oidor de la Audiencia de Santa Fe," 6 May 1584, AGI/S, SF 17, r.1, n.2, 1r.

72. In a later case in the community of Ubaque, an indio ladino named Usba, who called himself a capitán (a noble position that the cacique denied he held), was accused of the same sorts of abuses. His hold over the chontales was attributed to his facility in Spanish and his literacy skills. See "Usba, Francisco, indio de Ubaque. . . . Capítulos de la acusación que le formularon los caciques y capitanes de dicho pueblo sobre los delitos que había cometido," 1618–19, AGN/B, CI 57, doc. 20, 372–449. There are many more similar accusations against indios ladinos in the documentary record.

73. On the broadness of the category "indio ladino" and ambivalent attitudes toward those labeled as such, see Adorno, "Images of *Indios Ladinos* in Early Colonial Peru."

74. On prejudices against such intermediaries, see Yannakakis, *The Art of Being In-Between*, 35–38. On the dangers posed by Spanish-speaking, literate sons of southern Andean caciques, see Álvarez, *De las costumbres y conversión de los indios del Perú*, 267–74. There are other documents in the archival record that condemn mestizo caciques for abuses, using similar tropes. See, for example, the case of don Juan, cacique of Cunucubá, in chapter 5. See also "Olalla, Juan de, cacique de los indios de Ubaté. Capítulos de acusación que le puso, por los malos tratamientos que les daba y por otros actos delictuosos don Juan, capitán de la fracción de Quibatá, del dicho pueblo," 1618–19, AGN/B, CI 34, doc. 8, 106–237.

75. The missives run from folios 151v–163v.

76. Cañeque, "The Emotions of Power."

77. Burns, "Unfixing Race," 197–98.

78. "Carta de la Audiencia de Santa Fe (30-08-1583)," AGI/S, SF 16, r.27, n.203, 2r. Mestizo-led conspiracies had already been uncovered in the viceroyalty of Peru. See López Martínez, "Un motín de mestizos en el Perú (1567)."

79. "Carta de Francisco Auncibay y Bohórquez, oidor de la Audiencia de Santa Fe (10/2/1577)," AGI/S, SF 16, r.21, n.76-1, 3r.

80. "Carta del doctor don Lope de Armendariz (30/03/1580)," AGI/S, SF 16, r.24, n.99-1; "Carta del capitán Juan Prieto Maldonado, vecino y regidor de la ciudad de Tunja," 1580, AGI/S, SF 16, r.24, n.126; "Carta del licenciado Prieto de Orellana, visitador de Santa Fe (6/12/1582)," AGI/S, SF 16, r.26, n.169. On the imagery of the royal seal, see Rappaport and Cummins, *Beyond the Lettered City*, chap. 5.

81. Juan Rodríguez Freile, a contemporary of Monzón and Torres, argues that the cacique's predicted rebellion was entirely fabricated, the product of the jealousy of a Crown official's wife, who was thus impelled to lash out at Monzón through her husband (*El carnero*, 147).

82. In other words, this was not a fear of mestizo commoners like the ones

I introduced in chapter 2, even those like the mulatto Manuel Rodrí- guez who was charged with rebellion. True, Rodríguez's cocky dissing of the local priest had to be reprimanded, and the mulatto should not have been in Soatá at all, but he was not positioned to storm Tunja and steal the royal seal. Nor did the fear of men like Diego de Torres mirror the anxieties the Santafé cabildo expressed over ceding a seat to Diego García Zorro, a man who conformed more with the colonial system than did the cacique of Turmequé. By the seventeenth century, when few mestizos could claim the sort of elite positions occupied by Silva, Torres, or the García Zorros, such worries about mestizo rebellions drop out of the historical record in the Santafé-Tunja area.

83. Viewed through the lens of idolatry, Torres appears to be closer to the Peruvian mestizo Jesuit Blas Valera than to Garcilaso. Valera, like the cacique of Turmequé, was deprived of his position, ostensibly because of his mestizo identity, but even more so because of his stance in favor of Quechua as a language suitable for conveying Christian truth. The difference between the two cases is that the argument against Valera was more sophisticated than the jury-rigged accusation of Pedro de Torres. See Hyland, *The Jesuit and the Incas*. It may very well be that Torres participated as a distinguished guest at native ceremonies, much as Juan de Céspedes did at the biohote in Ubaque, although his ardent Catholicism might have kept him away from such events, much as don Francisco, Ubaque's cacique in the 1580s, eschewed non-Christian cer- emony. Pre-Columbian caciques applied red body paint to capitanes, who ritually presented them with tribute payments in the form of painted and red mantles. "Investigaciones que hiciera el Oidor Mi- guel de Ibarra, en la encomienda indígena de Alonso de Olmos—la de Pausada—de la jurisdicción de Santafé," 1594, AGN/B, VC 8, 381r. Cer- emonies of this sort were sometimes resignified in the context of the cacique-encomendero relationship, where the cacique would assume the part formerly occupied by the capitanes and the encomendero. See Rappaport and Cummins, *Beyond the Lettered City*, 247. Of course, in this case Pedro de Torres, the encomendero, would have painted Diego de Torres red, and it is unlikely that the encomendero would have con- demned his half brother for participating in an idolatrous ceremony in which he himself was a major actor. Nevertheless, we must keep in mind that in both instances the ceremonies were colonial in nature, in- volving both indigenous participation and encomendero acquiescence. I thank Santiago Muñoz for bringing these two issues to my attention.

84. Ares Queija, "*Mestizos en hábito de indios*"; Burns, "Gender and the Pol- itics of Mestizaje," 32.

85. Yannakakis, *The Art of Being In-Between*, 35–36. Wendy Lucas Cas- tro describes how North American colonists found it disconcerting that Christian Indians and bi-ethnics wore a patchwork of cloth- ing and adornment drawn from both the native and the European

traditions, suggesting that cross-dressing was, simply, felt to be peculiar ("Stripped," 113–14).

86. Guaman Poma, *Nueva corónica,* 787 [801].

87. "Carta del capitán Juan Prieto Maldonado, vecino y regidor de la ciudad de Tunja," 1580, AGI/S, SF 16, r.24, n.126, 3r.

88. Fuchs, *Exotic Nation,* chap. 4. See also Bernís, "Modas moriscas en la sociedad cristiana española"; Feliciano, "Muslim Shrouds for Christian Kings?"

89. Rodríguez Freile, *El carnero,* 156. Note that the witness's testimony was taken by the notary Juan de Albis, Alonso de Silva's employer.

90. Cornejo Polar, Santa Gadea, Tamayo Vargas, and Tauro del Pino, "Cinco preguntas en torno a Garcilaso," 20–21.

91. Collins, *Black Feminist Thought,* 11.

5. "ASI LO PARESÇE POR SU ASPETO"

1. "El fiscal contra Diego Romero," 1550–78, AGI/S, Just 509, n.1, 24r.

2. "Expediente de información y licencia de pasajero a indias de Gonzalo García Zorro, canónigo de la catedral de Santa Fe, con sus criados Luis de Chaves y Juan Morillo, al Nuevo Reino de Granada," 1589, AGI/S, Ct 5230, n.5, r.26. The document is badly damaged, so we can only glean small pieces of his physical description.

3. Ulises Rojas's paraphrasing of an order to capture Torres when he was accused of spearheading a mestizo rebellion (*El cacique de Turmequé y su época,* 192).

4. This particular brand was more common in Spain than in the New World, in the sixteenth century denoting a slave who was not an indigenous person born in the Americas. Juan Mulato was branded much later, however, which suggests that Otálora and Segura may have been copying an Iberian custom. On the branding of indigenous slaves in the Spanish early modern world, see van Deusen, "Global Indios."

5. "Segura, Juan, Causa criminal," 1607–20, AGN/B, CI 53, doc. 3, 76r. References to this document will henceforth be cited parenthetically in the body of the text. Perhaps Segura branded the child with a European mark so that he would *not* be taken as Pijao.

6. Newson, "The Demographic Impact of Colonization," 178. For an ethnographic account of the social relations that developed out of indigenous slavery written from the standpoint of female slaves, see van Deusen, "The Intimacies of Bondage." Segura and his wife were ultimately found guilty of enslaving a free Indian and were sentenced to two years of exile, a hefty fine, legal fees, and a sum to provide for Juan Mulato's maintenance, AGN/B, CI 53, doc. 3, 101r.

7. "Nación" refers here to the boy's insertion into a particular indigenous group. Also note that the prosecutor, in contrast, labels Juan as

a "mulatto boy . . . son of a Pijao Indian . . . being the aforementioned free and not subject to any servitude, being as he was, the son of the said Indian woman" (87r).

8. My discussion of the restricted nature of the terminology comes from Cahill, "Colour by Numbers." The designation "mulatto" was also an economic truth, which obliged the individual to pay a specific kind of tribute.

9. See Mörner, *Race Mixture in the History of Latin America*, 54, on the emergence of a pigmentocratic system in Spanish America. This is echoed to some extent by Cope, *The Limits of Racial Domination*, chap. 1.

10. Boyer, "Negotiating *Calidad*," 68–69. In modern Latin America, phenotype and behavior tend to trump genealogy, so that in everyday speech Juan would most likely be called "mulatto" unless he claimed membership in an indigenous community, in which case he would be identified as indigenous to the exclusion of his mulatto identification. However, observers would almost certainly note the discrepancy between his phenotype and his ethnic affiliation. See Cháves and Zambrano, "From *Blanqueamiento* to *Reindigenización*."

11. Real Academia Española, *Diccionario de autoridades*, 434.

12. In *Dreaming Equality* Robin Sheriff, an ethnographer, juxtaposes the intricate descriptive discourse of modern Brazilian color terminologies to the underlying, and considerably simpler, black-white racial dichotomy she was able to elicit from her informants, arguing that despite the profusion of terms classifying skin colors, black Brazilians see their social status as intimately affected by their blackness, the vast range of hues through which their skin color is described fulfilling a largely euphemistic purpose.

13. The simultaneous appeal to identification by calidad and by appearance is equally noticeable in documentation produced in Spain for travelers to the Nuevo Reino as it is in documents from the archives in Bogotá, which suggests that this is probably the case not only in Santafé but in the broader Spanish world, although comparative research would be necessary to highlight the specificities of each colonial or metropolitan context.

14. "Licencia de pasajero de Juan Zamorano, indio mestizo," 1595, AGI/S, Ct 5250, n.2, r.29, 3r. There is no explanation in the document of the meaning of the composite label "indio mestizo," which appears in the document's title in the AGI's catalog, but not in the document itself, which simply refers to him as an "indio." This suggests that the apellation is an artifact of a later historical period, when the document was catalogued. "Indio de nación" refers to Zamorano's condition of birth; in modern usage, he would be more properly described as "indio de nacimiento," or "Indian by birth." Later, I will include a reference to

Gabriel Sánchez, who is described as a "mestizo de nación," or "mestizo by birth." The Real Academia's *Diccionario de autoridades* includes a similar usage of "ciego de nación," or "blind by birth" (2:644). In other words, the usage of "nación" as "nacimiento" is different from the political affiliation of Juan Mulato, who was called a "Pijao de nación."

15. "El fiscal contra Diego Romero," 1550–1578, AGI/S, Just 509, n.1, 24r, emphasis added. See Martín Casares, *La esclavitud en la Granada del siglo XVI*, 448, on how "black" and "mulatto" were assimilated to "slave" in the early modern Granadan unconscious.

16. Porter, *Windows of the Soul*.

17. Carrera, "'El nuevo [mundo] no se parece á el viejo,'" 59.

18. In contrast, eighteenth-century casta paintings series from Mexico (and to a lesser extent, from Peru) shed light on how the visual conventions of the times depicted mestizos, mulattos, native people, Africans, and Spaniards, by showcasing the attributes that late colonial artists and, presumably, their compatriots thought were necessary to identify these groups. However, caste paintings do not reflect socioracial categories as they functioned on the ground. Instead, they are idealized representations of the Americas meant for European eyes, and thus cannot be taken as empirical evidence of the colonial classificatory system. See Carrera, *Imagining Identity in New Spain*; Katzew, *Casta Painting*; Majluf, *Los cuadros de mestizaje del Virrey Amat*. Casta series proposed logical sequences of intermarriage, resulting in a number of whimsical categories that had no legal status ("tente en el aire" or "hold yourself in the air" is a good example). As Tom Cummins writes in his review of Carrera's and Katzew's books, "Some terms are ultimately not understandable. They become something that is identifiable only through the images themselves, the pictured bodies. The differences and distinctions implied by such names can only be imagined as substantial by a comparison of the figures in one painting with the other figures in the series" ("Book Reviews," 186). In other words, the systematicity of the socioracial classification as represented in the casta series does not reproduce a system on the ground.

19. Registries in Spain sometimes included physical descriptions. In 1572 the Crown required that every Morisco in Granada be entered into a registry that indicated name, place of origin, residence, age, occupation, and "characteristics of stature and face [señas de estatura y rostro]." "Pragmática y declaración sobre los moriscos del Reyno de Granada" (Madrid: Casa de Alonso Gómez, Impressor de Su Magestad, 1572), Biblioteca Nacional de España, Sede de Recoletos, VE/36/8, 2v. I thank Kathryn Burns for sending me a copy of this document.

20. "Licencia de pasajero de Andrés Martín," 1615, AGI/S, Ct 5345, n.12, 1v. "Loro" denoted a dark, almost black, color. Note that I maintain the

early modern punctuation in these quotations (the equal sign instead of a comma or semicolon).

21. "Licencia de pasajero de Juan Meléndez, mestizo," 1601, AGI/S, Ct 5266, n.1, r.38.
22. "Descripción de los yndios de Cucunubá y Bobotá," 1580, AGN/B, VC, tomo 1, no. 5, 813r. Remember that in this period many Muiscas were still unbaptized, so identification as a Christian was more significant than we might suspect. Cucunubá was located in the province of Santafé, and is not to be confused with Cunucubá, mentioned below, in the province of Vélez.
23. Rostworowski, *Doña Francisca Pizarro*, 159.
24. Hulme, "Tales of Distinction," 163.
25. Groebner, "*Complexio*/Complexion," 376.
26. Nor could Gypsies and individuals condemned for heresy make the passage. See José Luis Martínez, *Pasajeros de Indias*. Notwithstanding these restrictions, there was a sizable population of New Christians in Spain's colonies, many of whom, as Irene Silverblatt documents for Peru in *Modern Inquisitions*, were victims of the Inquisition in the seventeenth century. See also Studnicki-Gizbert, *A Nation upon the Ocean Sea*.
27. In a nod to its centrality in the early modern Spanish imperial mission, the House of Trade is now the building that houses the Archivo General de Indias, where these certificates are archived.
28. Van Deusen, "Seeing *Indios* in Sixteenth-Century Castile."
29. This second scenario is adapted from Guevara-Gil and Salomon's portrayal of a visita, or royal census, in "A 'Personal Visit.'"
30. I could have collected hundreds more for Spaniards traveling to the Nuevo Reino between 1550, when these requests began to be submitted in large numbers, and 1630. I therefore limited myself to a year of documentation for every five years of accumulated certificates describing Europeans. Since considerably fewer mulattos, mestizos, and native people applied for these permits, most of them being Americans who had visited Spain (but who still required certificates for their legal return), I consulted all of those that were available for the eighty-year period.
31. On the physiognomic model, see Van der Lugt, "La peau noire dans la science médiévale," 444–47. For a Spanish physiognomy manual, see Cortés, *Fisionomia, y varios secretos de naturaleza*, chaps. 1–2. Cortés's writings mirror the conventions described by Rebecca Haidt and Martin Porter for European physiognomic discourse. See Haidt, *Embodying Enlightenment*, 126–27; Porter, *Windows of the Soul*, 122–23. For a copiously illustrated English-language manual, see Saunders, *Physiognomie, and Chiromancie, Metoposcopie*.
32. Guaman Poma, *Nueva corónica*, 535 [549].
33. Grasseni, "Skilled Vision," 41–42.

34. Goodwin, "Professional vision," 606.

35. Kagan, *Students and Society in Early Modern Spain*, chap. 2. I thank Richard Kagan for making clear to me in an extended phone conversation the educational level at which practices of skilled vision might have been included in the curriculum, as well as for alerting me to other contexts in which bureaucrats might have imbibed these descriptive conventions.

36. MacDonald, "Humanistic Self-Representation in Giovan Battista Della Porta's 'Della Fisionomia Dell'Uomo'"; Wilson, "Learning How to Read."

37. Groebner, *Who Are You?*, 129.

38. On the importance of the head, see Mason, "Reading New World Bodies," 159. For a description of horses that focuses on hooves and hair color, although also touching on eye color and distinct forehead and body markings, see "Ejecucion por suma de pesos, seguida por Alvaro de Zebreros a Diego Romero, como fiador de Domingo Gonzales," 1566, AGN/B, JCC 21, 744r–v. (It was almost impossible to encounter a document in late sixteenth-century Santafé that didn't make at least a passing reference to that Morisco-slave-turned-encomendero, Diego Romero.)

39. Dunn, "'De las figuras del arçipreste.'"

40. "Licencia de pasajero de Jerónimo Vicente Colomer," 1594, AGI/S, Ct 5246, n.1, r.32, 6v.

41. "Licencia de pasajero de Alonso del Pulgar con su hijo Alonso del Pulgar," 1598, AGI/S, Ct 5257, n.1, r.21, 2r.

42. "Licencia de pasajero de Juan García," 1605, AGI/S, Ct 5287, n.11, 6v.

43. "Licencia de pasajero de Magdalena Diaz Rodriguez," 1555, AGI/S, Ct 5218, n.45, 1r.

44. "Licencia de pasajero de Diego Prieto Dávila," 1590, AGI/S, Ct 5232, n.91, c.2, 2r. Note the reference to Toribia's having suffered from smallpox; pockmarks are a common feature, particularly in descriptions of native people, who suffered in the greatest numbers from smallpox epidemics, which were frequent into late in the colonial period. Silva, *Las epidemias de viruela de 1782 y 1802 en el virreinato de Nueva Granada*, chap. 1. Note also the mole behind her ear, a semi-hidden attribute. In the sixteenth and seventeenth centuries, even hidden moles and warts were used to identify individuals. For example, in a dispute over the ownership of a black slave in 1636, the man was described as "a black man with a wart on the left side behind the ear" ("Francisco Salgado contra José Gómez Sedero," 1636, AGN/B, NEB 13, 180v). Such features were of physiognomic significance, their presence on the face mirroring their positioning on the torso and extremities. See "A Treatise of the Moles," in Saunders, *Physiognomie, and Chiromancie, Metoposcopie*.

Despite their prominence in the narrative portraits, moles appear to have little bearing on sociracial classification.

45. In general, descriptions of Spaniards are more detailed than are those of other groups. Colonial North American physical descriptions also privilege individuals of European descent. See Prude, "To Look upon the 'Lower Sort,'" 149.

46. "Licencia de pasajero de Francisco de Albornoz," 1579, AGI/S, Ct 5227, n.4, r.16, 3r.

47. "Licencia de pasajero de Gabriel Sánchez, mestizo," 1605, AGI/S, Ct 5288, n.35, 2v.

48. Covarrubias Orozco, *Tesoro de la lengua castellana o española*, 164–66.

49. Ibid., 164.

50. Bly, "Beards in the Poema de Mio Cid." Covarrubias makes reference to the Cid's beard in his lengthy dictionary entry (*Tesoro de la lengua castellana o española*, 165).

51. Cortés, *Fisionomia, y varios secretos de la naturaleza*, 21. Beards were considered significant physiognomic attributes not only among Spaniards, but in the rest of Europe as well. The English author Richard Saunders dedicates a chapter of *Physiognomie, and Chiromancie, Metoposcopie* to the inner attributes indicated by different qualities of beards.

52. Sebastián de Covarrubias includes an image of a bearded woman modeled after Sánchez Cotán's portrait in his *Emblemas morales*, 164. See also Johnston, "Bearded Women in Early Modern England," 8–9; Konečný, "Una Pintura de Juan Sánchez Cotán, emblematizada por Sebastián de Covarrubias."

53. Fisher, "The Renaissance Beard," 158.

54. Cadden, *Meanings of Sex Difference in the Middle Ages*, 181. See also Israel Burshatin's "Elena alias Eleno," a fascinating study of Eleno de Céspedes, a sixteenth-century intersexed person (and mulatto/a), who was sometimes identified by his/her genitalia and sometimes by his/her behavior. Mary Beth Norton describes another intersexed person in colonial Virginia, who was examined and found to be sexually "incompletely masculine," but whose gender identity was feminine. The court required this person to wear articles of male and female attire simultaneously: a man's clothing, but with a woman's apron and cap. See Norton, "Communal Definitions of Gendered Identity in Seventeenth-Century English America." I thank Sarah Messer for leading me to Norton's illuminating study.

55. Biow, "Manly Matters," 333.

56. Najmabadi, *Women with Mustaches and Men without Beards*, 15, 16. I thank Steve Caton for alerting me to Najmabadi's book.

57. Fuchs, *Exotic Nation*.

58. This Sandobal is not the Jesuit author from whose work I draw later in this chapter, but a young retainer or possibly an adoptee—a criado—of a Spanish couple.

59. "Licencia de pasajero de Diego de la Cadena," 1620, AGI/S, Ct 5374, n.33, 3r.

60. Ibid., 8v–9r.

61. "Juan Ortiz Manosalva contra Jorge Vaca Moscoso," 1621, AGN/B, JC 18, doc. 23, 549r–v.

62. Ibid., 549v.

63. On the centrality of clothing in identifying individuals, an issue I have emphasized in previous chapters, see Groebner, *Who Are You?*, 82–89.

64. García, *Origen de los indios del Nuevo Mundo e Indias Occidentales*, 140. Other period texts also dwell on the significance of climatic influence among the ancient ancestors of indigenous people. In his late sixteenth-century *Problemas y secretos maravillosos de las Indias*, published in Mexico City, Juan de Cárdenas explains that native Americans did not have beards because their ancestors had been exposed to the elements during their travels, which caused their pores to close and blocked the exit of humors, thus inhibiting beard growth (but not hair growth on their crowns) (187v–189v).

65. Caillavet, "Imágenes del cuerpo."

66. Guaman Poma, *Nueva corónica*, 787 [801]. A zambaigo (also called a zambo) was the child of an Indian and a black; Francisco Suárez, the duplicitous suitor of doña Catalina Acero de Vargas, was a zambo. In chapter 1, I also explained that in colonial Ecuador a chola was a hispanized mestiza. Note that Guaman Poma is referring generally to lineage, not specifically to socioracial category, when he speaks of "bad caste."

67. By the late seventeenth century, European writers had begun to distinguish themselves from the men of other continents by pointing out the thickness of their beards. See Schiebinger, *Nature's Body*, 120–25. But in other social contexts, it was not as necessary for Spaniards to slight mulattos and mestizos by ignoring their beards: witness, for instance, Velásquez's portrait of his mulatto assistant, Juan de Pareja, complete with facial hair.

68. "Descripción de los indios de los pueblos de Cucunubá y Simijaca," 1586, AGN/B, VC 1, 844r–871r.

69. "Censo de población de los indios de Viracachá y otros pueblos," 1687, AGN/B, CI 10, doc. 40, 287–316.

70. Londa Schiebinger argues similarly that the reason the beard "could play such a role in racial evaluation in this period [was] only because anthropological classificatory interests focused almost exclusively on males" (*Nature's Body*, 124).

71. In fact, of the eighteen men and women identified as Spaniards whose physical descriptions I recorded for 1555, eight were identified

as "moreno," while none were described as having a "white face." A look at just one paragraph of the writings of Juan López de Velasco, a sixteenth-century chronicler, indicates that there were multiple color terms that could be deployed to identify the differing hues among native people: *membrillo cocho* (cooked quince), *bazo* (yellowish brown), *leonado* (tawny), *castaño* (chestnut) (*Geografía y descripción universal de las Indias*, 27). The same range of colors employed by López de Velasco to distinguish among American natives was used to identify Moriscos captured in the 1568–71 rebellion of the Alpujarras in Andalucía, although the vocabulary for describing the children of mixed Morisco-Christian unions was more limited, perhaps because observers could not distinguish between them and other Spaniards. Fuchs, "A Mirror across the Water," 9–10. Sixteenth-century indigenous slaves in Spain were identified in notarial registries by similar gradations of hue. Mira Caballos, *Indios y mestizos americanos en la España del siglo XVI*, 60. Nonetheless, most of these descriptive terms were not part of the physiognomic conventions employed in documentary narrative portraits, whose palette was more limited.

72. Covarrubias Orozco, *Tesoro de la lengua castellana o española*, 763.

73. Blacks, however, are never described as "moreno" in the travel documents, although Alonso de Sandoval does employ it to emphasize that there are "blacks of many types of blackness [negros de muchas maneras de negregura]" (*De instauranda aetiopum salute*, 10). Nowadays, "moreno" is a more polite way of saying "black," although modern Afro-Colombian political organizations urge people to recognize themselves as black.

74. "Licencia de pasajero de Antón Pérez," 1555, AGI/S, Ct 5218, n.13, 3v; "Licencia de pasajero de Bárbola Núñez," 1555, AGI/S, Ct 5218, n.19, 3v; "Licencia de pasajero de Miguel de Lizaso, escribano real," 1555, AGI/S, Ct 5218, n.35, 1r; "Licencia de pasajero de Pedro de Amendux," 1555, AGI/S, Ct 5218, n.33, 2r; the last of these was a member of the nobility. The earliest identification of a Spaniard as having a "white face" that I found dates to 1576. See "Licencia de pasajero de Juan de Basurto," 1576, AGI/S, Ct 5223, n.17, 2v.

75. Groebner, *Who Are You?*, 131–32.

76. Behrend-Martínez, "Manhood and the Neutered Body in Early Modern Spain," 1076. Cortés classifies European skin colors into four categories: "whiteish [blanquecino], as in ice, or lead, denotes a cold complexion"; "reddish [vermejo], and flushed [encendido], with a mixture of whiteness [blancura], and with many freckles, denotes a hot complexion"; "white [blanco], with a white thinness [una delgadéz blanca], and with traces of the color red [encarnado], signals a temperate complexion"; and "the color brown, or swarthy, indicates a good complexion [bruno, ó moreno dice buena complexion]" (*Fisionomia, y varios secretos de la naturaleza*, 1–3).

77. Lewis, *Hall of Mirrors*, 75–76.

78. References to white coloring become more common in requests for travel permits of the seventeenth century. See, for example, among numerous cases, "Licencia de pasajero de Alonso de Rivadeneira," 1594, AGI/S, Ct 5244, n.2, r.44; "Licencia de pasajero de Antonio de Herrera Montalbo, con su hermano Juan de Benavente," 1626, AGI/S, Ct 5394, n.60; "Licencia de pasajero de Andrés de Zapiaín," 1630, AGI/S, Ct 5406, n.33. "White" is equated with "Spaniard" in other documents I found for Santafé; for example, in one document a woman calls herself "a Spanish woman and white [vna muger española y blanca]" ("Demanda por el valor de servicios personas, de Juana Gonzalez, sobre los bienes mortuorios de Bartolome Gomez. Santafe," 1660, AGN/B, TC 7, 981r). On the meaning of the color white, see Groebner, *Who Are You?*, 137.

79. "Francisco Antonio de Colmenares contra Jacinto de Padilla," 1633, AGN/B, JCC 46, 65r. The use of terms that reference degrees of mixing, such as "quarteroon," appear occasionally in the seventeenth-century documentation, but not in that of the sixteenth century. Remember that Juana Galván's children were called "cuarterones."

80. "Indios de la Provincia de Santafé y Tunja, destinados a trabajos en las minas de Las Lajas y Santa Ana," 1628, AGN/B, CI 5, doc. 3, 603–56; AGN/B, CI 10, doc. 40, 287–316.

81. Cañizares-Esguerra, *Nature, Empire, and Nation*; Hahn, "The Difference the Middle Ages Makes"; Van der Lugt, "La peau noire dans la science médiévale," 448–55.

82. Sandoval, *De instauranda aethiopum salute*, libro 1, chap. 2.

83. Ibid. See also an English edition of Alonso de Sandoval's treatise containing an abbreviated version of this quotation, as translated by Nicole von Germeten (Sandoval, *Treatise on Slavery*, 18).

84. Sandoval, *De instauranda aethiopum salute*, ibid.; also Sandoval, *Treatise on Slavery*, 18–19. Sandoval uses "nación" in two senses here: first, in relation to Angola, he refers to the child's African ancestry; then, in relation to "negro," he refers to the child's birth.

85. Cohen, "On Saracen Enjoyment"; Hahn, "The Difference the Middle Ages Makes." Silvia De Renzi notes that resemblance did not constitute reliable evidence of paternity for early modern judges, who were likely to ascribe it to the maternal imagination, rather than to paternity. This provides further evidence of the disconnect in the period between physical appearance and lineage. De Renzi, "Resemblance, Paternity, and Imagination in Early Modern Courts," 64–66.

86. Forbes, *Africans and Native Americans*. Note that these color terms were employed within the framework of a very different definition of mulatto from that which came to be used in the Americas. Iberian mulattos, whose mixed parentage was European and North African, also appear in the requests for permission to travel to the Nuevo Reino. See, for example, "Ana, de color mulata, natural de Huelva, soltera, hija de

Cristóbal Beltrán y de Catalina Peguera, al Nuevo Reino de Granada, como criada del secretario Francisco Velázquez," 1565, AGI/S, Ct 5537, l.3, 122v; also see "Autos de bienes de difuntos de Pedro Montesdoca," 1591, AGI/S, Ct 485, n.4, r.5.

87. Martín Casares, *La esclavitud en la Granada del siglo XVI*, 146, 157.

88. "Licencia de pasajero de Juan Zambrano," 1615, AGI/S, Ct 5347, n.23, 1v.

89. "Licencia de pasajero de Pedro de Cabrera Bohorquez, indio," 1604, AGI/S, Ct 5280, n.51, 1v.

90. For "negros atezados," see "Licencia de pasajero de Agustín de Monroy," 1610, AGI/S, Ct 5317, n.2, r.18, 1v; AGI/S, Ct 5339, n.17, 1v, among others. "Loro," which dates to the Middle Ages, was used to refer to Muslim and East Indian slaves, as well as mulattos—in other words, to all of those slaves who could not be classified as European or black. It was also used to refer to the inhabitants of the Canary Islands and, in the first years of Spanish domination, to natives of the Caribbean. "Mulatto" as a color term appears to have largely replaced "loro" in the early sixteenth century (personal communication, Jean-Paul Zúñiga). On "loro" as a color, see Cejador y Frauca, *Vocabulario medieval castellano*, 253; Forbes, *Africans and Native Americans*, 26–27, 106–12. For individuals classified as "black slaves" and identified as of loro color, see AGI/S, Ct 5315, n.31, 2r. The diversity of shades of black was noted by early modern observers in treatises like the seventeenth-century Jesuit Alonso de Sandoval's *De instauranda aetiopum salute*, lib. 1, chap. 16. Sandoval's color terminology is analyzed in Eduardo Restrepo, "Eventalizing Blackness in Colombia," chap. 5. On "black" as a term for "slave," see Fracchia, "(Lack of) Visual Representation of Black Slaves in Spanish Golden Age Painting," 32; Tinhorão, *Os negros em Portugal*, 76–77.

91. David Waldstreicher argues that "white" was also not a relevant category in colonial north America ("Reading the Runaways," 257). I thank Michael Hill for alerting me to this literature. It was not until the late eighteenth century that color in general—that is, including "white"—shifted from being used "as an adjective describing a hue" to being used "as a noun describing a condition," at once an auto-ascription and an imposed category (Twinam, "Purchasing Whiteness," 154). I am inclined, however, to infer that "mestizo" and "mulatto" became colors only after being established as categories, whereas "white" was first a color, only much later becoming a category.

92. "Expediente de información y licencia de pasajero a indias de Juan Zamorano," 1595, AGI/S, Ct 5250, n.2, r.29, 3r. Zamorano was identified genealogically as "the son of Alonso Ruiz indio cacique and of Aryana Alonso india his wife from Funsa [hijo de Alonso Ruiz yndio caçique y de Aryana Alonso yndia su muger de Funsa]" (ibid., 1r).

93. "Don Juan, cacique de los indios de Cucunubá [*sic*], defensa de su cacicazgo," 1607–20, AGN/B, CI 11, doc. 6, 331v. Don Juan was also tagged

as mestizo because his body was "very hairy" (*muy vellado*) (ibid., 205r). Value judgments by local witnesses might lead us to inquire into how the Muisca described themselves. Ezequiel Uricoechea's compilation of colonial-era documentation on the Muisca language indicates that some colonial lexicographers struggled to fit native referents into physiognomic conventions, such as "es blanco de rostro" or "oba apquyhyzyn mague [he is white of face]," "es de color negro" or "oba amuyhyzyn mague [he is black in color]," and "es amulatado" or "amuynin mague [he is mulatto-like]" (Uricoechea, *Gramática, vocabulario, catecismo i confesionario de la lengua chibcha*, 93). I suspect, however, that these phrases reflect the Spanish palette, rather than Muisca categories.

94. AGN/B, CI 11, doc. 6, 264r, 547r.

95. Ibid., 551v. "Líquida" is a Spanish rendering of the Quechua word "lliclla," in this case referring to an indigenous-style mantle, although frequently those worn by elite native women were made from fine European cloth.

96. "Indios de la Provincia de Santafé y Tunja, destinados a trabajos en las minas de Las Lajas y Santa Ana," 1628, AGN/B, CI 5, doc. 3, 613r. Las Lajas became an important silver-mining center in the early seventeenth century and a destination for indigenous workers subject to labor levies. On the history of the mine, see Ruíz Rivera, *La plata de Mariquita en el siglo XVII*.

97. "Censo de población de los indios de Viracachá," 1687, AGN/B, CI 10, doc. 40, 292r and 302r.

98. "Cantor Agustín, nombramiento de gobernador de los indios de Ubatoque," 1699–1705, AGN/B, CI 56, doc. 17, 500r. The mother is also described as being "white in color [de color blanco]" or even as "an india of white caste [yndia de casta blanca]" (ibid., 550v, 501v). This suggests that although categories—now increasingly called "castes" in Santafé (although the quotation still appears to refer to lineage)—may have been solidifying, descriptors still moved with ease across a wide range of groups. The *Diccionario de Autoridades* (1726) defines "amulatado" as "a person who has a color that is not totally black, but very dark. The word is composed of the particle 'a' and the name Muláto, which means almost black, mestízo [mixture] of white and black" (278).

99. "Padron de los negros libres y mulatos que hay en la ciudad de Velez para la cobranza de los requintos," 1664, AGN/B, MC 54, doc. 16, 127v.

100. Cervantes Saavedra, *La ilustre fregona*, 36. The editor identifies Aroba as "probably the name or nickname of some notorious rogue" (ibid., 136). See also Querol Gavaldá, *La música en la obra de Cervantes*, 119–25. I thank Carlos Páramo for bringing my attention to this chacona.

101. Beusterian, *An Eye on Race*, 152–53.

102. Herzog, "Early Modern Spanish Citizenship." However, as I detail in chapter 6, in the eighteenth century, when the rural population became largely mixed, the term "vecino" appears to have been extended to all sorts of people.

6. THE PROBLEM OF CASTE

1. "Proceso de fe de Pablos de Orejuela, natural de Santa Fé (Granada) [*sic*], vecino de Santa Fé de Bogotá (Colombia), mestizo, labrador, seguido en el Tribunal de la Inquisición de Cartagena de Indias, por herejía. Fue condenado a sambenito y a destierro," 1621, AHN/M, ICI, 1621, exp.12. Orejuela was tried in Cartagena because there was no Inquisition tribunal in Santafé. For an excellent history of Usaquén, see Zambrano Pantoja et al., *Comunidades y territorios*, in particular, chap. 5 on the seventeenth century.

2. AHN/M, ICI, 1621, exp.12, 67v–69v, 78v–80r, 86r–v, 89v–90r, 93v, 156r–163v.

3. Ibid., 50r–53r. See also Flórez de Ocáriz, *Genealogías*, 2:34–36, 154–55.

4. AHN/M, ICI, 1621, exp.12, 54r–55v. The *juego de barras* originated in Aragón, Spain, and consisted of a court along which metal bars were thrown. I have not been able to determine with precision, however, if this was the same game Orejuela set up in his house.

5. "Cardoso Juana, vecina de Santafé; su denuncio y demanda por haberle sonsacado una india, su sirvienta, contra Pablo de Orejuela," 1629–32, AGN/B, CI 70, doc. 9, 220–45. Note that in this document, his mother speaks in his defense through an interpreter (ibid., 245r), suggesting that he maintained relations with her, despite the fact that he says so little about her at his trial. Whether or not Orejuela spoke his mother's language is unknown, and it is possible he had forgotten it, if he was brought up in his father's household.

6. Covarrubias, *Tesoro de la lengua castellana o española*, 282.

7. There is some debate over whether "casta" referred only to the mixed categories or to all socioracial categories. On the problematics of the meaning of "casta" in the scholarly literature on the colonial period, see Hill, *Hierarchy, Commerce, and Fraud in Bourbon Spanish America*, 204–11. Based on her survey of literary usage of the term, Hill argues that "casta" morphed from meaning "pure or noble lineage" to denoting both "impure" mixtures and groups that were not mixed at all, including Spaniards, Indians, Africans, Jews, and Moors.

8. Cope, *The Limits of Racial Domination*, 24. In *Hall of Mirrors* Laura Lewis routinely refers to the various social categories in seventeenth-century New Spain as "castas."

9. I thank Kathryn Burns, José Cornelio, Ruth Hill, Nancy van Deusen, and Marta Zambrano for enlightening me on the meaning of "casta"

in the Caribbean, Peru, and Santafé. On the relatively late appearance of caste in the Nuevo Reino, see Jaramillo Uribe, *Ensayos sobre historia social colombiana*, 163–203. In her study of calidad in eighteenth-century Mariquita, *Gobierno y calidad en el orden colonial*, Katherine Bonil Gómez almost completely eschews the term "casta" in favor of "calidad," which is ubiquitous in the late colonial documentary record for Nueva Granada.

10. Garrido, "'Free Men of All Colors' in New Granada." Later in this chapter, I return to the question of why color is mentioned.

11. Carrera, *Imagining Identity in New Spain*; Cummins, "Book Reviews"; Katzew, *Casta Painting*.

12. Bonil Gómez emphasizes this point continuously, in *Gobierno y calidad*.

13. Chance, *Race and Class in Colonial Oaxaca*, 127.

14. Frederick, "Without Impediment," 593.

15. Chance, *Race and Class in Colonial Oaxaca*, 127; Cope, *The Limits of Racial Domination*, chap. 4.

16. Lewis, *Hall of Mirrors*, chap. 7.

17. Correa Rubio, *El sol del poder*, 200; Francis, "Población, enfermedad y cambio demográfico, 1537–1636"; Francis, "The *Resguardo*, the *Mita*, and the *Alquiler General*"; Herrera Ángel, *Poder local*, 79–89.

18. Colmenares, *La Provincia de Tunja en el Nuevo Reino de Granada*, 61.

19. Friede, "De la encomienda indiana a la propiedad territorial y su influencia sobre el mestizaje," 48.

20. "Documentos referentes a la visita que practicara el Oidor Juan de Valcárcel en las encomiendas indígenas de Sogamoso, Monguí, Tópaga, Tutasá y Mongua," 1636, AGN/B, VB 8, 223v. Further citations of this document will be parenthetical.

21. On the history of the segregation of indigenous lands through the institution of the resguardo, see the classic text by Margarita González, *El resguardo en el Nuevo Reino de Granada*. On the loss of ancestral lands resulting from the creation of resguardos, see Herrera Ángel, *Ordenar para controlar*, 165–69.

22. Note that Pongota argues in his own defense that he sold these goods out of his house (as opposed to running a store). At the end of this chapter I clarify the meaning of this assertion.

23. It is unlikely that Pedro Rodríguez Mendo and Pedro Mendo are the same person, particularly since Rodríguez Mendo appears to have enjoyed more friendly relations with the indigenous authorities than Mendo did. Moreover, they do not have a common patronymic (although the use of patronymics and matronymics that is common today in the Spanish language was not as consistent in the colonial period).

24. Colmenares, *La Provincia de Tunja en el Nuevo Reino de Granada*, 69.

25. Álvarez M., Orlando Melo, Meisel, and Tovar, "La relevancia de la historia colonial en el mundo de hoy," 182–83.

26. Herrera Ángel, *Poder local*, 78.

27. Jaramillo Uribe, *Ensayos sobre historia social colombiana*, 164–69.

28. Bonfíl Batalla, *México profundo*, chap. 3.

29. Jaramillo Uribe, *Ensayos sobre historia social colombiana*, 169.

30. Fals Borda, "Indian Congregations in the New Kingdom of Granada," 342–43.

31. Silvestre, *Descripción del Reyno de Santa Fé de Bogotá*, 68. By this period, the term "casta" had come into general use in this sort of census document to refer to broad swathes of the population who were not native, European, or black. Nevertheless, the usage of the term "casta" remained highly restricted, in comparison to late colonial Mexico.

32. In "Conflict and Solidarity in Indian Village Life," Eric Van Young argues that the growth of commercialized agriculture in the rural hinterlands of Guadalajara, Mexico, caused many formerly homogeneous indigenous villages to cede territory to nonmembers, as well as to become internally differentiated by wealth and by cultural allegiance. Ethnic complexity also characterized the communities of the late colonial Bajío in northern Mexico. Tutino, *Making a New World*, 359–66. There is thus a critical mass of scholarship on late colonial Mexico, which opens still-unanswered questions for those of us working in more peripheral regions.

33. Bonnett Vélez, *Tierra y comunidad, un problema irresuelto*, 165; Herrera Ángel, *Poder local*, 91–95. Berdugo y Oquendo's report was published as "Informe del visitador real don Andrés Berdugo y Oquendo sobre el estado social y económico de la población indígena, blanca y mestiza de las provincias de Tunja y Vélez a mediados del siglo XVIII."

34. Bonnett Vélez, *Tierra y comunidad, un problema irresuelto*, 165–67. The various parts of Moreno y Escandón's report were brought together into a single published volume entitled *Indios y mestizos de la Nueva Granada a finales del siglo XVIII*. The figures were no less startling for the city of Santafé, which was 70 percent indigenous at the beginning of the eighteenth century, but midcentury censuses reported that only 10 percent of the population was native, with some 40 percent mestizo and mulatto. Vargas Lesmes, "Santafé a la luz de sus padrones (1778–1806)," 12–16.

35. Herrera Ángel, *Ordenar para controlar*, 177–80.

36. García Jimeno, *Conflicto, sociedad y estado colonial en el resguardo de Chiquiza, 1756-1801*, 64.

37. These figures come from Herrera Ángel, *Poder local*, 91–95. The 1758–60 visita of Aróstegui y Escoto was transcribed and published as "Informe de la visita que practico en la provincia de Santa Fe en 1758." Note that by this period, "blanco" (white) had become a category employed in all sorts of legal documents.

38. Bonnett Vélez, *Tierra y comunidad, un problema irresuelto*, 165–81.

39. Herrera Ángel, *Poder local*, 92–99. She also notes that doctrinal priests anxious to preserve their posts had compiled tributary lists that

exaggerated the size of the local population and the nature of the ethnic distribution within this population.

40. Múnera, *Fronteras imaginadas*, 39–40.

41. Phelan, *The People and the King*, chap. 7. The Comuneros Rebellion began in Socorro as an insurrection by whites and mestizos to repudiate administrative and tax reforms. On the ambivalences of indigenous participation in the Comuneros, see González, "Don Ambrosio Pisco, señor de Chía y príncipe de Bogotá."

42. I thank Marta Herrera for clarifying this point, which Fals Borda also makes very forcefully in "Indian Congregations in the New Kingdom of Granada." In the past two decades there has been a resurgence of Muisca identity, which had lain dormant for two centuries. See Cháves and Zambrano, "From *Blanqueamiento* to *Reindigenización*"; Gómez-Montáñez, "Patrimonio y etnopolíticas de la memoria."

43. Garrido, "'Free Men of All Colors' in New Granada," 167–68. The distribution of the four groups varied by region in Nueva Granada, with a more substantial indigenous population in Pasto in the southern part of the viceroyalty, a greater proportion of slaves on the Pacific coast, and a distinct majority of libres in the Cauca Valley and Antioquia. Gutiérrez de Pineda and Pineda Giraldo, *Miscegenación y cultura en la Colombia colonial, 1750–1810*, 1:109–11; Patiño Millán, "Las mujeres y el crimen en la época colonial," 80–81.

44. Herrera Ángel, "'Libres de todos los colores,'" 248.

45. Covarrubias Orozco, *Tesoro de la lengua castellana o española*, 191, 763, 775.

46. Real Academia Española, *Diccionario de autoridades*, 1:616.

47. Twinam, "Purchasing Whiteness." Even mestizos were concerned with notions of purity, despite the inherent contradiction this posed with their status as people of mixed parentage. Bonil Gómez highlights the use of color terms by individuals in Mariquita who legally solicited non-indio status: they used terms like "mestizo de color blanco [mestizo of white color]," "mestizo puro [pure mestizo]," or "mestizo limpio [clean or pure mestizo]" to identify themselves (*Gobierno y calidad en el orden colonial*, 154–60).

48. Herrera Ángel, "'Libres de todos los colores,'" 252.

49. Dueñas Vargas, *Los hijos del pecado*, chaps. 5 and 7.

50. Bonil Gómez, *Gobierno y calidad en el orden colonial*, 162–67.

51. Dueñas Vargas, *Los hijos del pecado*, 96–102. La Catedral was the barrio where two centuries earlier the mestizo regidor Diego García Zorro made his home.

52. López Bejarano, "Hommes fainéants et indolents, femmes dissolues," 188–92.

53. Ibid., 207.

54. López Bejarano, "Dinámicas mestizas," 16–19. See also López Bejarano's

analysis of the relationship between "Indian" and "mestizo" work in "Control y desorden en Santa Fe de Bogotá (Nueva Granada)."

55. I have just begun to study the eighteenth-century documentary record and, aside from the visitas, have as yet found no reference to the term "casta."

56. There is one known set of casta paintings from Peru. Majluf, *Los cuadros de mestizaje del Virrey Amat*.

57. Cummins, "Book Reviews," 186.

CONCLUSION

1. In his ingenious portrait of William Gooch, a forgotten ship's scientist who accompanied Captain James Cook on his second voyage to Hawai'i, Greg Dening concludes in *History's Anthropology* that the issue we should be concerned with when we write history isn't what "really" happened but what "actually" happened, pointing out that memory does its work in the present; Dening, *History's Anthropology*.

2. Merrell, *Into the American Woods*, 22–23, 75–77.

3. Rappaport, *The Politics of Memory*.

Audiencia   Representatives of the Royal Court in the Americas. After the Viceroyalty, the most inclusive administrative unit in the New World. Santafé was an Audiencia, achieving viceroyalty status only in the eighteenth century.

barrio   Quarter of a city or town.

bastardo/a   Child born out of wedlock, with at least one parent who was already married.

cabildo   Town or city council, or the council governing an indigenous *resguardo*.

cacica   Female hereditary lord, a member of the indigenous nobility.

cacicazgo   Hereditary chiefdom.

cacique   Male hereditary lord, a member of the indigenous nobility.

calidad   The plotting of individual status according to ethnicity or race, congregation, morality, privilege, and aspect.

cañas, juego de   Game of canes, an Iberian form of jousting.

capitán   Member of the indigenous nobility ranking under the *cacique*, heading a portion of a *cacicazgo*.

capitanía   Section of a Muisca community. Also called *sybyn* in the native vernacular.

casta   Caste; a socioracial umbrella category used in the late colonial period. In census records from Nueva Granada, it referred to people of mixed descent. "Casta" has also been employed by historians to refer to a hierarchical system of degrees of racial mixing, anchored by the "pure" poles of "Indian," "black," and "Spaniard."

casta painting   Eighteenth-century pictorial representations of degrees of racial mixing, mainly produced in Mexico for European consumption.

cédula   Royal decree.

chontal   Native person not fluent in Spanish. Also called *indio chontal*.

converso   Convert to Christianity. See "New Christian," "Old Christian."

criollo   Settler of Spanish descent, born in the New World. The term only rarely appears in the documentation from the Nuevo Reino de Granada.

cuarterón   Quadroon. Employed in the Nuevo Reino to refer to

Indian-Spanish admixtures where the Spanish side predominated.

doctrina   Village-level structure of Christian indoctrination.

don/doña   Forms of address to holders of noble title.

encomendero/a   Holder of a royal tribute grant.

encomienda   Royal tribute grant given to individuals who performed service to the Crown.

forastero   Individual who was not a formal member of the community, i.e., not on the tribute rolls. Although forasteros were frequently mestizos, mulattos, blacks, or Spaniards, they were sometimes Indians from other communities or other parts of Spanish America.

hijodalgo   Title of minor nobility.

hijo/a natural   Child born of unmarried parents; illegitimate child.

honor   Status.

honra   Virtue.

huauqui   Quechua term meaning "brother"; used in Santafé to refer to indigenous people from Quito.

indio/a   Category of indigenous person. The closest English equivalent is "Indian."

indio ladino   See *ladino*.

interrogatorio   List of questions put to witnesses in a legal case.

ladino   Native person who speaks Spanish. Sometimes it refers to Spanish-speaking members of indigenous communities; in other cases it refers to native people living in or near an indigenous community who are not formally affiliated with the community as tributaries.

libre   Eighteenth-century term denoting an individual of mixed parentage who inhabits the countryside and has no legal obligations. Also called *libres de todos los colores* (free men of all colors).

limpieza de sangre   Purity of blood, indicating the proven absence of Jewish, Muslim, or heretic ancestors.

méritos y servicios   Service report compiled by an applicant for official positions, *encomiendas*, and other favors. Includes a narrative of the services the applicant provided to the Crown and an inventory of his individual merits.

mestizo/a   Individual identified or identifying as of mixed indigenous and European descent. Also used to refer to types of mixing that were not genealogically based (such as a Spanish child drinking the milk of an Indian wet nurse) or that were not socioracial in nature (such as the child of a noble-commoner union).

mestiza en hábito de india   Mestiza habitually dressed in indigenous attire.

mestizaje   Process of racial mixing. In the twentieth century, *mestizaje* became a nationalist discourse, and "mestizo" acquired other meanings. The word "mestizaje" came into use only in the twentieth century.

moreno   Brown.

Morisco/a   Spanish Muslim.

mulatto/a   Individual identified or identifying as of mixed African and European or African and indigenous descent.

natural   Indigenous person; also, status acquired through birth in a specific place.

New Christian   Convert or descendant of converts to Christianity.

Nueva Granada   New Granada; eighteenth-century viceroyalty encompassing what is today Colombia.

Nuevo Reino de Granada   New Kingdom of Granada; sixteenth- and seventeenth-century Spanish colonial jurisdiction encompassing what today comprises Colombia and the location of the Audiencia de Santafé.

oidor   Judge of the *Audiencia*.

Old Christian   Individual who can prove through witnesses and documentation that he or she has no converts among his or her ancestors.

principal   A member of the indigenous nobility occupying a rank lower than that of *cacique*.

probanza   Documentary genre bringing together depositions of witnesses in response to questions (*interrogatorio*) provided by a legal actor.

pueblo de indios   Nucleated settlement established for an indigenous community and supervised by a doctrinal priest. Also called a doctrinal town. The pueblo was organized according to a grid, with a plaza that housed the church and the cacique's residence.

raza   Early modern term referring to membership in a lineage; used in particular to indicate membership in noble lineages, as well as to denote descent from Jews or Muslims.

recogimiento   Practice of cloistering unmarried women in their homes or in institutions.

Reconquista   The conquest of Muslim Spain by the Catholic Kings.

reducción   Planned indigenous town, organized in a grid pattern. See also *pueblo de indios*.

repartimiento   Indigenous community with tributary obligations.

República de Españoles   Administrative and judicial division covering Africans, mestizos, mulattos, and Spaniards.

República de Indios   Administrative and judicial division covering native people.

resguardo   Communal lands granted by royal title to an indigenous community in the New Kingdom of Granada, administered by a *cacique*; non-Indians were barred from residing there.

Santafereño/a   Person from Santafé; attribute pertaining to Santafé.

uta   Smallest social unit among the Muisca beyond the family.

vecino   Citizen of a city or town. In the eighteenth century, "vecino" also referred to non-indigenous smallholders in the countryside.

visita   A detailed census of native tributaries that included precise ethnographic descriptions of the structure and customs of communities, orders to be implemented by colonial officials, and minute tabulations of the names, ages, and families of tributaries.

visitador Crown official charged with compiling a *visita*.

zambo Indigenous-African admixture. Also called *zambaigo*.

BIBLIOGRAPHY

ARCHIVES

Archivio Generale della Compagnia di Gesù, Rome (AGCG/R): Novi Regni et Quitensis (NRQ)

Archivo General de Indias, Seville, Spain (AGI/S): Contratación (Ct); Escribanía de Cámara (Esc), Indiferente General (Ind), Justicia (Just); Mapas y Planos (MP), Patronato (Pat); Santa Fe (SF)

Archivo General de la Nación, Bogotá, Colombia (AGN/B): Caciques e Indios (CI); Curas y Obispos (CO); Empleados Públicos de Cundinamarca (EPC), Encomiendas (Enc); Historia Civil (HC); Juicios Civiles de Cundinamarca (JCC); Juicios Criminales (JC); Miscelánea de la Colonia (MC); Negocios Exteriores (Neg); Negros y Esclavos de Bolívar (NEB); Negros y Esclavos de Cundinamarca (NEC); Notaría 1a (N1); Notaría 2a (N2); Notaría 3a (N3); Policía (Pol); Testamentarias de Boyacá (TB); Testamentarias de Cundinamarca (TC); Visitas de Boyacá (VB); Visitas de Cundinamarca (VC)

Archivo Histórico Nacional, Madrid (AHN/M): Inquisición de Cartagena de Indias (ICI)

Archivo Histórico de Protocolos de Madrid (AHP/M)

WORKS CITED

Acevedo Latorre, Eduardo. *Atlas de los mapas antiguos de Colombia*. Bogotá: Litografía Arco, 1971.

Adorno, Rolena. "Images of *Indios Ladinos* in Early Colonial Peru." *Transatlantic Encounters: Europeans and Andeans in the Sixteenth Century*. Edited by Kenneth J. Andrien and Rolena Adorno, 232–70. Berkeley: University of California Press, 1991.

Ahmed, Sara. "'She'll Wake Up One of These Days and Find She's Turned into a Nigger': Passing through Hybridity." *Theory, Culture and Society* 16.2 (1999): 87–106.

Alaperrine-Bouyer, Monique. "Comment 'policer' les nobles indigènes:

Les stratégies d'une éducation au service du pouvoir colonial, Pérou XVIIe–XVIIIe siècle." *Transgressions et stratégies du métissage en Amérique coloniale*. Edited by Bernard Lavallé, 201–22. Paris: Presses de la Sorbonne Nouvelle, 1999.

Almansa Moreno, José Manuel. "Arquitectura doméstica en el Nuevo Reino de Granada." *Arquitectura vernácula en el mundo ibérico*. Edited by Ana María Aranda Bernal, 243–52. Seville: Universidad Pablo de Olavide, 2007.

Almorza Hidalgo, Amelia. "Género, emigración y movilidad social en la expansión Atlántica: Mujeres españolas en el Perú colonial (1550–1650)." PhD diss., History and Civilization, European University Institute, Florence, 2011.

Álvarez, Bartolomé. *De las costumbres y conversión de los indios del Perú: Memorial a Felipe II (1588)*. Edited by María del Carmen Martín Rubio, Juan J. R. Villarías Robles, and Fermín del Pino Díaz. Madrid: Ediciones Polifemo, 1998 [1588].

Álvarez M., Víctor, Jorge Orlando Melo, Adolfo Meisel, and Hermes Tovar. "La relevancia de la historia colonial en el mundo de hoy." *Fronteras de la Historia* 1.1 (1997): 177–98.

Anonymous. "Epítome de la conquista del Nuevo Reino de Granada." *No hay caciques ni señores: Relaciones y visitas a los naturales de América, siglo XVI*. Edited and transcribed by Hermes Tovar Pinzón, 163–88. Barcelona: Sendai Ediciones, 1988 [1547?].

Appelbaum, Nancy P. *Muddied Waters: Race, Region, and Local History in Colombia, 1846–1948*. Durham: Duke University Press, 2003.

Ares Queija, Berta. "El papel de mediadores y la construcción de un discurso sobre la identidad de los mestizos peruanos (siglo XVI)." *Entre dos mundos: Fronteras culturales y agentes mediadores*. Edited by Berta Ares Queija and Serge Gruzinski, 37–59. Seville: Escuela de Estudios Hispano-Americanos, 1997.

———. "Mestizos en hábito de indios: ¿Estrategias transgresoras o identidades difusas?" *Passar as fronteiras: Actas do II Colóquio Internacional sobre Mediadores Culturais, séculos XV a XVIII (Lagos–Outubro 1997)*. Edited by Rui Manuel Loureiro and Serge Gruzinski, 133–46. Lagos, Nigeria: Centro de Estudos Gil Eanes, 1999.

———. "'Un borracho de chicha y vino': La construcción social del mestizo (Perú, siglo XVI)." *Mezclado y sospechoso: Movilidad e identidades, España y América (siglos XVI–XVIII)*. Edited by Gregorio Salinero, 121–44. Madrid: Collection de la Casa de Velázquez 90, 2005.

Aróstegui y Escoto, Joaquín de. "Informe de la visita que practico en la provincia de Santa Fe en 1758." *Convocatoria al poder del número: Censos y Estadísticas de la Nueva Granada, 1750–1830*. Edited by Hermes Tovar Pinzón, Jorge Andrés Tovar Mora, and Camilo Ernesto Tovar Mora, 229–85. Bogotá: Archivo General de la Nación, 1994.

Arzáns de Orsúa y Vela, Bartolomé. *Historia de la villa imperial de Potosí*. Providence: Brown University Press, 1965.

Aubert, Guillaume. "'The Blood of France': Race and Purity of Blood in the French Atlantic World." *William and Mary Quarterly* 61.4 (2004): 439–78.

Baber, R. Jovita. "Categories, Self-Representation and the Construction of the *Indios*." *Journal of Spanish Cultural Studies* 10.1 (2009): 27–41.

Barth, Frederik, ed. *Ethnic Groups and Boundaries: The Social Organization of Culture Difference*. Boston: Little, Brown, 1969.

Behrend-Martínez, Edward. "Manhood and the Neutered Body in Early Modern Spain." *Journal of Social History* 38 (2005): 1073–93.

Berdugo y Oquendo, Andrés. "Informe del visitador real don Andrés Berdugo y Oquendo sobre el estado social y económico de la población indígena, blanca y mestiza de las provincias de Tunja y Vélez a mediados del siglo XVIII." Edited by Jaime Jaramillo Uribe, *Anuario Colombiano de Historia Social y de la Cultura* 1 (1963): 131–96.

Bergmann, Emilie L. "Milking the Poor: Wet-nursing and the Sexual Economy of Early Modern Spain." *Marriage and Sexuality in Medieval and Early Modern Iberia*. Edited by Eukene Lacarra Lanz, 90–114. New York: Routledge, 2002.

Bernal V., Alejandro. "Relaciones entre caciques y encomenderos en el inicio del período colonial: El caso de la encomienda de Guatavita." *Los muiscas en los siglos XVI y XVII: Miradas desde la arqueología, la antropología y la historia*. Edited by Jorge Augusto Gamboa M., 140–68. Bogotá: Universidad de los Andes, 2008.

Bernís, Carmen. "Modas moriscas en la sociedad cristiana española del siglo XV y principios del XVI." *Boletín de la Real Academia de Historia* 144 (1959): 199–226.

Beusterien, John. *An Eye on Race: Perspectives from Theater in Imperial Spain*. Lewisburg, PA: Bucknell University Press, 2006.

Biow, Douglas. "Manly Matters: The Theatricality and Sociability of Beards in Giordano Bruno's *Candelaio* and Sixteenth-Century Italy." *Journal of Medieval and Early Modern Studies* 40.2 (2010): 325–46.

Bloch, Marc. *The Historian's Craft*. Translated by Peter Putnam. New York: Knopf, 1953.

Bly, P. A. "Beards in the Poema de Mio Cid: Structural and Contextual Patterns." *Forum for Modern Language Studies* 14.1 (1978): 16–24.

Bonfíl Batalla, Guillermo. *México profundo: Reclaiming a Civilization*. Translated by Philip A. Dennis. Austin: University of Texas Press, 1996 [1987].

Bonil Gómez, Katherine. *Gobierno y calidad en el orden colonial: Las categorías del mestizaje en la provincia de Mariquita en la segunda mitad del siglo XVIII*. Bogotá: Ediciones Uniandes, 2011.

Bonnett Vélez, Diana. "Entre el interés personal y el establecimiento colonial: Factores de confrontación y de conflicto en el Nuevo Reino de Granada entre 1538 y 1570." Special edition of *Historia Crítica* (2009): 52–67.

———. *Tierra y comunidad, un problema irresuelto: El caso del altiplano cundiboyacense (Virreinato de la Nueva Granada), 1750–1800*. Bogotá: Instituto Colombiano de Antropología e Historia / Universidad de los Andes, 2002.

Bourdieu, Pierre, and Loïc Wacquant. "On the Cunning of Imperialist Reason." *Theory, Culture and Society* 16.1 (1999): 41–58.

Bouysse-Cassagne, Thérèse. "Etre métis ou ne pas être: Les symptômes d'un mal identitaire dans les Andes des XVIe et XVIIe siècles." *Cahiers des Amériques Latines* 12 (1991): 7–27.

Bowker, Geoffrey C., and Susan Leigh Star. *Sorting Things Out: Classification and Its Consequences*. Cambridge: Massachusetts Institute of Technology Press, 1999.

Boyer, Richard. "Honor among Plebeians: Mala Sangre and Social Reputation." *The Faces of Honor: Sex, Shame, and Violence in Colonial Latin America*. Edited by Lyman L. Johnson and Sonya Lipsett-Rivera, 152–78. Albuquerque: University of New Mexico Press, 1998.

———. "Negotiating *Calidad*: The Everyday Struggle for Status in Mexico." *Historical Archaeology* 31.1 (1997): 64–72.

———. "Respect and Identity: Horizontal and Vertical Reference Points in Speech Acts." *Americas* 54.4 (1998): 491–509.

Broadbent, Sylvia M. *Los chibchas: Organización socio-política*. Bogotá: Facultad de Sociología, Universidad Nacional de Colombia, 1964.

Brubaker, Rodgers, and Frederick Cooper. "Beyond 'Identity.'" *Theory and Society* 29 (2000): 1–47.

Burkholder, Mark A. "Honor and Honors in Colonial Spanish America." *The Faces of Honor: Sex, Shame, and Violence in Colonial Latin America*. Edited by Lyman L. Johnson and Sonya Lipsett-Rivera, 18–44. Albuquerque: University of New Mexico Press, 1998.

Burns, Kathryn. *Colonial Habits: Convents and the Spiritual Economy of Cuzco, Peru*. Durham: Duke University Press, 1999.

———. "Gender and the Politics of Mestizaje: The Convent of Santa Clara in Cusco, Peru." *Hispanic American Historical Review* 78.1 (1998): 5–44.

———. *Into the Archive: Writing and Power in Colonial Peru*. Durham: Duke University Press, 2010.

———. "Making Indigenous Archives: The Quilcaycamayoc of Colonial Cuzco." *Hispanic American Historical Review* 91.4 (2011): 665–89.

———. "Unfixing Race." *Rereading the Black Legend: The Discourses of Religious and Racial Difference in the Renaissance Empires*. Edited by Margaret R. Greer, Walter D. Mignolo, and Maureen Quilligan, 188–202. Chicago: University of Chicago Press, 2007.

Burshatin, Israel. "Elena alias Eleno: Genders, Sexualities, and 'Race' in the Mirror of Natural History in Sixteenth-Century Spain." *Gender*

Reversals and Gender Cultures: Anthropological and Historical Perspectives. Edited by Sabrina Petra Ramet, 105–22. London: Routledge, 1996.

Butler, Judith. *Bodies that Matter: On the Discursive Limits of "Sex."* New York: Routledge, 1993.

Cadden, Joan. *Meanings of Sex Difference in the Middle Ages: Medicine, Science, and Culture.* Cambridge: Cambridge University Press, 1993.

Cahill, David. "Colour by Numbers: Racial and Ethnic Categories in the Viceroyalty of Peru, 1532–1824." *Journal of Latin American Studies* 26.2 (1994): 325–46.

Caillavet, Chantal. "Imágenes del cuerpo: Divergencias, convergencias en España y América." *Mezclado y sospechoso: Movilidad e identidades, España y América.* Edited by Gregorio Salinero, 90:23–42. Madrid: Collection de la Casa de Velázquez, 2005.

Candelario, Ginetta E. B. *Black behind the Ears: Dominican Racial Identity from Museums to Beauty Shops.* Durham: Duke University Press, 2007.

Cañeque, Alejandro. "The Emotions of Power: Love, Anger and Fear, or How to Rule the Spanish Empire." *Emotions and Daily Life in Colonial Mexico.* Edited by Sonya Lipsett-Rivera and Javier Villa-Flores. Albuquerque: University of New Mexico Press, forthcoming.

Cañizares-Esguerra, Jorge. *Nature, Empire, and Nation: Explorations of the History of Science in the Iberian World.* Stanford: Stanford University Press, 2006.

Cardenas, Juan de. *Problemas y secretos maravillosos de las Indias.* Facsimile edn. Madrid: Ediciones Cultura Hispánica, 1945 [1591].

Carrera, Magali. "'El nuevo [mundo] no se parece á el viejo': Racial Categories and the Practice of Seeing." *Journal of Spanish Cultural Studies* 10.1 (2009): 59–73.

———. *Imagining Identity in New Spain: Race, Lineage, and the Colonial Body in Portraiture and Casta Paintings.* Austin: University of Texas Press, 2003.

Casilimas, Clara Inés, and Eduardo Londoño L., transcription. "El proceso contra el cacique de Ubaque en 1563." *Boletín del Museo de Oro* 49 (2001): 49–101.

Castro, Wendy Lucas. "Stripped: Clothing and Identity in Colonial Captivity Narratives." *Early American Studies* 6.1 (2008): 104–36.

Castro-Gómez, Santiago. *La hybris del punto cero: Ciencia, raza e ilustración en la Nueva Granada (1750–1816).* Bogotá: Editorial Pontificia Universidad Javeriana, 2005.

Cejador y Frauca, D. Julio. *Vocabulario medieval castellano.* Madrid: Visor Libros, 2005 [1929].

Cervantes Saavedra, Miguel de. *La ilustre fregona, el Licendiado Vidriera: Two of the Noveles Ejemplares of Miguel de Cervantes Saavedra.* Edited by F. A. Kirkpatrick. Cambridge: Cambridge University Press, 1909 [1613].

Chance, John K. *Race and Class in Colonial Oaxaca*. Stanford: Stanford University Press, 1978.

Charles, John. *Allies at Odds: The Andean Church and Its Indigenous Agents, 1583–1671*. Albuquerque: University of New Mexico Press, 2010.

Cháves, Margarita. "'¿Qué va a pasar con los indios cuando todos seamos indios?': Ethnic Rights and Reindianization in Southwestern Colombian Amazonia." Ph.D. diss., Anthropology, University of Illinois at Urbana, 2005.

Cháves, Margarita, and Marta Zambrano. "From *Blanqueamiento* to *Reindigenización*: Paradoxes of *Mestizaje* and Multiculturalism in Contemporary Colombia." *Revista Europea de Estudios Latinoamericanos y del Caribe* 80 (2006): 5–23.

Cobo Gutiérrez, Juan Fernando. *Mestizos heraldos de Dios: La ordenación de sacerdotes descendientes de españoles e indígenas en el Nuevo Reino de Granada y la racialización de la diferencia 1575–1590*. Bogotá: Instituto Colombiano de Antropología e Historia, 2012.

Cohen, Jeffrey Jerome. "On Saracen Enjoyment: Some Fantasies of Race in Late Medieval France and England." *Journal of Medieval and Early Modern Studies* 31.1 (2001): 113–46.

Collins, Patricia Hill. *Black Feminist Thought: Knowedge, Consciousness, and the Politics of Empowerment*. New York: Routledge, 1991.

Colmenares, Germán. *La Provincia de Tunja en el Nuevo Reino de Granada: Ensayo de historia social, 1539–1800*. Bogotá: TM Editores / Universidad del Valle / Banco de la República / Colciencias, 1997 [1970].

Colombia, República de. *Colombia una nación nulticultural: Su diversidad étnica*. Bogotá: Departamento Administrativo Nacional de Estadísticas, 2007.

Comaroff, John, and Jean Comaroff. *Ethnography and the Historical Imagination*. Boulder: Westview, 1992.

Cook, Karoline P. "Forbidden Crossings: Morisco Emigration to Spanish America, 1492–1650." Ph.D. diss., History, Princeton University, 2008.

Cook, Noble David. "The Mysterious Catalina: Indian or Spaniard?" *The Human Tradition in Colonial Latin America*. Edited by Kenneth Andrien, 64–83. Wilmington, DE: Scholarly Resources, 2002.

Cope, R. Douglas. *The Limits of Racial Domination: Plebeian Society in Colonial Mexico City, 1660–1720*. Madison: University of Wisconsin Press, 1994.

Cornejo Polar, Antonio, Luis Millones Santa Gadea, Augusto Tamayo Vargas, and Alberto Tauro del Pino. "Cinco preguntas en torno a Garcilaso." *Literaturas Andinas* 1.1 (1988): 19–27.

Corradine Mora, Magdalena. *Los fundadores de Tunja: Genealogías*. 2 vols. Tunja: Academia Boyacense de Historia, 2008.

Correa Rubio, François. *El sol del poder: Simbología y política entre los muiscas del norte de los Andes*. Bogotá: Universidad Nacional de Colombia, Facultad de Ciencias Humanas, 2004.

Cortés, Gerónimo. *Fisionomia, y varios secretos de la naturaleza*. Valencia: Librerías "Paris-Valencia," 1992 [1741].

Cortés Alonso, Vicenta. "Visita a los santuarios indígenas de Boyacá en 1577." *Revista Colombiana de Antropología* 9 (1960): 199–273.

Covarrubias Orozco, Sebastián de. *Emblemas morales*. Madrid: L. Sánchez, 1610.

———. *Tesoro de la lengua castellana o española*. Madrid: Castalia, 1995 [1611].

Cummins, Tom. "Book Reviews: Cummins on Casta Paintings." *Art Bulletin* 88.1 (2006): 185–89.

———. "Three Gentlemen from Esmeraldas: A Portrait Fit for a King." *Slave Portraiture in the Circum-Atlantic World (1660–1890)*. Edited by Agnes Lugo-Ortiz and Angela Rosenthal, 118–45. Cambridge: Cambridge University Press, 2013.

Dean, Carolyn. "Beyond Prescription: Notarial Doodles and Other Marks." *Word and Image: A Journal of Verbal/Visual Enquiry* 25.3 (2009): 293–316.

———. *Inka Bodies and the Body of Christ: Corpus Christi in Colonial Cuzco, Peru*. Durham: Duke University Press, 1999.

Dean, Carolyn, and Dana Leibsohn. "Hybridity and Its Discontents: Considering Visual Culture in Colonial Spanish America." *Colonial Latin American Review* 12.1 (2003): 5–35.

De Certeau, Michel. *The Writing of History*. Translated by Tom Conley. New York: Columbia University Press, 1988.

Dedieu, Jean-Pierre. "Entre religión y política: Los moriscos." *Manuscrits, Revista D'història Moderna* 12 (1994): 63–78.

de la Cadena, Marisol. "Are *Mestizos* Hybrids?: The Conceptual Politics of Andean Identities." *Journal of Latin American Studies* 37 (2005): 259–84.

———. *Indigenous Mestizos: The Politics of Race and Culture in Cuzco, Peru, 1919–1991*. Durham: Duke University Press, 2000.

———. "'Las mujeres son más indias': Etnicidad y género en una comunidad del Cusco." *Revista Andina* 1 (1991): 7–47.

Delaney, Patricia L. "Understanding *Qualidade*: Conceptions of Race, Color, and Status in Northeastern Brazil." Master's thesis, Anthropology, University of California, Los Angeles, 1991.

Demos, John. *The Unredeemed Captive: A Family Story from Early America*. New York: Vintage, 1995.

Dening, Greg. *History's Anthropology: The Death of William Gooch*. Lanham, MD: University Press of America / Association for Social Anthropology in Oceania, 1988.

De Renzi, Silvia. "Resemblance, Paternity, and Imagination in Early Modern Courts." *Heredity Produced: At the Crossroads of Biology, Politics, and Culture, 1500–1870*. Edited by Staffan Müller-Wille and Hans-Jörg Rheinberger, 61–83. Cambridge: Massachusetts Institute of Technology Press, 2007.

Diccionario y gramática chibcha: Manuscrito anónimo de la Biblioteca Nacional de Colombia. Edited by María Stella González de Pérez. Bogotá: Instituto Caro y Cuervo, 1987 [early seventeenth century].

Du Bois, W. E. B. *The Souls of Black Folk*. New York: Bantam, 1989 [1903].

Dueñas Vargas, Guiomar. *Los hijos del pecado: Ilegitimidad y vida familiar en la Santafé de Bogotá colonial*. Bogotá: Editorial Universidad Nacional de Colombia, 1996.

Dumont, Jean-Paul. *The Headman and I: Ambiguity and Ambivalence in the Fieldworking Experience*. Prospect Heights, IL: Waveland, 1978.

Dunn, Peter N. "'De las figuras del arçipreste.'" *"Libro de Buen Amor" Studies*. Edited by G. B. Gybbon-Monypenny, 79–93. London: Tamesis Books, 1970.

Durston, Alan. "Native-Language Literacy in Colonial Peru: The Question of Mundane Quechua Writing Revisited." *Hispanic American Historical Review* 88.1 (2008): 41–70.

Dyer, Abigail. "Seduction by Promise of Marriage: Law, Sex, and Culture in Seventeenth-Century Spain." *Sixteenth Century Journal* 34.2 (2003): 439–55.

Earle, Rebecca. "'Two Pairs of Pink Satin Shoes!!': Race, Clothing and Identity in the Americas (17th–19th Centuries)." *History Workshop Journal* 52 (2001): 175–95.

Ehlers, Benjamin. *Between Christians and Moriscos: Juan de Ribera and Religious Reform in Valencia, 1568–1614*. Baltimore: Johns Hopkins University Press, 2006.

Espinosa, Carlos. "Colonial Visions: Drama, Art, and Legitimation in Peru and Ecuador." *Native Artists and Patrons in Colonial Latin America*. Edited by Emily Umberger and Tom Cummins. Special issue, *Phøebus* 7 (1995): 84–106.

Fals Borda, Orlando. "Indian Congregations in the New Kingdom of Granada: Land Tenure Aspects, 1595–1850." *Americas* 13.4 (1957): 331–51.

———. *Mompox y Loba: Historia doble de la Costa—1*. Bogotá: Carlos Valencia, 1979.

———. *Peasant Society in the Colombian Andes: A Sociological Study of Saucío*. Westport, CT: Greenwood, 1976 [1955].

Feerick, Jean E. *Strangers in Blood: Relocating Race in the Renaissance*. Toronto: University of Toronto Press, 2010.

Feliciano, María Judith. "Muslim Shrouds for Christian Kings?: A Reassessment of Andalusi Textiles in Thirteenth-Century Castilian Life and Ritual." *Under the Influence: Questioning the Comparative in Medieval Castile*. Edited by Cynthia Robinson and Leyla Rouhi, 101–31. Leiden: Brill, 2005.

Figueroa Muñoz, Mario Bernardo, and Pío Eduardo San Miguel, eds.

¿*Mestizo yo?* Bogotá: Universidad Nacional de Colombia, Facultad de Ciencias Humanas, Colección CES, 2000.

Fisher, Andrew B., and Matthew D. O'Hara, eds. *Imperial Subjects: Race and Identity in Colonial Latin America*. Foreword by Irene Silverblatt. Durham: Duke University Press, 2009.

———. "Introduction: Racial Identities and Their Interpreters in Colonial Latin America." *Imperial Subjects: Race and Identity in Colonial Latin America*. Edited by Andrew B. Fisher and Matthew D. O'Hara, 1–37. Durham: Duke University Press, 2009.

Fisher, Will. "The Renaissance Beard: Masculinity in Early Modern England." *Renaissance Quarterly* 54.1 (2001): 155–87.

Flórez de Ocáriz, Juan. *Genealogías del Nuevo Reino de Granada*. Facsimile edn. in 3 vols. Bogotá: Instituto Caro y Cuervo, 1990 [1674].

Forbes, Jack D. *Africans and Native Americans: The Language of Race and the Evolution of Red-Black Peoples*. Urbana: University of Illinois Press, 1993.

Fracchia, Carmen. "(Lack of) Visual Representation of Black Slaves in Spanish Golden Age Painting." *Journal of Iberian and Latin American Studies* 10.1 (2004): 23–34.

Francis, J. Michael. "'La tierra clama por remedio': La conquista espiritual del territorio muisca." *Fronteras de la Historia* 5 (2000): 93–118.

———. "Población, enfermedad y cambio demográfico, 1537–1636: Demografía histórica de Tunja: Una mirada crítica." *Fronteras de la Historia* 7 (2002): 15–95.

———. "The *Resguardo*, the *Mita*, and the *Alquiler General*: Indian Migration in the Province of Tunja, 1550–1636." *Colonial Latin American Historical Review* 11.4 (2002): 375–406.

Frederick, Jake. "Without Impediment: Crossing Racial Boundaries in Colonial Mexico." *Americas* 67.4 (2011): 495–515.

Freyre, Gilberto. *The Masters and the Slaves: A Study in the Development of Brazilian Civilization*. New York: Knopf, 1956 [1933].

Friede, Juan. "De la encomienda indiana a la propiedad territorial y su influencia sobre el mestizaje." *Anuario Colombiano de Historia Social y de la Cultura* 4 (1969): 35–61.

———, ed. *Fuentes documentales para la historia del Nuevo Reino de Granada desde la instalación de la Real Audiencia en Santafé*. 8 vols. Bogotá: Biblioteca Banco Popular, 1976.

———. "La conquista del territorio y el poblamiento." *Nueva Historia de Colombia*. Edited by Jaime Jaramillo Uribe, 1:69–115. Bogotá: Editorial Planeta, 1978.

Fuchs, Barbara. *Exotic Nation: Maurophilia and the Construction of Early Modern Spain*. Philadelphia: University of Pennsylvania Press, 2009.

———. *Mimesis and Empire: The New World, Islam, and European Identities*. Cambridge: Cambridge University Press, 2001.

———. "A Mirror across the Water: Mimetic Racism, Hybridity, and Cultural Survival." *Writing Race across the Atlantic World: Medieval to*

Modern. Edited by Philip D. Beidler and Gary Taylor, 9–26. New York: Palgrave Macmillan, 2005.

Gálvez Piñal, Esperanza. *La visita de Monzón y Prieto de Orellana al Nuevo Reino de Granada*. Seville: Escuela de Estudios Hispano-Americanos de Sevilla, v. 225, 1974.

Gamboa, Jorge, ed. *Encomienda, identidad y poder: La construcción de la identidad de los conquistadores y encomenderos del Nuevo Reino de Granada, vista a través de las probanzas de mérito y servicios (1550–1650)*. Bogotá: Instituto Colombiano de Antropología e Historia, 2002.

Gamboa Mendoza, Jorge Augusto. *El cacicazgo muisca en los años posteriores a la Conquista: Del sihipkua al cacique colonial, 1537–1575*. Bogotá: Instituto Colombiano de Antropología e Historia, 2010.

García, Gregorio. *Origen de los indios del Nuevo Mundo e Indias Occidentales*. Madrid: Consejo Superior de Investigaciones Científicas, 2005 [1607].

García Jimeno, Camilo. *Conflicto, sociedad y estado colonial en el resguardo de Chiquiza, 1756–1801*. Bogotá: Ediciones Uniandes, 2008.

Garcilaso de la Vega, El Inca. *Royal Commentaries of the Incas*. Translated by Harold V. Livermore. Austin: University of Texas Press, 1970 [1609].

Garrido, Margarita. "Entre el honor y la obediencia." *Historia y Sociedad* 5 (1998): 19–35.

———. "'Free Men of All Colors' in New Granada." *Political Cultures in the Andes, 1750–1950*. Edited by Nils Jacobsen and Cristóbal Aljovín de Losada, 164–83. Durham: Duke University Press, 2005.

———. "La vida cotidiana y pública en las ciudades colonials." *Historia de la vida cotidiana en Colombia*. Edited by Beatriz Castro Carvajal, 131–58. Barcelona: Norma, 1996.

Gauderman, Kimberly. *Women's Lives in Colonial Quito: Gender, Law, and Economy in Spanish America*. Austin: University of Texas Press, 2003.

Glave, Luis Miguel. "Gestiones transatlánticas: Los indios ante la trama del poder virreinal y las composiciones de tierras (1646)." *Revista Complutense de Historia de America* 34 (2008): 85–106.

———. "Sociedad colonial, discurso literario e imaginario colectivo: Inés de Hinojosa y las mujeres extraordinarias." *Inés de Hinojosa: Historia de una transgresora*. Edited by Isabel Rodríguez Vergara, 32-49. Medellín: Editorial Universidad de Antioquia, 1999.

Gómez-Montáñez, Pablo F. "Patrimonio y etnopolíticas de la memoria: El pasado como aparato ideológico en la fiesta del Zocán en el Templo del Sol de Sogamoso." *Antípoda* 12 (2011): 165–86.

González, Margarita. "Don Ambrosio Pisco, señor de Chía y príncipe de Bogotá: Aspectos de la participación indígena en la Insurrección de los Comuneros." *Al Margen* 14 (2005): 16–51.

———. *El resguardo en el Nuevo Reino de Granada*. Bogotá: Editorial La Carreta, 1979.

González Alonso, Benjamín. "La fórmula 'obedezcase, pero no se cumpla' en el derecho castellano de la baja edad media." *Anuario de Historia del Derecho Español* 50 (1980): 469–87.

González Holguín, Diego. *Vocabulario de la lengua general de todo el Peru llamada lengua qquichua o del inca.* Lima: Editorial de la Universidad Nacional Mayor de San Marcos, 1989 [1608].

Goodwin, Charles. "Professional Vision." *American Anthropologist*, n.s., 96.3 (1994): 606–33.

Graff, Gary W. "Spanish Parishes in Colonial New Granada: Their Role in Town-Building on the Spanish-American Frontier." *Americas* 33.2 (1976): 336–51.

Grasseni, Cristina. "Skilled Vision: An Apprenticeship in Breeding Aesthetics." *Social Anthropology* 12.1 (1004): 41–55.

Graubart, Karen. "The Creolization of the New World: Local Forms of Identification in Urban Colonial Peru, 1560–1640." *Hispanic American Historical Review* 89.3 (2009): 471–99.

———. "Hybrid Thinking: Bringing Postcolonial Theory to Colonial Latin American Economic History." *Postcolonialism Meets Economics.* Edited by Eiman O. Zein-Elabdin and S. Charusheela, 212–34. London: Routledge, 2004.

———. *With Our Labor and Sweat: Indigenous Women and the Formation of Colonial Society in Peru, 1550–1700.* Stanford: Stanford University Press, 2007.

Groebner, Valentin. "*Complexio*/Complexion: Categorizing Individual Natures, 1250–1600." *The Moral Authority of Nature.* Edited by Lorraine Daston and Fernando Vidal, 361–83. Chicago: University of Chicago Press, 2004.

———. *Who Are You?: Identification, Deception, and Surveillance in Early Modern Europe.* New York: Zone, 2007.

Gruzinski, Serge. *The Mestizo Mind: The Intellectual Dynamics of Colonization and Globalization.* Translated by Deke Dusinberre. London: Routledge, 2002 [1999].

Guaman Poma de Ayala, Felipe. *Primer nueva corónica y buen gobierno.* Edited by John Murra and Rolena Adorno. Mexico: Siglo XXI, 1980 [1615].

Guevara-Gil, Armando, and Frank Salomon. "A 'Personal Visit': Colonial Political Ritual and the Making of Indians in the Andes." *Colonial Latin American Review* 3.1–2 (1994): 3–36.

Gutiérrez de Pineda, Virginia, and Roberto Pineda Giraldo. *Miscegenación y cultura en la Colombia colonial, 1750–1810.* 2 vols. Bogotá: Ediciones UniAndes / Colciencias, 1999.

Gutiérrez Ramos, Jairo. *El mayorazgo de Bogotá y el marquesado de San Jorge: Riqueza, linaje, poder y honor en Santa Fé, 1538–1824.* Bogotá: Instituto Colombiano de Cultura Hispánica, 1998.

Hahn, Thomas. "The Difference the Middle Ages Makes: Color and Race before the Modern World." *Journal of Medieval and Early Modern Studies* 31.1 (2001): 1–37.

Haidt, Rebecca. *Embodying Enlightenment: Knowing the Body in Eighteenth-Century Spanish Literature and Culture.* New York: St. Martin's, 1998.

Hanks, William. *Intertexts: Writings on Language, Utterance and Context.* Lanham, MD: Rowman and Littlefield, 2000.

Haskett, Robert. *Indigenous Rulers: An Ethnohistory of Town Government in Colonial Cuernavaca.* Albuquerque: University of New Mexico Press, 1991.

Henderson, Hope, and Nicholas Ostler. "Muisca Settlement Organization and Chiefly Authority at Suta, Valle de Leyva, Colombia: A Critical Appraisal of Native Concepts of House for Studies of Complex Societies." *Journal of Anthropological Archaeology* 24 (2005): 148–78.

Hering Torres, Max S. "Color, pureza, raza: La calidad de los sujetos coloniales." *La cuestión colonial.* Edited by Heraclio Bonilla, 451–69. Bogotá: Universidad Nacional de Colombia, 2011.

Herman, Susan. "The Conquista y Descubrimiento del Nuevo Reino de Granada, Otherwise Known as El Carnero: The Coronica, the Historia, and the Novela." PhD diss., Yale University, 1978.

——. "La encomienda de Chivatá: El caso de doña Inés de Hinojosa y la cuestión del (mal)tratamiento a los indígenas." *Inés de Hinojosa: Historia de una transgresora.* Edited by Isabel Rodríguez Vergara, 1–21. Medellín: Editorial Universidad de Antioquia, 1999.

Herrera Ángel, Marta. "Autoridades indígenas en la provincia de Santafé, siglo XVIII." *Revista Colombiana de Antropología* 30 (1993): 9–35.

——. "'Libres de todos los colores': El ordenamiento social en las llanuras del Caribe, siglo XVIII." *El Caribe en la nación colombiana: Memorias X Cátedra Anual de Historia Ernesto Restrepo Tirado.* Edited by Alberto Abello Vives, 248–68. Bogotá: Ministerio de Cultura / Observatorio del Caribe / Museo Nacional de Colombia, 2006.

——. *Ordenar para controlar: Ordenamiento espacial y control político en las llanuras del Caribe y en los Andes centrales neogranadinos, siglo XVIII.* Bogotá: Instituto Colombiano de Antropología e Historia / Academia Colombiana de Historia, 2002.

——. *Poder local, población y ordenamiento territorial en la Nueva Granada—siglo XVIII.* Bogotá: Archivo General de la Nación, 1996.

Herrera Ángel, Marta, and Diana Bonnett Vélez. "Ordenamiento espacial y territorial colonial en la 'región central' neogranadina, siglo XVIII: Las visitas de la tierra como fuente para la historia agraria del siglo XVIII." *América Latina en la Historia Económica* 16 (2001): 11–32.

Herzog, Tamar. *Defining Nations: Immigrants and Citizens in Early Modern Spain and Spanish America.* New Haven: Yale University Press, 2003.

——. "Early Modern Spanish Citizenship: Inclusion and Exclusion in the Old and the New World." *New World Orders: Violence, Sanction, and Authority in the Colonial Americas*. Edited by John Smolenski and Thomas J. Humphrey, 205–25. Philadelphia: University of Pennsylvania Press, 2005.

Hill, Ruth. "Between Black and White: A Critical Race Theory Approach to Caste Poetry in the Spanish New World." *Comparative Literature* 59.4 (2007): 269–93.

———. "Casta as Culture and the *Sociedad de Castas* as Literature." *Interpreting Colonialism*. Edited by Philip Stewart and Byron Wells, 231–59. Oxford: Voltaire Foundation, 2004.

———. *Hierarchy, Commerce, and Fraud in Bourbon Spanish America: A Postal Inspector's Exposé*. Nashville: Vanderbilt University Press, 2005.

———. "Toward an Eighteenth-Century Transatlantic Critical Race Theory." *Literature Compass* 3.2 (2006): 53–64.

Hoyos García, Juan Felipe. "El lenguaje y la escritura como herramientas coloniales: El caso de Santa Fé y Tunja, durante el siglo XVI." Trabajo de Grado, Departamento de Antropología, Universidad Nacional de Colombia, Bogotá, 2002.

Hoyos García, Juan Felipe, and Joanne Rappaport. "El mestizaje en la época colonial: Un experimento documental a través de los documentos de Diego de Torres y Alonso de Silva, caciques mestizos del siglo XVI." *Boletín de Historia y Antigüedades* 94.836 (2007): 301–18.

Hulme, Peter. "Tales of Distinction: European Ethnography and the Caribbean." *Implicit Understandings: Observing, Reporting, and Reflecting on the Encounters between Europeans and Other Peoples in the Early Modern Era*. Edited by Stuart B. Schwartz, 157–97. Cambridge: Cambridge University Press, 1994.

Hyland, Sabine. "Illegitimacy and Racial Hierarchy in the Peruvian Priesthood: A Seventeenth-Century Dispute." *Catholic Historical Review* 84.3 (1998): 431–54.

———. *The Jesuit and the Incas: The Extraordinary Life of Padre Blas Valera, S.J.* Ann Arbor: University of Michigan Press, 2003.

Ibarra Dávila, Alexia. *Estrategias del mestizaje: Quito a finales del siglo XVIII*. Quito: Ediciones Abya-Yala, 2002.

Israel, J. I. *Race, Class and Politics in Colonial Mexico: 1610–1670*. Oxford: Oxford University Press, 1975.

Jaramillo Uribe, Jaime. *Ensayos sobre historia social colombiana*. Bogotá: Editorial Universidad Nacional de Colombia, 1968.

Johnson, Lyman L., and Sonya Lipsett-Rivera. "Introduction." *The Faces of Honor: Sex, Shame, and Violence in Colonial Latin America*. Edited by Lyman L. Johnson and Sonya Lipsett-Rivera, 1–17. Albuquerque: University of New Mexico Press, 1998.

Johnston, Mark Albert. "Bearded Women in Early Modern England." SEL *Studies in English Literature 1500–1900* 47.1 (2007): 1–28.

Jones, Ann Rosalind, and Peter Stallybrass. *Renaissance Clothing and the Materials of Memory.* Cambridge: Cambridge University Press, 2000.

Julien, Catherine J. *Reading Inca History.* Iowa City: University of Iowa Press, 2000.

Kagan, Richard L. *Lawsuits and Litigants in Castile, 1500–1700.* Chapel Hill: University of North Carolina Press, 1981.

———. *Students and Society in Early Modern Spain.* Baltimore: Johns Hopkins University Press, 1974.

Katzew, Ilona. *Casta Painting: Images of Race in Eighteenth-Century Mexico.* New Haven: Yale University Press, 2004.

Kellogg, Susan. *Law and the Transformation of Aztec Culture, 1500–1700.* Norman: University of Oklahoma Press, 1995.

Konečný, Ludomir. "Una Pintura de Juan Sánchez Cotán, emblematizada por Sebastián de Covarrubias," *Actas del 1 Simposio Internacional de Emlemática, Teruel, 1 y 2 de Octubre 1991,* 823–34. Teruel: Instituto de Estudios Turolenses, 1994.

Kuznesof, Elizabeth Anne. "Ethnic and Gender Influences on 'Spanish' Creole Society in Colonial Spanish America." *Colonial Latin American Review* 4.1 (1995): 153–76.

Langebaek Rueda, Carl Henrik. *Noticias de caciques muy mayores: Orígen y desarrollo de sociedades complejas en el nororiente de Colombia y norte de Venezuela.* Bogotá: Ediciones UniAndes / Medellín: Editorial Universidad de Antioquia, 1992.

———. "Resistencia indígena y transformaciones ideológicas entre los muiscas de los siglos XVI y XVII." *Concepciones de la Conquista: Aproximaciones interdisciplinarias.* Edited by Felipe Castañeda and Matthias Vollet, 281–328. Bogotá: Editorial UniAndes, 2001.

Larsen, Nella. *Passing.* New York: Courier Dover, 2004 [1929].

Larson, Brooke. *Trials of Nation Making: Liberalism, Race, and Ethnicity in the Andes, 1810–1910.* Cambridge: Cambridge University Press, 2004.

Lee López, R. P., Fray Alberto. *Clero indígena en el Arzobispado de Santa Fé en el siglo XVI.* Bogotá: Editorial Kelly, 1962.

Lepore, Jill. *New York Burning: Liberty, Slavery, and Conspiracy in Eighteenth-Century Manhattan.* New York: Vintage, 2006.

Lesbre, Patrick. "Un représentant de la première génération métisse face à l'aristocratie acolhua: Juan Bautista Pomar, Tezcoco (fin XVIe–début XVIIe siècle)." *Transgressions et stratégies du métissage en Amérique coloniale.* Edited by Bernard Lavallé, 183–200. Paris: Presses de la Sorbonne Nouvelle, 1999.

Lewis, Laura A. *Hall of Mirrors: Power, Witchcraft, and Caste in Colonial Mexico.* Durham: Duke University Press, 2003.

Lipsett-Rivera, Sonya. "De Obra y Palabra: Patterns of Insults in Mexico, 1750–1856." *Americas* 54.4 (1998): 511–39.

Lizárraga, Fray Reginaldo de. *Descripción breve de toda la tierra del Perú,*

Tucumán y Río de la Plata. Vol. 141. Madrid: Biblioteca de Autores Españoles, 1968 [1605].

Lockhart, James. *The Nahuas after the Conquest: A Social and Cultural History of the Indians of Central Mexico, Sixteenth through Eighteenth Centuries.* Stanford: Stanford University Press, 1992.

———. *Spanish Peru, 1532–1560: A Colonial Society.* Madison: University of Wisconsin Press, 1968.

Londoño, Eduardo. "Mantas muiscas una tipología colonial." *Boletín del Museo del Oro* 27 (1990): 120–26.

López Bejarano, María del Pilar. "Control y desorden en Santa Fe de Bogotá (Nueva Granada): En torno a las reformas urbanas de finales del siglo XVIII." *Brocar: Cuadernos de Investigación Histórica* 30 (2006): 111–37.

———. "Dinámicas mestizas: Tejiendo en torno a la jerarquía, al trabajo y al honor: Nueva Granada, siglo XVIII." *Nuevo Mundo Mundos Nuevos,* Debates, 2008. Accessed 14 October 2011. http://nuevomundo.revues .org/19263.

———. "'Hommes fainéants et indolents, femmes dissolues . . .': Paresse et travail à Santa Fe de Bogotá (Nouvelle-Grenade)—XVIIIe siècle." PhD diss., Histoire et Civilisation, Ecoles des Hautes Etudes en Sciences Sociales, Paris, 2007.

López de Velasco, Juan. *Geografía y descripción universal de las Indias.* Madrid: Establecimiento Tipográfico de Fortanet, 1894 [ca. 1571–74].

López Martínez, Héctor. "Un motín de mestizos en el Perú (1567)." *Revista de Indias* 24 (1964): 367–81.

López Rodríguez, [Celina de las] Mercedes. "Ficciones raciales: Representaciones de raza y género a través de la literatura y las artes visuales en Colombia 1830–1875." PhD diss., Latin American Literature, Georgetown University, 2012.

———. *Tiempos para rezar y tiempos para trabajar: La cristianización de las comunidades indígenas muiscas durante el siglo XVI.* Bogotá: Instituto Colombiano de Antropología e Historia, 2001.

Loveman, Mara. "Is 'Race' Essential?" *American Sociological Review* 64.6 (1999): 891–98.

MacDonald, Katherine. "Humanistic Self-Representation in Giovan Battista Della Porta's 'Della Fisionomia Dell'Uomo.'" *Sixteenth Century Journal* 36.2 (2005): 397–414.

Majluf, Natalia, ed. *Los cuadros de mestizaje del Virrey Amat.* Lima: Museo de Arte de Lima, 2000.

Mangan, Jane E. 2009. "A Market of Identities: Women, Trade, and Ethnic Labels in Colonial Potosí." *Imperial Subjects: Race and Identity in Colonial Latin America.* Edited by Andrew B. Fisher and Matthew D. O'Hara, 61–80. Durham: Duke University Press.

Mannarelli, María Emma. *Private Passions and Public Sins: Men and*

Women in Seventeenth-Century Lima. Translated by Sidney Evans and Meredith D. Dodge. Albuquerque: University of New Mexico Press, 2007.

Mannheim, Bruce. *The Language of the Inka since the European Invasion.* Austin: University of Texas Press, 1991.

Marchena Fernández, Juan. "Los hijos de la guerra." *Actas, Congreso de Historia del Descubrimiento (1492–1556)*, 311–420. Madrid: Real Academia de Historia, 1992.

Martin, Cheryl English. "Popular Speech and Social Order in Northern Mexico, 1650–1830." *Comparative Studies in Society and History* 32.2 (1990): 305–24.

Martín Casares, Aurelia. *La esclavitud en la Granada del siglo XVI.* Granada: Universidad de Granada / Diputación Provincial de Granada, 2000.

Martínez, José Luis. *Pasajeros de Indias: Viajes transatlánticos en el siglo XVI.* Madrid: Alianza Editorial, 1984.

Martínez, María Elena. "The Black Blood of New Spain: *Limpieza de Sangre*, Racial Violence, and Gendered Power in Early Colonial Mexico." *William and Mary Quarterly* 61.3 (2004): 479–520.

———. *Genealogical Fictions: Limpieza de Sangre, Religion, and Gender in Colonial Mexico.* Stanford: Stanford University Press, 2008.

———. "Interrogating Blood Lines: 'Purity of Blood,' the Inquisition, and *Casta* Categories." *Religion in New Spain.* Edited by Susan Schroeder and Stafford Poole, 196–217. Albuquerque: University of New Mexico Press, 2007.

Martínez-Alier, Verena (Verena Stolcke). *Marriage, Class and Colour in Nineteenth-Century Cuba: A Study of Racial Attitudes and Sexual Values in a Slave Society.* Cambridge: Cambridge University Press, 1974.

Mason, Peter. "Reading New World Bodies." *Bodily Extremities: Preoccupations with the Human Body in Early Modern European Culture.* Edited by Florike Egmond and Robert Zwijnenberg, 148–67. Aldershot: Ashgate, 2003.

Mazzotti, José Antonio. *Coros mestizos del Inca Garcilaso: Resonancias andinas.* Lima: Fondo de Cultura Económica, 1996.

McFarlane, Anthony. *Colombia before Independence: Economy, Society and Politics under Bourbon Rule.* Cambridge: Cambridge University Press, 1993.

Mejía Espinosa, María Emilia. "La preocupación por el honor en las causas judiciales seguidas por adulterio en la Nueva Granada entre 1760 y 1837." Monografía de grado, Programa de Historia, Universidad Colegio Mayor de Nuestra Señora del Rosario, Bogotá, 2011. Accessed 21 October 2011. http://repository.urosario.edu.co/handle/10336/2355.

Merrell, James H. *Into the American Woods: Negotiators on the Pennsylvania Frontier.* New York: W. W. Norton, 1999.

Messer, Sarah. *Red House: Being a Mostly Accurate Account of New England's Oldest Continuously Lived-in House*. New York: Viking, 2005.

Mira Caballos, Esteban. *Indios y mestizos americanos en la España del siglo XVI*. Frankfurt: Vervuert / Madrid: Iberoamericana, 2000.

Molénat, Jean-Pierre. "Hornachos fin XVe–début XVIe siècles." *En la España Medieval* 31 (2008): 161–76.

Morales Pradilla, Próspero. *Los pecados de Inés de Hinojosa*. Bogotá: Plaza and Janés Editores Colombia, 1986.

Moreno y Escandón, Francisco Antonio. *Indios y mestizos de la Nueva Granada a finales del siglo XVIII*. Edited by Jorge Orlando Melo. Transcribed by Germán Colmenares and Alonso Valencia. Bogotá: Biblioteca Banco Popular, v. 124, 1985 [1770–79].

Mörner, Magnus. *La corona española y los foráneos en los pueblos de indios de América*. Madrid: Ediciones de Cultura Hispánica, Agencia Española de Cooperación Internacional, 1999.

———. "Las comunidades de indígenas y la legislación segregacionista en el Nuevo Reino de Granada." *Anuario Colombiano de Historia Social y de la Cultura* 1 (1963): 63–88.

———. *Race Mixture in the History of Latin America*. Boston: Little, Brown, 1967.

Müller-Wille, Staffan. "Figures of Inheritance, 1650–1850." *Heredity Produced: At the Crossroads of Biology, Politics, and Culture, 1500–1870*. Edited by Staffan Müller-Wille and Hans-Jörg Rheinberger, 177–204. Cambridge: Massachusetts Institute of Technology Press, 2007.

Múnera, Alfonso. *Fronteras imaginadas: La construcción de las razas y de la geografía en el siglo XIX colombiano*. Bogotá: Editorial Planeta, 2005.

Muñoz Arbeláez, Santiago. "Espacio y autoridad en el valle de Ubaque, 1550–1600." Master's thesis, Departamento de Historia, Universidad de los Andes, 2010.

Najmabadi, Afsaneh. *Women with Mustaches and Men without Beards: Gender and Sexual Anxieties of Iranian Modernity*. Berkeley: University of California Press, 2005.

Navarrete, María Cristina. "Judeo-conversos en la Audiencia del Nuevo Reino de Granada: Siglos XVI y XVII." *Historia Crítica* 23 (2003): 57–68.

Newson, Linda A. "The Demographic Impact of Colonization." *The Cambridge Economic History of Latin America*. Edited by V. Bulmer-Thomas, John H. Coatsworth, and Roberto Cortes Conde, 143–84. Cambridge: Cambridge University Press, 2006.

Nirenberg, David. *Communities of Violence: Persecutions of Minorities in the Middle Ages*. Princeton: Princeton University Press, 1996.

———. "Figures of Thought and Figures of Flesh: 'Jews' and 'Judaism' in Late-Medieval Spanish Poetry and Politics." *Speculum* 81 (2006): 398–426.

———. "Race and the Middle Ages: The Case of Spain and Its Jews." *Rereading the Black Legend: The Discourses of Religious and Racial Difference in the Renaissance Empires.* Edited by Margaret R. Greer, Walter D. Mignolo, and Maureen Quilligan, 71–87. Chicago: University of Chicago Press, 2007.

Norton, Mary Beth. "Communal Definitions of Gendered Identity in Seventeenth-Century English America." *Through a Glass Darkly: Reflections on Personal Identity in Early America.* Edited by Ronald Hoffman, Mechal Sobel, and Fredrika J. Teute, 40–66. Chapel Hill: University of North Carolina Press, 1997.

Olaechea, Juan Bautista. *El mestizaje como gesta.* Madrid: Colecciones Mapfre, 1992.

Ortiz, Fernando. *Cuban Counterpoint: Tobacco and Sugar.* Translated by Harriet de Onís. Introduction by Bronislaw Malinowski. Prologue by Herminio Portell Vilà. New introduction by Fernando Coronil. Durham: Duke University Press, 1995 [1940].

Ospina, William. "Lo que le falta a Colombia." *Número* 7 (September 1995). Accessed 8 August 2013. http://app.idu.gov.co/boletin_ alejandria/1306_100518/doc/e_libro/loquelefaltaacolombia.pdf.

O'Toole, Rachel Sarah. *Bound Lives: Africans, Indians, and the Making of Race in Colonial Peru.* Pittsburgh: University of Pittsburgh Press, 2012.

———. "From the Rivers of Guinea to the Valleys of Peru: Becoming a *Bran* Diaspora within Spanish Slavery." *Social Text* 25.3 (2007): 19–36.

Pagden, Anthony. "Identity Formation in Spanish America." *Colonial Identity in the Atlantic World, 1500–1800.* Edited by Nicholas Canny and Anthony Pagden, 51–93. Princeton: Princeton University Press, 1987.

Palacios Preciado, Jorge. "El cacique de Tibasosa: Don Alonso de Silva" *Revista Memoria*, segundo semestre (1997): 40–53.

Pardo Tomás, José. "Physicians' and Inquisitors' Stories?: Circumcision and Crypto-Judaism in Sixteenth–Eighteenth Century Spain." *Bodily Extremities: Preoccupations with the Human Body in Early Modern European Culture.* Edited by Florike Egmond and Robert Zwijnenberg, 168–94. Aldershot: Ashgate, 2003.

Patiño Millán, Beatriz A. "Las mujeres y el crimen en la época colonial: El caso de la ciudad de Antioquia." *Las mujeres en la historia de Colombia.* Edited by Magdala Velásquez, 2:77–119. Bogotá: Norma, 1995.

Pech, Sarah. "L'influence des nourrices sur la formation physique et morales des enfants qu'elles allaitent selon les médecins et moralistes espagnols des XVIème siècles." *Paedagogica Historica* 43.4 (2007): 493–507.

Peñalosa y Mondragon, Fray Benito de. *Libro de las cinco excelencias del español que despveblan a España para sv mayor potencia y dilatacion.* Pamplona: Carlos de Labayen, 1629.

Phelan, John Leddy. *The People and the King: The Comunero Revolution in Colombia, 1781.* Madison: University of Wisconsin Press, 1978.

Piedrahita, Lucas Fernández de. *Noticia historial de las conquistas del Nuevo Reino de Granada*. 2 vols. Bogotá: Ministerio de Educación Nacional/Instituto Colombiano de Cultura Hispánica, 1973 [1688].

Poloni-Simard, Jacques. *La mosaïque indienne: Mobilité, stratification sociale et métissage dans le corregimiento de Cuenca (Équateur) du XVIe au XVIIIe siècle*. Paris: Éditions de L'École des Hautes Études en Sciences Sociales, 2000.

Ponce de Leiva, Pilar. *Certezas ante la incertidumbre: Élite y Cabildo de Quito en el siglo XVII*. Quito: Ediciones Abya-Yala, 1998.

Porro Gutiérrez, Jesús María. *Venero de Leiva: Gobernador y primer presidente de la Audiencia del Nuevo Reino de Granada*. Valladolid, Spain: Secretariado de Publicaciones, Universidad de Valladolid, 1995.

Portelli, Alessandro. *The Death of Luigi Trastulli and Other Stories*. Albany: State University of New York Press, 1991.

Porter, Martin. *Windows of the Soul: Physiognomy in European Culture 1470–1780*. Oxford: Clarendon, 2005.

Powers, Karen Vieira. "The Battle for Bodies and Souls in the Colonial North Andes: Intraecclesiastical Struggles and the Politics of Migration." *Hispanic American Historical Review* 75.1 (1995): 31–56.

———. *Women in the Crucible of Conquest: The Gendered Genesis of Spanish American Society, 1500–1600*. Albuquerque: University of New Mexico Press, 2005.

Prude, Jonathan. "To Look upon the 'Lower Sort': Runaway Ads and the Appearance of Unfree Laborers in America, 1750–1800." *Journal of American History* 78.1 (1991): 124–59.

Puente Luna, José Carlos de la. "Into the Heart of the Empire: Indian Journeys to the Habsburg Royal Court." PhD diss., Texas Christian University, Fort Worth, 2010.

Querol Gavaldá, Miguel. *La música en la obra de Cervantes*. Alcalá de Henares, Spain: Ediciones del Centro de Estudios Cervantinos, 2005.

Quiroga, Marcela. "Las unidades sociopolíticas muiscas en el siglo XVI." *Los muiscas en los siglos XVI y XVII: Miradas desde la arqueología, la antropología y la historia*. Edited by Jorge Augusto Gamboa M., 94–115. Bogotá: Universidad de los Andes, 2008.

Quiroga, Pedro de. *Coloquios de la verdad*. Edited by Daisy Rípodas Ardanaz. Valladolid, Spain: Instituto de Cooperación Iberoamericana / Casa-Museo de Colón, Seminario Americanista, 1992 [1562].

Rama, Ángel. *The Lettered City*. Edited and translated by John Charles Chasteen. Durham: Duke University Press, 1996 [1986].

Ramírez, María Himelda. *De la caridad barroca a la caridad ilustrada: Mujeres, género y pobreza en la sociedad de Santa Fe de Bogotá, siglos XVII y XVIII*. Bogotá: Universidad Nacional de Colombia, 2006.

Ramírez, Susan Elizabeth. "*Amores Prohibidos*: The Consequences of the Clash of Juridical Norms in Sixteenth Century Peru." *Americas* 62.1 (2005): 47–63.

———. "The 'Dueño de Indios': Thoughts on the Consequences of the Shifting Bases of Power of the 'Curaca de los Viejos Antiguos' under the Spanish in Sixteenth-Century Peru." *Hispanic American Historical Review* 67.4 (1987): 575–610.

Rappaport, Joanne. *Intercultural Utopias: Public Intellectuals, Cultural Experimentation, and Ethnic Pluralism in Colombia*. Durham: Duke University Press, 2005.

———. *The Politics of Memory: Native Historical Interpretation in the Colombian Andes*. Durham: Duke University Press, 1998.

Rappaport, Joanne, and Tom Cummins. *Beyond the Lettered City: Indigenous Literacies in the Andes*. Durham: Duke University Press, 2012.

Ray, Jonathan. *The Sephardic Frontier: The Reconquista and the Jewish Community in Medieval Iberia*. Ithaca: Cornell University Press, 2006.

Real Academia Española. *Diccionario de autoridades: Edición facsímil*. 3 vols. Madrid: Editorial Gredos, 1990 [1726].

Restall, Matthew. *The Maya World: Yucatec Culture and Society, 1550–1850*. Stanford: Stanford University Press, 1997.

Restrepo, Eduardo. "El negro en un pensamiento colonial de principios del siglo XVII: Diferencia, jerarquía y sujeción sin racialización." *Genealogías de la diferencia: Tecnologías de la salvación y representación de los africanos esclavizados en Iberoamérica colonial*. Edited by María Eugenia Chaves Maldonado, 118–76. Bogotá: Pontificia Universidad Javeriana.

———. "Eventalizing Blackness in Colombia." PhD diss., Anthropology, University of North Carolina at Chapel Hill, 2009.

Restrepo, Luis Fernando. "Narrating Colonial Interventions: Don Diego de Torres, *Cacique* of Turmequé in the New Kingdom of Granada." *Colonialism Past and Present: Reading and Writing about Colonial Latin America Today*. Edited by Alvaro Félix Bolaños and Gustavo Verdesio, 97–118. Albany: State University of New York Press, 2002.

———. *Un Nuevo Reino imaginado: Las Elegías de varones ilustres de Indias de Juan de Castellanos*. Bogotá: Instituto Colombiano de Cultura Hispánica, 1999.

Restrepo Posada, José. *Arquidiócesis de Bogotá. Tomo IV: Cabildo Eclesiástico*. Bogotá: Academia Colombiana de Historia, Biblioteca de Historia Eclesiástica "Fernando Caycedo y Flórez," vol. 6, 1971.

Rivas, Raimundo. *Los fundadores de Bogotá*. 2 vols. Bogotá: Editorial Selecta, Juan Casis, 1938.

Rodríguez, Pablo. *En busca de lo cotidiano: Honor, sexo, fiesta y sociedad s. XVII–XIX*. Bogotá: Universidad Nacional de Colombia, Facultad de Ciencias Humanas, 2002.

———. *Seducción, amancebamiento y abandono en la Colonia*. Bogotá: Fundación Simón y Lola Guberek, 1991.

Rodríguez Freile, Juan. *El carnero*. Bogotá: Instituto Caro y Cuervo, 1984 [1620–38].

Rodríguez Jiménez, Pablo, ed. *Testamentos indígenas de Santafé de Bogotá, siglos XVI–XVII.* Bogotá: Alcaldía Mayor de Bogotá D.C., Instituto Distrital de Cultura y Turismo, 2002.

Rodríguez Vergara, Isabel, ed. *Inés de Hinojosa: Historia de una transgresora.* Medellín: Editorial Universidad de Antioquia, 1999.

———. "Mujeres transgresoras (criollas, indias y brujas) en la Colonia," *Inés de Hinojosa: Historia de una transgresora.* Edited by Isabel Rodríguez Vergara, 60–89. Medellín: Editorial Universidad de Antioquia, 1999.

Rojas, Ulises. *El cacique de Turmequé y su época.* Tunja: Imprenta Departamental de Boyacá, 1965.

———. *Escudos de armas e inscripciones antiguas de la ciudad de Tunja.* Tunja: Talleres de la Cooperativa Nacional de Artes Gráficas, 1939.

Román, Ángel. "Necesidades fundacionales e historia indígena imaginada de Cajicá: Una revisión de esta mirada a partir de fuentes primarias (1593–1638)." *Los muiscas en los siglos XVI y XVII: Miradas desde la arqueología, la antropología y la historia.* Edited by Jorge Augusto Gamboa M., 276–313. Bogotá: Universidad de los Andes, 2008.

Roncancio, Andrés, ed. *Fuentes documentales del Archivo Regional de Boyacá.* Bogotá: Instituto Colombiano de Antropología e Historia, 2002.

Root, Deborah. "Speaking Christian: Orthodoxy and Difference in Sixteenth-Century Spain." *Representations* 23 (1988): 118–34.

Rostworowski, María. *Doña Francisca Pizarro: Una ilustre mestiza, 1534–1598.* Lima: Instituto de Estudios Peruanos, 2003.

Ruggles, D. Fairchild. "Mothers of a Hybrid Dynasty: Race, Genealogy, and Acculturation in al-Andalus." *Journal of Medieval and Early Modern Studies* 34.1 (2004): 65–94.

Ruíz Rivera, Julián B. *La plata de Mariquita en el siglo XVII: Mita y producción.* Tunja: Ediciones Nuestra América, 1979.

Safford, Frank. "Race, Integration, and Progress: Elite Attitudes and the Indian in Colombia, 1750–1870." *Hispanic American Historical Review* 71.1 (1991): 1–33.

Sandoval, Alonso de, S. J. *De instauranda aetiopum salute: Historia de Aetiopia, naturaleza, policía sagrada y profana, constumbres, ritos y catechismo evangélico, de todos los aetiopes con que se restuara la salud de sus almas.* Madrid: 1647.

———. *Treatise on Slavery: Selections from De instauranda Aethiopum salute.* Edited and translated by Nicole von Germeten. Indianapolis: Hackett, 2008 [1647].

Saunders, Richard. *Physiognomie, and Chiromancie, Metoposcopie: The Symmetrical Proportions and Signal Moles of the Body.* London: Printed by R. White for Nathaniel Brooke, 1653.

Schiebinger, Londa. *Nature's Body: Gender in the Making of Modern Science.* Boston: Beacon, 1993.

Schwaller, Robert C. "Defining Difference in Early New Spain." Ph.D. diss., History, Pennsylvania State University, 2010.

———. "'For Honor and Defence': Race and the Right to Bear Arms in Early Colonial Mexico." *Colonial Latin American Review* 21.2 (2012): 239–66.

———. "The Importance of Mestizos and Mulatos as Bilingual Intermediaries in Sixteenth-Century New Spain." *Ethnohistory* 59.4 (2012): 713–38.

Schwartz, Stuart B., and Frank Salomon. "New Peoples and New Kinds of People: Adaptation, Readjustment, and Ethnogenesis in South American Indigenous Societies (Colonial Era)." *The Cambridge History of the Native Peoples of the Americas*, vol. 3, *South America*. Edited by Frank Salomon and Stuart B. Schwartz, part 2, 443–501. Cambridge: Cambridge University Press, 1999.

Seed, Patricia. *Ceremonies of Possession in Europe's Conquest of the New World, 1492–1640*. Cambridge: Cambridge University Press, 1995.

Seth, Vanita. *Europe's Indians: Producing Racial Difference, 1500–1900*. Durham: Duke University Press, 2010.

Sheriff, Robin E. *Dreaming Equality: Color, Race, and Racism in Urban Brazil*. New Brunswick: Rutgers University Press, 2001.

Sicroff, Albert A. *Los estatutos de limpieza de sangre: Controversias entre los siglos XV y XVII*. Madrid: Taurus, 1985.

Silva, Renán. *Las epidemias de viruela de 1782 y 1802 en el virreinato de Nueva Granada*. Medellín: La Carreta, 2007.

———. *Saber, cultura y sociedad en el Nuevo Reino de Granada—siglos XVII y XVIII*. Bogotá: Centro de Investigaciones, Universidad Pedagógica Nacional, 1984.

Silverblatt, Irene. *Modern Inquisitions: Peru and the Colonial Origins of the Civilized World*. Durham: Duke University Press, 2004.

Silvestre, Francisco. *Descripción del Reyno de Santa Fé de Bogotá: Escrita en 1789 por D. Francisco Silvestre, Secretario que fue del Virreinato y antiguo Gobernador de la Provincia de Antioquia*. Bogotá: Universidad Nacional de Colombia, Dirección de Divulgación Cultural, 1968 [1789].

Simard, Jacques P. "Problèmes et tentatives d'identification des métis à travers la documentation coloniale: L'exemple de Cuenca." *Transgressions et stratégies du métissage en Amérique coloniale*. Edited by Bernard Lavallé, 11–31. Paris: Presses de la Sorbonne Nouvelle, 1999.

Simón, Fray Pedro de. *Noticias historiales de las conquistas de Tierra Firme en las Indias Occidentales*. 8 vols. Bogotá: Biblioteca Banco Popular, 1981 [1627].

Solórzano Pereira, Juan de. *Política indiana*. Madrid: Matheo Sacristan, 1736.

Stepan, Nancy Leys. *"The Hour of Eugenics": Race, Gender, and Nation in Latin America*. Ithaca: Cornell University Press, 1991.

Stolcke, Verena. "Invaded Women: Gender, Race, and Class in the Formation of Colonial Society." *Women, Race, and Writing in the Early Modern Period*. Edited by Margo Endricks and Patricia Parker, 272–86. London: Routledge, 1994.

Stoler, Ann Laura. *Carnal Knowledge and Imperial Power: Race and the Intimate in Colonial Rule*. Berkeley: University of California Press, 2002.

Studnicki-Gisbert, Daviken. *A Nation upon the Ocean Sea: Portugal's Atlantic Diaspora and the Crisis of the Spanish Empire, 1492–1640*. Oxford: Oxford University Press, 2007.

Sweet, James H. "The Iberian Roots of American Racist Thought." *William and Mary Quarterly* 54.1 (1997): 143–66.

Tavárez, David. "Legally Indian: Inquisitorial Readings of Indigenous Identity in New Spain." *Imperial Subjects: Race and Identity in Colonial Latin America*. Edited by Andrew B. Fisher and Matthew D. O'Hara, 81–100. Durham: Duke University Press, 2009.

Taylor, Jean Gelman. *The Social World of Batavia: European and Eurasian in Dutch Asia*. Madison: University of Wisconsin Press, 1983.

Terraciano, Kevin. *The Mixtecs of Colonial Oaxaca: Ñudzahui History, Sixteenth through Eighteenth Centuries*. Stanford: Stanford University Press, 2001.

Therrien, Monika. "Indígenas y mercaderes: Agentes en la consolidación de facciones en la ciudad de Santafé, siglo XVI." *Los muiscas en los siglos XVI y XVII: Miradas desde la arqueología, la antropología y la historia*. Edited by Jorge Augusto Gamboa M., 169–210. Bogotá: Universidad de los Andes, 2008.

Therrien, Monika, and Lina Jaramillo Pacheco. *"Mi casa no es tu casa": Procesos de diferenciación en la construcción de Santa Fe, siglos XVI y XVII*. Bogotá: Instituto Distrital de Cultura y Turismo, Alcaldía Mayor de Bogotá, D.C., 2004.

Tinhorão, José Ramos. *Os negros em Portugal: Uma presença silenciosa*. Lisbon: Caminho, 1988.

Toquica, Constanza. *A falta de oro: Linaje, crédito y salvación*. Bogotá: Ministerio de Cultura / Instituto Colombiano de Antropología e Historia / Universidad Nacional de Colombia, Facultad de Ciencias Humanas, CES, 2008.

Tovar Pinzón, Hermes. *La batalla de los sentidos: Infidelidad, adulterio y concubinato a fines de la colonia*. Bogotá: Ediciones Fondo Cultural Cafetero, 2004.

Trinh, T. Minh-ha. *When the Moon Waxes Red: Representation, Gender and Cultural Politics*. London: Routledge, 1991.

Trouillot, Michel-Rolph. *Silencing the Past: Power and the Production of History*. Boston: Beacon, 1995.

Tutino, John. *Making a New World: Founding Capitalism in the Bajío and Spanish North America*. Durham: Duke University Press, 2011.

Twinam, Ann. *Public Lives, Private Secrets: Gender, Honor, Sexuality, and*

Illegitimacy in Colonial Spanish America. Stanford: Stanford University Press, 1999.

⸻. "Purchasing Whiteness: Conversations on the Essence of Pardoness and Mulatto-ness at the End of Empire." *Imperial Subjects: Race and Identity in Colonial Latin America.* Edited by Andrew B. Fisher and Matthew D. O'Hara, 141–65. Durham: Duke University Press, 2009.

⸻. "Racial Passing: Informal and Official 'Whiteness' in Colonial Spanish America." *New World Orders: Violence, Sanction, and Authority in the Colonial Americas.* Edited by John Smolenski and Thomas J. Humphrey, 249–72. Philadelphia: University of Pennsylvania Press, 2005.

Uricoechea, Ezequiel. *Gramática, vocabulario, catecismo i confesionario de la lengua chibcha segun antiguos manuscritos anónimos e inéditos.* Paris: Maisonneuve y Cia, 1871.

Van der Lugt, Maaike. "La peau noire dans la science médiévale." *Micrologus* 13 (2005): 439–75.

van Deusen, Nancy E. *Between the Sacred and the Worldly: The Institutional and Cultural Practice of* Recogimiento *in Colonial Lima.* Stanford: Stanford University Press, 2001.

⸻. "Diasporas, Bondage, and Intimacy in Lima, 1535 to 1555." *Colonial Latin American Review* 19.2 (2010): 247–77.

⸻. "Global Indios." Manuscript.

⸻. "The Intimacies of Bondage: Female Indigenous Servants and Slaves and Their Spanish Masters, 1492–1555." *Journal of Women's History* 24.1 (2012): 13–43.

⸻. "Seeing *Indios* in Sixteenth-Century Castile." *William and Mary Quarterly* 69.2 (2012): 205–34.

Van Young, Eric. "Conflict and Solidarity in Indian Village Life: The Guadalajara Region in the Late Colonial Period." *Hispanic American Historical Review* 64.1 (1984): 55–79.

Vargas Lesmes, Julián. "Fiestas y celebraciones públicas en Santafé." *La sociedad de Santafé colonial.* Edited by Julian Vargas Lesmes, 297–341. Bogotá: Centro de Investigación y Educación Popular, 1990.

⸻. "La mita urbana: Trabajos y oficios en Santafé." *La sociedad de Santafé colonial.* Edited by Julian Vargas Lesmes, 85–118. Bogotá: Centro de Investigación y Educación Popular, 1990.

⸻. "Santafé a la luz de sus padrones (1778–1806)." *La sociedad de Santafé colonial.* Edited by Julián Vargas Lesmes, 11–45. Bogotá: Centro de Investigación y Educación Popular, 1990.

Vargas Lesmes, Julián, and Marta Zambrano. "La población indígena de Santafé." *La sociedad de Santafé colonial.* Edited by Julián Vargas Lesmes, 49–84. Bogotá: Centro de Investigación y Educación Popular, 1990.

Vasconcelos, José. *The Cosmic Race: A Bilingual Edition.* Translated and edited by Didier T. Jaén. Baltimore: Johns Hopkins University Press, 1997 [1925].

Villamarin, Juan A. "El concepto nobleza en la estratificación social de Santa Fé de Bogotá en la época colonial." *Estudios Andinos* 14 (1998): 47–62.

———. "Encomenderos and Indians in the Formation of Colonial Society in the Sabana de Bogotá Colombia—1537 to 1740." PhD diss., Anthropology, Brandeis University, 1972.

Villamarin, Juan A., and Judith E. Villamarin. "The Concept of Nobility in Colonial Santa Fe de Bogotá." *Essays in the Political, Economic and Social History of Colonial Latin America.* Edited by Karen Spalding, 125–53. Newark: University of Delaware, Latin American Studies Program, Occasional Papers and Monographs, no. 3, 1982.

———. "Epidemic Disease in the Sabana de Bogotá, 1536–1810." *"Secret Judgments of God": Old World Disease in Colonial Spanish America.* Edited by Noble David Cook and W. George Lovell, 113–41. Norman: University of Oklahoma Press, 2001.

———. "Kinship and Inheritance among the Sabana de Bogotá Chibcha at the Time of the Spanish Conquest." *Ethnology* 14.2 (1975): 173–79.

Vincent, Bernard. "The Moriscos and Circumcision." *Culture and Control in Counter-Reformation Spain.* Edited by Anne J. Cruz and Mary Elizabeth Perry, 78–92. Minneapolis: University of Minnesota Press, 1992.

Vives, Juan Luis. *Instruccion de la mujer christiana: Obra compuesta en latin por, el célebre Juan Luis Vives, que traduxo á la lengua castellana Juan Justiniano.* Madrid: En la Imprenta de don Benito Cano, 1793 [1524].

Wade, Peter. *Music, Race, and Nation: Música Tropical in Colombia.* Chicago: University of Chicago Press, 2000.

———. "Rethinking *Mestizaje*: Ideology and Lived Experience." *Journal of Latin American Studies* 37.2 (2005): 239–57.

Waldstreicher, David. "Reading the Runaways: Self-Fashioning, Print Culture, and Confidence in Slavery in the Eighteenth-Century Mid-Atlantic." *William and Mary Quarterly* 56.2 (1999): 243–72.

Weiditz, Christoph. *Authentic Everyday Dress of the Renaissance: All 154 Plates from the "Trachtenbuch."* New York: Dover, 1994 [1529].

Weismantel, Mary J. *Cholas and Pishtacos: Stories of Race and Sex in the Andes.* Chicago: University of Chicago Press, 2001.

———. *Food, Gender, and Poverty in the Ecuadorian Andes.* Long Grove, IL: Waveland, 1998.

White, Richard. *The Middle Ground: Indians, Empires, and Republics in the Great Lakes Region, 1650–1815.* Cambridge: Cambridge University Press, 1991.

Whitehead, Colson. *The Intuitionist: A Novel.* New York: Anchor, 2000.

Wilson, Bronwen. "Learning How to Read: Giovanni Battista Della Porta,

Physiognomy, and Printed Portrait-Books." Paper presented at the Visual Knowledges Conference, University of Edinburgh, 17–20 September 2003. Accessed 22 March 2011. http://webdb.ucs.ed.ac.uk/malts/other/VKC/dsp-all-papers.cfm.

Wood, Robert D., S.M. *"Teach Them Good Customs": Colonial Indian Education and Acculturation in the Andes.* Culver City, CA: Labyrinthos, 1986.

Woolard, Kathryn A. "Bernardo de Aldrete and the Morisco Problem: A Study in Early Modern Spanish Language Ideology." *Comparative Studies in Society and History* 44.3 (2002): 446–80.

Yannakakis, Yanna. *The Art of Being In-Between: Native Intermediaries, Indian Identity, and Local Rule in Colonial Oaxaca.* Durham: Duke University Press, 2008.

Zambrano Escovar, Marta. *Trabajadores, villanos y amantes: Encuentros entre indígenas y españoles en la ciudad letrada, Santa Fe de Bogotá (1550–1650).* Bogotá: Editorial Instituto Colombiano de Antropología e Historia, 2008.

Zambrano Pantoja, Fabio, et al. *Comunidades y territorios: Reconstrucción histórica de Usaquén.* Bogotá: Corporación Horizontes, 2000.

Zúñiga, Jean-Paul. *Espagnols d'outre-mer: Émigration, métissage et reproduction sociale à Santiago du Chili, au 17e siècle.* Paris: Éditions de l'École des Hautes Études en Sciences Sociales, 2002.

———. "La voix du sang: Du métis à l'idée de métissage en Amérique espagnole." *Annales* HSS 54.2 (1999): 425–52.

INDEX

Page numbers in italics refer to illustrations.

aspect (*aspecto*), 171, 175, 200, 230, 233; *calidad* and, 178, 303; categorization and, 202; classification vs., 197; construction of, 177; conventions of, 183; descriptions of, 188, 198; dress and, 282n46; identification and, 210; physical appearance as, 172

Audencia, Nuevo Reino de Granada, 107, 140, 144, 153, 173, 303; allies of, 107; Alonso de Silva' petition, 136; case of Inés de Hinojosa and, 1, 144; case of Juan Mulatto and, 173; lawyers of, 108, 125, 152; officials of, 116, 123, 125, 145, 163, 181, 215, 272n64, 276n95, 305; Pedro de Sotelo and, 107; petitions to, 136; of Quito, 261n101; records of, 215; Santafé as capital of, 1, 2, 64, 95, 96, 135, 142, 162, 241, 242, 245n1

Baber, Jovita, on sociocial terms, 8–9, 248n21

baptisms, 98, 147, 182; of Moors, 43; records of, 62, 223, 236, 264n31, 267n1, 268n3

La Barbuda de Peñaranda (Juan Sánchez Cotán), 189

Barth, Fredrik, on ethnic boundaries, 12

Basques, 9, 100, 144, 159

beards, 27, 241, 291n51, 292n64, 292n67; *calidad* and, 188–93; Cid's, 291n50; as generational markers, 178, 190; masculinity and, 188–93, 203; as mode of identification, 173, 178–93; natives generally lacking, 178, 192–93, 291n64; new, 187–88, 191; scant, 43, 172, 189, 191, 193, 239, 242; on Spaniards, 172, 203; on women, 189, 291n52

behavior, 106, 148, 165, 172, 197, 210, 230; *calidad* and, 40, 49; as form of *mestizaje*, 17, 83, 160; of Francisco Suárez, 31–37; groupness and, 9; heretical, 205; of non-Christians in Spain, 45; public, 63, 124; racial

identity and, 98, 197; social rank and, 7

Bermúdez, Luis, 53–54, 261n89

betrothal: legality of, 109; promise of, 20, 106–15, 241

Birves, Juan, 231, 241, 271n48; in cast of characters, 240; story of, 106–15; tryst of, 40, 124, 130

black, blacks (*negro*), 71, 122, 247n16; as caste group, 208; as category, 32, 179–80, 196–97, 221, 252n6, 254n29; coherence of term, 7; groupness of, 25; identified by origins, 9; marriages of, 211; *moreno* and, 193, 195, 293n73; in *pueblos*, 160; racial interactions of, 69–70, 75, 174, 211, 292n66; as slaves, 74, 127, 191, 196, 197, 288n15, 290n44, 295n90; as stable term, 4, 5, 6. *See also* Africa, Africans; mulatto; *zambaigos*; *zambo*

blood: certification of purity of, 47–48, 181–82, 221; Christian and European lines of, 26, 36–38, 44, 140, 154–56, 228, 235; discrimination and, 38, 275n92; impurity of, 39, 47, 97, 98, 157; mixing of, 29–30, 98; mother's milk as type of, 19; purity of, 17, 44–49; redemption of indigenous, 133, 155; as somatic referent, 18; Spanish, 14, 26, 38, 133, 154–57, 208, 242. *See also* lineage; mixed parentage; mixing, mixed ancestry; parentage

Bogotá. *See* Santafé

Bohórques, María de, 100

Bonfíl Batalla, Guillermo, 217

Boyacá province, 88, 216, 245n1

Boyer, Richard, 123, 175, 247n13

branding, 286n4; of livestock, 44; of Juan Mulato, 173–74, 242, 286n5

brown, 35, 189–94, 221; *bazo*, 27, 293n71; as category, 193–94; as complexion, 42, 171–73, 176, 179, 187–88, 239, 241, 293n76; *loro*, 27, 197, 288n20, 295n90. See also *moreno*

Brubaker, Rodgers, "Beyond 'Identity,'" 5–6, 8, 247n14
bureaucracy, bureaucrats, 27, 33, 172, 184–86, 290n35; colonial, 136, 202; of Crown, 88. *See also* archives; *and names of specific offices*
Burns, Kathryn, 104, 162, 258n67, 268n3, 278n5

cacicas (female *caciques*), 50, *51*, 270n25, 303. *See also names of individual* cacicas
cacicazgo (hereditary chiefdom), 17, 97, 133, 149, 303; *calidad* and, 40; mestizos as, 62; Muisca, 138, 143, 146–48, 153, 241; of Tibasosa, 135–36, 151–54, 242, 274n78; of Turmequé, 149, 155–58, 167, 242. See also *cacicas; caciques*
caciques (hereditary lords), 8, 17, 146, 157–61, 250n47, 303; beards and, 192; Christianity and, 64, 141, 147, 149; Diego de Torres as, 228; of Fontibón, 65, 68; of Guatavita, 19; mestizos as, 14, 26, 62, 143–46, 198, 277n3, 281n40; power of, 139, 146, 161, 223, 275n92; rebellious, 15; schools for sons of, 136; as sons of conquistadores, 12; strategic marriages of daughters of, 100; succession of, 149–55; taxes and, 137, 285n83; of Tibasosa, 97; of Turmequé, 15; *visita* and, 73. *See also names of individual* caciques
Cajicá, Jesuit mission in, 81
Cali, 97, 101, 104, 231, 241
calidad (quality), 111–13, 175, 303; aspect and, 172, 176–78, 201; beards and masculinity and, 188–93; classifications of, 186; construction of, 236; as designation of lineage, 7, 34; determination of, 39, 62, 106, 220–23; ethnicity and, 32, 70; as fluid, 63, 67, 87, 91–92, 196; of Francisco Suárez, 171; as identity, 75, 287n13; meaning of, 38–41, 97, 210; mestizos and, 62, 96; nobility

and, 106; passing and, 31–32; physiognomy and, 188; prejudices engendered by, 176; travel papers and, 181–83; unmarked, 11; use of, 201, 225, 231–32
Cárdenas, Luis Zapata de, Archbishop of Santafé, 82, 273n69, 273n70
carpenters, 50, 234, 274n84; Francisco de Reyna as, 119–25; as honorable occupation, 223; mestizos as, 20
Cartagena de Indias, 37, 111, 195–97; Inquisition in, 48, 205, 243, 253–54n18, 297n1
Carvajal, don Gabriel de, 1639 *visita* of, 74–76
Casa de los Niños Expósitos (Foundlings Home), in Santafé, 19
casta (caste), 91–92, 150, 208, 296n98, 297n9, 299n31, 303; beards and, 192; fluidity of, 4, 27, 210, 224, 229, 265n40; Indians and, 217; lineage and, 225, 247n15, 250n46, 282n50; mestizo and, 13, 16, 35, 192, 217, 267n58; in Mexico, 4–7, 27, 28, 209; paintings, 4, 224–25, 247n11, 288n18, 301n56, 303; problems with, 28, 205–26, 297n7, 298n9; *raza* and, 44, 225, 247n15; socioracial categories and, 41, 224, 250n46, 297n7, 297n8; system of, 4–5, 7, 92, 207–10, 220, 224–27, 267n58, 292n66
castizos, 208, 246n8, 257n54, 265n40, 267n2
categorization, 6, 13, 57; *casta* paintings and, 4, 288n18; caste and, 205–26, 297n7; challenges to, 72–79, 175, 201; fluidity and, 3, 4, 15, 49, 61, 129, 230, 233; on Iberian Peninsula, 7, 196; interpreted situationally, 5, 172; kin groups and, 151; legal context of, 21; mestizo and, 7–18, 29, 42, 51, 61–93, 229, 248n27; in Mexico, 7, 39, 40; process of, 28, 39, 220, 293n76. *See also* socioracial classification

Facatativá, 118, 241, 258n64, 273n70
Fals Borda, Orlando, 217, 300n42;
  *Peasant Society in the Colombian
  Andes*, 73
Feerick, Jean, on blood as somatic
  referent, 18
fiestas, 65, 68, 71, 85–86
Flórez de Ocáriz, Juan, 105; on
  Captain García Zorro family, 127,
  253n125; on Catalina Tafur, 56; on
  Céspedes family, 271n57; *Genealogías del Nuevo Reino de Granada*,
  22, 34, 91, 99, 100, 106, 121; on
  Juan de Penagos, 101, 270n25; on
  mestizos, 268–69n14
fluidity: of *calidad*, 52, 63, 67, 196; of
  caste designations, 4, 91–92, 210;
  of mestizo category, 15, 49, 64, 67,
  114, 230; of socioracial classification, 23–29, 87, 129–31, 176, 224,
  255n33
Fontibón, 69, 124, 231, 240, 262n8,
  263n14, 267n56; *cacique* of, 127;
  difficulty of classification in,
  64–68, 231; Jesuit mission in, 81;
  tributaries of, 214
forastero (outsider), 16, 68, 79–82,
  213–14, 304; influence of, 65, 70,
  74, 81, 92, 151, 154; mestizo as metaphor for, 16, 79, 212–16, 219, 234,
  266n46; unattached, 68, 90, 202
Frederick, Jake, on *casta* system, 209
freedpersons, 9, 43, 55, 71, 200
French (language), 233; terms for
  mestizo in, 17–18
Freyre, Gilberto, *The Masters and the
  Slaves*, 71
Friede, Juan, 211
Fuchs, Barbara, 58, 59, 166, 190
Fusagasugá, 127

Gachancipá, 97
Gallque, Andrés Sánchez, *Three
  Mulatto Gentlemen from Esmeral-
  das*, 57
Galván, Juana, 87–93, 201, 207; in
  cast of characters, 240; children

of, 206, 294n79; family of, 76, 82,
  90–91; as mestiza, 214–17, 234,
  236; misclassified, 76–80, 90,
  265n41
García, Gregorio (*Origen de los indios
  del Nuevo Mundo e Indias Occidentales*), 192
García Zorro, Captain Gonzalo, 121,
  125
García Zorro, Diego, 97, 119–25,
  133–34, 140, 143, 199, 236, 274n84,
  300n51; in cast of characters, 241;
  mestizo identity of, 22, 121–24,
  127–30, 215; as Spanish elite, 127–
  30, 229, 285n82; will of, 126–28
García Zorro, Fr. Gonzalo, 55, 127–28,
  134, 182; appearance of, 172; in
  cast of characters, 241; family of,
  121, 123, 125, 126; mestizo identity of, 121, 123–24, 215; ministry
  of, 118–19, 125–26; as speaker of
  Muisca, 273n69, 273n70
Garcilaso de la Vega, El Inca, 14, 136,
  139, 168
Garrido, Margarita, 109, 220
gender: beards and, 189, 190, 192;
  caste and, 27; colonial *mestizaje*
  and, 22, 231; elite *mestizaje*
  and, 100; elites and, 4; factor of
  identification, 6, 7, 21, 41, 95, 233,
  246n6; intersection of status, race,
  and, 254n19; mestizos and, 95–131,
  231; native garments and, 165;
  race and, 60, 98, 256n46; social
  process and, 26, 76, 236; transculturation and, 234
*Genealogías del Nuevo Reino de
  Granada* (Flórez de Ocáriz), 22, 34,
  99, 101, 106, 121
géneros, 225, 256n46; as genres of
  people, 40–41
gente decente ("decent" folk), 121,
  209
gente de razón ("rational" people),
  209
Gómez, Katherine Bonil, on *calidad*,
  113, 222, 298n9

(*hijo sacrílego*), 265n39; mestizos as, 14, 69, 76, 98, 279n7; paternal recognition of, 33, 77, 265n39; as servants, 91; of Spanish couples, 19. *See also names of specific individuals*

Inca, 13, 14, 134, 136, 154, 168; Atahualpa as, 137; costume of, 57–58; royalty of, 105, 139

india, indio (Indian) , 8, 10, 13, 17, 71–79, 87, 197, 200, 254n27, 304; ambiguity of, 129, 230; as ascriptive classification, 7, 32, 40, 176, 247n10, 282n41; aspect of, 197–98; as caste group, 208–10; classification of, 196, 222; fiestas and, 65, 68; as floating descriptor, 172; freedom of, 174; groupness of, 25; intermarriage of, 211, 215; isolation of, 212, 219; mestizos as, 95; of Mexico, 9, 63; permeability of classification, 64–69, 129; racial interaction of, 69–72; rebellion and, 199, 216; as relational category, 115; as servants, 64, 87, 253n8; in society, 100, 233–34; as slaves, 253n8; as stable term, 4, 5, 6; tribute to Crown from, 8, 74–75; urban migration of, 64, 88, 260n80

indigeneity, 3, 27, 26, 175

indio ladino (Spanish-speaking native person), 82, 83, 304; abuses by, 284n72; as ascriptive classification, 68, 95, 124; *forasteros* and, 214; Francisco Pongota as, 213; Indians and, 212, 265n35; Juan de Salazar as, 65–69, 95; Manuel Rodríguez and, 80, 85–87; mestizos and, 69, 235; passing by, 266n50; religion and, 280n17; Spanish language and, 15, 64, 72

indio tributario (tribute-paying native person), as ascriptive classification, 8, 95. *See also* tribute

inheritance, 41, 150, 151, 221; illegitimacy and, 14–15, 56, 101, 104; matrilineal, 133, 138, 146; mestizos

and, 114, 116, 127, 160, 231, 236; patrilineal, 136; race and, 44; of virtue, 38

Inquisition, 47–48, 206, 243, 260n78, 289n26; Indians exempt from, 8, 63; Jews and, 258–59n69; mestizos and, 205, 253n18, 297n1; in Mexico, 63–64; trials of, 209, 289n26

Instruccion de la muger christiana (Juan Luis Vives), 35

Islam, 38, 45, 58, 166, 196; *amoriscados* and, 19; converts from, 15, 17, 24, 43, 168, 181. *See also* Moors; Morisca, Morisco; Muslims

Israel, J. I., on Mexican mestizos, 61

jewelry, 57, 128; rights to wear certain, 8, 50

Judaism, Jews, 16, 19, 38, 44, 45; ancestors of, 208, 258–59n69, 304, 305; converts from, 15, 17, 259n69; mixing of, 34–35, 47, 49, 157, 297n7

language, 8, 72, 86, 117; as distinguisher, 7, 179, 202; as racial marker, 14, 32, 52, 83, 100, 129, 141, 188, 260n78; status and, 39, 108, 165. *See also specific languages*

La Palma, 40, 106–7, 112–15, 240, 241

Lara, Juan de, royal interpreter and mestizo son of Juan de Lara, 117, 151

Larsen, Nella, *Passing*, 140, 262n103

laws, legal system: betrothal and, 109, 110; cases of passing, 30, 36, 232; caste and, 208, 209; ethnicity in, 124; Muisca and, 74, 151; *obedezco pero no cumplo*, 122, 275n86; petitions to Crown, 99, 124, 161; physiognomy and, 179, 180, 185–88, 198, 300n47; socioracial categories and context of, 10, 21, 62, 63, 78, 95–98, 113, 157, 174–75, 212–14, 226–28, 231, 234, 237, 248n20, 262n6, 268n3; sumptuary, 17, 50, 52, 55, 259n74; wills and, 127; women in, 53 *lengua* (interpreter), 82, 86, 117

Lepore, Jill, *New York Burning*, 24

Lewis, Laura, *Hall of Mirrors*, 27–28, 297n8

libres de todos los colores (free men of all colors), 208, 220–24, 304

Libro de las cinco excelencias del español (Fray Benito de Peñalosa y Mondragón), 38–39, 157

Lima, Limeños, 2, 145; grandees and nobles of, 24, 30, 31, 39, 60, 68, 99, 239; Jews in, 258n69; *morenos* in, 194; social mobility in, 231; viceroy in, 143; women in, 36, 98, 99

lineage, 34, 44, 104, 117, 157; modern notion of race as, 25, 38, 48, 49; protection of, 26, 56, 90, 109, 111; status and, 17, 18, 24, 26, 30, 35, 47, 56, 90, 130, 133, 134, 156, 201–2, 235; terms for, 7, 37, 208, 225, 250n46, 297n7

literacy: of *caciques*, 147, 165; of indigenous populations, 64, 228, 284n72; of mestizos, 118, 138, 161–64; notaries and, 134; passing and, 31, 36–37, 232; of *vecinos*, 219

Lizárraga, Fray Reginaldo de, 19

López Bejarano, María del Pilar, 223, 233

Madrid, 40, 118, 134, 137, 242

Malasmaños, Juan, 77

Mangan, Jane, 52

Manuel de Hoyos, doña Antonia, 53–55, 239

Mariquita, 80, 113, 134, 145, 222, 240, 300n47; as mining center, 174, 280n28

marriage, 17, 209, 211; absent in Muisca culture, 151; *calidad* identified in registers of, 222, 226, 236, 264n31, 267n1, 268n3; elite mestizas groomed for, 56, 99; ethnically unmarked due to, 130; inter-, 157, 223, 288n18; promises of betrothal and, 20, 109, 254n19; to repair honor, 110; as strategic,

72, 91, 98, 100, 101, 104–6, 133, 268n11, 269n20

Martin, Cheryl English, 123

Martínez, María Elena, on blood purity, 47–48

masculinity: beards and *calidad* and, 188–93; brown and, 194; of mestizos, 99, 167

Medina, Juan de, 64–69, 72, 240, 262n8, 263n14

memory, historical, 99, 105, 119, 168, 301n1; nature of, 22–23, 228

Mendo, Pedro, 213, 298n23

Mendoza, Ana de, 100–101, 104, 105

Mendoza, Leonor de, 106

Merrell, James H., 233, 235

mésalliance ("misalliance"), 17

Mestiza, Isabel, 83–85

mestiza, mestizas, 2–3, 304; children of, 11, 76–78, 87, 91, 98, 211, 216–17; education of, 99; elite, 25; as epithet, 231; femininity and, 99; in Indian habit, 12, 31, 42, 50–59, 177, 229; marital strategies of, 72, 99, 100, 101; meaning of, 21; in Mexico, 61; mobility of, 100, 130; multiple identities of, 58, 78; as nuns, 13; social barriers and, 99, 130; unmarked status of, 90, 98, 130. *See also* mestizo, mestizos; *and names of specific individuals*

mestizaje, 27, 237, 247n9; ethnography of colonial, 20–24, 62, 129, 251n65; forms of, 17; gendering of, 22, 130; in hinterlands, 212, 216; process of, 88; as stain, 3

mestizo, mestizos, 6, 10–11, 29–30, 61–62, 98, 100, 229, 304; ambiguity of classification, 95, 96, 198; no boundary between Spanish and, 25; as *casta*, 208; caste system and, 207–8, 211–12; as children of rape, 69; as contagion source, 15–16; demographics of, 36; "disappearance" of, 61–87; as elite, 116–19, 123, 130, 235–36, 285n82; fail to transcend mixed ancestry, 116,

117; family lives, 100; fiestas and, 65, 68; as *forasteros*, 213, 234; as group, 61–93; in Indian habit, 58, 260–61n87, 261–62n101; as Indians, 10, 63–64, 72–79; literacy and, 161–64; as majority, 28; masculinity and, 99; misidentified, 63–69, 76–79; Muisca language and, 48, 134; occupations of, 11, 72, 117, 222–23; permeability of classification, 64–69, 72, 96, 129, 230–32; physical appearance and, 172; as plebeian, 125, 199, 236; as priests, 117–19; in *pueblos*, 201, 215–18, 224; racial interaction of, 69–72, 87; rape by, 83; rebellion and, 15–16, 163–64, 199, 216, 284n78, 285n82, 300n41; religion and, 164–68; in seventeenth century, 199, 215–16; social barriers and, 99, 122–24, 199; social mobility and, 72, 117, 129; in society, 126, 227; as Spanish, 222; of unmarked *calidad*, 62, 81, 91, 96, 128, 130; as *vecinos*, 218. *See also* mestizo (as term); passing, racial

mestizo (as term), 13; as bilingual, 82; blood as making, 29; as caste group, 208, 210; as category, 7–12, 32, 199; child of Muisca woman considered Indian, 61; classification of, 5, 40; as colonial label, 4, 176, 199, 247n9, 249n32; as color term, 196–97, 221, 295n91, 300n47; as exclusionary category, 13–15; fluidity of, 15, 87, 91–93, 114, 129–31, 172, 174; gendering of, 26, 72, 95–131; as hereditary, 250n53; as identifying marker, 3, 58, 61–62; incoherence of, 8; inscrutability of term, 7, 92–93; as metaphor for "outsider," 16; Moors referred to as, 18; as relational category, 115; as slight, 66–68; as surname, 11
methodology of book, 21–24
métis (mestizo), 17, 159, 233
Mexico, 208, 224–25; *calidad* in, 39,

40; *casta* in, 4–5, 27, 91, 209; *casta* paintings in, 247n11, 288n18; documentation of, 228; Inquisition in, 63–64; mestizos in, 52, 105, 220; Mexico City, 2, 52, 194; passing in, 252n6, 254n29

mining, mines: emerald, 2, 101, 179, 248n19; gold, 144; indigenous laborers in, 179, 199; at Mariquita, 174; silver, 2, 181, 280n28, 296n96

mita, 17, 36, 64, 211, 234–35, 260n80
mixed parentage, 61, 304; of *caciques*, 142, 154, 275n92; Church and, 118; citizenship and, 202; classification of people of, 216, 232, 234; of Diego García Zorro, 128; disappearance and, 10, 74, 105; discrimination against, 11; of elites, 130; as growing minority, 207, 218, 236; illegitimate, 67; of Isabel de Sotelo, 22, 113; of Juana Galván, 90, 104; in law, 174; of Manuel Rodríguez, 79–80, 90; marginal status of people of, 89, 97; of mestizos, 199, 300n47; of mulattos, 175, 294n86; of office seekers, 123; of Pedro de Penagos, 116; between Spanish and blacks, 86; tribute grants and, 108; urban women of, 12, 42. *See also* mixing, mixed ancestry; parentage
mixing, mixed ancestry, 7; in Americas, 15; appearance of, 174; children of, 82; discrimination against, 11–12, 121–24, 199, 201, 275n92; of elite Spaniards and native women, 96; erasure by hispanicization, 105; genealogy and, 24; groupness of, 61–93; laws and, 174; meaning of, 15–20; mestizo and, 16; nongenealogical, 18–19; race and, 99, 104; racial, 69–72, 92; as routine, 11; social milieu and, 96, 97; in upper social strata, 99, 130. *See also* mixed parentage

mobility, social, 60, 111, 252n6, 254n29; downward, 57, 129; of elite mestizos, 18, 96, 117, 130, 199; through marriage, 72, 104, 133; of mestizas, 60, 100

Mondragón, Fray Benito de Peñalosa y, *Libro de las cinco excelencias del español*, 38–39, 157

Mongua, 212

Monguí, 212

Montour, Andrew, 159, 233

Monzón, Juan Bautista de, 144, 162, 280n31

Moors, 18, 24, 274n78, 297n7; in Bogotá, 42–49; clothing of, 58, 166–68; color of, 193; conversion of, 259n70; as slaves, 171, 196. *See also* Islam; Morisca, Morisco; Muslims

Morales Pradilla, Próspero, *Los pecados de Inés de Hinojosa*, 2–3, 239, 246n7

moreno (brown), 193–94, 221, 292–93n71, 304; blacks and, 293n73; race and, 31; *de rostro*, 172, 179, 187, 191, 293n76

Morisca, Morisco, 304; as caste group, 208; circumcision and, 45–46; Diego Romero as, 42–45, 130; forbidden as wet nurses, 19; in New World, 48; *raza* and, 44, 258n67; registration of, 288n19. *See also* Islam; Moors; Muslims

Mörner, Magnus, 41

mother's milk, as type of blood, 19, 304. *See also* wet nurses

Moyachoque, doña Catalina de, 136, 156

Moyquitiva, don Juan, 81, 86

Muisca, 8, 25; *cacicazgos* of, 146–49; in colonial society, 233–35; descent system of, 18, 61, 92; heartland of, 79–87; as laborers, 2; mestizos and, 48, 92, 214–17; movement of, 211; nobility of, 100, 143, 156–59, 216; as wet nurses, 19; women as, 18

Muisca (language), 12, 72, 216, 233;

mixed children and, 74, 82; priests and, 273n69, 273n70

La mujer barbuda (José de Ribera), 189

Mulato, Juan, 197, 203, 286n4, 288n14; branding of, 173–76; in cast of characters, 242

Mulato, Lázaro, 75–76, 141, 201, 206, 229, 275n92; in cast of characters, 240; children of, 80, 82, 87–92, 95; as mestizo, 215–16; as *natural*, 79–80, 84, 90–91

mulatto, 100, 305; as ambiguous identity, 61, 95, 172, 174; as apparently stable term, 6; as bilingual, 82, 86–87; broader classification of, 7; caste system and, 207–8, 210; as category, 32; as classification, 40, 47; colonial definition of, 175, 176; as color term, 196–97, 221, 295n90, 295n91; fiestas and, 65; Francisco Suárez as, 130; as freed-person, 9, 200; incoherence of, 8; as Indian, 10, 72–79; marriages of, 211; as outsiders, 234; perme-ability of classification, 92–93, 129, 229–30; as racial interaction, 69–72, 87; rape by, 83; as slave, 9; in society, 126, 227; as *vecinos*, 218. *See also names of specific individuals*

Múnera, Alfonso, 219–20

murder, murderers, 1, 43, 46–47, 239; adultery and, 232, 239

Muslims, 19, 44–48, 162, 258n69, 259n70. *See also* Islam; Moors; Morisca, Morisco

Muzo, 8, 179, 248n19; emerald mines of, 101

myth of the three races, 246n8

naciones (nations, populations). *See* nationality, nations

Najmabadi, Afsaneh, 190

narrative approach, 24

Nasa, 234–35

nationality, nations, 62, 157, 174,

246n8; of blacks, 9, 196, 248n23; as determining factor in racial categories, 32; Iberian, 248n22; Portuguese, 259n69; recognized by Crown, 8

naturales (indigenous natives), 8, 9, 13, 82, 128, 213, 305; *caciques* and, 17; mixed bloods as, 79

negro (black), 7, 32, 172, 176. *See also* Africa, Africans; black, blacks

networks of social relationships, 22, 25, 123–29

New Christians, 38, 44–47, 172, 201, 252n5, 289n26, 305. See also *conversos*; Old Christians

New Laws (1542), 143, 174

Nicaragua, 82, 141, 160, 280n28

Nirenberg, David, on race, 44

nobility, 17, 30, 34, 100, 101, 116, 120, 155; bloodlines and lineage of, 38, 39, 44–47, 53, 104–5, 149, 151, 156, 157, 208, 235, 253n18, 297n7; *calidad* and, 106, 221; in determining race, 30, 32, 210; Diego Romero as, 42–43; *don*, 34, 98, 100, 304; *doña*, 1, 3, 205, 261n89, 304; executions of members of, 1; honor and, 59, 109, 210; Iberian and Spanish, 4, 24, 169, 167, 194, 199, 239, 241, 253n12; indigenous, 18, 57, 75–78, 86, 97, 105, 134–39, 142–43, 152, 212, 218, 241; mestizos and, 4; minor, 38, 75, 111, 136, 144, 304; Muisca, 143, 156, 158, 159, 216; posers of, 32, 49, 231, 239; project in process in colonial situation, 104; status of, 1, 6, 17, 36, 38, 56, 130, 139, 143, 226; women as, 24, 53, 76, 78, 97, 117, 165, 239, 241. See also *caciques*; conquistadors; elites; *encomiendas, encomenderos*; *hidalgos*

notary, notaries: Alonso de Silva as assistant to, 134–36, 139, 140, 149, 152, 232, 242, 278n7; documentation by, 22, 96, 97, 125, 181, 182, 274n84, 293n71; Juan de Albis as,

286n89; Juan de Penagos as receptor, 116; Juan Flórez de Ocáriz as, 22, 269n20, 271n57; Iñigo de Aranza as, 144; marital ties to, 101, 116; mestizos excluded from office of, 13, 278–79n7; occupation of, 32, 161, *183*, 185, 278n5

novels: Colson Whitehead's *The Intuitionist*, 262n103; Nella Larsen's *Passing*, 140, 262n103; Próspero Morales Pradilla's *Los pecados de Inés de Hinojosa*, 2–3, 239, 246n7, 245n8

Nueva Granada, viceroyalty, 44, 210, 217, 220–21, 224–25, 236, 305

Nuevo Reino de Granada, 305; archival record of, 7, 233; as Audencia, 1–2, 107, 245n1; *castas* in, 208, 210, 217; central highlands of, 18, 24; classificatory practices in, 5, 210, 221, 224–26; conquest of, 43, 45, 101, 141, 168; demographic of, 300n43; genealogies of, 22, 34, 99, 121, 253n12; mestizo caciques and reform in, 143–46; mestizo population of, 15, 92, 220, 227, 233; rural towns of, 12; secondary literature on, 28; Spaniards in, 172; as viceroyalty, 1–2, 208, 245n1. *See also* Colombia

Núñez, Lorenzo, 107, 112, 114, 256n41, 270n36

Núñez, Úrsula, 114, 116, 271n51

nuns, mestizas as, 13

obligations: of mestizos, 8,11, 29, 32, 53, 58, 90, 129, 208, 235–36, 261n101, 264n32; of Muisca, 211, 217; of *reservados*, 73; of slaves, 9, 208, 220, 234

occupation: as basis of identification, 6–7, 11, 21, 32, 72, 121, 129, 130, 222–23, 229, 234; socioracial hierarchy and, 41, 71, 130, 223, 226, 233–34, 236

Old Christians, 31, 34, 168, 194, 201, 252n5, 305

Oquendo, Andrés Berdugo y, visita by, 217–19

Oran, 43, 239

orejones, 218

Orejuela, Pablos de, 205–8, 211, 215–18, 297n5; accused of heresy, 253–54n18, 297n1; in cast of characters, 243

Origen de los indios del Nuevo Mundo e Indias Occidentales (Gregorio García), 192

origin, place of, 70, 231; collectivities based on, 9, 13; identity based on, 10, 76, 83, 129, 226, 233, 288n19

Oropesa, Juana de, 137

Padilla, Jacinto de, as stereotypical untrustworthy mestizo, 20, 21

Panches, 8

parentage, 3, 83, 84, 126, 129; African, 29, 49; as basis of identification, 6, 10, 93, 210; *calidad* and, 40; of mestizos, 10, 93, 96, 123, 140, 141, 214, 227, 236, 275n92; of mulattos, 30, 260n78, 275n92; Muslim, 47; nature of, 18; of Spaniards, 9–10, 140. *See also* lineage; mixed parentage

passing, racial, 29–30, 60; *calidad* and, 31–32; costume and, 51–52; of Francisco Suárez, 30–31, 35, 36, 37, 49; identity and, 33, 59, 130, 255n33; ladinos as, 266n50; mestiza in Indian habit, 50–59; methods of, 31; in Mexico City, 252n6, 254n29; modern notions of, 25, 253n11; social milieu and, 114; as Spaniard, 45–46; through written communication, 31, 36–37. *See also names of individual mestizos who passed*

Penagos, Juana de, 104–6, 119, 231; in cast of characters, 241; as daughter of Juan de Penagos, 97, 98, 101

Penagos, Juan de (conquistador), 97, 101, 104, 241, 270n25; genealogy of, *102*, *103*, 270n25; sons unable to

achieve nobility, 116; strategy to hispanicize daughter, 106

Penagos, Juan de (son of Juan de Penagos), 101, 270n25

Penagos, Juan de (son of Pedro de Penagos), 116, 270n25

Penagos, Pedro de, 101, 270n25; death of, 271n59; efforts to rise above *mestizaje*, 116–17

Pereira, Solórzano, 279n7

Peru, 2, 16–18, 30, 115, 141, 208, 228; Andean core of, 100, 229; categories in, 258n67; creoles in, 19; ladinos from, 82; mestizos in, 56, 105, 139, 165; Pizarro in, 43, 180

physiognomy, 27, 197–201; beards and, 188–93; classification based on, 177–78, 200; descriptions of, 183–86, 193–95; diversity of, 178–83; narrative portraits and, 186–88, 193; racial, 171; reactions to, 176; skin color, 193–98

Pijao, 75, 127, 173–76, 229

Pizarro, Francisco, 180

Pizarro, Pedro, 180

plebeians, 92, 96, 125, 128, 129, 233; artisans as, 5; cautions against marriage to, 34; distinguishing of, 3, 25–26, 42, 209; laborers as, 12, 126; mestizos as, 56, 72, 199, 229; milieu of, 21, 71, 91, 100, 133, 215, 216, 236, 241; social landscape of, 69, 207, 209, 223, 231, 234; solidarity of, 88, 89, 91, 92, 100; status of, 7; women as, 3. *See also* commoners

Poloni-Simard, Jacques, on colonial Cuenca, 53, 268n13

Pongota, Francisco, 213–14, 298n22

Popayán, 18, 231, 247n16; *caciques* from, 101, 270n25; mestizos in, 272n62; Nasa in, 234–35

Porta, Giovanni Battista Della, 185

portugués, 13, 71, 97, 134, 151, 259n69

Powers, Karen, on mestiza in Indian habit, 52

Presidio de Carare, 66

priests: as category, 41, 71, 73, 118; mestizos as, 13, 40, 48, 62, 96, 117–19, 272n68; need for interpreter, 82, 265n35; offspring of, 265n39; as outsiders, 74, 82; preaching in Muisca, 134, 273n69. *See also* doctrinal priests; *and names of specific individuals*

property owners: mestizos as, 11, 74, 128, 213; as sign of social standing, 104, 117, 119

protectores de indios, 205

pueblo de indios, 77, 79, 137, 205, 211, 242, 266n46; defined, 305; ethnic purity of, 216; localities of, 8; mestizos in, 18, 63, 84, 90, 201, 214–17, 224; Muisca, 26; non-natives in, 201, 219; Usaquén as, 205. *See also* Mulato, Lázaro; *visita*; *visitador*

quadroons, quarteroons (*cuarterones*), 11, 77–78, 214, 294n79, 303–4

Quechua, 55, 72, 100, 129; words in, 252n3, 263n15, 263n17

Quesada, Gonzalo Jiménez de, 101

Quesada, doña Isabel de, 85–86

Quiroga, Pedro de, 83, 235

Quito, Quiteños, 263n15, 263n17; costume in, 53; elites of, 270n31; Francisco Pongota from, 213; *huauquis*, 31, 59, 69, 252n3; *indias* from, 117, 231; Juan de Salazar and, 23, 66, 95, 124, 263n15; mestizos in, 260n85, 261n101; mulattos in, 24; revolts in, 162–63; social mobility in, 18, 231

rape, 83–85, 87; by employers, 69, 253n8; mestizos as children of, 69, 98–99; women and, 110

raza (race), 7, 44, 104, 305, 258n67; *casta* as, 225; classification of, 172, 207; defined, 305; gender and, 98; interaction between, 69–72, 87;

interpretation of, 59, 209; lineage and, 17, 37, 38, 48, 49, 25, 104; meaning of, 37–42, 254–55n33; mixed parentage and, 4, 104–5, 174; physiognomy and, 171, 175–78; in Spanish America, 3, 60; as term, 6, 37–38, 42. *See also* passing, racial; sociocial classification

rebellion: Comuneros, 220, 300n41; of *encomenderos*, 145; fear of, 235; indigenous, 199, 284n81; Manuel Rodríguez and, 79, 81–83, 240, 285n82, 286n3; mestizos and, 15–16, 62, 144, 161–67, 199, 216, 275n92, 285n82, 286n3; Morisco, 168, 293n71; in Peru, 43

recogida, mujer (sheltered woman), 31, 35, 91, 239

regidor (city alderman): Diego García Zorro as, 119–26, 130, 134, 140, 143, 241, 274n84

religion: as basis of identification, 6, 53, 196; *calidad* and, 31; confraternities of, 11, 62, 81, 266n46; convents and, 56; in determining race, 30, 38, 44; discrimination by, 46; as hereditary, 258n67, 259n72; mission schools and, 64; mystics of, 35; *raza* designates, 7, 44. *See also* doctrinal priests; priests; *and names of religious faiths and practitioners*

reservados (exemptees from tribute obligations), 73

resguardos (lands set aside for indigenous communities), 70, 212–13, 235, 262n6, 305; mestizos living on, 63, 215, 263n22; redistribution of, 224

residentes (residents), as basis of identification, 6, 9

Reyna, Francisco de, 119–21, 123, 274n78

Ribera, José de, 189

Río, Brígida del, 189

Riohacha, 80

Rioja, Lope de, 125

ritual, 58, 62, 147, 153; church, 266n46; indigenous, 64, 83, 141, 145, 165, 285n83; of marriage, 110; Spanish public, 8

Rivas, Esteban de, 120–21, 128

Rodríguez, Manuel, 79–90, 207, 217, 236; in cast of characters, 240; company kept by, 85–89; as *forastero*, 79–81; Muisca spoken by, 216; as rapist, 83–85, 87; as rebel, 81–83, 285n82; relationship with indigenous communities, 80–82, 86–87, 92

Rodríguez, Pablo, 109

Rodríguez Freile, Juan, 105; *El carnero*, 1–3, 22, 166–67, 239, 245n1, 284n81

Rodríguez Mendo, Pedro, 215, 217, 298n23

Romero, Diego (Diego Hurtado), 42–49, 256n52; appearance of, 171–72; in cast of characters, 239; concealed identity of, 43–49, 59–60, 176; as *encomiendo*, 42–43, 48, 49, 261n87; family of, 257n64, 272n67; lawsuit of, 181; as *Morisco*, 42–45, 130, 274n78; as mulatto, 47, 48, 49, 258n65; offspring of, 48–49, 257–58n64; rivalries of, 272n67

Romero, Fr. Alonso, 48, 258n64

Romero, Fr. Andrés, 48, 258n64, 272n67

Romero, Isabel, 116, 257n64

royalty, Aztec and Inca, 105, 139

Salazar, Juan de, 23, 64–69, 72, 95, 124, 214, 231, 263n15; in cast of characters, 240

Salomon, Frank, on mestizo as term, 12–13

sanbenito, 205

Sánchez Cotán, Juan, *La Barbuda de Peñaranda*, 189

Sandoval, Alonso de, 37, 195, 293n73, 295n90; *De instauranda aethiopum salute*, 195–96

Sangrelinda, Juana, 126–29, 276n104

San Jacinto, 119, 123, 128

Santa Bárbara (barrio), 116–17, 120, 272n64, 274n78

Santafé, 74, 146, 163, 171, 245n1; archives of, 20, 26, 31, 64, 133, 136, 142, 185, 212, 247n16, 287n13; authorities of, 30; as capital of Audencia, 1, 2, 64, 95, 96, 135, 142, 144, 162, 241, 242, 245n1; caste system in, 210; chronicles of, 1; city council, 97; convent of, 20, 56; demographics of, 36, 63, 282n41, 299n34; elites of, 22; foundlings home in, 19; goldsmiths in, 20; intermarriage in, 223; mestiza in Indian habit in, 53; mestizos in, 11, 13, 22, 24, 29, 62, 63, 84, 205–6, 211–12, 216–20, 224, 229–32, 247n17; Moors in, 42–49; nobility in, 22, 34, 42, 60, 62; notaries in, 13; passing in, 33; plebeian laborers in, 12; racial interaction in, 71–72, 87; as refuge for native people, 8; suburbs of, 205

scenarios, 226; ethnographic, 21–24, 57, 69, 112, 121, 173, 227; legal, 231

Schwaller, Robert C., 39–40

Schwartz, Stuart, on mestizo as term, 12–13

self-identification, 182, 202; of *casta* groups, 209; of mestizo elite, 130; of mestizos, 62, 91, 217; of *naturales*, 79–80; of Spaniards, 193, 218

servants, 71; *criados*, 126, 276n95; mestizas as, 20, 53–59; mestizos as, 11, 62, 84, 91; native people as, 15, 86, 107, 126, 207, 253n8; prospective, 88

Seth, Vanita, 37, 255n33

Seville: archives of, 26–27, 31, 133, 182, 250n38, 274n85; natives of, 9

shoemakers and cobblers, 32, 65, 85, 86, 184, 234; as honorable, 223; Juan de Salazar as, 23, 64, 66–68,

95, 124, 214, 240; ladinos as, 81; mestizos as, 11; patron saints of, 266n51

signifier: floating, 15; "mestizo" as empty, 16

Silva, don Alonso de, 19, 26, 97, 133–69, 215; as *cacique* of Tibasosa, 12–16, 62, 97, 137–43, 154–57, 281n40, 285n82; in cast of characters, 242; as mestizo, 229, 232; right to govern of, 40, 143–46, 283n54

Silvestre, don Francisco, 217

Simón, Pedro de, 70

Sirita, doña Juana, 97, 134, 149–50

skilled vision, and physiognomy, 184–85

slavery, slaves, 111, 123, 137, 200; blacks and Africans as, 7, 9, 11–13, 55, 71, 74, 127, 141, 179, 196, 197, 201, 235, 242, 247n16, 248n23, 290n44, 295n90; branding of, 286n4, 286n5; categorization of, 220, 224; clothing of, 55–56; color of, 292n71, 295n90; defined by nature of bondage, 9, 11; escapes of, 121–22; in Europe, 196; groupness of, 10; housing of, 128; indigenous, 181, 242, 253n8, 263n18, 276n102, 286n4, 286n6, 293n71; Juan Mulatto as, 173–75; miscegenation and, 71; Moors as, 46, 59, 171, 176, 290n38, 295n90; murders by, 43; passing of, 31; as racial marker, 32; sales of, 22, 125, 178, 27n84; status of, 32, 174; white children of, 196; as witnesses, 191

Soatá, 79–89, 207, 217, 236, 266n50, 285n82

sociracial classification, 5–7, 21, 23, 32, 72, 175, 226, 236; ambiguity of, 95, 201, 208–9; appearance and, 176–78, 193–98; barriers and mixed ancestry males, 99, 120–24; *calidad* and, 32, 39–42, 106; categorization and, 23, 27, 32, 41, 48, 52, 115, 172–83, 192–203, 230,

232, 247n10, 254n29; deindianization and, 220; epithets and, 222; fluidity of, 27, 87, 91–92, 129–31, 176; by functionaries, 61; hardening of categories, 207; hierarchy and, 178; of Isabel de Sotelo, 112, 130; mestizo as, 29; in Mexico, 39, 40; narrative portraits and, 180; by "nation," 9; origins and criminal record, 97; petitions to change, 33, 73, 90, 124; physical appearance and, 171–203; processes of, 229; in rural communities, 72–81; of rural mestizos and mulattos, 25; skin color and, 177, 193–98, 200; travel papers and, 181, 196; unmarked status and, 98, 100, 114, 125; visual clues for, 175–78. *See also* passing, racial

Sogamosos, 8, 68; indigenous populations in, 212–15, 218, 234, 236

Sotelo, Alonso de, 107, 113–14

Sotelo, Isabel de, 130, 215, 231, 236, 256n41, 270n36; in cast of characters, 241; change in sociracial classification of, 112, 124, 215; color of, 171; illegitimate birth of, 14, 22, 107; suitor and, 106–14

Sotelo, Pedro del Acebo, 106–7, 111, 131, 241; as father of Isabel de Sotelo, 107; lawsuit of, 112–14

Spain: Alpujarras revolt and, 162; Andalusia, 3; beards and, 178, 192; blood purity and, 44, 47–49, 157, 181, 182, 201, 222, 258n65, 265n39, 269n19; branding of slaves in, 286n4; Christian determination and, 58; Córdoba, 53, 105, 205; escape from, 43, 239; ethnic boundaries in, 57, 97, 134, 162, 174, 196, 199; honor and, 120; "Jew" as term in, 16; legal matters and, 42, 46, 107, 137–38, 143–44; physiognomic conventions in, 27, 176, 184, 202, 287n13, 288n19, 293n71; religious rulings from, 118; travel from 179, 191, 201, 289n30

Spanish (language): definition of "mestizo" in, 16; in Muisca towns, 25; as pure, 246n8; spoken by *caciques*, 14, 89; spoken by children of mixed parentage, 74, 198; spoken by Indians, 15, 23, 64

Spanish, Spaniards (*español, española*), 97, 104; ambiguity of classification, 96, 230; as ascriptive classification, 7, 176; *calidad* and, 208, 210; costume of, 198, 282n46; as dark-complexioned, 172; as dominant population, 233; facial hair and status of, 192; gender and, 98, 112, 130, 231, 248n25; groupness of, 25; heterogeneity of category of, 26; interact with mestizos, 62, 70; label "*español*," 97, 247n10; marriage to *indios* by, 211; mestizo children of, 76, 91, 92, 105, 127–28, 133, 257–58n64; as model, 71; Muisca invaded by, 18; nationalities of, 9; people of mixed descent integrated into, 10, 130; permeability of classification, 114, 129; privileges and duties of, 9, 11; racial interaction, 69–72; as racial term, 4, 5, 6, 246n8; as relational category, 115; rights of, 8, 13; self-identity of, 3; servants of, 64, 86, 91, 92, 253n8; travel papers and, 181–83; unmarked, 9–10; as *vecinos*, 218; as white, 194

speech-acts: classifications and, 5, 186; ethnic labels as, 123, 175

status, 7; *calidad* and, 34, 45; cues for establishing, 176; economic, 32, 39, 92, 93, 97, 106, 223, 236; elite, 36, 56, 114, 130, 139; as free or slave, 32, 174; honor and, 22, 253n8; marital, 233; mestizo, 60, 75, 77, 91, 100, 125, 131, 142, 155, 264n32; moral, 32; noble, 1, 6, 17, 36, 38, 56, 120, 130, 139, 143, 226; occupational, 11, 223; social, 1, 11, 17, 29, 39, 56, 99, 110, 114, 121, 142, 201, 231–36, 287n12; socioracial,

33, 98; Spanish, 99; strategies to protect, 96; tributary, 73, 93, 222; unmarked, 100, 125, 127

Suárez, Francisco, 139, 213, 239; appearance of, 171, 188, 198; attempt at passing, 30–39, 49, 59–60, 130, 252n3; in cast of characters, 239; as *huauqui*, 59, 68–69; as *indio*, 231; as *zambo*, 231, 292n66

subjectivity, subjectivities, 21; of researcher, 23

sumptuary laws, 17, 50, 52, 55, 259n74. *See also* clothing

Tafur, Catalina, 106, 229–30, 261n89; in cast of characters, 239; "disappears" twice, 106; education of, 91, 99; as mestiza in Indian habit, 53–60, 85, 177; unmarked status of husband of, 105

Tafur, Isabel, 54, 105, 139

Tafur, Captain Juan, 53–56

tailors, 81, 85–86, 122; as honorable, 223; indigenous, 71, 234; mestizos as, 11

Tamalameque, 111, 114–15, 240–41

tanners: *indios ladinos* as, 64, 65, 66; mestizos as, 11; natives as, 234

Tavárez, David, 63, 67, 260n78

taxation, 52, 58, 197; *caciques* and, 137; of free mulattos, 9, 11, 90, 287n8. *See also* tribute

Tesoro de la Lengua Castellana o Española (Sebastián de Covarrubias Orozco), 41, 44

theft, 20, 21, 144, 145, 163

Tibasosa, *135*, 149–54, 161, 278n4; Alonso de Silva and, 242; *cacicazgo* of, 135, 146, 149, 274n78; cacique of, 14–15, 62, 97, 133–36, 139, 149, 152; indigenous tributaries of, 141, 153; Miguel Holguín and, 138, 278n4; noble lineages of, 149–51, *150*, *153*; power struggles in, 161

Tocancipá, 97

Toledo, 9, 45, 101

Tópaga, 212

Toro, Christóbal del, 175

Torres, don Diego de, 133–68, 285n83; appearance of, 167, 172, 180; arrested, 163; as *cacique* of Turmequé, 14, 15, 38, 62, 199, 261n100, 281n40, 285n82; in cast of characters, 242; lineage of, 155, 235, 279n15; as mestizo, 12–16, 215, 228, 232; right to govern of, 38, 40, *156*; self-narratives of, 26

Torres, Juan de, 136, 158

Torres, Pedro de, 138, 158, 160–66, 215, 283n53, 285n83

transeunte (transient), 9, 80

travel permits, identifiers in, 191–93, 197, 294n78

tribute: *caciques* exempt from, 17; *encomiendas* and, 43, 46, 108, 304; exemptions from, 73, 208, 235, 264n32; flight from, 211, 260n80, 261n101; mestizos and mulattos and, 10, 53, 58, 74; paid by Indians to Crown, 8, 11, 36, 56, 74–76, 87, 114, 201; records of, 73, 76–79, 88, 211, 240; request to change status of, 73, 90, 264n32; system of, 234; women exempt from, 53, 73, 90. See also *indio tributario*; taxation

Truxillo, Catalina de, 113, 114

Tunja, 1, 144–45, 210–11, 224, 235, 245, 285n82; demographics of, 36, 207, 219, 254n27, 282n41; don Diego de Torres and, 136–38, 142, 152, 155–57, 163–64, 242; documents from, 6, 179; fear of elite mestizos in, 162; indigenous population of, 8, 218, 220, 254n27, 282n41; Manuel Rodríguez and, 80–81, 85–86, 240; mestiza in Indian habit, 50, 53, 165; mestizos in, 11, 12, 24–28, 32, 74, 84, 117, 169, 206, 212, 218–20, 229–32, 246n8, 247n17, 250n53; migrants and, 260n80; nobility in, 62; plebeian laborers in, 12, 88; *pueblos* near,

26; racial interaction in, 71–72, 87–90, 231; Spaniards in, 10, 88, 97

Tunjuelo, 118, 241

Turmequé, 62, 154–55, *156*, 160–63

Tutasá, 212

Twinam, Ann: on color, 221; on passing, 33, 221, 253n8

Ubaque, 165, 285n83; cacique of, 129, 147–48, 235; rituals and, 153; Usba and, 284n72

Ubaque, don Diego de, 100, 106

Ubaque, don Francisco de, 147–48, 153, 159, 165, 235, 269n20, 282n46, 285n83; in cast of characters, 241

Ubaté, 218

Ugarte, doña María Arias de, 74–76

Umayyad dynasty, 105

Usaquén, 205–7, 211, 297n1

Valcárcel, Juan de, *visita* by, 212–15, 266n47

Valera, Blas, 285n83

Valero de Tapia, Alonso, 97, 101

Valverde, García de, 43, 272n64

van Deusen, Nancy, 263n18, 280n22, 285n16, 285n19, 302n4, 302n6

Vargas, Juan de, 30–39, 239, 252n3, 253n8

vecino (citizen), 8, 97, 111–12, 122, 134, 138, 179, 218, 236, 247–48n17, 305; as category, 32, 70, 97, 139, 160, 181, 202, 219, 222; denied right of, 202; informal, 79; rural not necessarily elite, 297n102; Spanish men as, 9. *See also* citizenship

Vélez, 219, 224; don Juan Cunucubá and, 198, 242, 249n37; free mulattas in, 200; Juana Galván in, 76, 89–92, 206, 240; mestizos in, 24, 224; racial interaction in, 71–72, 92

Venero de Leiva, Andrés Díaz, 1, 2, 144, 145, 242, 246n4, 280n27

Venezuela, 1, 2, 23

visita (royal inspection tour), 305–6;
1580 report, 40; of 1636, 212,
266n47; 1639 report, 79, 240; of
1755, 217; of 1758–60, 219; auction
of native lands and, 220; *castas*
limited to, 224, 301n55; of Chocontá, 73–79; demography and, 63,
73, 212, 219–20; Juan Birves and,
113; in eighteenth century, 218; by
Juan de Valcárcel, 212; mestizos
in *pueblos* and, 63, 92; not routine,
92, 218; Prieto de Orellana and,
145; women in, 73
visitador, 162, 202, 306; audiencia
and, 144, 145; in Chocontá, 73–76,
79; demographics and, 217–20;
mestizos and, 92, 212–13; physiognomic descriptors in, 178, 202,
217. *See also names of specific
individuals*
Vives, Juan Luis, *Instruccion de la
muger christiana*, 35
Voto, Jorge, 1

wet nurses, 19–20, 137
white (*blanca*): as category, 32,
194–97, 220, 223, 295n91; as complexion, 35, 175, 180, 194, 196, 221;
"not-white," 232, 236; passing for,
140; white children born to black
slaves, 196
Whitehead, Colson, *The Intuitionist*,
262n103
woman, women, 10, 26, 31, 35, 73,
100, 117, 130, 177, 195; assumes
identity of husband, 3; beards
and, 189, 190; betrothal and, 109,
110; *calidad* and, 39; character
of, 184, 188–89, 293n71; church

seating of men and, 81; clothing
of, 50, 55, 129, 271n48, 296n95;
as concubines, 83; confined to
convents, 36, 56; *criollas*, 268n8;
elite mestiza assuming unmarked
socioracial status, 98, 130, 231; as
encomenderas, 249n36; ethnicity
of, 98; family honor and, 34–36;
india, 17; fluid socioracial categories and, 129; indigenous, married
to mestizos, 211, 213, 214, 250n53;
intersection of race and gender
and, 4, 72, 98, 231; legitimacy in
native society of, 151; mestiza in
Indian habit, 42, 50–60, 165, 217,
260n85; mixed parentage and, 25;
Muisca descent system and, 18, 61;
noblewomen, 34, 98; rape of, 69,
83–85, 240; recognition of "libre"
and, 220; sheltering of high-born
unmarried, 36, 269n16; social
mobility through marriage and,
104, 207, 268n11; travel papers
and, 182; as wet nurses, 19–20, 137;
wills and, 128. *See also españolas;
mestiza, mestizas; and names of
specific individuals*

zambaigos, 74, 86, 212, 292n66, 306
zambo (*indio zambo*): defined, 30, 86,
306; Francisco Suárez as, 30–35,
39, 59–60, 231, 239, 252n3, 292n66
Zamorano, Juan, 287n14, 295n92;
characterized as Indian, 176,
197–98
Zipacón, 118, 241
Zipaquirá, 218
Zúñiga, Jean-Paul, 104, 156–57,
259n90, 262n3

CPSIA information can be obtained
at www.ICGtesting.com
Printed in the USA
JSHW040804310322
24359JS00007B/173

9 780822 356363